Titan of the Thames

Titan of the Thames
The Life of Lord Desborough

Sandy Nairne and Peter Williams

unbound

First published in 2024
Unbound
c/o TC Group, 6th Floor, Kings House, 9–10 Haymarket,
London, United Kingdom SW1Y 4BP

www.unbound.com

Text design by Ellipsis, Glasgow

A CIP record for this book is available from the British Library

ISBN 978-1-80018-279-0 (hardback)
ISBN 978-1-80018-280-6 (ebook)

Printed in Great Britain by Clays Ltd, Eclograf S.p.A.
1 3 5 7 9 8 6 4 2

Our many thanks go to Christine and Andrew Hall, Leander Club, Randy Lerner, and Alan and Virginia Lovell for their generous contributions as patrons.

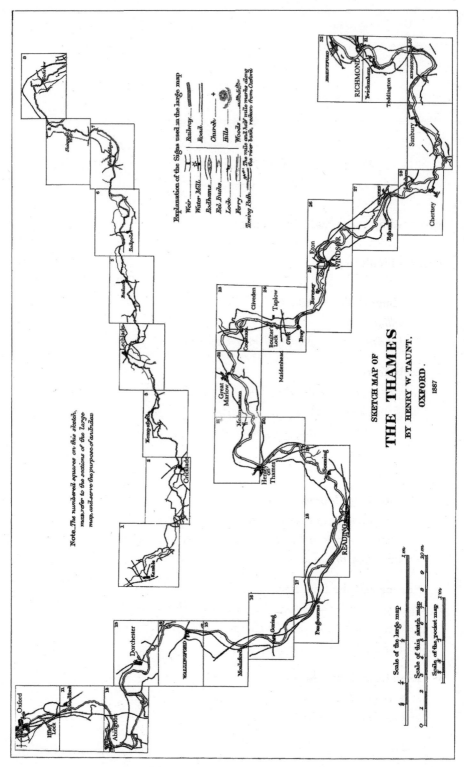

Henry W. Taunt, *A New Map of The River Thames from Thames Head to London*, 5th Edition, Taunt & Co., Oxford, 1887

CONTENTS

PUBLIC GAIN, PRIVATE LOSS

FOREWORD

Dame Katherine Grainger, Chair, UK Sport

Why should a man born in the nineteenth century, when the British Empire was flourishing, be relevant to us today? Why should someone like Lord Desborough matter?

Yet for a man from such a distant world, he has arguably never felt more relevant. Lord Desborough offers a wonderful mix of challenging contradictions. He became a titled, privileged member of the elite, but also a devoted public servant, displaying deep integrity and a voracious desire to make a difference. Across his varied career he inhabited a range of roles from being a Member of Parliament and serving in the House of Lords to Chairman of the Lawn Tennis Association, the Amateur Athletic Association, the British Olympic Association and the MCC.

He was a devoted husband and father who suffered his share of tragedy, losing two sons in the First World War and a third in a motoring accident. Nevertheless, his personal losses didn't dim his enthusiasm for life and he continued to throw himself with passion into countless projects.

Lord Desborough is a superb example of someone who knew sport had a role far beyond just physical competition. He instinctively understood that sport had a great contribution to make to society and was pivotal in bringing the 1908 Olympic Games to London, the first time the Games were held in Great Britain. His vision of what hosting the Olympics could do helped transform public ambitions for sport in this country.

From being a successful sportsman himself – including competing in the Oxford v. Cambridge Boat Race, swimming across the basin of Niagara Falls, rowing the English Channel, winning international medals in fencing, and being a triple punting champion – Lord Desborough recognised the enormous benefit sport could give both to the wider public and to specific communities. He also realised that in promoting international competition in sport, it might help make the world a better, and better connected, place. In the polarised world of today, Lord Desborough's attitude – of optimism and action – would go a long way.

Some of his interests might appear to be from another time, but he was a very modern thinker. He supported the early days of air flight; he argued at length for a fixed date for Easter; he campaigned tirelessly to open sport to wider participation. He worked hard as Chairman of the Thames Conservancy to modernise the Thames and created projects to lessen the impact of flooding.

Lord Desborough is a magnificent figure who has, for whatever reason, gone missing from British history. Sandy Nairne and Peter Williams have done an extraordinary job of bringing him vividly back to life, where he can stride through the world exuding energy and delight once again. This wonderful book, with its detailed research and engaging storytelling, will hopefully restore him to the place he deserves in our collective memory, where his example can continue to entertain and inspire, educate and enrich. Lord Desborough and his legacy has never felt more relevant, and more necessary, than now.

Family Tree – William Grenfell, Lord Desborough

Pascoe Grenfell 1761–1838

m. (1) Charlotte Granville 1765–1790 ·············· m. (2) Georgiana St Leger 1777–1818

Charlotte Granville c. 1787–1845

George Granville 1789–1853

Charles Pascoe 1790–1867 — m. — **Georgiana Frances Molyneux** 1793–1826

Maria Georgiana 1820–1900
m.
Colonel Frederick Paget 1807–1866

Charles William 1823–1861
m.
Georgiana Caroline Lascelles 1826–1911

Henry Riversdale 1824–1902
m.
Aletha Louisa Adeane 1829–1923

Louisa Henrietta 1825–1911
m.
Theodore Walrond 1824–1887

Caroline Georgiana 1853–1881
m.
Colonel Robert Meade 1835–1898

William Henry 1855–1945
m.
Ethel Priscilla Fane 1867–1952

Charles Molyneux 1857–1915
m.
Mabel Blanche Mills 1865–1936

Claud George 1858–1900

Algernon Granville 1859–1927

Constance Isabella 1860–1923
m.
Frederick Aylmer 1849–1918

Julian Francis 1888–1915

Gerald William 1890–1915

Monica Margaret 1893–1973
m.
Sir John Maitland Salmond 1881–1968

Ivo George Winfred 1898–1926

Alexandra Imogen Clair 1905–1969
m.
Henry Rainald, 6th Viscount Gage 1895–1982

Julian John 1926–2006
m.
Brigid Louise Wright 1928–2000

Rosemary Laura 1928–1991
m.
Nicholas Mosley, Lord Ravensdale 1923–2017

George John 7th Viscount Gage 1932–1993
m. (1) Valerie Dutch
m. (2) Deirdre Kingsbury

Nicolas 8th Viscount Gage 1934–
m. (1) Lady Diana Beatty
m. (2) Alexandra Templeton

Camilla Jane 1937–
m. Sir Edward Cazalet

This offers an abbreviated account of the family and descendants of William Henry Grenfell. For information on the wider Grenfell family visit: grenfellhistory.co.uk

I

——◆——

The Importance of Athens

Travelling to Athens – Vesuvius erupts – epée contests – 1908 Olympics for London – central point in Lord Desborough's career

On 4 April 1906 Mount Vesuvius erupted. Few could have imagined the chain of events that this would trigger, nor the consequences for William Grenfell, newly ennobled as Lord Desborough. It was the worst eruption since the seventeenth century and it soon became clear that Italy could no longer stage the next Olympic Games in Rome. A new host city would be needed for 1908.

The fifty-year-old all-round sportsman Lord Desborough sailed – literally and metaphorically – into this vacuum, and within months was offered the leadership challenge of his life: to stage an international event in London at a scale never previously seen, with no set budget, no government support and with an almost impossibly tight timescale. How this came about, and the success of the London Olympics that followed, proved to be pivotal in his career and critical to the development of sport in Britain.

It was by chance that in the days following the eruption, Desborough was visiting Athens for the first time, as a member of the British Olympic fencing team, participating in an 'interim' set of Games held that spring (known as the Intercalated Games). He met with other team members in Naples, including Lord Howard de Walden, in whose new steam yacht *Branwen* they would sail to Athens. Desborough, however, was already worried: about the impact of the volcano, about his physical fitness and the suitability of the boat.

Branwen, *a steam yacht owned by Lord Howard de Walden, off Naples, by Antonio De Simone.*

For an accomplished sportsman, his nervousness is surprising: an aspect of his private self never visible in public. After leaving Marseille, he wrote to his wife, Ettie: 'There may be trouble at Naples but I hope the worst is over – though the worst will not be over till the fencing is!'[1] Arriving in Naples, he described how 'Vesuvius is not to be seen. Two days ago it was very bad here – but nothing is falling at the moment. Everything, roofs etc. is deep in dust. I have seen our little yacht . . . She is very small, but I hope safe.'[2]

The weather rather than the eruption made their next stage hazardous: by Wednesday 18 April they had only reached Messina, and Desborough wrote: 'We have just put in here after a most awful day, a sort of hurricane & we have only done about 4 knots. Everything in "my cabin" was drenched, so it is far from comfortable and no one turned up all day except Howard de Walden. I hope we shall not be storm bound here so as to make us late for everything. I do not see how anyone can fence after all this: & we now have to face the Adriatic in this little boat: she is only 68 tons nett.'[3]

Yet despite these storms, the *Branwen* was safely docked in Athens by the weekend and Desborough could focus his mind on his double role: as a competitive fencer, with *épée* his speciality, and as sporting diplomat: being Chairman of the British Olympic Association and one of two British official representatives at the Games.[4]

He wrote to Ettie from the Hotel Imperial:

> *My dearest – We have at last arrived here very battered. I lunched with the Legation to meet the King and Prince of Wales, who were most kind. Then we processed with the other competitors round the stadium before 50,000 people, including the King and Queen, P & Princess of Wales, K of Greece etc. etc.*

A display by boy gymnasts in the restored Olympic Stadium, Athens, 1906.

and now we are at the Hotel & just going to do a bit of fencing.

It was very silly coming here on a little yacht, nothing could have been worse. We fight the Germans on Tuesday: I do not know how good they are . . . Athens is fascinating as far as I have seen it: we first went into Piraeus, & then to Phalerum where the yacht, absurd little boat, is now lying . . . The Greeks, I have come to the conclusion, know nothing whatever about the management of any form of athletic sports.

I am scratching this with the most awful row going on. Very best love, yr loving Willy.[5]

Soon after his arrival in Athens, Desborough found himself in discussion as to whether London could be the location for the 1908 Olympic Games. He immediately regarded this as an exceptional opportunity – both national and personal – and shrewdly recognised that royal approval might be critical to making it happen.

King Edward VII was in Athens for the Games as a guest of his brother-in-law, King George I of Greece. Desborough had known Edward, when Prince of Wales, as a fellow sporting enthusiast (they joined the same shooting parties, and fencing was a shared interest). Athens provided a perfect opportunity for consultation with the King if Desborough could fit this in around his fencing matches.[6]

*The 1906 British fencing team in Athens (left to right): Charles Newton-Robinson,
Sir Cosmo Duff-Gordon, Lord Desborough and Edgar Seligman (with an official behind).*

Still very nervous, he wrote to Ettie on 23 April:

> *I have been spending the morning at the palace where Seymour Fortescue* sent for
> me to see the King – Our Queen was there, and says she is coming to see us fence
> the Germans tomorrow, & Princess Victoria and all the Greek Royalties, to say
> nothing of the King & Prince of Wales; it will be awful, we fight the German
> team at 11 o'clock, & I hope I shall beat them. The King has asked me to drive
> down with him to the fencing . . . but it will be awful if I get whacked by these
> Germans. I will wire. It will be dreadfully hot fencing.*[7]

In the same letter he confessed to Ettie that were Rome to fall through as host
city, as anticipated, he was already sketching out what might be entailed for
London to take it on:

> *I spoke to the King about it this morning and he highly approved. We could
> run at the Queen's Club, Fence at Olympia, row on the Thames, Swim at*

---

* Seymour Fortescue was a former naval officer and equerry in the King's service.

Highgate Ponds – and I think make much more business like arrangements than they have here, but it would give me a lot to do as President of the Olympic Committee – we have no Stadium, which [here] is seriously glorious, with the Acropolis above you in the sun, but could make a fine show at Olympia to wind up with; massed bands & crown the Victors . . .[8]

While the eruption of Vesuvius had been an act of nature, Desborough's exploitation of the opportunity was not. Once in Athens, discussing a London Olympics with the King was part of a plan quickly formulated with his fellow fencers and with Theodore Cook, who had organised the trip.[9] Desborough's forceful imagination was at work, and he was soon committing himself to the huge task of bringing the Olympic Games to fruition in London.

Desborough and the *épée* team won their match against the Germans, but his opportunism and diplomacy were of much greater significance. [See *Chapter 15 Bringing the Games to Fruition.*] The 1908 Olympics turned out to be a pivotal achievement in Lord Desborough's life, and characteristic of his work as an all-round sportsman, a brilliant sports administrator and a committed public servant.

William Grenfell, Lord Desborough, was the right man at the right time, but many elements in his earlier life – as a sportsman, politician, businessman and writer – pointed towards the unfolding events of 1906, and many achievements after 1908 flowed from his Olympic success. Any sense of luck (and privilege) would belie the degree to which he had created his own success, and many came to regard him as an ideal English gentleman, his early fame as an exceptional all-round sportsman gradually matched as an outstanding leader of public institutions and crucially as a 'man who could get things done'.[10] In his time, Lord Desborough's name became a byword for duty, integrity, humility, diplomacy and generosity of spirit. And while some might choose to regard these as specifically English virtues, his own aspiration was to contribute – internationally, nationally and locally – to a better organised and more stable world.

Desborough's life neatly spanned the second half of the nineteenth century and the first half of the twentieth, and as the nature of English society changed, so too did the roles of privileged and educated men. England was still deeply marked, despite political reform, by hierarchies of class, gender and culture, and Britain in this period was vigorously pursuing imperial expansion. Desborough was a man of his time, and his own interests focused on the 'settled dominions', with particular business and sporting interests in Canada. At the same time, he was devoted to creating a more open and participative society: he was a traditionalist in style and temperament but a believer in change. He wanted the Empire to be a force for good in the world and for others to be inspired by individual achievement (as demonstrated by the Olympics). He also wanted sport more generally to be a positive symbol, not just of intense competition but of wider collaboration and team effort.

If public service, within and beyond Parliament, was a key theme in his life, his relationship with the River Thames was its central thread. His later years in charge of the Thames Conservancy followed not just from sporting achievements on the water and management of his Thames-side estate at Taplow Court in Bucking-hamshire, but also from knowing those families, across generations, who worked and played on the river. His tall, powerful oarsman's frame was complemented by an approachable manner, and although occasionally reticent in company, he offered rousing but thoughtful words when speaking at public events.

Alongside his life of public achievement, his marriage to Ethel Fane (known always as Ettie) – a famously elegant and intriguing figure among the Souls, a group of like-minded society hosts of the late Victorian and Edwardian period – was a mainstay. By the 1890s the Grenfells, first as a couple and then as a family, were much in the public eye: in civic circles locally in Maidenhead, in London society, when visiting great country houses, or as they mixed with prominent figures in politics or public affairs and at Court. Though conventional in appearance, Grenfell was always smartly dressed and frequently had the flourish of a carnation worn prominently in his buttonhole.

Desborough's life was not one of scandal or intrigue – there were no mistresses or hidden identities – but it *was* one of tragedy. Within seven years of the Olympics, their two elder sons, Julian and Billy, had been killed. The Desboroughs were perceived, like so many who lost close relatives in the Great War, as figures struck by cruel misfortune. The family was dealt a further terrible blow by the death of their youngest son, Ivo, from injuries following a car accident in 1926.

Led by Lord Desborough, London rescued a nascent Olympic movement that might never have survived. The determination and professionalism with which he tackled the Olympics – establishing many of the principles and tenets of the modern Games – was mirrored in the many enterprises and projects of a long and fulfilling life, explored in the chapters that follow. In their heady mix of sport and politics, glorious victory with tragic defeat, visionary leadership with detailed organising, national significance with international cooperation, the 1908 Olympics represented the challenge of public service that he pursued so relentlessly and passionately.

2

---·---

Early Years

Coming of age – the Grenfell family – deaths of father and grandfather – inheritance – Georgiana's journal – Harrow – Oxford entrance examination

On Monday 30 October 1876, the Mayor of Maidenhead, Mr E. W. Mackie, with the Town Clerk, councillors and members of the Oddfellows and Foresters Lodges, took carriages to Taplow Court and presented an illuminated document (on vellum) to Mrs Georgiana Grenfell.* It was addressed to her eldest son, William, known as Willy, on the occasion of his twenty-first birthday, and expressed (in the formal language of the period) how they:

> deem it a duty respectfully to approach you with their most cordial congratulations on the auspicious occasion of the attainment of your majority. Mindful that your honoured family have, for several generations, ever stood at the front as amongst the chief and most liberal supporters of our local institutions, we desire heartily to welcome your succession to the hereditary estates, constituting you the principal landed proprietor in our midst; and we sincerely trust that, in health and happiness, you may long live to enjoy the proud position you now attain.[1]

Given that Willy Grenfell's father had died in 1861 and his grandfather in 1867, a formal response was offered by his uncle, Henry Riversdale Grenfell. Having

---

* William Henry Grenfell was born on 30 October 1855 at 7 Chesham Place, Belgrave Square, where his parents were living in the 1850s.

thanked the Mayor and Corporation, Henry Grenfell said he was sorry that his nephew wasn't present to thank them in person, because: 'His nephew . . . was working at his studies at Oxford, and, as they all knew, an interruption of his studies and labours at such time would be very undesirable – the more so since he had taken to those studies and labours as a serious matter, and with the desire to fit himself for the position which awaited him.'[2]

Referring to the long-standing connections between the Grenfell family and the borough – as well as to the early death of his elder brother, Charles William Grenfell, Willy's father – he hoped that:

> his nephew would use the gifts which God had given him to the advantage not only to himself but of those around him. The speaker made allusion, in words broken by emotion, to the duty which had devolved upon those nearly related to the heir in the absence of the care and guidance of one who was not with them, and expressed his gratification that up to the present time his nephew had proved everything they could wish.

However, as a further address was about to be read (and to everyone's surprise), the young Willy Grenfell himself 'opportunely arrived from Oxford, and entered the room amid applause'.

Once the 'young squire' was back at Taplow Court after the end of term, further celebratory events were staged: on 21 December he hosted a large dinner for all tenants (and the Mayor and Corporation) at which his health was toasted by Mr Webster, the oldest Taplow tenant; on 3 January 1877 a ball was held for servants and their friends, and apparently 'the general company did not separate till 6am, when some distant visitors retired in punts to their watery homes'; and on the 5th two plays were performed for a 'large audience of children and friends from Taplow and the neighbourhood', but 'unfortunately some were unable to reach Taplow Court on account of the obliteration of the roads by the floods'.[3]

The date of 30 October 1876 marked the point when Willy Grenfell became the acknowledged heir, within the formalities of Victorian civic ritual in Maidenhead, to the extensive estate largely accumulated by his great-grandfather, Pascoe Grenfell (1761–1838).[4] In 1794 Pascoe Grenfell had acquired Taplow House, halfway up the hill from the Buckinghamshire bank of the Thames (on the opposite side from the town centre of Maidenhead in Berkshire).

Circumstantial evidence suggests that an earlier forebear, Pascoe Grenfell (1636–65), born in St Just in Penwith, was an illiterate Cornish tinner.[5] But by the eighteenth century the interests of the Grenfell family had expanded into trading extensively in metals.[6] The later Pascoe Grenfell was born at Marazion, and while inheriting from his father and uncle in the 1780s their business as 'merchants and large-scale dealers in tin and copper ores', profitably threw in his lot with Thomas Williams of Anglesey and of Temple House, Bisham. Williams was a considerable and enterprising figure, dubbed the 'Copper King' by his great commercial rival Matthew Boulton, and at the height of his commercial powers controlling the marketing and sale of all the copper raised in Anglesey and Cornwall.[7]

After Thomas Williams's death in 1802, the business partnership of Pascoe with Williams's son Owen took over the smelting works at Middle and Upper Bank in Swansea, with copper ores primarily from Cornwall.[8] Pascoe was elected MP for Great Marlow in 1802 (in succession to Thomas Williams) and, after 1820, represented Penryn in Cornwall. In 1829 Owen Williams withdrew from the business and the Swansea firm became Pascoe Grenfell and Sons. In Parliament, Pascoe Grenfell was a persistent critic of the Bank of England, argued for a silver standard – initiating a multigenerational Grenfell family linkage to silver (rather than gold) – and was a supporter of the abolition of slavery and Catholic emancipation.[9]

Charles Pascoe Grenfell (1790–1867), Willy's grandfather, was one of three children born to Pascoe Grenfell's first wife and cousin Charlotte Granville, who died within days of his birth. Pascoe fathered a further twelve children by his second wife, Lady Georgiana St Leger, whom he married in 1798. Charles Pascoe continued what was becoming a Grenfell pattern: of marrying daughters of the landed aristocracy. In his case, Lady Georgina Frances Molyneux, daughter of the 2nd Earl of Sefton, whom he married in 1819. They had two sons and two daughters before Georgiana died young in 1826, shortly after giving birth to a third daughter who did not survive. On the death of his father in 1838, Charles Pascoe became head of the family copper-smelting business. He was a director of the Bank of England and served two terms as MP for Preston. In 1852 he purchased for £12,000, and then rebuilt, Taplow Court, on the hill above his father's house, Taplow House, which had been sold in 1839.[10]

His eldest son, Charles William Grenfell (1823–61), Willy's father, married Georgiana Lascelles in 1852, and served, in the family tradition, as a Liberal politician. But he died in May 1861 at the age of thirty-eight, six years before his father. His death certificate records 'atrophy' as the cause of death.* His younger brother, Henry Riversdale Grenfell (1824–1902), also briefly an MP, was active in the family business, as well as being a founding member of the Bimetallic League and a director (and, for a short term, Governor) of the Bank of England.†

As the nineteenth century progressed, male members of the family, increasingly well connected, contributed to the civic, political, banking and business life of the country.

Historian of the Grenfell family, Penny Watts-Russell, in researching their Cornish origins, has described the Grenfells' upward social mobility in relation to Willy's great-great-grandfather, Pascoe Grenfell: 'it may be truer to say that when resident in Marazion they [the Grenfells] more readily fell into the "middling sort" classification. An income derived from trade differentiated them economically from the poorer sort below, while it enabled a standard of living that allowed for the education of their eight offspring. A payer of land tax marks Pascoe out as belonging to a reasonably prosperous section of society.'[11]

The social and economic progress of the enterprising Grenfells meant that by the time Willy reached his majority in 1876, he inherited considerable wealth and a valuable estate, which ensured that he was very comfortably provided for.[12] As Watts-Russell emphasises, 'the Grenfells were to be relative latecomers to land ownership, it was not to be in Cornwall that vast swathes of acres would accrue to them. Full entitlement to the status of landed gentry and country landowner had come with Pascoe's procurement of manors (in the process of which he acquired the title of Lord of the Manor of Bray) in the neighbourhood of his country residence in Buckinghamshire.'[13]

A document in the Hertfordshire Archive, entitled 'Epitome of Articles of Partnership', sets out the family's financial arrangements for the young William Henry Grenfell. It refers to his grandfather's estate and is dated 10 January 1877. It provided him with three shares in the family businesses out of

---

* The death certificate gives no explanation as to why his life was cut so short, and 'atrophy' could indicate a number of different health conditions.

† One of Charles William's sisters, Maria Georgiana (1820–1900), married Colonel Frederick Paget MP (1807–66, grandson of the 1st Earl of Uxbridge and nephew of the 1st Marquess of Anglesey); another sister, Louisa Henrietta (1825–1911), married Theodore Walrond, who became a Civil Service Commissioner. Charles William's cousin Francis Grenfell (1841–1925) was a distinguished soldier in the Victorian period, becoming a Field Marshall and created 1st Baron Grenfell in 1902. Grenfell Tower in west London was named after Grenfell Road, itself named after the 1st Baron Grenfell; Grenfell Tower was destroyed in a catastrophic and tragic fire in 2017.

a total of twenty, each valued then at £10,000, together worth some £1.35 million today.[14] These monies were in trust, but provided Willy with considerable security, as also his ownership of the Taplow estate and the surrounding farms and properties which his grandfather had acquired, including the large Taplow paper mill operated by Charles Venables & Co. In the early 1870s the Taplow estate had also acquired the Orkney Arms, which became famous as the Maidenhead riverside inn known as Skindles.[15]

We know little of the short life of Charles William, Willy's father. He and his brother Henry commenced their studies at Christ Church, Oxford, at the same time in October 1842. Charles went on to pursue business interests and become MP for Sandwich between 1847 and 1852 and then Windsor between 1852 and 1859. Following their wedding, he and Georgiana took an extensive European honeymoon tour, and his surviving diary depicts both their cultural explorations and glimpses of their relationship. In December 1852 he wrote: 'The last day of the happiest year of my life, in which I not only made sure of my Georgy, but married her, and had not repented of that, the most important step of anyone's life. I believe firmly that no two people can be more suited to one another, and I am sure a better little creature does not exist, a more faithful and devoted wife, or a more pleasant companion, I very often think that I am not good enough for her.'

The diary offers a snapshot of the couple (accompanied by their servant Theodore) enjoying visits to cathedrals and art collections in the Netherlands and Belgium, and travelling to Germany where, in Dresden, Charles had contacts from previous business excursions. They go south to Venice and he records: 'Thurs Oct 21st . . . to San Zaccaria . . . a very curious church . . . Of course there was a Giov. Bellini and a Tintoretto or two.' And then on to Florence, where they attended the English church (hiring a pew for a month), he studied Italian, and Georgy acquired a sketching permit for the Uffizi. They arrived in Rome on 6 December, and, intriguingly, Charles noted, 'we took a look at my old quarters . . . the Hotel de Minerva'.

After the revolutions of the late 1840s, 1852 was a year of relative calm in Europe (though the couple may have avoided France, as Napoleon III's coup d'état had only taken place in December 1851) and the journal conveys the delight of a wealthy young couple enjoying their own version of a Grand Tour before settling into the conventional combination of well-heeled business and family life.

Their happy relationship was reflected in the birth of six children over the next eight years. Their second child, William, was six when his father died, and only twelve when his grandfather passed away. As eldest son, he therefore inherited the house and estate. But whatever the impact of these family traumas, he had a secure place in the supportive clan of Grenfells, which offered well-established connections intertwined with business interests and a pattern of civic, political and military service.[*]

After Willy's grandfather died in 1867, his uncle, Henry, became guardian to the six children. And while Willy's mother Georgiana was a devoted matriarch, her journal acknowledges support from Willy's aunt Maria, known as Aunt Dotty who also lived at Taplow Court (and whose own husband, Colonel Frederick Paget, had died in 1866).

On the steps of Taplow Court, 1865. Standing (left to right): Aunt Louey, Georgiana Grenfell, unknown, Aunt Dotty and Charles Pascoe Grenfell. Seated: Caroline (Lina), William, Charles, Claud, Algernon and Constance (Connie).

---

[*] Such a pattern was exemplified by his uncle, Henry Riversdale Grenfell, his father's cousin Field Marshal Francis Grenfell GCMG, a distinguished soldier and the first Lord Grenfell, and his younger cousin Edward, also a politician, who became 1st Baron St Just, having helped establish the international bank of Morgan Grenfell.

The ten-year-old Willy – William was known interchangeably as Willie or Willy all his life – appears in an 1865 photograph, which features the six children on the front steps of Taplow Court, with his grandfather standing on the right.* A doctored version of the same photograph in the family albums shows Uncle Fred (Paget) pasted into the centre of the image, replacing the unknown female figure, perhaps honouring his memory after his early death.

Glimpses of Willy's childhood emerge from Georgiana's entries in The Children's Journal which she started writing in 1864, three years after her husband's death, and continued until 1909 (two years before her own death).[16] For Tuesday 2 August 1864, for example, she recorded that she was in Wales, on a visit to Penmaenmawr in North Wales, staying at Plas Dyffryn Hall, and gives a delightful everyday account of the 'boys': Willy (aged eight and a half), Claud and Charles playing cricket; and how Aunt Dotty and Uncle Fred are seen off at the station, having stayed for a few days.

At the end of August, 'Uncle Henry, Willy, Lizzy and Martha [family friends] got up very early to ascend Snowdon, it was a bright morning & they had a very good view. Willy despised a pony & was not the worse for the rough walking.' Back home, on Thursday 8 September, she noted that 'Mr and Mrs Gladstone & Lady Mary Farquhar came to tea. They looked out of the window & saw Willy, Charles & Claud walking in procession along the top of the high garden wall, which was very dangerous.' Gladstone was Chancellor of the Exchequer at this point – becoming Prime Minister for the first time four years later – thus highlighting Willy's mother's social connections. Samuel Wilberforce, Bishop of Oxford, was an occasional teatime guest, while Georgiana's sister Henrietta (married to William Cavendish, 2nd Baron Chesham) was often visited at Latimer House, nearby in Buckinghamshire.

As a boy Willy already showed some physical prowess, and his mother records for 13 September 1864 how, 'We drove to Llandudno . . . we had tea with Mrs Charlie Molyneaux & saw her three little boys. Mama and Willy walked along the cliffs . . . Willy ran quick out of sight, so Mama was obliged to ask some gentlemen if they had seen him & and they said they had met a little boy in a red shirt running at 20 miles an hour so Mama knew he was safe.'[17]

---

* Throughout his life William Grenfell signed his letters as 'Willy', but his wife Ettie always wrote to him as 'Willie'.

Drawing of a 'mishap' on the Thames by William Grenfell, aged eleven.

The Thames played a prominent part in the childhood of the Grenfell children. Georgiana recorded (with herself referred to as 'mama' in the third person) the celebration of Claud's eighth birthday in August 1866: 'Uncle Henry gave us a Tea on Monkey Island – he & Mr Newton rowed us there, with mama . . . and Mrs Drummond & Mrs Willoughby joined us. The three eldest can row pretty well now – & Lina has a Jacket & Cap like the boys – One day mama fell into the river, as she held a tree, & the Punt slipped away – Willy fastened the boat, & Uncle Henry pulled her out.' This mishap was vividly sketched by the young Willy, and the drawing pasted by Georgiana into her journal.

Following the death of Uncle Fred (not yet fifty-nine), there was further sadness the following year with the death in 1867 of Willy's grandfather, Charles Pascoe Grenfell: 'March Thursday 21 – Before 9 in the morning we heard of the great misfortune that had fallen upon us in the sudden death of our dear grandfather, whose tenderness & love to us will be always one of the most precious recollections of our childhood . . . Willy had just returned from school (back from Mr Elpea's) & allowed to go to the Funeral on Thursday March 28.'

The sense of close maternal encouragement is complemented by an expectation that the twelve-year-old Willy should already be taking up social and estate duties; for example, on 24 June 1868: 'Mama gave a party from 3 to 7 to all the neighbourhood – about 200 were asked . . . People walked about and admired the new view of the weir . . . Willy helped Mama to receive. He is at home because he is reading with Mr Carter at Hitcham for a Harrow Scholarship . . . It went off well.'

Willy's education is prominent in the journal, and on Monday 27 July 1868 his mother notes: 'To Harrow for scholarship exams – stayed 2 nights at the King's Head. The heat was so intense & Willy <u>knew</u> he should fail.' But the next day Georgiana recorded, 'Willy was all day at the Examinations, turning back to the Inn occasionally to say he was doing very badly & we might as well go home – he did not know till 7.30 that he was amongst the 12 kept on till the next day. It was not pleasant. Mama saw Dr Butler [headmaster] & Mr and Mrs Rendall [potential housemaster and his wife] & sat in the beautiful old churchyard.' But by Thursday the 30th, the agony of waiting was over: 'Mama heard from Dr Butler that Willy had done very well & was 4th on the list next to the 3 scholars – This was exactly what Uncle Henry & Mama wished, as they really wanted him to work & to take a good place at Harrow. Mr Carter had taken great pains with him . . . & all are much pleased.'

After starting at Harrow in September 1868, Willy's achievements, both academic and sporting, were scrupulously recorded by his mother, leavened here and there with additional news, such as noting in July 1870: 'Willy is delighted to have a foxhound puppy.' Willy's own letters to his mother give boyish accounts of boarding-school life and challenges, always keen to make the most of the many and various sporting opportunities at Harrow. Notable sporting successes emerged towards the end of his time at school, and a newspaper cutting is pasted into his mother's journal from July 1873, covering the notorious Eton v. Harrow cricket match in which Willy took part. Headlines referred to an 'Extraordinary scene! – Harrow won by one run – a fight – a "vulgar brawl"'. [See *Chapter 7 Outstanding Sportsman*.] When, in the same year, aged eighteen, a question was raised about his health, he wrote to seek his mother's permission to continue with running, having already secured the support of his Harrow housemaster, Mr Rendall: 'I have been running ever since last year almost every day as hard as I can, without having the very slightest symptoms of anything at all: and now I am suddenly told I must not run.'[18]

He explained that Dr Plummer had examined him and said he was 'quite sound', which he took as unqualified encouragement to continue. He challenged his mother by saying that she had considered him 'such a consummate and unmitigated ass as to wish to run'. And whatever the doctors thought, he was, with determination, now playing cricket, and boxing and fencing as well.

Although his letters testify to an early passion for sport, it is hard to discern whether the Harrow that Willy experienced provided the well-ordered moral framework that the headmaster Dr Butler hoped for. Or whether it fitted with an alternative picture painted a little later in *The Harrovians*, an autobiographical novel by Arnold Lunn.[19] Lunn's novel aimed to tell a truer story of the rough and tumble – and occasional cruelty – of school life, in which boys looked more for survival than moral enhancement. Lunn's protagonist, Peter, notes that 'it was a relief to be able to sleep in form. Footer was our real work.'[20] In the book, Peter triumphs against the odds, but when he looked back to his time at Harrow, it was:

> with a certain grim pleasure. He had learned many salutary lessons. He owed a great debt to his training . . . But he could not mark down any period of his life as 'the happiest days of his existence.' Joy came not according to pattern and direction, but in stray, detached moments, casual and unsought. It would be idle to pretend that life at school marks the supreme point of human happiness for all but a few exceptional, and, perhaps, exceptionally stupid, boys. It is a preparation, and the wise man finds the play more real than the rehearsal.[21]

Given that Willy Grenfell was a fatherless elder son wishing to prove himself within a particularly competitive environment, the context of his schooling is considered at greater length in the next chapter, *Chapter 3 Manhood and Morals*.

Willy applied to Balliol College, Oxford, and took the entrance exam in October 1873. His letters to his mother describe how he travelled to Oxford with his uncle Henry, but arrived an hour late on a Friday morning for the exam (10 a.m. instead of 9). He had more exams on the Saturday, and a viva, before returning to Harrow, though this took longer, as he boarded the wrong train. A telegram had arrived before him, opened by his brother Claud, and his success was known before midnight.[22]

The Balliol offer was to start the following January, in 1874, but when Willy asked if he could stay at Harrow until the summer, his uncle Henry wrote to request a postponement. However, the Master of Balliol, the celebrated Dr Benjamin Jowett, replied saying:

> *I cannot accede to your nephew's wish that he should defer his residence at Balliol though I should gladly have done so if the application had been made six months ago.*
>
> *I am obliged to have fixed rules about the admission of residents in College. We cannot allow the candidate to change his mind after the Examination*

doubt he is as obstinate as a pig.

he said he would write to the Pig-ass.

Two of Willy Grenfell's caricatures of Dr Jowett, included in letters to his mother, 1873.

because a set of rooms has been reserved for him which would in that case remain vacant.

My own impression is that every boy ought to leave school at about 18 or 18½ as was usually the case in our generation. I do not agree with school-masters & tutors in detaining boys at school. After a long university course which is somewhat longer than formerly they get too late into life.[23]

Writing two days later to his mother, Willy explained that he was deeply frustrated by Jowett's refusal, and boldly asserted that he would 'like to know what he means by it, the little ass'. He claimed that if he stayed at Harrow through the following year it would make all the difference both for work and for cricket, and suggested that Jowett was as obstinate as a pig, and illustrated his impertinent view of Dr Jowett.

He added, somewhat arrogantly, 'I've no doubt that the Ass-pig is an estimable man but I should like to flatten his nose.'[24] By the end of November the matter was still not resolved, and his housemaster, Mr Rendall, reported that Jowett refused to change his mind. In early December Willy wrote his own letter to Jowett, for which a draft has survived:

Dear Rev. Dr. Jowett,

I hope you will forgive me troubling you upon a question which has already occupied too much of your attention.

My Uncle has allowed me to do what I can in this matter and has no objection to my staying on at Harrow if possible but says he cannot interfere any more himself.

I have a strong desire to become a scholar and feel perfectly certain that it is of paramount importance for me to stop on here for two more terms: I am not yet advanced enough to be able to cast off regular School discipline without the greatest disadvantage.

I have several times talked the matter over with Dr Butler and Mr Rendall and know that their opinion entirely coincides with mine.

I should not have thought of this request without good authority, and feel sure that a thorough education is as important in my case as in any.

If it is impossible to stay away after having passed the Examination is there any objection to my coming up to be examined again? If I failed then I should have no right to be a member of your college. Of course I should not do this without my Uncle's sanction.

My excuse for making this request is that I had no idea that it was necessary to go up to College immediately after having passed the examination.

I hope you will overlook my boldness in writing to you: nothing would have induced me to do so, had I not felt the question to be one of the greatest importance.

I remain, Yrs very humbly, W. H. Grenfell[25]

It isn't clear whether Willy's thinking was entirely based on scholastic considerations, given that he hoped to be head of house and play cricket for another season. But his negotiating tactic of offering to be examined again produced a change of heart and Dr Jowett wrote back to Grenfell on the 12th:

I very much disapprove of breaking an engagement at the last moment which is what you have done, though unintentionally. The consequence is

that a set of rooms has to be kept vacant & the College loses its rent &
tuition fees & the servant his payment for attendance.

But as you let me think you did not understand the rule & that you
remain at Harrow for the sake of becoming a better Scholar I shall not
enforce it in your case.

I shall expect you to be examined again after Easter & to show us that
you are really a better Scholar than you were last October.[26]

The further examination was successful, and Willy matriculated to read Greats at Balliol on 20 October 1874. Before he left Harrow that summer, Willy achieved a significant record in athletics that stood for many years – running the mile in 4 minutes and 37 seconds. Not surprisingly, his mother's care and interest took her to his final Speech Day at Harrow, after which she noted that 'Grenfell Snr played Sir Anthony Absolute in Sheridan's "The Rivals"' (his younger sibling Claud having joined him at the school).

At Oxford, Willy continued to write regularly to his mother, conveying at one point, somewhat out of character that: 'You may be surprised to hear that I am taking lessons in dancing. I am getting on all right except I get fearfully giddy.'[27] Georgiana's journal entries, however, become more sporadic in the later 1870s and '80s.

When Grenfell inherited Taplow Court, home since the early 1850s to the Grenfells, whose links with the borough of Maidenhead dated back to the family's forty-four-year occupation of Taplow House, he took on more than simply a house and land. It encompassed an expectation of engagement with the local community. Ownership included the employment and care of staff and the management of business and family tenancies, and stood for a set of social and economic relations within the wider life of Maidenhead. As Willy grew up, some of these connections matured into service in the governance of county and town, including as High Steward and Mayor. [See *Chapter 12 Trusted Servant.*] Other connections developed through sport and charitable work, including the forms of companionship offered through membership of the Oddfellows and the Masons. He joined the Apollo Lodge at Oxford (alongside Oscar Wilde) and remained linked to the Masons throughout his life, including in Maidenhead and Taplow.*

---

* William Grenfell became a freemason and was initiated into the Apollo University Lodge, no.357, Oxford, on 23 February 1875 (the same day as Oscar Wilde); on 26 August 1884 he became a member of Ellington Lodge, no.1566, Maidenhead.

And after 1880, as a Member of Parliament – on and off for twenty-five years – he was connected to his constituents, albeit in other parts of the country: they had elected him to Parliament, and he had responsibilities to them.

Willy Grenfell may have been a somewhat arrogant, self-regarding and privileged young man at Harrow and Oxford (he looks awkwardly away from the camera in numerous sporting photographs), and someone who was yet to grow up and find a public persona. However, having lost while young a father and grandfather, he quickly learned, through family, college, sport and politics, the true value of networks: to serve others and equally to ensure continuing support for himself.

Sport and Adventure

3

———•———

Manhood and Morals

Dr Arnold and Tom Brown's School Days *– muscular Christianity – sport at Harrow – 'play the game' – sport and empire – Tom Brown at Oxford*

William Grenfell's schooling at Harrow in the 1870s exemplified significant developments in private education during the second half of the nineteenth century. The dominant ethos and priorities in such schools had been vividly portrayed in Thomas Hughes's *Tom Brown's School Days*, published in 1857. Although fictional, it was based on Rugby School, led by its famous headmaster, Dr Thomas Arnold, between 1828 and 1841. Grenfell might well have read the book as a boy, given that it went into five editions in its first year and emerged as a classic text.

In a passage from Chapter VI, 'After the Match', a senior student named Old Brooke is about to complete his time at Rugby School. He is described as 'cock of the school, and head of the School-house side, and the best kick and charger in Rugby'. After a notable victory on the field, he addresses the younger schoolboys:

> Gentlemen of the School-house . . . Each of us knows and can depend on his next-hand man better – that's why we beat 'em to-day. We've union, they've division – there's the secret – (cheers). But how's this to be kept up? How's it to be improved? That's the question . . . I know I'd sooner win two School-house matches running than get the Balliol scholarship any day – (frantic cheers).[1]

The book was widely influential, but while the novel's depiction of team sports dominating school life contained considerable truth, this didn't entirely correspond with Dr Arnold's own thinking at Rugby. His priorities focused on promoting Christian virtues and morals more than organised games. Nevertheless, the fictional depiction consolidated something frequently experienced: that sport at boys' public schools, which had been rowdy and unregulated in the early nineteenth century, was from mid-century better codified, offered wider participation and had higher status. 'Playing the game' now mattered, and amplified the emerging concept of 'muscular Christianity', ensuring that organised sports would play an influential part in the formation of masculine identity in Britain in the second half of the century.[2] Grenfell himself became an exemplar of that identity.

The sports historian J. A. Mangan describes how: 'Physical exercise was taken, considerably and compulsorily, in the sincere belief of many, however romantic, misplaced or myopic, that it was a highly effective means of inculcating valuable instrumental and impressive educational goals: physical and moral courage, loyalty and co-operation, the capacity to act fairly and take defeat well, the ability to both command and obey.'[3]

One former pupil and notable follower of Thomas Arnold was Charles Vaughan. When appointed as headmaster of Harrow School, aged twenty-eight in 1845, he applied himself as a Christian educator and talented administrator and revived the fortunes of the former grammar school: improving teaching, refocusing the curriculum, extending facilities and thereby increasing pupil numbers from fewer than seventy to over 460.[4] Willy attended Harrow in the 1860s under his successor, the Revd Montagu Butler, though Vaughan's influence was still strong. Sport at Harrow became more prominent with the formation of the Harrow Philathletic Club in 1853 – an elite of thirty pupils elected from the sixth- and fifth-form students – and this countered the wildness and irresponsibility attributed to earlier Harrow boys.[5] Sporting development can also be charted through a striking increase in the land given over to sport: from approximately eight acres in 1845 to 146 acres by 1900, made possible through the support of a wealthier set of parents and alumni.[6] Sport infiltrated many aspects of the lives of boys at Harrow, and Mangan comments how with sport, in a short space of time, 'resented innovation became respected tradition'.[7]

The Clarendon Royal Commission of 1864 examined nine prominent public schools in great detail, including Eton, Harrow, Rugby and Winchester: investigating their governance, admissions, teaching quality, curriculum and facilities.[8] Amid many recommendations for Harrow, the Commission said that

W. H. Grenfell (back row, left, ball in hand) in the Harrow School cricket 1st XI, 1873.

'The attention of the Governors should be directed to . . . the insufficiency of the cricket-ground, and the desirableness of acquiring more space for cricket.'[9] The Commission nonetheless noted that 'The average time given to cricket is estimated at about fifteen hours in the week; "a boy who took every opportunity" would make it twenty. That the importance assigned to games in the estimation of the boys is somewhat greater than it should be, is admitted by a witness who was for two years captain of the eleven. But it is frequently the case, at Harrow as elsewhere, that diligent and distinguished cricketers are also diligent and distinguished in school work.'[10]

This last comment may *not* have applied entirely to Willy Grenfell, as his determination to stay on for extra terms at Harrow appeared to be largely dictated by his keenness to achieve further success at cricket and athletics, while hoping that he wouldn't fall behind academically. The Commission wanted reforms, but its rousingly positive conclusion set a tone of expectation for the public schools themselves:

the English people are indebted to these schools for the qualities on which they pique themselves most – for their capacity to govern others and control themselves, their aptitude for combining freedom with order, their public spirit, their vigour and manliness of character, their strong but not slavish respect for public opinion, their love of healthy sports and exercise. These schools have been the chief nurseries of our statesmen; in them, and in schools modelled after them, men of all the various classes that make up English society, destined for every profession and career, have been brought up on a footing of social equality, and have contracted the most enduring friendships, and some of the ruling habits, of their lives; and they have had perhaps the largest share in moulding the character of an English gentleman.[11]

Sir Theodore Cook – one of Grenfell's closest collaborators in the creation of the 1908 Olympic Games – published a book titled *Character and Sportsmanship* in 1927, a year after the General Strike. As he looked back, he offered a rallying cry 'amidst these days of turmoil, of uncertainty, of civil strife', and called for a response by which:

We must be worthy of our heritage. We shall keep it by that sense of fair play which is bred in our bone and courses through our blood, which makes a boy play the game outside the schoolroom walls even if he does not achieve much intellectual distinction inside them. We shall keep it by the readiness to take up responsibility and make his own decision, which is ingrained in every English schoolboy as he rises among his comrades whether in work or play, and as he feels the influence of the higher forms of sportsmanship upon his life and character.[12]

This male-centred rhetoric is typical of the many expressions of what Mangan describes as 'patriotic self-pride in noble muscularity'.[13] And it exemplifies the ethos of 'muscular Christianity' which surrounded Willy Grenfell as he progressed through Harrow and Oxford. The term was associated both with Thomas Hughes and the writings of cleric, novelist and historian Charles Kingsley (who was married to Willy's great-aunt Frances Eliza Grenfell).[14] Muscular Christianity emphasised the virtues of self-sacrifice, endurance, stoicism and discipline, and linked an assertive masculinity to patriotic service for the nation, and equally to moral probity and physical prowess through organised sport. It was presumed, though certainly not always true, that time spent at school (and particularly public school) would inculcate boys with these virtues, and serve them well as they went on to university or to public service in the military, politics, the church or an expanding empire, and, equally, in business and family life.

As historians Mangan and Walvin put it, 'In time, on both sides of the Atlantic, the cult [of muscular Christianity] became so potent that it formed, in effect, a distinctive and powerful moral code; it offered a set of values applicable to each and every facet of personal and collective life.'[15]

This was both a practical matter of how much time might be spent on sporting activities at school, university and beyond, and the promotion of a moral framework, as much through school magazines as sermons in chapel. That framework included the presumption of fair play – playing by the rules – and an implication that highly competitive sportsmen would not allow their competitiveness to get ahead of their sense of duty.[16] Grenfell's headmaster at Harrow, Montagu Butler, asserted at his eightieth birthday dinner in July 1912 that, 'whether it be a matter of cricket . . . or politics or professional engagements, there is hardly any motto which I would more confidently commend . . . than "Play the Game"!'[17] The more widely popular version of the cliché was later encapsulated by the American sportswriter Grantland Rice when he wrote in the last lines of his 1941 poem 'Football' that when you are marked by the Great Scorer it won't matter whether you lost or won but 'how you played the game.'[18]

This moral dimension, which promoted fair play (and looked down on betting), fed into the growth of amateur sport, including association football and rugby football, and had an impact in established professional sports (such as rowing, horse-racing, boxing and running) in which prize money or the interests of those betting on the outcome had previously predominated. Lincoln Allison explains that while the public schools and the universities were influential in the development of modern sport, they represented only 3 per cent of the population, so that, despite the apparent dominance of the upper classes, it was the establishment of many kinds of sporting clubs across the country, both working and middle class, that made the larger difference to the growth of organised sport.[19] The adoption of colours, costume, rituals and rules amplified the precepts of teamwork and fairness.[20] And although women were beginning to participate in several sports, such as croquet, tennis and gymnastics, the emphasis was on masculinity: sporting heroes were mostly male, English, white, and from middle- or upper-class families.

The distinguished biographer Sir Leslie Stephen (father of Virginia Woolf and Vanessa Bell) wrote slightly cynically in 1875 (in marked contrast to the Clarendon Commission): 'An English public school . . . is a miniature world; and, certainly, the world is in many respects a big public school. The training it gives is of the rough and ready order, with plenty of hard blows and little allowance for sentiment. The men who succeed in later life generally owe that good fortune to the same qualities which raise a boy to be leader among his fellows.'[21]

As the British Empire expanded in the second half of the nineteenth century, particularly in the 'settled dominions' of Canada, South Africa, Australia and New Zealand, empire builders took with them those sports that had developed in Britain. Cricket, football, rugby, tennis and rowing were pursued in the dominant British communities around the world. And as sports were standardised and bureaucratised, overseen by club officials and committees, the national arena opened up to opportunities for international competition. David Cannadine emphasises how much the development of empire involved both strict racial hierarchy and the promotion of 'status' and its perception, and how the social roles and interests of British overseers served this, together with their growing number of ceremonies, pageants and medals:

> Underpinning all these mid-century settler regimes, with their traditional, transoceanic loyalties and their 'imported social hierarchies', was the view . . . that a mature settler society was necessarily a graded, layered society. That, in essence, was what they were seeking to establish in these new far-distant realms: in part by the export of authentic British aristocrats overseas, who would set the tone and the social standard; in part by the emulative creation of their own indigenous landed gentry.[22]

Organised sport, from cricket to game hunting – particularly hunting, which was transformed from pioneer survival, as Willy Grenfell first took part in it in the 1880s, to elite ritual – played its part in this expansion, and in reinforcing the layered hierarchies.[23] The expansion of public schools ensured that they could fulfil the demand for empire administrators.[24] From school to university, and to the armed forces, sport and the values of middle-class amateurism were spread around the world. By the end of the century, as historian Roberta J. Park has noted, there was a cult-like sense that an athletic hero would be a moral leader: a 'man who was an "aristocrat of character" not an aristocrat by birth'.[25]

As this ethos of the moral virtue of sport spread, there were other effects. Baron Pierre de Coubertin, founder of the modern Olympic Games, followed the idea (rather than the actuality) of Thomas Arnold's philosophy at Rugby.

De Coubertin was invited to England by Dr William Penny Brookes, who had already been promoting an international revival of the Olympics, to attend a special autumn edition of his Olympian Festival at Much Wenlock in Shropshire in October 1890.[26] As Luke Harris points out, it was de Coubertin's idealisation of British sport and the public-school system, alongside his myth-laden view of the ancient Games of Greece, that ensured a central Olympic principle was based on an amateurism much nurtured in Britain, something largely unchanged into the 1970s.[27]

Tom Brown at Oxford, Thomas Hughes's lesser-known sequel to *Tom Brown's School Days*, was first published in book form in 1861. Once at Oxford, Tom takes to the river, and gradually achieves success as an oarsman at the fictional St Ambrose's College.[28] His sporting adventures give Hughes the chance to make some ironic comments about the concept of muscular Christianity, a philosophy with which he, as a writer, was identified:

> Our hero on his first appearance in public some years since, was without his own consent at once patted on the back by the good-natured critics, and enrolled for better or worse in the brotherhood of muscular Christians, who at that time were beginning to be recognised as an actual and lusty portion of general British life. As his biographer, I am not about to take exception to his enrolment; for, after considering the persons up and down Her Majesty's dominions to whom the new nick-name has been applied, the principles which they are supposed to hold, and the sort of lives they are supposed to lead; I cannot see where he could in these times have fallen upon a nobler brotherhood.[29]

The implication is that Tom is to some degree an innocent, and potentially indifferent to the moral debates swirling around the public schools and Oxford at the time. This may equally have been true of Willy. However, Grenfell's belief in the significance of sport, both to individuals and to society, was forged in this period. Alongside his studies, his sporting life took new forms, including rowing, and also mountaineering, riding, hunting, boxing and cricket (as we discuss later). One senses that without becoming an evangelical Christian, he began to see the importance of Christian values – as the most appropriate moral framework – for life and work, and for sport.

4

---·---

Rowing and the Boat Race

*Rowing at Oxford – Oxford University Boat Club – the 1877
dead-heat Boat Race – rowing the Channel – defining amateurs – an
ambassador for rowing*

William Grenfell's close bonds to the River Thames were forged through two
of the sports to which he became devoted: rowing and punting. He lived by
the river, he used the river frequently and considered it hugely significant.

An article in *Baily's Magazine of Sports and Pastimes* in 1890 noted that despite
living beside the river for much of his childhood, Grenfell didn't take up rowing
as a sport until he went to university, as Harrow wasn't a rowing school.[1] But local
accounts suggest that he was already well known on the river at Taplow, and this
will have involved both punting and rowing. In the same year, Grenfell wrote an
article titled 'Rowing at Oxford', in which he followed the progress of a would-be
oarsman 'Graham' at the fictional 'St Giles College' as he progresses from beginner
in college rowing to joining the university Blue Boat.[2] This appears to be a thinly
veiled account of his own earlier rowing career at Oxford – the likenesses are striking: 'Graham' came from a non-rowing school and his supposed weight of 12
stone 6 pounds matched that of Grenfell. He was strong, athletic and determined,
but with flawed technique. After being offered an initial try-out on the river, our
hero Graham 'got out of the boat with the conviction firm upon him that rowing,
or at all events rowing in racing form, was a very much more complicated exercise
than at first sight it appeared, still he felt that he had received sufficient encouragement from the coach to make it worthwhile to come down to the river again –
besides which the rowing men . . . seemed such good sorts and so ready to take
any amount of trouble over people they had never seen before'.[3]

Balliol College VIII 1875, William Grenfell, standing, second from left.

Grenfell arrived in Oxford in the autumn term of 1874 with a reputation as an accomplished all-round athlete.[4] It wasn't surprising that he continued in both athletics and cricket (competing in both college and inter-college events), but as a 'dry bob' (slang for a schoolboy who goes in for field sports in preference to rowing) it was unexpected that he embraced the river with enthusiasm and made rapid progress with his rowing.[5] Within months he was in the Balliol first eight, rowing at number 4 in the Spring Torpids of 1875. He represented the college throughout his time there, rowing on bow side at 5 (in 1877 he rowed at 7). In October 1875 he became Secretary of the Balliol Boat Club, progressing to Captain in 1876. But it wasn't always straightforward with Balliol and, writing to his mother from Oxford on Vincent's Club* notepaper towards the end of that year, he says:

> I am disgusted with Balliol; it is peopled with little men with big heads
> who think themselves clever and don't wash. As to setting a decent boat
> on the river it is absurd to dream of it, as most of those men who can
> row won't, as they are in for Schools, and those who will row would

---

* The dining club in Oxford for those who have been awarded a university blue.

look much better on the bank . . . I think we have a bad boat this summer. I shall never get into the Varsity as one can't learn to row properly if half the crew are all over the place for the first quarter mile and have to be pulled over the rest of the course.[6]

He went on to be re-elected as Balliol Captain in 1877 and 1878, only resigning in the summer of 1879.[7] However, although he had taken part in trials for the university in 1875 without success, his ambition was such that he emerged as one of a group of powerful new oarsmen considered for the university in late 1876. He also competed in the intervarsity athletics match in the same year, coming second in the three-mile race. Grenfell was trained by T. C. Edwardes-Moss, the experienced Blue Boat President and, rowing at 4, his aptitude for hard training was noted.[*] Despite this evident willingness and application, he continued to struggle with technique. The *Daily Telegraph* reported harshly on 12 March 1877:

University crew, 1877, with Grenfell rowing at number 4.

---

[*] At the point at which Grenfell became successful at rowing, it became clear that he was unlikely to progress further with his cricket career.

He (Grenfell) is the strongest man in a boat that boasts little but strength. Considering his weight (12st 13lb), Mr Moss must be congratulated on the progress his pupil has made. He is by no means a perfect oar, and has not a good style. Occupying as he does the place No.4 he ought to be careful of the swing, and try to catch it with No.6, for No.2 is dependent upon him for swing and time. It is however, in his swing back and forwards that Mr Grenfell seems most faulty . . . The result is that disagreeable roll and unsteadiness in the Oxford crew which has never forsaken them since the first day they took to their racing ship.

Selected to row at number 4 in the spring of 1877, weighing in at 12 stone 10 pounds, he played his part in the famous dead-heat Boat Race.[8]

The 1877 Oxford Boat crew, both strong and heavy, was improving all the time. It was clear from the outset that the 'intervarsity boat race' (as it was called) was going to be closely fought, even with a more experienced Cambridge crew – all of whom were blues and regarded as superior in technique. Cambridge were considered favourites.

W. H. Grenfell (back row, left) in the Oxford University Boat Club crew, 1877.

The Boat Race has been described as one of the most 'brutal, harsh and uncompromising struggles[s] in all of sport' and it has always taken place in the public eye.[9] It was normal in this period for the build-up to involve intensive press coverage, with daily reports on the progress of the two crews as they trained on their home waters and then on the Tideway. Grenfell was firmly entrenched as number 4 and 'was tied to the boat' (though he had still found time to run in both the Mile and Two Mile handicap races in a college athletics meeting on 14 February that year).

By race day (24 March 1877) the odds on the crews had shifted to evens, suggesting a very close result. The race was started shortly after eight in the morning, when the tide was at its most favourable. Interest was intense and, despite the early start and poor weather, crowds gathered. As the *Standard* reported: 'Albeit turning out at sunrise on a March morning is not, in the metropolis at least a popular amusement, many scores of thousands of well to do Englishmen and Englishwomen performed the feat for that occasion.'[10]

Astonishingly, we are still able to hear Grenfell's view of the race through a BBC sound recording made in 1938, with John Snagge as interviewer.[11] Grenfell insisted that Oxford had won by a small margin, but accepted it was a close call:

The crews appearing in The Penny Illustrated Paper *and* The Illustrated and Dramatic News, *24 March 1877.*

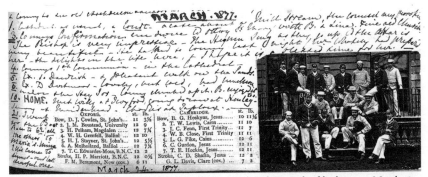

A page from The Children's Journal, with crew lists and a photograph of both crews, March 1877.

The wind was from the west northwest, the worst quarter, and blowing hard, and the tide was very slack when the race was started at eight twenty-seven on March twenty-fourth. Cambridge used their slides well and had done fast times in practice. Oxford had a redoubtable body swing set by H. P. Marriott, stroke, and by T. C. Edwardes-Moss, number seven, who had rowed together for four years for Brasenose College.

The race was a ding-dong one to Barnes, where Oxford were a length ahead and going away, when the boat suddenly felt like a barge. Bow's oar had given away at the button in the very rough water above Barnes, and all that D. J. Cawles, who was rowing bow, could do was to hold it in the middle and try to keep the ends out of the water. Cambridge, though a tired crew, immediately shot up, but Oxford, with the advantage of the inside bend, struggled on till the end. We thought we had won by a small margin. I was rowing number four and seemed to be on a level with the Cambridge two, and the boats were close together. We put away our boats first, and had taken up our places in the bows of the barge when we were told it was a dead heat. Much to our disappointment.

Rowing the last part of the course with effectively seven men inevitably saw Oxford's lead whittled away, and it is no surprise that the finish was tight.[12] The race became notorious because of the initial confusion as to who had won. The waterman acting as finishing judge, 'Honest John' Phelps, declared 'a dead heat to Oxford by four feet', though there were spurious claims that he was either drunk, asleep or both.*[13]

---

* At this date there was no finishing post – the judge simply had to decide the winner by eye as the boats passed by. Phelps lost his job as a consequence of this event.

The race umpire, Mr Chitty QC, wanted to understand more before he would announce the result. It proved impossible to achieve that at Mortlake, where the race ends, and Chitty had to return to central London almost immediately to conduct pressing legal matters. As a consequence, a deliberation (and thus the announcement of an official result) was delayed until later that morning, when Phelps had made his way to Chitty's chambers, adding to the drama surrounding the whole event. Chitty had no argument with the dead-heat decision, and the controversy surrounding it should not obscure the fact that this was a fine race, hotly contested. As the official record of the Thirty-Fourth University Boat Race rightly commented:

> Those who accompanied the race will not easily forget the intense excitement of that last desperate struggle, and the sudden pause of anxious inquiry as to the actual result when the crews ceased rowing. It is perhaps too much to expect, even from the stoical discipline of Old Blues, a unanimous acquiescence in a verdict of 'dead heat', than which no conclusion can be more unsatisfactory to the competitors themselves. We think it is but just, however, to a faithful old servant to say that no good grounds have been shown for doubting the rightness of John Phelps's decision. Surely whatever feelings of discontent may have existed in either crew in the heat of the moment may well give place to hearty satisfaction at having taken part in so grand a race.[14]

As training commenced for the 1878 Boat Race, concerns were raised about Willy's fitness and he underwent close examination of his heart (though his own view was that running, not rowing, affected him more). He wrote to his mother on 14 February:

> *You needn't be the least alarmed as regards my health as I am all right. Acland [Sir Henry Acland, the university doctor] asked me to breakfast yesterday and then made me run round the room & jump over a lot of chairs – can you imagine anything more likely to make one's pulse wrong than an amateur hurdle race round a small room immediately after a heavy breakfast – he then said I wasn't all right, which I could have told him, as I had scraped all the skin off my knuckles over one of his beastly chairs – in the afternoon I rowed ten miles in the crew and worked as hard as I could and felt better for it.[15]*

Willy was eventually passed as fit, and having tried out at number 6, he reoccupied the 4 position.[16] Oxford won by forty seconds, more than seven lengths (a record that lasted for 103 years). Having included the crew list and group photograph for the Boat Race of 1877 in her journal, Georgiana Grenfell had failed to mention the controversial dead-heat result. But for 1878 she records Oxford's victory on 23 March, observing that she 'saw them get into their boat – Willy looks very thin & pale & so do most of them'. Health concerns continued that year with a diagnosis of quinsy, a form of tonsillitis, leading Willy to take time out from the university. And in 1879, although now elected as President, a broken collarbone prevented him from rowing – he consulted numerous doctors to secure permission to row but failed to find support – and fell back on coaching the crew (which was unsuccessful).[17] In the following year Willy switched to a pass degree and graduated on 19 June 1879. After leaving Oxford, he continued to coach, and regularly hosted the Oxford crew at Taplow Court.[18]

Grenfell's retrospective view of his rowing career at Oxford is reflected in the persona of the fictional Graham: 'As he looks at his oars and trophies and thinks over the lessons of generosity in victory, good-humour in defeat, of self-denial in training, of self-sacrifice and esprit de corps, of obedience and authority, he is well assured that not the least valuable of the lessons of his University career have been taught him on the river, and that all the toil he has gone through has been more than thrice repaid.'[19]

The 1883 Oxford crew training at Taplow Court.

In 1879 Willy was made honorary Captain of the recently formed Maiden-head Rowing Club, a position he held until 1945, as well as becoming President in 1934 on the death of Viscount Burnham. He was thus Captain for some sixty-six years, and President for twelve.[20] At the club's Annual Dinner in 1879, shortly after becoming Captain, Grenfell described how: 'Not only was it a manly sport, but it called forth qualities which could not be too highly esteemed. A man must not only pull well himself, but he must consider others, and maintain good temper and good fellowship. The one great necessity was that a crew should pull together, and this principle, so prominent in rowing was equally important in greater things.'[21]

This sentiment reverberated through many of Grenfell's activities – for him sport and life were intertwined.

A version of the portrait by Arthur Stockdale Cope, on loan from the Borough Council, hangs prominently in the stairwell of Maidenhead Rowing Club, along with Grenfell's blade from the 1877 dead-heat Boat Race. His enthusiasm for rowing was such that he rowed for Leander Club (to which he had been elected in 1877) in the Grand Challenge Cup at the 1881 Henley Regatta while a Member of Parliament for Hereford, and then again in 1885 as MP for Salisbury. In the same year he rowed as stroke across the Channel in a clinker eight fitted with sliding seats and outriggers (each crew member apparently equipped with a jam jar for bailing). In 1889, perhaps seeking further boating triumphs, Grenfell rowed in a team of three (with a cox weighing 13 stone) from Oxford to Putney (a distance by river of 105 miles) in a time of twenty-two hours, having not rowed for the previous two years.

Two Grenfell oars hanging at Maidenhead Rowing Club.

Grenfell was elected as a Steward of Henley Royal Regatta in 1882 and served until 1939.[22] As with other sports, he continued his involvement well beyond his days as an active participant, being engaged with rowing for well over sixty years and despite his late start.

William Grenfell's role as an ambassador for rowing grew out of his distinguished record as an oarsman. He made himself readily available for dinners, meetings and public events. While he may be considered the Establishment personified, it was no coincidence that he gave the Desborough Cup for champion eights on the Thames to the National Amateur Rowing Association (NARA), which, unlike the Amateur Rowing Association (ARA), admitted manual labourers. Similarly, towards the end of his life, as Lord Desborough, he opened the new Imperial College boathouse on 21 October 1938 – a strikingly modernist building designed and built by the club's founder, Charles Bristow. The commemorative plaque from the occasion reads: 'May all who use this boathouse in it find such happiness and make such friendships as may endure throughout their lives.' If these were not Desborough's words, they mirrored his wholehearted belief in the capacity of team sports to build trust and long-lasting friendships.

The image of someone so thoroughly immersed in sport – in this case rowing – might lead to an easy assumption that all that he had to offer was 'brawn not brains'. Colin Clifford, in discussing the friendship between Margot Asquith and Ettie Desborough, makes the jibe that 'She was married to Willy Grenfell, Lord Desborough – six foot five and with a physique to match. Grenfell was an Oxford rowing blue and an Olympic fencer but his intellect was as puny as his body was athletic.'[23]

The basis for this assertion is unclear, although Clifford is not alone in making it. However, it is a long way from the truth, as would become evident from Grenfell's substantial contributions in so many spheres of public life.

Grenfell revealed more of his intellectual capacities in two articles, exemplifying his influence beyond the sport itself.[24] First was his contribution to Alfred Watson's edited volume on *English Sport*, published in 1903. Here he reflected first on the growth of rowing as a sport and the relative merits of amateur and professional rowing, and then on the design of the Oxford boat in 1901.* He then moved on to consider the question of entry qualifications

---

* Professional river sports pre-date amateur, for the obvious reason that those who earned their living on the river were the first to organise contests. The Tyne and the Thames were the principal centres of professional rowing.

for the Henley Regatta and the impact of its growing international ambition on amateur rowing in England.

He set out a passionate case for keeping Henley as a 'genuine amateur regatta' and questioned whether some crews from other countries met the criteria for amateur status. He noted that 'for the Diamond Sculls there have been at least four entries much open to suspicion' and argued that the 'greater the competition, especially if international rivalry be added, the greater the danger of sport becoming professionalized'. In essence, the suspicion was that competitors from overseas might have the benefit of greater strength and fitness, due either to their manual occupations or from additional training and coaching. This was seen as giving them an advantage over British amateurs, for whom the sport was a leisure pursuit secondary to their occupations.[25]

Grenfell was influenced by Dr Edmond Warre, headmaster of Eton College and a senior Steward at Henley, who had raised this question in 1901. Grenfell subsequently wrote to *The Times* to say that he proposed that entries should be confined to the British Isles. His motion was considered by the Stewards in November of that year but the vote was decisively (by nineteen votes to five) in favour of foreign crews rowing at Henley. This debate rumbled on for decades.

The definition of an amateur was a point of major dispute between the two national organisations for rowing in England, with the ARA opting to keep manual labourers out of membership, while the NARA welcomed them in. Desborough backed the NARA, even though he was unhappy about the issue of foreign crews.[26] The battle concerning the definition of an amateur found some accommodation in the inter-war period, but it wasn't until 1956 that the two organisations were merged and a new Amateur Rowing Association, with a new constitution, was born.

Grenfell's second written contribution was *The Story of the Oar*, a lecture delivered on 22 February 1910 at the Philosophical Institution in Edinburgh and subsequently published in *The Field* in March 1910.[27] In this rather earnest dissertation, complete with illustrations, he set out a chronology of the historical evolution of rowing boats and oars, from the ancient world to the turn of the century.[28]

Desborough remained closely associated with rowing throughout his life, not least through his long-standing connections with Oxford University Boat Club, Leander Club and as a Steward of Henley Royal Regatta. Through him (and with others) the sport would have access to influence in high places.

There is also the nice point that with rowing – as with tennis and other sporting interests – he was joined by Lady Desborough. In 1923 she was appointed
as founding President of the Women's Amateur Rowing Association (WARA);
a small but significant milestone for the sport. [29]

*Lord Desborough, as a long-serving Steward of Henley Royal Regatta and member of
Leander Club, accompanying the Duke and Duchess of York (the future King and Queen),
at the Regatta, July 1931.*

5

Exploits and Expeditions

*Lost in the Rockies – swimming at Niagara Falls – Suakin and the
battle of McNeill's zareba*

Alongside his growing dedication to sport, William Grenfell had a substantial
appetite for adventure, combined with a lifelong passion for hunting animals,
some of which was fulfilled in the wide-open spaces of Canada and the United
States. He sought out risk, believing that 'The presence of a certain element of
danger adds to the excitement and attractiveness of any sport.'[1] He took on danger
well beyond the level of everyday sport, and in the 1880s, in his twenties and
before marrying, Grenfell's adventurous spirit dominated his life, in contrast to
rather less exciting periods of parliamentary service. He published accounts of
getting lost in the Rockies in 1884, his Niagara swims and of his time in Suakin.[2]

The incident in the Rockies revealed a degree of naivety – mixing reckless-
ness and self-pity – in how Grenfell handled himself when surviving in the
wilderness. There was little evidence of the 'outstanding sportsman'. His two
swims across the basin below the Niagara Falls, one in 1884, the other in 1888,
also revealed a certain foolhardiness, perhaps borne out of an assumed infalli-
bility. By the time he was pursuing large game in India in the early 1890s or
giant tarpon in the Gulf of Mexico in the late 1890s, he was much more
assured as a sportsman and public figure. [See *Chapter 7 Outstanding Sportsman* and *Chapter 8 The Great Amateur*.]

HUNTING IN THE ROCKIES
In 1884, at the age of twenty-nine, Grenfell travelled to the Rocky Mountains
with fellow Harrovian and MP Gilbert Leigh. Leigh had made a number of

trips to the Rockies (this was his fifth) and was four years older than Grenfell. They travelled by boat, train and then wagon to the Bighorn Mountains in Wyoming, with the intention of hunting bear. They were accompanied by two hunters and a cook. This proved to be an ill-fated expedition, recounted in an eleven-page article by Grenfell that provides valuable insight into his skills as an outdoorsman and his character and ambition as a writer.[3]

Grenfell captures with some humour the setting up of their camp, the selection of horses and the challenge of getting fresh meat, on which a bet was made. This required him to leave camp early, as he describes:

Silently and sleepily I pulled out my rifle and collected the cartridges, not forgetting pipe, tobacco and lights, and slipped quietly out in the still frosty air. Outside the tent the grass lay white and crisp with hoar frost under the dusky sky, and not a sound was to be heard. Now for the deer! But first to mark the camp. Well that is easy enough, for our two little tents lie below the most remarkable eminence that we have come across in our wanderings. The hill facing the camp rose slowly on the left hand fringed with burnt timber till it reached a great height, and then dropped sheer down to the sage-brush plain below – a solid wall and frowning

Studio images of William Grenfell in New York and in a studio in Wyoming, 1884.

precipice of red rock, with a profile resembling that of the most versatile and most prominent statesman of our time. There it stood, a plain mark for all the country round, and if this massive rock can only be kept in view, the way back to the camp will not be hard to find. With the surroundings being taken in and carefully noted, the long streaks of dawn are getting brighter and brighter; there is but little time to lose. At twelve o'clock it has been arranged that the camp will be struck, and a move made further into the mountains in hope of finding wapiti and bear and before twelve o'clock a deer must be slain, meat must be got for the camp, and one dollar won and five saved.

Grenfell sets off along the edges of the forest and then into the forest itself, but to no avail. The deer had given him the slip and with the sun high in the sky, he decides to return to camp. He finds the hill 'as red and menacing as ever, but a welcome sight – and though chaff at my failure is to be expected, still a hot cup of tea will more than wash it down after this long morning walk'. But it isn't to be: there is no sign of the camp even from higher up the hill. He fires shots and yells 'but no answer comes back save for silence. The sun is beginning to decline – horrors – I shall have to pass the long cold night without food or shelter.' He resolves to stop his search and focus on eating and finding shelter before the light gives out. He makes a fire, but 'sleep is out of the question – the wood burns so quickly that the fire requires constant attention; as soon as it burns a little low, the intense cold of the frosty night makes one start up to replenish it'.

Dawn comes and he renews his search. A grouse flies up and he shoots it 'not so bad for a starving shot'. He crosses a series of canyons in his search for a valley to descend before dark sets in again. He now recognises he is completely lost. He has abandoned searching for the camp (he also thinks that his companions may have moved) and is focused on finding human habitation. He climbs down into a canyon to reach a stream, and water to drink, and prepares for his second night, lighting a fire and attempting to cook the grouse ('not being well versed in the culinary art – how to cook it?'). He makes a spit of some sort, but in the event, 'I feel too dispirited to care for so scanty a meal and a very small portion suffices.' His narrative continues:

And now begins the second night, a night infinitely more dreadful than the first – more dreadful because more hopeless. The first was bad enough; it is not exhilarating to pass any night without shelter, food, or companion, but the first night there was always hope: there was hope of reaching the valley and of finding human beings. But now it had been reached and denied all help and here I am a second night at the bottom of a gloomy canyon, not knowing which way to go – one way no better than another and apparently in a country devoid of human beings. Through the long dark hours there is time for many thoughts . . . The same thoughts occur over and over again. What a fool I am to die here slowly of starvation when I might have been comfortably in camp or, better still at home in bed! Why did I go out alone to die here like a rat in a trap when I feel so strong and well. Why did I come out at all to die three thousand miles from home with important rage at my heart? How do men die here of starvation? . . . When will this night come to an end? What shall I do when it does? If only I had started on horseback – a horse would support one in more ways than one for some time. Then would come fits of anger and bitterness, and my hand would instinctively feel my pocket to find if the two precious cartridges were still safe which I had put by in case the worst should come to the worst – anything is better than to die inch by inch like this.

As luck would have it, the next day he comes across a man named Frank Sykes, who lived in the area entirely alone. Sykes was familiar with the hunters leading this party and returned Grenfell to the camp on horseback, explaining that the terrain was very confusing, with many similar mountains which 'you could hardly tell apart'. Sykes had seen him coming and had considered avoiding him altogether but his 'woe-begone appearance had arrested his attention'.

So, Grenfell made it back to camp and rejoined the expedition. He had gone out in tennis shoes and on foot. He had a compass and telescope, but told no one he was going out and was unfamiliar with the terrain. It was in hindsight a foolhardy response to his companions' bet on finding food! The hunters who were running this trip might well have reflected on the naivety of the two Englishmen, but the story didn't end there. Within a week, on 14 September, his companion Gilbert Leigh got lost, fell from a precipice and died. Grenfell and the party spent several days searching before discovering the body on the 21st. They had to carry Leigh's body over the mountains for twenty-three miles before beginning a wagon journey of 130 miles to reach the railway and ultimately back to England.[4]

NIAGARA

On 24 August 1875 Matthew Webb, aged twenty-seven, became the first person to swim the English Channel without the use of artificial aids. Although known already for his life-saving exploits, this achievement catapulted him to international prominence and he became a professional swimmer, undertaking exhibition swims of one kind or another.[5] In July 1883 he undertook his most dangerous challenge when he set out to swim through the Whirlpool Rapids on the Niagara River.

From the 1860s there was a 'Niagara craze', with numbers of people going over the Falls – most survived, some didn't. Some of these 'daredevils' attracted considerable crowds and, in a few cases, substantial prize money. Webb, deemed by some to be the greatest swimmer in the world, announced he would swim down the Niagara from just below the Falls and proceed through the rapids within the narrow gorge towards the railway suspension bridge. He attempted to secure sponsorship for this venture, but this failed and, despite many warnings, he went ahead.[6] Some thought it inevitable he would fail and, tragically, despite brave efforts, he went ahead on 24 July 1883 and died.

Grenfell was in North America a year later for his hunting trip in the Rocky Mountains and visited the Falls to swim the Niagara River.[7] This exploit was likely to have been prompted by the publicity surrounding Webb's death, as well as his own love of adventure.[8] Years later, in a speech for the unveiling of a memorial to Webb in Dover in June 1910, Grenfell explained further:

> It so happens that I myself might in some degree be said to be associated with him (cheers). I happen to have swum across the Pool of Niagara – (cheers) – but that is nothing. But in 1884, the year after Webb's death in Niagara, I jumped out of the boat which Webb had jumped out of the previous year, and I then swam across the Pool, which strangely enough Webb had never attempted . . . [and] had a vivid description given me of when Webb tried to swim down the Niagara Rapids.[9]

Although he used the same boat and presumably the same ferryman as Webb, he wasn't trying to swim through the rapids. There is no public record of Grenfell's first swim, and he undertook a second swim some four years later because no one witnessed the first and he was apparently challenged as to whether he had done it.[10]

N. Y. 101 General View of Niagara Falls

One of several postcards of the Niagara Falls purchased by William Grenfell.

However, as it happens, two Harrovians, Frederick Hamilton and Cecil Baring, were also at Niagara in the summer of 1884, and Hamilton later recorded:

> We were standing at the foot of the American Falls, when we noticed a little board inscribed, 'William Grenfell of Taplow Court, England . . . swam Niagara at this spot.' I looked at Baring, Baring looked at me. 'I don't see why we shouldn't do it too,' he observed, to which I replied, 'We might have a try'.[11]

The *Coleraine Telegraph* followed up the story from 25 August 1884 with helpful detail:

> They jumped into the water at the foot of the American Falls on the American side, and struck out diagonally across the stream . . . They both swam safely through the rough water, being carried down some by the current, which is very violent there, and reached the smooth water on the Canadian side . . . Mr Baring swam on . . . and landed a hundred yards below the new suspension bridge, none the worse for his novel bath.[12]

Grenfell, Hamilton and Baring took different and shorter routes than Webb and focused their efforts on swimming diagonally across the Pool, i.e. that part of the river below the two sets of falls and before the rapids through the gorge. Grenfell was twenty-nine years old for his first swim and thirty-three for the second. This was in 1888, a year after he married Ettie, swimming from America to Canada and 'close to where the fall strikes the water and fills the air with spray'. This swim is documented through primary and secondary sources, with the *Dundee Evening Courier* reporting on this event in 1896 and noting Grenfell's comment that 'it was mainly a matter of keeping the legs up during the swim, so as to avoid the eddies known locally as the flams'. Grenfell added that 'the second time I did it I was for a while in a terrible funk, I can tell you, for I got in the backwash and could feel it carrying me under the falls'.

Grenfell was staying in Buffalo with the lawyer and prominent Democrat John G. Milburn, whom he had met on the White Star liner RMS *Celtic* as he and Ettie sailed across the Atlantic.[13] On 7 September 1888 he wrote to Ettie in a 'confessional' manner, and acknowledged this was a somewhat foolhardy venture, having just got married and started a family:

> *My darling – just off – You had better come here – a good place – We're at Milburn, 1168 Delaware Street, Buffalo – a good sort. Walter Long is here. I couldn't help swimming across as they didn't believe it – a very rough day and rather hard work. I will tell you all about it. Your loving Willy.*[14]

And then on 8 September he added:

> *Milburn was very good to me at and about Niagara & is very known there . . . It was an awful day & blowing half a gale which made it much worse for swimming but I had to do it as Milburn was incredulous – I expect all his Buffalo friends will have a go at it now. I hope you will not think me a beast for doing it – but I don't call it risky really – & I mean to take great care in the Rockies & just walk about very gingerly and not run any chances. I don't think it is anything like so risky as riding across country.*[15]

In a separate account Grenfell wrote:

> *On Saturday morning, Sept 8th, and showed him [Milburn] how to swim the pool which he only half believed I had done. This time I got no assistance from the men who would not row the boat for me or anything – so I went across in the Maid of the Mist and got a boy and a flat bottomed boat from*

the Canadian side – we had the greatest difficulty in getting the boat up towards the falls as it was blowing half a gale of wind and she filled twice near the shore – so I got on and undressed – near the fall – getting of course drenched through and through from the spray. The boy took my wet clothes and rowed across to the Canadian side and I jumped in. It was such a rainy rough day that I didn't get up to the right place and jumped in off a rock not close enough to the falls – the consequence being that I met the back-wash which made it harder work – getting out of this I struck the current where the water was very broken and soon after the Maid of the Mist came by – too close and I yelled at her, being afraid of the wash.[16]

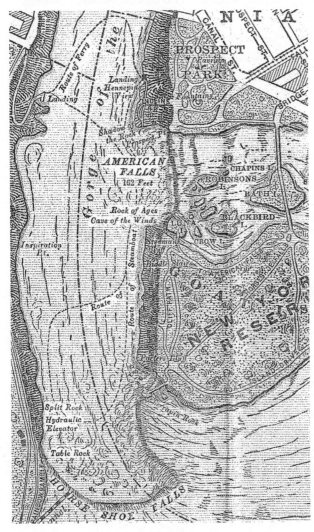

Detail from the Matthews-Northrup 1893 map of Niagara River and the pool below the Horseshoe Falls.

In conjunction with Grenfell's letter, an 1893 map makes it possible to understand something of the geography of his swim. He catches the sightseeing boat (*Maid of the Mist*) from the American side to the Canadian side, from east to west. He then hires the flat-bottomed boat to take him up towards the Falls. It's possible he aimed for the Rock of Ages as a jumping-off point (but perhaps got as far as Split Rock, which is where he may have jumped in). After shouting at the *Maid of the Mist* for coming too close, he swam downstream, with the current, over to the Canadian side, though his precise landing point is unclear. Throughout Grenfell's life, his swimming achievements were celebrated as iconic moments and made a real connection with the public, given the impact Niagara already had on the popular imagination.

North America was the first of the continents where Grenfell travelled and hunted, and was perfect both for 'manly' pursuits and for investigating a new country. At the end of 1884, travelling through New York on his way back from Canada, he makes notes in his diary about how 'American girls are very quick and lively and easy to get on with but . . . I saw none in NY whom one could call a beauty'. He further comments that 'society goes entirely by wealth and is much smaller and meaner than in London', and how 'chivalry, honour, self-sacrifice and politeness are very generally looked down upon and each man is for himself'. On 15 December he met Thomas Edison and noted that he had 'extraordinary bright eyes' and was 'rather hypnotic'. He was impressed when Edison showed him a telephone on which he was talking to someone 300 miles away in Boston and a 'new way of transmitting hand writing by electricity', which he thought 'the most interesting thing I saw in America'.[17]

Given the Grenfell family's long involvement with mining and minerals, it is logical that Grenfell would explore opportunities for potential investment as part of these visits to America and Canada. Initially for hunting, they were combined in later years with Desborough's role as President of the Imperial Chamber of Commerce. His sporting prowess on this continent made him a respected figure and his swims at Niagara reinforced his reputation for physical achievement and gave him a certain calling card for later imperial meetings. [See *Chapter 18 Commerce, Empire, War and Peace.*]

THE SUAKIN INTERLUDE

Although Grenfell was new to politics in the early 1880s, it is surprising that someone who had, as a young MP for Salisbury, expressed a desire for a long-term career in Parliament should decide, in early 1885, to become a special correspondent for the *Daily Telegraph*, covering the ongoing Mahdist war in the Sudan. But it was more adventure.

Muḥammad Aḥmad, who claimed to be the Mahdi – a messianic Islamic leader – had declared an outright rebellion against the Egyptian government in the Sudan, who were backed by the British. General Gordon was sent to Khartoum in early 1884 to help evacuate the city, which he partially accomplished before settling in to organise its defence. This was much against the British government's wishes and, as the siege of the city continued, so pressure grew from the British public to send a relief force. This was ultimately despatched in late 1884, but arrived in Khartoum two days after Gordon had been killed on 26 January 1885.

An enormous outpouring of public dismay followed Gordon's apparent martyrdom to Britain's imperial ambitions in Africa. The British government came under immediate pressure to punish the Mahdi. In 1884 and 1885 General Sir Gerald Graham VC had led troops aiming to remove Mahdist forces from around Suakin, a port in north-eastern Sudan (thus protecting the Red Sea route to British interests in India – the Suez Canal having opened in 1869). The second expedition of the Suakin Field Force left Aldershot in mid-February 1885, arriving in March, with the purpose of clearing Mahdist forces under Osman Digna, one of their most able generals, as well as supervising and protecting the construction of the Suakin to Berber Railway.

Grenfell joined this force as a special correspondent.[18] The *Daily Telegraph* had more than ten in the Sudan, and Grenfell noted that 'most of the papers had one or more paid assistants' and they were able to report very openly on the plans and action (there was no Official Secrets Act), and with great frequency (cabling reports back to London more than once a day).[19] Bennet Burleigh was the best known of the *Telegraph's* correspondents, but they all wrote under the same by-line, so it is impossible to identify any specific reports by Grenfell. The *Maidenhead Advertiser* in 1895 included an interview with Grenfell in which he looked back to his experiences in the Sudan: he explained that because he had failed to join the mounted infantry, he simply contacted the proprietor of the *Daily Telegraph*, whom he knew, and offered to go.

It seems from his diary that Grenfell travelled by mail train to Brindisi, by boat on to Alexandria (taking about a week) and then south on a steamer for another week. His Suakin diary is sparse, but mentions leaving the ship at Jeddah (which he notes to revisit) on the east of the Red Sea before crossing to Suakin, and then inland to engage with the enemy, and observe a first action on Wednesday 20 March at Hasheen, a week after arrival.[20]

He witnessed the Berkshire regiment taking a hill – an action he describes as unnecessary, a view supported by an officer who was present.[21] A review of this officer's narrative noted that 'it was an account that avoids striving after sensational effects'.[22] The author observed how the public was reliant upon the news through Bennet Burleigh and the other correspondents, whom he describes as 'amateur military critics'. Apparently the military actions were frequently chaotic skirmishes and the officer describes the action at Hasheen by saying, 'all that was gained . . . was the possession of two small hills which we secured without firing a shot, and before the fighting began (and without taking possession of the nearby waterhole)'. He suggested that both sides regarded it as a victory. The reports from special correspondents also demonstrated the confused nature of the war, and with non-combatants being exposed to considerable risk.[23]

The force moved on a few miles and on Sunday the 22nd the Battle of Tofrek (or, as Grenfell refers to it in his *Maidenhead Advertiser* interview, 'the affair of McNeill's Zareba') took place between 3,000 British and Indian troops and around 2,000 Arab soldiers. The Arab forces made a surprise attack on the British, who were in the process of building a zareba – a fortress using

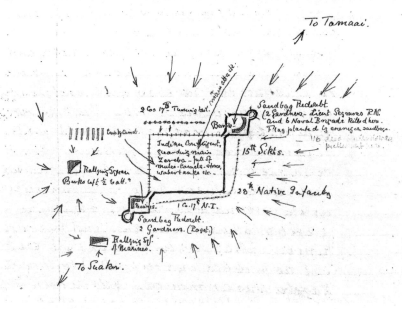

Diagram from Grenfell's diary of the battle of McNeill's zareba.

native bush, stones and sand to create a barricade inside which an encampment could be created. With the troops were large numbers of camels and mules and the drivers who had brought all the equipment up in a convoy. These were now being readied for return to Suakin and Grenfell was planning to go back with them. As the convoy assembled, Grenfell describes how 'with fiendish yells the enemy were upon them – there was no square and two sides of the zareba were not finished – many of the men had their arms piled up and were cutting bushes in their shirt sleeves . . . Every mule and camel driver and all the camels stampeded.'

In the chaos, in which it 'was hard to distinguish friend from foe', Grenfell became isolated from the zareba and it was impossible for him to get back. He came under fire from the British troops inside the zareba, his horse went head over heels and he lost it in the bush. He was totally unarmed and 'had to trust his legs which fortunately served me in good stead'. He came under fire (three shots) from an Arab behind him, but fortunately he wasn't hit. Grenfell continued and 'after going some little way I had the luck to catch a horse and so get along to Suakin'.

Another special correspondent for the *Daily Telegraph*, Phil Robinson, recalled: 'I may perhaps mention that the riderless horse that galloped past me in Sunday's affair, and that I caught by heading it, oddly enough was that of Mr. W. H. Grenfell upon whom I afterwards came in the bush, he having mounted another runaway. We were astonished at meeting one another, for each thought the other had been overtaken by the enemy.'[24]

McNeill's Zareba, Tofrek, 22 March 1885, by Charles Edwin Fripp, who worked as a 'special artist' for the Daily Graphic.

Grenfell told the correspondents he only had his umbrella with him in the event of a hand-to-hand fight, and was knocked down six times in the crush of camels, carts, camp followers and rushing Arabs.[25]

Grenfell often commented that, though a non-combatant, he saw a degree of 'active service', not least in the sudden onslaught on that Sunday morning.[26] Although the battle was won, he noted that the losses were considerable: 300 British and Indian dead or wounded, 200 drivers killed, along with 723 camels lost. Four hundred and fifty of the enemy were killed.

IN MEMORY OF
THE GALLANT MEN
WHO
IN THE DISCHARGE OF THEIR DUTY
AS
SPECIAL CORRESPONDENTS
FELL IN
THE CAMPAIGNS IN THE SOUDAN
1883 ~ 1884 ~ 1885.
EDMOND O'DONOVAN,
"DAILY NEWS". KASHGIL, NOVEMBER 1883

Detail of the plaque in the crypt of St Paul's Cathedral commemorating the lives of seven special correspondents killed in the campaigns in the Sudan between 1882 and 1885.

Grenfell stayed in the Sudan for about three weeks, proceeding with the force on the road to Tamai before returning to Suakin. He left on 8 April, boarding the ship *Geelong* at Suez on the 12th. He was back in England by late

April and arrived just in time to attend a meeting of the Maidenhead, Cookham and Bray Angling Association at Skindles hotel.[27]

For what it is worth, Grenfell's diary indicates that he was unimpressed with the leadership of the campaign, highlighting poor tactics and contradictory orders. It seems the Gladstone government agreed with him, for within two months it decided to abandon both the railway and its military campaign. General Graham and his Field Force were evacuated from Suakin on 17 May 1885.[28] However, the Tobrek incident almost certainly enhanced Grenfell's 'action man' image, which captured people's imaginations and may have served his political interests. Before the end of the year a General Election enabled him to win back the now reformed single-seat constituency of Salisbury.

6

Racing Punting

Punting on the Thames – racing punting – Grenfell and Beesley – Amateur Champion – the Thames Punting Club

Alongside rowing, William Grenfell's great love in terms of river activity was punting – both racing and for leisure. He owned a number of punts, and Taplow Court had two small boathouses (neither survives) and employed a waterman.[1] As we have seen, he inherited Taplow in 1867 at the age of twelve and had easy access to the river. It seems likely that he started to punt there and we know that he was competing and winning in college and local punting events, such as the Maidenhead Regattas, in his twenties and thirties.

Looking back to this period, the *Maidenhead Advertiser* spelt out his early association with the river and with punting:

> It was his skill at aquatic sports and his love of the river that really endeared him to the sport-loving youth of the district and he soon became a familiar on local reaches of the Thames. He took up punting and became an expert with the pole: in the late 70s and early 80s he was often seen [training] with such champions of the ryepeck[*] as Ned Andrews and Abel Beesley.[2]

Given that punting, and especially racing punting, is much less popular today than in the late Victorian and Edwardian period, because it was so much a part of Grenfell's life, it is worth giving a brief introduction to its development.

---

[*] A ryepeck is a stake driven into the riverbed around which punts race.

Fishing Punt.

Illustration from The Book of the Thames, From its Rise to its Fall, *Mr and Mrs S. C. Hall,
Virtue & Co., London, originally 1867, revised version, 1877, p.178.*

THE EVOLUTION OF PUNTS AND PUNTING

Robert Rivington provides the best account of the early days of punting on
the Thames, with flat-bottomed shallow-draft boats called 'punts' in regular
use by fishermen and ferrymen.[3] Racing was not uncommon by the mid-1800s:
professional boatmen competing for a purse provided by a wealthy backer
with others placing wagers on the outcome. Punting seems to have been a
recreation at Eton College in the nineteenth century, with punts hired from
local watermen, the first race recorded there in 1830. These continued until
banned by the headmaster in 1852.

As towns along the Thames expanded, so regattas came into being in the
1840s. The Henley Regatta, founded in 1839, had a punting match between
local watermen as early as 1841 and there was a steady growth in competitions
for watermen and gradually also for 'amateurs'. In 1876 Henry Tagg issued a
challenge in *Sporting Life* to 'punt any man in England, in best and best
punts, two miles straight against the stream'. Abel Beesley, a famous waterman
and punter based in Oxford, was expected to take up the challenge, but
ultimately the race took place between two other watermen on 2 October 1877
on what became known as the Maidenhead Mile, a course used for every
professional championship race bar one (1920) up to 1948.

While Cambridge or Oxford are presumed today to be the natural homes
of leisure punting, it was not an established social or sporting activity in the
early nineteenth century. Boatmen used heavily built punts on the river to

ferry passengers, livestock and other goods, and fishermen employed them for commercial angling as well as for guiding amateur anglers. But as rowing became established as a sport through the 1870s and 1880s, so the work of watermen expanded to include a variety of service and support activities.

These professional watermen were extremely competent punters, as Grenfell himself acknowledged in the 1890s:

> The navigation of this craft required both skill and strength, more skill and strength than is wanted to keep a tolerably straight course in its much lighter successors which are now seen in such numbers up and down the river Thames. The old Thames fishermen were adept at the art; they were acquainted with each eddy in the stream and knew the bottom no less well than the surface, and the way they pushed their heavy loads up some swift rushing stream was a triumph of art not easy to acquire.[4]

Oxford Regatta began in 1841 and offered punt races for watermen from 1842. There was a gradual expansion of punts on the river, with boat builders and hirers responding to growing demand by replacing fishing punts with leisure 'saloon' punts. Salters in Oxford, for example, had twenty punts in 1861, thirty-one by 1875 and thirty-four by 1879. However, only half of these were punts used for leisure hire; the others were 'rowing' punts (i.e. assisting oarsmen) and ferries. By 1903 Salters had nearly one hundred and by 1927, 140.[5] The company still runs 'steamers' today, and offers punts for hire at Folly Bridge.

Punts on the River Thames at Oxford c. 1900 during the inter-college summer races.

Lucien David,
'A Punting Expedition',
Illustrated London News,
17 September 1887.

By the 1860s undergraduates were increasingly accustomed to using the river in the ways they do today and colleges took to acquiring their own punts. Leisure punting in Oxford mainly took place on the Cherwell, with the river said to 'be covered at intervals with punts occupied by students typically reclining on cushions reading a book, whilst smoking a pipe'.[6] Caricatures of punts and punting abounded, with standard mishaps emphasised.

By the mid-1880s the expansion of leisure activity up and down the Thames had become very pronounced – and was often referred to as the 'boating craze'. Punting in particular enjoyed huge popularity, with the numbers of punts and punters more numerous than rowing boats.* They were relatively stable, could accommodate several people and pushing them along with a pole was fairly simple, even if there were still challenges![7]

---

* By 1900 there were said to be 1,000 punts available for hire downriver at Richmond-on-Thames.

Abel Beesley and William Grenfell, professional and amateur champions, late 1880s.

GRENFELL AND PUNTING

Punting was a regular part of the Balliol College regatta programme and Grenfell's own records of his sporting achievements show that he won a cup for punting in the college regatta in 1878, so it was already part of his sporting repertoire. Bertram Symons-Jeune, writing in 1907, refers to Lord Desborough taking up punting at Oxford thirty years previously and being trained by Abel Beesley, the acclaimed punter and Professional Champion from 1877.[8] Beesley was Grenfell's first coach and they formed a continuing relationship. In the later 1880s they posed for the camera.

An article concerning Grenfell's athletic prowess in the *Lock to Lock Times* in January 1889 refers to his role as rowing coach to the Oxford crew after leaving the university and that 'he is even a greater adept with the punt pole than with the oar and last year won the Amateur Championship of the Upper Thames'. Noting his support for all athletic clubs in his neighbourhood, it continued: 'and he spends the greater part of his time on the river, where he is one of the best-known figures, and it is but a few of frequent visitors to Maidenhead waters who have not come across a herculean form propelling a racing punt at a terrific speed – a model of good form to others and with evident enjoyment to himself'.[9]

An interview in the same journal in 1890 on the conclusion of Beesley's last professional championship race records this exchange: "'No more running around the park every morning Abel", said Mr Grenfell to the champion. "No sir" replied Abel with a hearty laugh and a significant wink, "none of that tomorrow". Prior to the championship meeting Abel had to run a certain number of times round Mr Grenfell's park to "get into condition" and he was not likely to escape this training while under the eye of such a veteran athlete as W. H. Grenfell.'

As this suggests, Beesley and Grenfell admired each other and worked closely together in Oxford and Taplow. Grenfell recognised that Beesley needed to earn a living if he was to practise his chosen sport, whereas he, as a 'gentleman amateur', could indulge as he chose. In Abel Beesley's obituary in the *Oxford Journal Illustrated* in 1921 it was noted that 'many were the fine tussles these two had in their trials'.

Grenfell also made use of the skills and prowess of Edward Andrews, Professional Champion prior to Beesley, in 1876. Grenfell's victory in the Amateur Punting Championship of the Upper Thames in 1888 provoked the following comment:

The superiority of Mr W. H. Grenfell is so marked, and, moreover, so well known, as to leave little uncertainty about the result and I can bear testimony to the fact that the victor did full justice to his trainer and himself. Apart from his powerful physique, which gives him a marked advantage over his competitors, Mr Grenfell owes much to the excellent teaching he has received at the hands of the well-known ex-champion, E. Andrews, who I was glad to see about on Thursday.[10]

Ned Andrews was, in Grenfell's view, 'the most practised exponent' of running a punt – the dominant style in the early years.[11] This involved running down the punt towards 'the stern' pushing the pole back as you went, what Grenfell calls 'the old method'. Running was prevalent when the punts were the heavier boats used for fishing. Beesley had beaten Andrews a decade earlier in 1877 using the new method – pricking – standing still with a long shove – and was its 'most successful exponent'. Grenfell used both methods, but pricking was what he employed in the light 'best' boats in which he typically raced.

Grenfell had initially, and cleverly, employed the best proponents of both of these styles to coach him.[12]

In 1887 Grenfell was beaten by F. Tomkins in the third heat of the Amateur Championship by some six lengths. A week earlier, and at the Maidenhead Amateur Regatta, he also competed in the Championship of the Upper Thames as this report from the *Maidenhead Advertiser* of 10 August 1887 reveals:

> *Final heat – No1 station Gardner, No3 station Grenfell, No2 station Matthews, No4 station Baker.* Grenfell went away with a fairly good lead, but at the end of Mrs Graham-Smith's lawn he was very badly fouled by Baker, and as he was righting himself Gardner passed him, and managed to reach the rye-peck a couple of lengths in front. Turning well, he came home an easy winner by a length clear. Matthews beat Baker by about a quarter of a length. Gardner 'pricked' his punt, and thus the same style of punting won the amateur as well as the professional championship. Had not Grenfell been fouled, he would have run Gardner very close, and probably have proved the 'amateur champion'.[13]

In that year Tomkins became the first Amateur Champion, winning under the auspices of the Thames Punting Club and beating E. V. Gardner. Grenfell then beat Gardner in the singles race at the 1887 Sunbury Regatta (Gardner was disqualified 'for being pushed off the shore by a spectator, when he ran into the bank some one hundred yards from the finish') before losing again to Tomkins in the final.[14]

William Grenfell and Abel Beesley in training, late 1880s.

*Grenfell's Amateur
Punting Championship
medal for 1889.*

William Grenfell, aged thirty-three, started a string of successes by beating F. Tomkins, Amateur Champion, by around five lengths at Sunbury in 1888: his first championship win. Then in 1889 he defeated W. Searle by the huge margin of thirty lengths.

He followed this in 1890 by beating A. M. Kilby by two lengths and in a time of 7 minutes and 29 seconds.[15] Grenfell had risen quickly and brilliantly through the ranks of the best punters, or 'puntists' as they were sometimes known, aided by his excellent coaches and fast boats.[16] He did not compete again for the Championship and a year later the *Sunday Times* reflected on his decision to retire: 'It will be a very long time before we see his like again. In him immense power was combined with a graceful style that made his performances a treat to watch. He had learned his art under the tuition of Abel Beesley, the professional champion, and a race between these two, if it could have been brought about, would have been most interesting.'[17]

Grenfell was able to afford top-quality racing punts and, given that this was an era in which designs and construction methods were evolving, he obtained 'the best'. One of his racing punts may survive in the Rose Collection of River Thames pleasure boats, though seemingly impossible to prove: a 'cross-laced' 'best boat' with traces of blacklead (graphite) on the hull.[18] Grenfell was noted as having his racing boats prepared in this way to ensure optimum speed, as a report from September 1890 confirmed: 'The racing punts he uses are of the lightest description, exceedingly narrow, and he usually has them blackleaded so as to slip through the water more easily.'[19]

Cross-laced racing punt 'best boat', 1890s, Rose Collection.

Grenfell 'resigned' after competing in the Amateur Championship in 1890, partly because competition was limited and also to allow others to come through. Other champions have subsequently done the same, and Abel Beesley was apparently persuaded by Grenfell to retire from professional racing at the same time – the waterman thus sacrificing income as well as status. Asked if he retired to let somebody else have a chance, Beesley replied, 'exactly'.[20] However, as the *Lock to Lock Times* reported in its August 1893 edition, he was compensated to a degree with a 'purse of Gold subscribed to by nearly every well-known puntist on the Thames'.[21]

Beesley went on to work for the Oxford University Humane Society (part of the Royal Life Saving Society, with which Desborough was linked) for forty-seven years – effectively a river safety organisation rescuing those who fell in and risked drowning. He became Chief Inspector and died in 1921 at the age of seventy.

Grenfell and the sport of racing punting are intertwined. Indeed, the image on the medals awarded at the annual punting championships to this day is that of Grenfell posed in a racing punt.[22] He served as Chairman of the Committee of the Thames Punting Club (TPC) from 1890 and also as President from 1899 on the death of the Duke of Beaufort up until his own death in 1945. In 1924 he was appointed Patron of the newly formed Dittons Skiff and Punting Club and served for the rest of his life.[23]

In 1900 Grenfell was himself presented with the TPC Gold Medal and a miniature medal in recognition of his achievement in winning the Championship

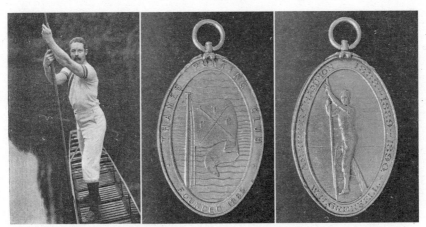

William Grenfell, photographed by Marsh Brothers, and the miniature medal marking his three years as Amateur Champion 1888–1890.

three years running (and before the Challenge Cup was instituted), as well as his services as Chairman since 1890.

He had been instrumental in the relaunch of the TPC in 1886 and its subsequent development, including the incorporation of watermen's punt racing into regulated professional racing. He was an active umpire throughout his life – not least for the professional races – and a generous benefactor. He conducted business with considerable humour, and could be an amusing raconteur, as when he remarked that 'Although Britannia ruled the waves she did not appear to be able to rule the bottom of the Thames, as there were holes and other conditions which made it difficult to get a fair course.' As with rowing, Grenfell was keen to embrace innovation and to make good use of the enthusiasm of others.

He was fortunate that his period in office, at least up until 1919, coincided with two highly competent TPC Secretaries – first Henry Faija and then Peter W. Squire. Faija's own boathouse at Sunbury was used first as the headquarters of the TPC at its inception. Faija introduced the canvas-rigged 'best and best racing punt', which was a much narrower craft built for its owner (a sort of bespoke punt), its depth reflecting the weight and height of the punter. The term 'best and best' began to mean the *best punter* in his or her *best punt*.

The TPC Report of 1893 noted that the Committee had concluded that the cost of building racing punts was a factor in the decline in regatta entries. It resolved therefore to introduce if possible 'a regulation sized punt' intended to be scaled between the best and best punts and the ordinary pleasure punt, and

Posters for the Amateur and Professional Championships, 1900.

not be subject to variation year by year. The club had two punts built to the 'dimensions specified' so that they could be used in club races and lent out to other regattas.[24]

Sadly, Henry Faija died suddenly of cancer and the 1894 TPC Report recorded his contribution as Secretary and Treasurer.[25] Peter Squire was appointed as Honorary Secretary and served until his own death in 1919.[26] Squire was described as 'courteous and energetic' and awarded a very handsome silver salver in recognition of his great services. In the *Maidenhead Advertiser*'s report of the 1901 Professional Championships much is made of Mr Grenfell's role, but the report then notes: 'We should not omit to mention the very valuable assistance Mr Squire (as starter and umpire) received from his estimable wife, who is a punting enthusiast and knows as much about the art and rules and regulations that govern it as most of the members of the committee of the TPC. She was one of the official timekeepers of the day.'[27]

Squire acquired his house on the Middlesex bank, which he subsequently renamed The Ryepeck, in 1901. It was located next to the punting course at Sunbury and a very logical home for the Secretary of the TPC. He then went a substantial step further by building a boathouse, complete with an underground punt harbour and a pavilion. Only the former remains, complete with punt racks and the shallow harbour itself and a gated entrance onto the river.[28]

The boathouse and punt harbour at The Ryepeck with racing punts, c. 1906.

The input of Faija and Squire sits alongside William Grenfell's great contribution to the sport, as participant and champion, and as Chairman and President of the TPC. As with the Thames Conservancy, Grenfell engendered immense loyalty from the people who worked with him.

Grenfell took the time to write commentaries on punting.[29] His short piece in Frederick Aflalo's 1899 book on the cost of sport is particularly intriguing because it details the expense associated with punting, and some insight into his views on racing punting in particular. He commented that 'Punt-racing is an exhausting performance and requires thorough preparation, and a light racing punt wants "living in", if justice is to be done to her.' And, reflecting on the expense of training and the fees paid to professionals, he offered wise advice: 'A professional can be dispensed with if you know of an amateur better than yourself who will train with you, but it is essential to have someone alongside in order to get accustomed to the wash, and to get disillusioned in the matter of your own pace, which, when punting alone, always seems much faster than it really is.'

Punting was central to Desborough's world of the Thames, and he was central to the development of this new sport. He hoped many people might take part, though in fact it has remained a somewhat exclusive sport, partly because of the very considerable demands it places on acquiring the skills as well as the general decline in punting on rivers. He showed a great appetite to improve technical aspects of the sport: seeking, for example, to enhance the punts being raced. Having excelled among the very best – and with his significant physical and speaking presence – Desborough was able to contribute throughout his life, reinforcing that what mattered for him was not just 'winning his own events'.

Desborough continued to punt in later years and records show him competing in a scratch two-foot punting race in 1894 at Bray. In the final of what appeared to be four-person teams, Grenfell's team lost when he broke his pole. The *Lock to Lock Times* periodically noted him out in a punt, for example with Lady Desborough and their sons in 1893.

Ettie with Willy punting an East Anglian gun punt at Whiteslea, Hickling Broad.

Much later in life he was seen poling a gun punt at the Hickling Point Regatta in 1932. And in the 1940s an account is given by Apsley Cherry-Garrard (whose celebrated book *The Worst Journey in the World* recounted the ill-fated Antarctic expedition led by Robert Falcon Scott, of which he was a member) of being invited to Panshanger with his wife Angela, and how 'Lord Desborough, once a great athlete, took Angela punting on the section of the Mimram river that flowed through the grounds of Panshanger'.[30]

The climber and poet, Geoffrey Winthrop Young wrote elegiacally about Willy's punting:

He would come drifting out of the Taplow backwater, over the river reflections under the green drooping Cliveden woods, a tower of a figure in white with a reddish wave of hair, balancing with dripping pole upon the long narrowish spar that looked like a spillikin under him. Suddenly, he would crash into motion and swirl upstream, with a water-rip of the driving pole and a fleeting silver wake behind; at the pace of a four oar or a steam launch, and faster than any professional puntsman. It was an unforgettable impression of superb movement and power, of perfect balance and rhythm. And I have never since seen it surpassed as an exhibition of human strength coordinated.[31]

7

———•———

Outstanding Sportsman

Athletics – cricket and the Triangular Tournament – fencing – game hunting – mountaineering – Grenfell v Fry

William Grenfell (later as Lord Desborough) was frequently admired not just as an oarsman or a racing punter but as a sporting 'all-rounder'. *The Times* used the phrase to headline an editorial about him after his death, and significant sporting journals of the day – such as *Baily's Magazine of Sports and Pastimes* in 1890, *Fry's Magazine* in 1906, the *Illustrated Sporting and Dramatic News* in 1923 and *Country Life* in 1983 – referred to him as a distinguished all-round sportsman.[1] This reflected not only what he achieved in his chosen sports but also their number and remarkable diversity. As well as competing, he frequently took on the mantle of Chairman or President and provided guidance and leadership. [See *Chapter 8 The Great Amateur.*]

Grenfell, of course, had flexibility in his work and enough money to indulge his passion for sport. He also had the physique. Even from early photographs at Harrow, it is evident that he was tall for his age and equipped with powerful shoulders and long arms. He thus had a certain natural advantage in sports such as rowing, punting and fencing. The sports he played or were associated with through his lifetime included: athletics, bartitsu, boxing, bowls, cricket, croquet, coaching and four in hand, fencing and épée, fishing, game hunting, golf, harriers and drag hounds, mountaineering, racing punting, rowing, stické and lawn tennis, swimming and life-saving, and wrestling.

Several of these eighteen sports – such as bartitsu and stické – have now almost disappeared. In others Grenfell triumphed, achieving a silver medal in fencing at the Intercalated Games in Athens (regarded as an Olympic equivalent until 1949), blues in both rowing and athletics at Oxford, and three national championship medals in racing punting. Athletics and cricket predominated at school and he was a noted athlete at Oxford.[2] He ran in the three-mile Varsity match race and became President of the university athletic club (at the same time being President of the university boat club: a unique distinction to this day).

Grenfell apparently favoured the expression *'festina lente'* – make haste slowly – and planned physical exertion seems to have been part of his day. Separate consideration of his contributions on the river have been charted earlier [see *Chapter 5 Rowing and the Boat Race* and *Chapter 6 Racing Punting*] but here we examine his other favourite sporting activities: athletics, cricket, fencing, game hunting and mountaineering.

ATHLETICS

At Harrow, Grenfell won the mile race in the exceptional time of 4 minutes and 37 seconds, a school record for many years, as well as running the steeple-chase, sprinting and throwing the hammer.[3] He continued to pursue athletics at Oxford, where he focused on distance events (three miles), and in *50 Years of Sport at Oxford and Cambridge* his running is described as follows:

> In his undergraduate days Grenfell was a regular glutton for work on and off the path . . . [and] it may be said that a more determined runner and finer judge of pace seldom put on a shoe. His trouble was, as was demonstrated at [the Varsity match in 1876], that he was of little use when it came to sprinting. Ordinary opponents he could wear down by taking them along uncomfortably fast and allowing them no time to take a pull; but in Goodwin [the Oxford first string] he met a man who could live with him and yet raise a spurt at the finish. When the two men ran the first mile in 4 min. 51 secs. and completed two in 10 min. and 5 secs., many knowledgeable spectators prophesied that one or other must crack. As a fact the third mile was faster than the second and the winner cut yet another Varsity record.[4]

Grenfell came in second in front of some 12,000 spectators at Lillie Bridge in Fulham. His subsequent interest in athletics was focused through his presidency of the Oxford University Athletic Club and through many years of work with the Amateur Athletic Association (AAA), which he supported at numerous athletic meetings and in a variety of official roles.[5]

Prince Albert, the future King George VI, aged 13, with his tutor Mr Henry Peter Hansell and Lord Desborough, attending the AAA meeting organised to test the new Olympic Stadium. Daily Mirror *6 July 1908.*

In 1908, in a speech to the Polytechnic Harriers, he argued 'for success in sport but also for fair play'. Athletics was perhaps under press scrutiny more than any other sport and required his considerable diplomacy at the 1908 Olympics. [See *Chapter 15 Bringing the Games to Fruition*.]

A photograph from 1929 shows him taking the salute from nearly 1,000 young athletes competing at the Schools Athletic Association, Fifth Inter-County Championship meeting at Stamford Bridge in London on Saturday 22 July. Perched on the podium, Desborough might have seemed something of a relic from a bygone age, standing tall with his traditional boater firmly in place. Importantly, given what was to unfold in Germany from the early 1930s, the Olympic salutation is not to be confused with the Nazi salute.* The event was run under a headline 'Come and see sport that is keen and clean' – an indication of some of the tensions that existed in athletics.

---

* The Olympic salute (right arm raised and directed to the side) understandably fell into disuse given potential confusion with the Nazi salute (right arm held aloft and directed forward), especially after the Olympic Games in Berlin in 1936.

*Lord Desborough taking the 'Olympic salute' at the Inter-County Championship,
Stamford Bridge, 22 July 1929.*

The following year, after being a Vice President for some time – now in his seventies and in the final decade of his 'full on' involvement in sports – he became President of the AAA. In the same year, he contributed a foreword to the AAA's Jubilee souvenir, *Fifty Years of Progress*, and reminded readers how the organisation had gone far to remedy the defects of *shamateurism*, meaning substantial prizes and betting which had characterised this and other sports.[6] He noted that even defining 'gentlemen amateurs' was a problem. The AAA had 'broken down the distinctions between athletes and so had helped to make athletics one of the great democratic sports both in England and all over the world'. Desborough announced in 1935 that he was standing down 'with utmost regret', and was succeeded by Lord Burghley.

In 1925 he had created one element of legacy in the field of athletics by donating the Desborough Perpetual Challenge Cup for the long jump to the Women's Amateur Athletic Association, and he remained linked with the very successful Achilles Club, formed in 1920 for athletes who had competed for either Oxford or Cambridge. Desborough was appointed as President at the outset and remained in post until 1945, another remarkably long term of office.

CRICKET

When, in May 1911, Lord Desborough was announced as the new President of the Marylebone Cricket Club (MCC), there was considerable surprise in cricketing circles. While all accepted that, as William Grenfell, he had been an acclaimed sportsman, his cricketing credentials were modest compared with his achievements in other sports.

It was forty years since Willy had played as a schoolboy in the annual Eton v. Harrow match at Lord's – a significant event in the London social calendar.[7] At Harrow he had played cricket for his form, house, and the school, primarily as a bowler. He played in the school team in 1873 against the MCC and Gentlemen, taking eight wickets in the first innings – five of them bowled. In the same year at Lord's he took four wickets for twenty-seven runs in the first innings, and a further wicket (for forty-three) in the second.[8]

He didn't play for the university side at Oxford but turned out for Balliol, and after leaving Oxford played for various local sides, probably until the turn of the century. He also joined and played for both MCC (known then as the Marylebone) and I Zingari (a 'wandering' cricket club with no home ground).[9]

Although his MCC appointment was a surprise to some, his standing was such that it was regarded as entirely sensible. According to *Athletic News*: 'Such is the titular head of the most famous of all cricket clubs, and no more representative sportsman has ever filled the chair at St John's Wood – although the long roll of presidents includes many men of fame. His practical and active sympathy with sport is universal.'[10]

As it turned out, Desborough's diplomatic skills – familiar from his work on the 1908 London Olympic Games – were required from the outset, not least because of the planned three-way cricket competition, a Triangular Tournament, between Australia, England and South Africa.[11] This had been floated in 1909 at the Imperial Cricket Conference, with the first series to be held in England in 1912.[12] The series got off to an inauspicious start when simmering tensions between Australian players and the heavy-handed Australian Board of Control (ABC) finally boiled over, and six leading Australian players (including the Captain) refused to travel to the tournament. This action by the 'Big Six', as Patrick Ferriday calls them, resulted in Pelham ('Plum') Warner, the official Captain of the England side, then touring Australia, sending a telegram to Lord Desborough on 8 March 1911, as he and the team were about to embark on a steamer from Adelaide at the end of their tour.[13]

A meeting of the MCC Committee was promptly convened in the Junior Carlton Club at 4.30 p.m. on 11 March. The Secretary reported on cable messages received from Australia from Plum Warner and from Mr Bailleau from Melbourne, a member of the Victoria State government and sent on behalf of the public of Victoria. The minutes give a verbatim report of the cable sent in reply:

> As President, Marylebone, I am certain the counties and all English cricketers bitterly disappointed if Australia not represented in the Triangular contest by best team, please publish, Desborough.

The message was that the ABC, as a national body, in contrast to the state-run associations, should exercise the authority that it was slowly establishing over players.[14] The Australian players had previously selected their own player manager for tours, and much else. It is notable that the ABC did not reply to Desborough's message (Warner felt this 'savoured of discourtesy').[15]

Whatever the rights and wrongs, it was clear from a subsequent after-dinner speech given by Lord Desborough to the Incogniti Cricket Club (another wandering club) where his sympathies lay. In relation to tours, his view as reported in the *Sportsman* magazine was that 'As President of the MCC, he had . . . some knowledge of the difficulty in getting an eleven together; some would not go under one captain, some declined to be led by another.'[16] His speech continued: 'They seemed to live in an age of insubordination in the athletic world – not only in athletics but in other branches of sport the deleterious influence had spread and even Boards of Control did not exercise to the full the influence under which they did their duty.'

He expressed the hope that in the forthcoming Triangular Tournament, 'the true spirit of sportsmanship would obtain', though when the tournament went ahead, with a restructured Australian side, it was with doubts about whether it was a desirable venture at all.[17] In the event, bad weather and limited spectator appetite for the games between Australia and South Africa (making up three of the nine game series) meant it was not a great success. Given some frustration from the English county teams that it was restricting their activities, the press reaction after the series was less than positive. The *Illustrated Sporting and Dramatic News* commented: 'The tale of the Triangular Tournament is indeed a tale of woe. Another match came to an unhappy end at Nottingham, this week, when rain interrupted play on the last day of the

Triangular Tour dinner card, 1 May 1912, 'The Court of King Cricket', for the MCC Australian team, with a banner listing Desborough as 'in the chair'; designed by George Hillyard Swinstead.

engagement between Australia and South Africa, and a further dull page in cricket history was handed down to posterity.'[18]

Sporting Life reported on the final game between England and Australia at the Oval, won by England by 244 runs (therefore winning the Tournament): 'Much cold water has recently been thrown upon the Triangular Tournament – not without some reason. But if the interest has been lukewarm with regard to the Tournament as a whole, the old interest very plainly remains in matches between England and Australia.'[19]

The Triangular series must have dominated Desborough's year as President. He might have taken comfort from the thought that if the weather had been better, the response might have been more positive – but the concept has never been repeated.[20] He would have been busy with the Imperial Cricket Council, as the England representative, the regular meetings of the Advisory County Cricket Committee and the MCC Committee meetings, along with numerous dinners and the Annual Meeting. In the history of cricket little is made of his tenure as President. But the ambition to stage sporting contests from across the Empire gave the Triangular Tour particular significance.

William Staveley, left, representing the Epée Club, against William Grenfell, Oxford Fencing Club, 1904.

FENCING

Fencing was a particular passion for Grenfell and he continued to participate well into his seventies. He took up fencing at school, competing in foils, and also at Oxford. But he only returned seriously to fencing in his late forties, being recorded in 1902 as 'fencing everyday' at the London Fencing Club.[21] He was elected as President of the Amateur Fencing Association from its inception in 1902, was a member of the Epée and Sword Club and very active in promoting the sport and participating in competitions, including their annual tournaments and international fixtures.[22] It was suggested that his style was particularly suited to the épée (sword) rather than the foil. When fencing in the Oxford v. Cambridge veterans' competition in 1902, *The Times* observed that he was 'gifted with strength, a long reach and untiring activity . . . one of the mainstays of the team'.[23]

In May 1903 the paper offered a similar report: 'Mr W. H. Grenfell, though in some respects not a stylish fencer, possesses two advantages which in épée play more than make up for lack of finish and correctness – great personal strength and an unusually long arm; and if he relies on his vigorous offensive methods he should disconcert more experienced opponents.'[24]

This was a reference to his participation in the Coupe Internationale d'Épée in Paris as part of the British team. In a letter to Ettie prior to the tournament he aired his doubts, saying 'my aim is very bad, and I don't think I shall do well I am afraid'.[25] In a further letter he continued:

> It was a great nuisance having a weak elbow, and prevented my fighting hard, but all the same nobody did better than I did taking the two fights together, and I had two ridiculous decisions against me; however this often happens in fencing – but I am sure no foreign team will <u>ever</u> win in Paris as the Jury will see to that: they cannot help going for their own side, & I believe the Italians are as bad. We have done much better than I expected.[26]

He returned to fence in the same tournament in 1904 and also appeared at the Épée Championship at the Military Tournament in 1904 and 1906. By this stage he was familiar with international contests, so was pleased to be selected for the first British fencing team to take part in an Olympic Games in 1906.* Travelling to Athens via Marseille and Naples, he confided to Ettie:

> I am frightfully afflicted as my right arm has got bad again: I suppose I gave it a twist playing golf, not having played for so long – it will quite spoil my fencing if it does not get right. However, I hear that the French and Belgian teams are so good that they will beat us anyhow – still it will be a great mortification if I do very badly myself – I suppose this will be my last Fencing expedition.[27]

The team was notable for its age (an average of forty-six) but defeated Germany and Belgium before meeting France in the final, Desborough noting, 'We scored all right today against the Germans . . . I began with the Captain of the German team and pursued him to the ropes & got in a rib roaster, which was a good beginning: & I had three fights and was not hit – so all was well.'[28] He continued:

> We beat the Belgians this morning & did very well. Then we fought the French and made a tie, & were finally beaten by 3 points: we really won but

---

* These games were recognised by the International Olympic Committee as official Olympics until removed by IOC President Avery Brundage in 1949.

the judges treated us most unfairly, especially me which they all allow – I hit three straight off & was not allowed one. It was quite ridiculous and I am frightfully annoyed.[29]

The match ended in a dead heat (after judging which he described as 'nothing short of scandalous'). The match was refought and France won the gold medal with a 9–6 score, with the British taking silver. Edward VII, himself a keen fencer and, as Prince of Wales, an early member of the London Fencing Club, was a spectator. It is rumoured that he won a substantial bet with the King of Greece that Britain would beat Germany (as they had in the earlier round).

At the Amateur Epée Championship in 1909 a testimonial presentation was made to Lord Desborough for services to British fencing as President of the Olympic Council during the 1908 Games. This was a replica of a fine statuette of Desborough in fencing costume, elegantly posed, by V. C. Bonanni. [30] He greatly treasured this statuette, even if he hadn't himself been the most stylish of fencers.[31]

Lord Desborough with the statuette by V. C. Bonanni, July 1909.

GAME HUNTING

Visitors to Taplow Court instantly surmised that Grenfell was a hunter and most especially a big-game hunter, a commonplace sport among the wealthy in the late nineteenth century, and another particular passion for him. The walls in the central hall, his gymnasium and his study were adorned with antlers (there were fifty sets of red deer antlers in his study alone), stuffed heads (including the head of a giraffe) and other mementos of his numerous expeditions. He later claimed that 'Sport would seem to imply the pursuit of some quarry, even if it were only rats, and if there is a spice of danger attending it, so much the better.'[32]

He went on big-game hunting trips to America (he was twice in the Rocky Mountains) and in 1884, as we have seen, was briefly lost in the Bighorn Mountains in Wyoming.[33] He travelled to Canada in the same year (hunting at Lake Megantic in Quebec) and in 1888, 1911 and 1920, and to India in 1883 and 1891–92, where he shot Asiatic lions, ibex and other big game – and had hoped to shoot a tiger that was marauding a village where he travelled.[34] He pursued big-game fishing in America and the Mediterranean and regularly joined stag hunts in Scotland.[35]

His journal for 1888 recorded his trip to the USA and Canada with Ettie. In late August they sailed on the RMS *Celtic* from Liverpool. 'Ettie was rather ill the

Lord Desborough's study, Taplow Court.

whole way' across and it was on this voyage that he met Milburn, an American lawyer, who had expressed amazement at his swim across the Niagara basin. Ettie and Willy visited Newport, Rhode Island, before he headed off by train on 5 September to stay with Milburn and onwards to hunt wolves, grizzly bear, caribou and deer in British Columbia. He then travelled down to San Francisco to meet Ettie. Similarly, in a journal for 1920, he was back in Canada for a Chamber of Commerce Congress before taking two weeks afterwards to go hunting.

Hunting and shooting were a constant preoccupation, as they were for many of Grenfell's class. The challenge of the chase, with respect for the animals pursued, was seen as part of the management of nature as well as a 'manly' and competitive pursuit. Adventure mixed with competition and socialising were at the heart of it, with almost no consideration for the welfare or lives of animals. While both of them were in India in early 1892, Ettie stayed in Government House, but wrote to Willy to protest that 'it can't be quite necessary to run between the legs of a lady elephant on a narrow path and enter into single combat' and refers to him 'being attacked by 17 wild elephants and a tiger, but I confess it makes me quite sick and I cannot bear to think of it except to be glad in a general way that you are happy. But do be careful.'[36]

A competitive spirit often led him on, and only later in life did questions of wildlife conservation become a much greater consideration. Writing in 1932, he acknowledged that in terms of 'different loads, velocity of shot, pressures and patterns, the weapons of today are very much superior' but there used to be 'more crack shots than perhaps there are now'.[37] He noted that the late Marquess of Ripon did not often miss, and the astonishing fact that 'in 1881 his year's total was 12,148 head of game. In 1882 the total was 3,000 head less, but . . . it included two rhinoceroses, two tigers, and six buffalos.'[38]

Family holidays on the Duke of Sutherland's estate in Assynt in the Northern Highlands were opportunities to stalk deer as well as enjoy the company of his family. Indeed, one such visit prompted a letter to *The Field* on the question of whether a stag's horns had blood circulating in them.[39] He observed that the artist Sir Edwin Landseer was often criticised for an over-sentimental portrayal of stags with broken and bleeding horns. Grenfell observed a fight between two stags at Assynt, with one losing a horn from which blood was seeping. He suggested that on the basis of his own evidence, Landseer was avenged of his critics. Grenfell is recorded as having 'killed upwards of 1,300 red deer' through his lifetime.

Monica, Billy, Ivo and Julian with Willy on the Hill, Assynt, Sutherland, 1902.

His letters to Ettie are filled with references to his hunting exploits. In 1895, writing to her from Sutherland, he noted that his foot was now better and he had 'been able to walk well and I think the typhoid did me good; had a long day yesterday and up till now have been shooting well; not missed a chance or haunched' (a reference to hitting the body and thus damaging the meat of a stag).[40]

In 1897, when shooting at Holkham in East Anglia, he wrote: 'We had a splendid shoot today & I never saw people shoot better! Even Leicester was most complimentary & said he had <u>never</u> seen the birds better killed – though he qualified it by saying any fool can shoot pheasants now.'[41]

In a series of letters from 1904 he wrote about shooting in West Dean Park, Chichester, and sitting next to the King at dinner. In December he was again shooting, this time in Nottinghamshire, and noted that 'the King arrived yesterday with lots of people – we are just off shooting pheasants'. Then by mid-December he was back in East Anglia shooting – commenting, 'a great shoot today – 3000 head – The King did not perform.'[42]

During the First World War, Desborough used his skills to contribute to the work of the so-called Venison Committee, a Ministry of Food supply committee formed under the leadership of Lord Lovat with the express purpose of boosting

Shooting party, Sandringham, Ettie Grenfell seated far left and Willy at far right, 1890s.

meat supplies by culling deer herds on landed estates. An article in *Country Life* reported him as having walked and cycled 1,200 miles in 1916 and accounting for eighty stags, 'In September 1919, using an old single .303 he got four stags in four shots . . . Clearly he was an accomplished shot!'[43] Two years previously he wrote to Ettie from Loch Merkland, having already shot sixty-five stags that season, and dispatched venison across the country, noting that 'Lloyd George is delighted with his haunch: he has written twice!'[44]

Panshanger, the Cowper estate in Hertfordshire that Ettie inherited, was often the location for shooting parties, but it was Whiteslea and Hickling Broad in Norfolk that was Desborough's best-known shooting estate. It was leased as a wildfowl shoot and as a sanctuary for protecting and expanding rare breeds such as the marsh harrier and bittern. It had been bequeathed to their son Ivo, but following his death in 1926, Willy inherited the property. [See *Chapter 21 Last Years*.]

Whiteslea provided Grenfell with a base for numerous wild fowling shoots with significant bags of game taken each time, often with detailed notes in his hunting diary. It was described in 1934 as 'probably the best all-round wild fowl shoot in England' with over 1,000 duck and between 2,000 and 3,000 coots killed every year.[45]

The family made full use of this lodge, as it was so secluded, while its proximity to Sandringham further enhanced its attractions. Winter shooting parties included visits by George V and George VI. A manuscript written in 1939 by Desborough (on Sandringham paper) entitled 'The King/The Last 2 Shoots when I was there' gave the numbers of birds shot at Hickling as '16th August

(408) and 19th September 1939 (307)'. It also noted that 'The shooting does not interfere with the bird sanctuary.'[46] Willy was for many years a Fellow (by subscription) and one of forty Vice Presidents of the Royal Society for the Protection of Birds, and Whiteslea was a focus for his interests in conservation, working to foil the attempts by thieves to steal the eggs of rare species.[47]

MOUNTAINEERING

Finally, mountaineering was a sport at which Grenfell briefly shone but didn't pursue. He joined the Alpine Club in 1876 while a student at Oxford and (as with so many sports) remained a member until his death.[48] In his second long vacation he travelled to Switzerland, as was fashionable at the time. Within eight days, and having never climbed before, he ascended the Little Matterhorn (the Klein Matterhorn, 3,883 metres), the Matterhorn (4,506 metres), Monte Rosa (4,634 metres), the Rothorn (3,103 metres) and the Weisshorn (4,506 metres), along with other nearby peaks. He subsequently climbed the Matterhorn by two other routes. Given that the Matterhorn had been climbed for the first time only twelve years earlier, these were significant accomplishments.[49] As a complete amateur, the ascents and descents were guided, but *Sporting Life* commented that 'this was an "eye opener" to the guides who were astonished to a man at such a smart noviciate'.[50]

He appears to have had only two Zermatt 'seasons'. Writing in the *Alpine Journal*, Geoffrey Winthrop Young said he had the impression that Grenfell thought he had exhausted the possibilities of mountaineering, though realised that he might have achieved more. Grenfell apparently remarked that of all his sporting activities, mountaineering was the most worthwhile, but he didn't return to climb the peaks. However, he remained a loyal member of the club and even made room for its library to be housed at Panshanger during the Second World War.[51]

GRENFELL – A GREAT ALL-ROUNDER

Grenfell was seen as a great all-rounder, a concept widely understood in the Victorian and Edwardian period among 'gentlemen players', when it was more commonplace for talented athletes to participate in many sports. This reflected the shorter length of seasons, as well as less rigorous training regimes and slightly less exceptional levels of skill than in the twentieth century. Teams were often selected from a relatively small elite class of amateurs, while choices today are made from much larger cohorts of players.

William Grenfell, 1890, and C. B. Fry, 1894, caricatured by 'Spy' in Vanity Fair.

Another great all-rounder of the late Victorian and Edwardian period was Charles Burgess Fry, who provides a suitable yardstick against which to understand Grenfell's achievements.[52] Grenfell earned a blue in rowing and athletics and was President of both clubs in the same year, while Fry, born in 1872, matched that with blues in athletics and cricket and also achieved a blue in football (and came very close to a rugby blue) and captained all three clubs.

Both were lauded as being at the centre of Oxford sporting life, while Fry appears to have been the more flamboyant character. Although Grenfell went on to achieve a silver medal at the Intercalated Games in 1906, Fry captained England at cricket and was a joint world-record holder for the long jump.[53] On this basis Fry was the better all-rounder in terms of standards achieved in two or more sports, but Grenfell was probably stronger in terms of a wider spread of achievements.

Fry's sporting afterlife was rather less distinguished, despite his best efforts to amplify it: revisiting his world record and its duration, his performance in various sporting events, his invitation to be considered for the throne of

Albania, or his role in the League of Nations. Grenfell was the opposite and did little other than let his efforts speak for themselves; an interested public and the media ensured his achievements were noted. Both men benefited from being members of a social elite that facilitated their successes. But in character they were poles apart. There is a certain irony that it is Fry who is remembered now as the great all-rounder rather than Grenfell: Fry was possibly the more distinguished sportsman in terms of standards, but Grenfell was the more truly versatile.

8

The Great Amateur

Drag hounds and harriers – coaching and four in hand – fishing – tarpon fishing – swimming and the Bath Club – tennis – stické – boxing and wrestling – bartitsu – croquet – cricket and the Julian Cup – amateurism

As a gentleman with time and resources to devote to the sports of his choice, Grenfell met the description of 'great amateur': not only did he compete at a high level in the sports discussed in Chapter 7, but in an array of other activities, more akin to the repertoire of a typical country gentleman. To these he added several more, including newly created sports such as the martial art of bartitsu and stické tennis, both now largely forgotten.

He believed in the virtues of amateurism and wanted to see sports dominated by amateurs rather than professionals. He saw sport in general, and team sports in particular, as having an important social function through the example of teamwork and common purpose.

DRAG HOUNDS AND HARRIERS

Early in life, Grenfell adopted the style of the country squire in becoming an active drag and harrier huntsman. At Oxford he became Master of the University Drag Hounds in succession to Cecil Rhodes, who had been Master of the pack in 1877.[1] Apparently, 'he got a very good pack together . . . and built kennels at Taplow so as to keep the hounds together and exercise them in vacations.'[2] As Grenfell himself recalled: 'when I first went to Oxford in 1874 there were two drags, the Christ Church and the University College. They were combined when I was Master and called the University Drag. There were

Willy pictured with the Oxford University Drag Hounds, 1878.

excellent lines all round Oxford, stone walls round Woodstock, fine fences and grass towards the Thames and fine intermediate country with big brooks.'[3]

In late 1888 Grenfell took over a pack of harriers that had previously been owned by the Prince of Wales (up to 1869) and then by Sir Robert Harvey.[*] It was renamed the Bucks and Berks Harriers, becoming a 'subscription pack', paid for by members including local farmers. The season ran from late November to the end of March, and alongside hunting on horseback for hares and deer (hares on Tuesdays and deer on Fridays), there were Harrier Hunt race meetings at Windsor and a steeplechase in April at the end of the season.[4] The pack regularly met at Taplow Court and Willy was Master until 1894. He was also an enthusiastic point-to-pointer and described as a fine horseman.

In 1923 the *Illustrated Sporting and Dramatic News* ran a series of articles on Distinguished British All-Round Sportsmen, including Desborough: 'It is said of him that, on one occasion, neither a broken arm nor a bandaged head –

---

* Harriers are a medium-sized dog breed of the hound class, used for hunting hares by trailing them. They resemble English foxhounds but are smaller (though not as small as beagles).

and he carried both – was sufficient to restrain his ardour for the chase when a stiffish post and rails obtruded itself, only to be cleared in a fashion which certainly did not suggest that the horseman was suffering from so severe a handicap.'[5]

COACHING AND FOUR IN HAND

In 1905 Desborough became President of the Coaching Club (CC), an elite organisation established in 1871 and comprised of aristocrats who had a passion for driving coaches with a team of horses around Hyde Park on selected Saturdays.[6] Some of the participants would continue on to venues such as the Ranelagh or Hurlingham clubs in South-West London, capable of hosting the coaches and perhaps a hundred to 150 people for lunch or dinner.[7] Desborough remained President until his resignation in 1933.

Typically, there were two meets a year, in May and June. Like others in this close-knit circle, he also joined the Four-in-Hand Driving Club (FIHDC), also devoted to driving teams of four horses around Hyde Park, but with a larger programme of meets.[8] It had been formed earlier, in 1856, and was the senior of the two clubs, often with members of the Royal Family participating as passengers or spectators.[9] He became its President in 1912, though it closed in 1926.

For either club the typical turnout was up to twenty coaches – the roads in the park were closed to other users – watched by several thousand spectators.

Lord Desborough with Mary Curzon, Four-in-Hand Driving Club meet, Hyde Park, June 1912.

It was a regular summer activity for the aristocracy, closely covered by the press. Much of the focus was on what the lady participants were wearing and not least if they were riding as well as driving. Desborough had a team of four Cleveland bays, described by one commentator as 'large animals not quite suited to the London scene'. Position in the procession was drawn by lots, overtaking forbidden, and a speed limit imposed. Members had to turn out at least once a year. Membership was restricted for practical reasons, and once the FIHDC membership was full, at fifty, it was inevitable that another club would be formed, and the CC set its own membership limit at one hundred.

FISHING

Fishing was one of Willy's continuing preoccupations, whether of the big-game variety overseas, or more conventional river fishing in Great Britain. He fished along the Thames at Taplow and on the Mimram at Panshanger and elsewhere. As a member of the Flyfishers' Club from 1902 (and President in 1922), he was noted for catching two trout in the lake at Buckingham Palace – a story recounted by the late Queen Mother when she visited the club in 1985.[10]

Desborough was also active in fish conservation. When Chairman of the Thames Conservancy, he made significant efforts to sustain and enhance the fish population of the Thames, particularly salmon and eels. He was appointed Chairman of a Board of Agriculture and Fisheries committee, set up to inquire into the wartime supply of freshwater fish, with special reference to eels, and two reports were produced in 1917.[11] The publicity surrounding the reports and their promulgation of the food value of eels, 'one pound of eels is better than a loin of beef', prompted *Punch* to publish a 'Ballad of the Eels', in which the opening verse ran:

> When lowering clouds refuse to lift
> And spread depression far and wide
> And when the need to strenuous thrift
> Is loudly preached on every side
> What Boundless gratitude one feels
> To DESBOROUGH, inspiring chief
> For telling us; 'One pound of eels
> Is better than a loin of beef'.[12]

*Tarpon fishing in the Gulf of Mexico with rod and line; photograph by
tarpon fisherman Otis Mygatt.*

He was also appointed founding Chairman of the Thames Salmon Association
(TSA), though it had limited success and salmon are no longer found in the
Thames (other than in exceptional circumstances).[13] At the 1907 AGM of the
Salmon and Trout Association (STA), of which Desborough was a Vice President, it was reported that the Thames Salmon Association was stepping back
after seven years of work on hatching, rearing and placing young salmon in
the Thames.[14] Some 12,000 well-grown parr (very young salmon) had been
released in the river in 1903 but had yet to return. The TSA had also tried to
establish Danubian non-migratory salmon, which they had bred in the
Denham hatcheries and released into the river at Hedsor and Taplow, but
sadly there was little success, as river pollution undermined these efforts.

TARPON FISHING

Grenfell's passion for hunting trophy species extended to big-game fishing. In
1899 he undertook a fishing expedition to the Gulf of Mexico to hunt for

giant tarpon* at the start of what became the 'tarpon craze'.[15] Ettie joined him on board the yacht *Decoy* before travelling on ahead to Ottawa. Not only did he make a record catch – landing a tarpon weighing 182 pounds and 7 feet 2 inches in length after an hour of hard work – but altogether landed one hundred of these huge fish in the space of the three-week trip, apparently using an ordinary 7-foot rod and a thin salmon line with lures or bait.[16]

In a letter to Ettie of 30 April 1899 he wrote: 'Yesterday I got five – 172lbs, 135lbs, 111lbs, 108lb, 101lbs – had another big one on the shore when the reel broke & wouldn't turn, & I lost him. Over 160lbs at least.'[17] By 3 May he was claiming, 'I hope to make up 100', but by the 6th he was writing, 'the Tarpon are pretty shy now, only got four yesterday. Hope I shall make up the 100 – doubt it . . . The lines I have now (Myers ones) are first rate, nothing breaks them. I caught a big shark yesterday through one fin, but he never broke the line. I had a Tarpon on yesterday & the rod flew into three pieces, but we let him run all the line out & fixed up another rod, & caught him . . . I am enjoying this enormously.'[18] By 10 May he reported the total score as ninety-one.

Cartoon by John Hassall (with a racist caricature of a local boy) of W. H. Grenfell as Chair of the Fly Fishers' Club, 1904.

---

* Giant tarpon are saltwater game fishes, prized for their great size, their ability to leap and to put up a sustained fight. As a consequence they are deemed by many to be at the peak of fishing challenges.

Grenfell later wrote a substantial article on tarpon fishing, giving a vivid description of the fight put up by these giant fish, while emphasising the importance of a good guide and the best equipment. He explained what took him to the Pass of Boca Grande, which forms the main entrance to Charlotte Harbor in Florida:

The presence of a certain element of danger adds to the excitement and attractiveness of any sport, and the element of danger is not wholly wanting in the Pass. I do not allude to such commonplace risks of tarpon-fishing as cutting the finger with the line, or breaking the thumb with the reel handle when the fish makes a sudden and unexpected rush, but rather to three possible sources of danger ... the presence of enormous quantities of sharks, some of great size; the chance, by no means remote, of being carried out to sea; and the risk of fish jumping into the boat itself.[19]

By 1905 tarpon fishing had become fashionable among the aristocracy, as reported in the *Maidenhead Advertiser*:

So great has the fame of Tampico as a tarpon fishing point become ... that Sir Frederick Johnstone and the party aboard the English yacht came all the way from England for the fishing. The party is having considerable success, the ladies of the party having landed some fine specimens of the big fish. The record fish was caught in front of the Tampico docks, and the angler played the tarpon for two-and-a-half-hours before he succeeded in landing him. This is one of the longest battles between a man and a fish that is on record.[20]

The same article continued:

It may be noted that Mr W. H. Grenfell, M.P., of Taplow Court, when tarpon-fishing in Florida early in April, 1899, captured a tarpon weighing 145lbs, while Mrs Grenfell secured one of 60lbs. Guests at the High Steward's banquet [in Maidenhead] in the following November found at their allotted places at the table tarpon scales on which each guest's name was inscribed. Most of the guests still possess these interesting souvenirs of Mr Grenfell's hospitality and of his skill as a tarpon-angler.[21]

In 1901 Grenfell travelled to the Aegadian Islands off Sicily to fish for Atlantic bluefin tuna, another significant game fish with notable fighting capabilities. As with tarpon fishing, Grenfell was determined to use rod and line rather than nets or other devices, but he arrived in late May when the tuna don't feed. He was unlikely to catch any tuna, but he witnessed the historic *mattanza*, a netting operation that slowly corrals the fish into a small area where they are slaughtered and processed. In a letter to Ettie on 31 May he described how 'they caught 700 this morning and then we went round the factories where they are all cut up and tinned: this place belongs to Florio who has a good looking wife and most of what is worth having in Sicily'.[22] Grenfell wrote about his visit and the history of 'tunny fishing' in the Mediterranean in an article in the *Nineteenth Century Magazine* in October that year.[23]

SWIMMING AND THE BATH CLUB

Grenfell was an excellent swimmer, as his exploits at the Niagara basin confirm. Indeed, in 1908 the Amateur Swimming Association supported the proposal to create a memorial for Captain Webb, and Desborough was asked to be Patron of the Webb Memorial Fund.[24] A portrait bust in bronze was commissioned from the sculptor Francis William Doyle-Jones and Desborough unveiled the memorial in Dover in 1910.[25] He later became President of the Channel Swimming Association from 1928 to 1945.

Lord Desborough unveiling the Captain Webb Memorial, Dover, 8 June 1910.

THE BATH CLUB

The Bath Club was established in 1894 as a gentlemen's club at 34 Dover Street in Mayfair. Grenfell was one of the founding members (and an investor) and became its first President, serving until 1942, a year after the club's premises were closed as a consequence of being badly damaged by a fire.[26] It rapidly became a leading London club, partly on account of the facilities it offered to those with sporting interests. There was a swimming pool (a rarity even now in London), a boxing ring, and in 1907 a miniature rifle range opened by Earl Roberts, with A. J. Balfour (Leader of the Opposition) in attendance.[27] The club was notable in admitting women, albeit using a separate entrance in Berkeley Street, and for encouraging the training of young people in swimming.

It had an extensive programme of activity for both men and women, and the Grenfells' daughter Monica won three swimming competitions in the pool. By the time of the AGM of 1897 Grenfell noted, 'There are now 1087 gents and 271 ladies, total 1358.'[28] Women were allowed to use the sporting facilities three days a week. In 1913 there was a controversy over the conversion of the library into men's bedrooms and half the ladies' dining room into a new library. This was approved by members, but Desborough reportedly mis-counted the votes and had scheduled the meeting later in the day when few women were present. In 1932 the admission of new female members was suspended.

There were regular aquatic events, including water polo, swimming races (such as the Varsity match), life-saving demonstrations and tableaux of various kinds, with the balconies filled with spectators.[29] Edward VII and Queen Alexandra visited the club in 1903 to watch a water polo competition – the first international competition for His Majesty's Cup, won by England with Hungary as runner-up – and the Queen was reported as 'standing up at times to get a better view of it'.[30]

The Bath Club often provided the pool facilities needed by the Life Saving Society, an organisation with which Desborough had a long association, serving as acting President and then as their longest serving President (1901–44). For many years he encouraged the Royal Life Saving Society to share its work around the world, and spoke of it when he travelled.[31]

Desborough often used the Bath Club to write letters if he was in town, and as somewhere to meet with colleagues or friends. In the inter-war period one of the members, Miss Amy Daly, was given the job of helping Princesses

Princesses Elizabeth and Margaret with their mother the Queen, and with Ettie Desborough, watching a swimming display at the Bath Club, 1938.

Elizabeth and Margaret learn to swim and life-save in their own pool at Buckingham Palace, and it was at the Bath Club that the Princesses subsequently gained their life-saving qualifications.*

Before he was raised to the peerage, Grenfell had also been instrumental in the foundation of the Queen's Club in Fulham, in 1887, as the home of racquet sports such as real tennis, lawn tennis, rackets and squash. It also had a stické court and promoted a variety of other sports (including ice skating and bicycling). Grenfell was an initial shareholder and became President in 1891–2.[32]

TENNIS

Taplow Court had at least six outdoor tennis courts (one hard court and a number of grass courts) and these were well used by the family and weekend visitors. In June 1921 Desborough hosted the Prince of Wales and Prince

---

* In 1937 Elizabeth passed her Elementary Certificate and the following year the Intermediate Certificate, while Margaret passed the Elementary Certificate. In 1939 the Princesses won their age groups in the Children's Challenge Shield at the Bath Club. Lord Desborough was the referee for the competition.

Henry to lunch, and tennis was played afterwards. He had a lengthy association with the game, though probably played little more than 'social' tennis himself. He was President of the Lawn Tennis Association from 1907 to 1926, and debates on amateurism were ever present, as in so many sports. In 1911 he was reported as commenting at the Annual Meeting, when: 'He had not a word to say against professionalism but that was not the point. If they decided not to adhere to the clause [by which a professional in any other sport could not be an amateur under lawn tennis rules] as it stood there might be individual cases of hardship, but they must look at what had happened in other sports and, personally he was in favour of the clause as it stood.'[33]

Elsewhere in the debate Desborough highlighted that the definition of 'amateur' the committee proposed to adopt was very strict. He noted that, 'As it read it would disqualify the King . . . because his majesty was engaged in sport for which money prizes were given, and if he won the Derby, as they hoped he would, then he would be disqualified . . . though whether his Majesty would derive any pecuniary advantage from his turf winnings was another question . . . his view [Desborough] was that each governing body of expert(s) must work out its own salvation, and frame its own view for amateurs.'

In 1925, on suggesting that he might stand down, Desborough was persuaded by the Wimbledon finalist Frank Riseley to stay as President for one more year, writing that 'the Lawn Tennis Association & the game generally would sustain a great loss if you were to carry your suggestion into effect'.[34]

STICKÉ

Stické tennis was invented by the Royal Artillery as an indoor game similar to rackets or real tennis: tennis rackets are used, and lower pressure – and thus softer – tennis balls. The game is easy to learn and can be played all year round and by men and women. In 1892 Grenfell built a stické court at Taplow Court, reputedly to his own patented design.[35] The building was always multi-purpose, being referred to as the 'covered tennis court' (with a penthouse down one side like a court for real tennis), as it could also double as a meeting or dining room. The court still exists at Taplow, where it is now used as a canteen.

Lord Desborough photographed at the top of the stairs outside his stické court with nurses getting respite at Taplow Court during the First World War.

Stické was a favourite sport for members of the Souls when visiting Taplow. Grenfell played enthusiastically, including on his hunting trips to India in 1883 and 1891–2, when staying with the Maharajah of Cooch Behar. Stické still has dedicated players, though there are only two courts in Great Britain in regular use, at Hartham Park, Wiltshire, and Knightshayes Court, Devon.[36]

BOXING AND WRESTLING

In *Fifty Years of Sport at Oxford and Cambridge, Volume 2*, it is noted that 'Willy Grenfell . . . left Oxford long before the inception of the club (the University Boxing Club being established in 1881) but from the first has been an honorary member and has often fought for Oxford.' However, there don't appear to be records of his fights, and the same is true of wrestling, another sport he engaged with; he was later appointed President of the Wrestling Association. He presided over the London-based Stadium Club, which was a rendezvous for amateur sportsmen, including boxers, and the Bath Club had its own boxing ring. In the 1930s Desborough was still attending dinners hosted by the Amateur Boxing Association, and a 1936 Pathé News clip shows him attending the finals of the Federation of Boys' Clubs boxing champion-ships at the Royal Albert Hall.[37]

BARTITSU

Grenfell was an early supporter of a form of Japanese 'scientific wrestling' and self-defence introduced by Edward Barton-Wright, who learned it while living in Japan.*

Barton-Wright gave a demonstration in March 1899 at a Ladies' Night at the Bath Club and by June that year Grenfell was championing the sport and the creation of a Bartitsu Club.[38] In an interview with the *Daily Mail* in June 1899 he explained: 'The idea is to establish an athletic class for people of good standing, and it seemed to us best to establish it in the form of a club so as to be able to exclude undesirable persons. So members will be able to come themselves and to send their children and the ladies of their family for instruc-tion with every assurance that they will be running no risk of objectionable associations . . . Athletic exercises of many kinds and physical culture will be taught.'[39]

Here Grenfell's class prejudice was fully on display, and in contrast to his general interest in widening participation in sport to all classes. The Bath Club, however, was an ideal venue, as it combined facilities with a member-ship of the 'right' social standing. Barton-Wright established his own school elsewhere in London and the sport was briefly fashionable from 1898 to 1902, although there have been modest signs of revival.[40]

CROQUET

Croquet was another sport Grenfell rarely played competitively (though Taplow Court had a croquet court on the west lawn) but with which he became associ-ated. In 1919, in advance of the AGM of the Croquet Association, the Chairman told the meeting that Lord Desborough had written, explaining:

Alas! I have a committee at the House of Lords on Thursday afternoon, and I am afraid that I cannot come to the Annual Meeting of the Croquet Club after all, which I much regret, and for which I apologise. Now that croquet will soon recuperate after the war I think that you should have an active and working President and a fit exponent of the

---

* Bartitsu combined boxing, jujitsu, cane fighting and kick boxing.

game, so the time has come for me to retire gracefully, which I accordingly do, so that you may elect a more fit and more proper President.

The Chairman then continued:

Now, ladies and gentlemen, you will all agree with me that it is a proposition to which we cannot give our assent ('Hear, hear'). It is quite true that Lord Desborough is not a very active croquet player, but in the world of sport his name is a name to conjure with, and he makes a most admirable Chairman at any meeting over which he presides . . . and I hope you will unanimously refuse to accept his resignation, and empower me to write to Lord Desborough and tell him so.

Desborough continued as President until 1933.

CRICKET AND THE JULIAN CUP

Desborough became President of the MCC (and, as we have seen, the only President to host a Triangular Tournament) but he is better remembered for his part in what became known as the Julian Cup and the birth of limited-over cricket aimed at stimulating wider participation by amateurs and which may have begun in Maidenhead.[41]

In 1924 Arthur Brooks (headmaster of Maidenhead County Boys' School, now Desborough College) suggested that workers might enjoy an evening's sport at the cricket club. He wrote to the *Maidenhead Advertiser* on 6 February:

Dear Sir, During the long summer evenings it would be possible to play off a 'knock out' cricket tourney next summer greatly to the encouragement of cricket and to the benefit of people who deserve recreation from their work and worries. The time factor usually gives trouble and it is generally only one or two players who stay at the wicket so long. I suggest that if a batsman is not out at the end of the twelfth over from when he came in he should retire 'not out' on a signal from the scorer. Most games could then be finished between six and nine pm or on a Saturday afternoon.

He suggested Maidenhead Cricket Club or the games committee at the school would organise this and appealed for someone to present a Maidenhead Challenge Cup.

Photo feature in the Sunday Mirror *captioned 'Cricket Pitches as War memorials', 5 June 1921.*

There was already a link between the school and Desborough, who had donated land for a cricket pitch in memory of his sons Julian and Billy, and then himself offered to donate a cup.[42] The competition became known as the Julian Cup and appropriately the first ever match in the series was won by Taplow Cricket Club while White Waltham Cricket Club went on to win the first final.[*]

The press commented: 'The Julian Rule continues to prove that cricket of the good old English style can be restored, where all sorts of people enjoy bright, short games where men hit out and don't potter about; and where every man gets his whack between 6.30pm and 9.00pm.' Desborough had been due to present the Cup but was held up in the House of Lords and Brooks extemporised in a long speech, reminding the audience that the Julian Rule meant 'get on or get out': 'It is a matter of intense importance that good

---

[*] In the first final of the competition, White Waltham won by ninety-one runs and were proclaimed the first winners of the Julian Cup. Central to the competition was the Julian Rule: by which batsmen retired at the end of the twelfth over. Brooks often reminded his audiences that 'This rule was in place to respect the memory of Julian Grenfell who along with millions of brave young men, gave up four fifths of their possible lives for the sake of others.'

cricket should be brought within the reach of ordinary Englishmen with only Saturday afternoons and evenings to spare for it . . . The competition had shown how delighted people were to pay to watch cricket when time is limited and they are certain that there will be something happening the whole time.'[43]

Desborough remained patron of the Julian Cup, frequently attended matches and often presented the Cup himself.[44] In 1934 he commented that the invention of the Julian Rule was 'by far the best solution of the cricket difficulty regarding . . . time' and although it has been suggested that 'it would encourage batsmen to "slog" . . . this idea has long since been exploded'.[45]

Arthur Brooks was the guiding force and remained close to the competition until his own death in 1955. He worked hard to maintain the Cup's standards, including no Sunday matches, a focus on amateurs and fairness. The competition has had its ups and downs but continues with the Cup itself sitting on a pyramid of plinths covered with the names of winning clubs: a fine tribute to both Brooks and Desborough.

AMATEURISM

The closing words of Desborough's speech at the 1912 Incogniti Jubilee Dinner underlined his determination that amateur sport should be encouraged: 'He

Hash Hussain, left, and Vishal Arjan of Stoke Green Cricket Club, Julian Cup winners, 2019.

confessed that he was in favour of amateur sport; that is as the more diffused sport as against the freak. He should explain himself. He would rather that one hundred should play cricket as against one freak bowler who could win a Test match. He had no desire to take away from the credit due to the freak, but he did not prefer the super excellence on the part of one or two.'[46]

This was quite something, given that he was President of the MCC, but his enthusiasm for amateur sport links with the wider theme of amateurism, and a set of questions running through all his activities. He never belittled professionals nor 'elite' players but remained fully committed to promoting wider participation across all classes and would frequently speak out, not least at the many AGMs at which he presided. Whether in tennis, rowing, punting or cricket, he would make his position known in support of amateurs, while recognising the symbiotic relationship between amateurism and professionalism: each one feeding off the other. This is evident in the sports in which he engaged and his willingness to 'cross the line', not least by awarding cups for professionals to race for. His commitment was to the sport and the ideals that underpinned it rather than how it was organised.

Desborough promoted the benefits of exercise and always maintained that to 'look fit one had to live fit'. For him sport was a central part of life.[47] This chapter has explored the exceptional diversity of Grenfell's sporting interests and the length of his association with many individual sports, as competitor and patron. He was competing in fencing into his fifties and this was also probably true of cricket, tennis and stické. He became President in six of the sports described here (and at the Bath and Queen's Clubs) and his combined length of service across all these amounted to nearly 150 years. Fulfilling the annual round of AGMs and dinners as President kept his diary full, but he was also active in committees and judging. The sheer energy and scale of his engagement across all these sports is staggering.

Family and Society

9

Ettie and the Souls

Ethel Priscilla Fane – wooing and marrying – Taplow Court and children – Arthur Balfour and the Souls – conversations and games

The politician Arthur Balfour recalled his early days of playing lawn tennis in his 1930 autobiography:

> The game which I first played on the lawns at Latimer was afterwards, in the early 'eighties, transferred to the gardens of Devonshire House in Piccadilly, and these became, as the game developed, a regular centre of afternoon amusement. Lady Desborough, then still Miss Fane and in her teens, has told me since how from the upper windows of her uncle Henry Cowper's house in Stratton Street, where she lived at this period, Devonshire House gardens could be seen. She well remembers that during the intervals of her being prepared for confirmation, she would look out from the school-room window and see all the Latimer party, including Alfred Lyttleton, myself and her own future husband, Willie Grenfell, and many others, amusing themselves in this new fashion.[1]

Ethel Priscilla Fane was born on 27 June 1867 into a family wealthier than Willy Grenfell's, and was part of an extensive aristocratic network. Her family losses, however, were even more acute: Ettie (as she was always known) was not yet two when her mother, Adine Cowper, died after the birth of her brother, Johnnie. Her diplomat father, Julian Fane, died when she was only three. And Ettie was just nine when her seven-year-old brother caught whooping cough, which developed into bronchitis, and died in March 1876. Such losses were by no means unusual in families in the late nineteenth century, but nonetheless were shattering blows.

Her father had designated his sister, Rose Weigall, and the children's uncle, Henry Cowper, as guardians for the two orphans and arranged that their year would be divided between their two grandmothers: Lady Westmoreland in Portman Square on the Fane side, and with the great heiress Anne Florence, Lady Cowper, at Wrest Park in Bedfordshire.[2] After Johnnie's death, the Cowper family became increasingly important for Ettie, particularly her uncle Francis (7th Earl Cowper) and his wife Katie at Panshanger House in Hertfordshire, though she also spent time with her uncle Henry Cowper's family at Brocket Hall, also in Hertfordshire. Amid this tumult, Ettie formed a lifelong attachment to Nanny Wake, whom she later engaged at Taplow Court to help bring up her own children.[3]

Ettie grew up in London high society and, amid the activities and trappings of wealthy country house life, spending her childhood both with Tory-leaning Fanes and Westmorelands as well as Whig and Liberal-connected Cowpers. Christianity was important and a strong personal religious faith was instilled early on. However, the primary expectation for young women was that of finding a suitable husband. Ettie's biographer, Richard Davenport-Hines, explains how, alongside the losses, Ettie benefited (particularly with the Cowpers) from 'a very precocious engagement with adult social life', and was launched, not yet eighteen – though attractive and assured – into the London season of spring 1885.[4] Her success, as he describes it, was 'swift, assured and striking', as 'she combined a natural, eager manner with an air of contrivance, leaving men to puzzle whether there were far-reaching intentions behind quite simple remarks'.[5] In this first season of 1885, Ettie caught the eye of three titled suitors, but she also met a persistent admirer of lesser status: William Grenfell, ten years older, handsome and a famous sportsman. As a commoner he was less well placed, but he was about to be re-elected as MP for Salisbury and would serve as Private Secretary to Sir William Harcourt, one of Ettie's godparents.

Later in life, Willy and Ettie's daughter Monica joked that her mother had fallen for Willy because she 'loved the idea of water parties [and] had been taken down to Taplow for one, when Kitty Drummond, a young married woman, was the chaperone. She told me so often that she married Daddy because the special brand of ginger beer at Taplow was so good, that I still almost believe it.'[6]

Willy wooed Ettie through 1886, and seems gradually to have won her over. In March Ettie's close friend Mabell (recently married to the Earl of Airlie) advised:

My darling Puppy, First and foremost about W.G . . . If you do not absolutely hate him I should marry him, I think; first everyone says he is an absolute angel; and he may be a little dull, but after all what a comfort it is to be cleverer than one's husband! Then he has got awfully nice relatives, and he is altogether so sweet, and if you care for that sort of thing you could get him made a peer any time. My goodness me, you could do anything you liked! But if you make up your mind for him I should go at him hammer and tongs and not look at another man till you have finished him off – because when a man really wants to marry a girl he is so awfully particular. You don't mind me saying this do you?[7]

Despite this fulsome encouragement, Ettie hesitated, and towards the end of the year Willy wrote to say, 'Dear Miss Fane, I meant to find out on Sunday whether you cared for me at all, but somehow I couldn't as I felt like an owl. But I hope you will not mind me writing to you now.'[8] Something further was offered – and agreed – as two days later, on 9 December, he wrote from Hothfield Place in Kent:

I cannot say how delighted I was to get your letter today – I can get out of this place tomorrow if I can see you – if you will send me a telegram 'most important, come at once' . . . you can sign it Snooks or Tomkins or Dr Jeykel [sic] and I can make up something – though I am rather a bad hand at it . . . they shoot tomorrow but there are plenty of guns without me – could I come to dinner I wonder? What do you think your respected relatives will say? Mine will be delighted, and with good reason . . . but perhaps yours will think I am not nearly good enough, in which case they will be quite right. I wonder what you thought when you got my letter. I suppose you laughed. Yours aff. William G.[9]

Despite Willy's nervousness, four days later they despatched a joint letter to Sir William Harcourt, writing, 'As a god-daughter and a late (and inefficient) Private Secretary are about to unite their fortunes they take the earliest opportunity to write to their godfather and chief to express the hope that their action may meet with his approbation.'[10] Approval was offered from all sides and the wedding was arranged for only two months ahead, in February 1887 (a month after Willy's younger brother Charles would marry the Hon. Mabel Mills (daughter of Lord and Lady Hillingdon) on 12 January). Willy's mother noted on 11 December that 'Willy came early to tell us all was settled. Most delightful. We were all very happy' and on 30 January recorded in her journal that she 'Gave Ettie my Bible and Quilt – She is quite charming'.[11] Willy's sister Constance had written to Ettie in late December to say, 'I must write at once to say how <u>delighted</u> I am. It is wonderful to think of having you for a sister & I long to see you to tell you how happy it makes me to think of it. It seems difficult to believe that something so delightful should come true.'[12]

The wedding took place at St George's, Hanover Square, on 17 February 1887, with Frederick Temple, Bishop of London, officiating, the Prince of Wales as a witness and an extensive range of society guests, some of whom joined the family for luncheon at the Cowper family house at 4 St James's Square. The guest list ranged from princesses, counts and ambassadors to earls and marquises, and the newspapers took considerable interest. The report in the *Hertfordshire Mercury* carried not only the guest list but detailed the wedding presents. Those given to Ettie, some 125 items, included an astonishing array of jewellery, with three diamond peacock feathers from Earl Cowper, and a large diamond dragonfly with ruby eyes and a diamond ring (and an inlaid table) from Countess Cowper. The groom received seventy-five gifts from well-wishers, with silver candlesticks and salvers from the tenants and staff at Taplow Court. The couple received, between them, no fewer than ten clocks and six inkstands.[13]

Studio photographs from Ettie and Willy's wedding day, 17 February 1887, in the album of Georgiana Grenfell.

Willy's mother, Georgiana, noted after the ceremony how 'at the end the bishop asked for a time for prayer for the Bridegroom & the Bride – he told me afterwards he liked so much the way Willy looked straight up afterwards & felt sure he <u>meant</u> every word he had said – & that he knew Ettie was a most fortunate woman. All went well . . . except that thick darkness came on just before the breakfast & one could hardly recognise one's friends.'

For some, by worldly standards Willy Grenfell may not have been the best match that Ettie could achieve, but in Taplow Court he had a well-located house and a large estate supplemented by income from family business. Perhaps more important was the fact that, as art historians Jane Abdy and Charlotte Gere comment, 'He adored her and put her on a pedestal for ever; he was of sterling quality, "the finest kind of Englishman" who could always be relied on to behave with perfect integrity.'[14] Ettie's friend Mabell Airlie wrote to Ettie sixty years later, 'When we married what *children* we were; and how we leaped into our happiness with such trusting faith.'[15]

For their honeymoon, Willy and Ettie travelled to Paris, then on to Cannes, Venice and Rome, where they despatched the servants and most of their luggage back to England before proceeding via Brindisi to Cairo. Returning home seven weeks later, they were met on Saturday 9 April at the station by villagers and townspeople. A newspaper account was headed 'Welcome home of Mr and Mrs W. H. Grenfell. Rejoicings at Taplow':

> Five triumphal arches had been erected, and there was everywhere in that part of the village through which the happy pair passed a lavish display of bunting . . . As the horses and carriage . . . arrived near the church a halt was made, and the horses were unharnessed and a rope fixed to the carriage, and half a hundred of the artisans and labourers employed on the estate prepared to do the work of the animals.[16]

An illuminated congratulatory address was presented by the Oddfellows and the Foresters, embellished with elaborate decoration, including 'two hearts bound together by a wreath of flowers [with] . . . two flames which mingle in a spiral form, two arrows piercing them diagonally'. Mr Grenfell offered thanks, adding: 'I have been something of a traveller . . . There is one thing about travelling which always strikes me and that is the more you travel the more you appreciate your own country and your own home, and the warmth of your welcome has made me even more glad to get back.'[17]

In the evening the 'artisans and labourers employed on the estate partook of a substantial repast provided for them by estate bailiff and manager, Mr E. Lodge'. And after this celebratory welcome from the staff, Ettie took up her place overseeing the management of the house, while Willy continued his oversight of the estate, with Mr Lodge as his long-standing agent.[18] A surviving account book from Taplow from February 1887 lists all the crockery and linen being transferred from the oversight of Mrs Georgiana Grenfell to the new Mrs Ettie Grenfell, and charts extensive holdings of: 'Table Linen, Slips, Damask Napkins, German Tablecloths, German Napkins, Towels [some marked WHG and some marked CPG], Sheets, Servants Sheets, Pillow Cases, Glass Cloths, Servants Table Cloths, Toilet Covers' . . . and more.[19]

In the first year of married life at Taplow Court Ettie's first pregnancy was welcomed. But on the evening of Friday 13 January 1888 it was disrupted when, as the dinner bell rang, and the household was occupied on the ground floor, burglars climbed into Ettie's dressing room and ransacked every drawer, cupboard, dressing case and handbag. They stole jewellery worth about £4,000, including a particularly fine pearl necklace given by Willy's mother, and many of the wedding gifts previously (and perhaps unfortunately) made public. Though Willy offered a reward of £200 for recovery of the jewellery (and a further £50 for information leading to conviction), the thieves were never caught. Ettie, now seven months pregnant, commented to a friend, 'I can't help being rather thankful they got away before W and the servants got in – a hand to hand fight would have been so awful.'[20]

Two months later, on 30 March, she gave birth to their first child, Julian Francis Henry Grenfell, at 4 St James's Square. Following this happy event, with the invaluable support of Nanny Wake and other Taplow staff, Willy and Ettie were able to establish the complex mix of private, social and public life, including trips overseas, which characterised the next twenty years of their marriage.

Even as the family grew – with the arrival of William Gerald (Billy) on 29 March 1890, Monica (Casie) Margaret in 1893, Ivo George Winfred in 1898 and Alexandra Imogen Clair (Mogs) in 1905 – they maintained a multi-stranded social life with a cycle of entertaining at Taplow from winter through to summer, including an annual civic dinner and summer fête, interspersed with visits to houses of others in their circle, travel overseas, summer with the Cowpers at Panshanger and holidays in Scotland (including for Willy to shoot) in the autumn. When apart, they would write – Willy sometimes every day – using their private terms of affection by which he addressed Ettie as 'Catts' and signed his letters as 'your Gent'.

Family album photograph of Ettie and Willy in the 1890s.

As a fashionable young couple, they often appeared in society columns in the papers, and for more Thames-oriented readers their comings and goings were charted in summer editions of the *Lock to Lock Times* in the late 1880s and 1890s.

Their surviving grandchildren – Nicolas, Viscount Gage and Camilla Cazalet – describe the creation of a 'mystique of the Grenfells' as something that Ettie nurtured.[21] She disliked being photographed, but as their social and political position advanced, so their public image began to consolidate, reflected in the pair of full-length pastel portraits they commissioned from Ellis Roberts in 1891: Ettie portrayed in romantic eighteenth-century costume, Willy dressed as a hunter.

Portraits in pastel by society portrait painter Ellis William Roberts, 1891, as reproduced in
Tracery, *an account of family life by Desborough's daughter Monica Salmond.*

By the time John Singer Sargent made a charcoal drawing of Ettie in 1909, her status as a society hostess was well established, and by 1911, when Willy was also drawn by Sargent, he had become an Establishment figure, now Lord Desborough.

Willy and Ettie Grenfell – Ettie as a hostess most particularly – were central figures in the social circle known as the Souls that emerged in the 1880s. This loosely defined but well-connected group was drawn together through a shared interest in socialising: enjoying house parties, dinners, witty conversation and games, rather than the more formal sporting activities at the centre of much mid-Victorian aristocratic life or the gambling characteristic of a circle around the Prince of Wales.

Arthur Balfour thought 'the name of "Souls" . . . meaningless and slightly ludicrous. It seems to imply some kind of organisation and purpose, where no

Charcoal portraits by John Singer Sargent: Lady Desborough, 1909; Lord Desborough, 1911.

organisation or purpose was dreamed of. It seems to suggest a process of selection, possibly even of rejection, by a group which, in so far as it had any separate existence, was a spontaneous and natural growth, born of casual friendship and unpremeditated sympathy.'[22]

The core figures included Balfour himself, George Curzon, members of the Baring, Charteris, Lister, Lyttleton and Wyndham families, John and Frances Horner, the Tennant sisters, older figures such as Francis and Katie Cowper, younger politicians such as Winston Churchill, and writers including Godfrey Webb and (slightly less central) Wilfrid Scawen Blunt.

One of the key characteristics of the Souls was the absence of any single political association, although Arthur Balfour, one of the most intellectual and complex politicians of the period, Conservative Prime Minister in 1902 and later Foreign Secretary, was a central figure. Margot Asquith (the sixth daughter of Sir Charles Tennant) who married H. H. Asquith – Liberal Prime Minister in 1908 – recorded a significant exchange with Balfour:

Arthur Balfour: 'Do you imagine that I could have asked any Liberal to dine with me either in Carlton Gardens or in the House of Commons before I knew you? Never. They would have said, "A man who entertains Liberals – men like Asquith, Haldane, Edward Grey, or any other

Liberal – is not fit to be a Conservative Prime Minister." Believe me, you, and your friends, changed the customs of London society, and had an enormous influence over it.'[23]

Balfour's biographer, Max Egremont, confirms his central place among the Souls, but emphasises the limit to his involvement and how, although he may have been the most distinguished member, 'his approach to life and human relationships was very different to that of most of his disciples. They were romantics, seekers after romance and feeling; he was a realist, proud of his powers of balanced appraisal, reluctant to commit himself to personal intimacy.'[24] Alongside his social life as a bachelor, Balfour remained a keen sportsman: playing lawn tennis and devoting a month each year (even when Prime Minister) to playing golf. Willy and Ettie's daughter Monica, one of his godchildren, later remarked, 'His family were more surprised when he won an insignificant golf tournament than when he was made Prime Minister of Great Britain.'[25]

Monica and other children of the Souls grew up experiencing country-house life within this spirited and enterprising milieu of male politicians, writers, businessmen and estate-owning aristocrats. They also saw how women were prominent in organising their social gatherings and all-powerful in selecting their guests. Monica later commented that part of what was wonderful in staying in great houses was that it was 'the "lady of the house" who called the tune. This was true of Lady Manners, Lady Wemyss, Lady Horner and my own Mother [Ettie], whose personalities, beauty and gift for living, all held the keys to the special spice and flavour of visits in their lovely houses.'[26] She described how:

My Mother and all her generation, and her clever friends of all ages, were brimming over with vitality and zest for life: it may even give a false impression of heartiness and joviality. They threw so much into the pool themselves, intellect, appreciation and spontaneous fun made out of thin air . . . Nothing was superficial, they felt both joy and sorrow to the full, there was no self-consciousness, and any form of pretension was treated like some deadly infectious disease. (Though infectious diseases actually were treated casually.)[27]

This vivid mix of cultivated amusement and sociable games (rather than serious sport) may appear distant from Willy's own interests, but he and Ettie evidently collaborated in establishing Taplow as a favoured location for 'Saturday to Monday' parties (as they were called) or lunch parties on Sundays each summer. What had changed from his father's and grandfather's generations – devoted though they were to business and political networking – were the elements of modern life, including railway travel and the telephone, intruding into what was seen as a pre-war gilded age.

In her detailed study of Balfour and his circle of friends and supporters, Nancy Ellenberger points out the important place of humour and wit, and how 'In after-dinner drawing rooms . . . the Souls played games in which the point was to be openly funny and intellectually competitive – and where literary parodies, writing contests and guessing games allowed women to shine as well as men.'[28] Favourite games for the Souls included Clumps,* Telegrams, Epitaphs and Styles. And although the games might imply considerable showing-off, they emphasised common intellectual ground and shared reading (Ettie was a voracious reader, less interested in music or the visual arts), allowing men and women to enjoy extensive conviviality. Ellenberger suggests that 'these forms of cleverness were also suited to an age that rewarded mental prowess in men', such that Balfour practised his wit through parlour games, thus honing his successful oratory in House of Commons debates.[29]

The Souls inevitably attracted both positive and critical comments. Wilfrid Scawen Blunt described them as 'bent on pleasure of a superior kind, eschewing the vulgarities of racing and card-playing indulged in by the majority of the rich and noble, and looking for their excitement in romance and sentiment'.[30] The politician Lord Haldane wrote in his autobiography how 'They care for literature and art, and their social gifts were so high that people sought much to be admitted into their circle', but 'They sometimes took themselves much too seriously, and on the whole it is doubtful whether their influence was on balance good.'[31] Ettie published an anonymous riposte to Haldane in *The Times*:

> *Never can there have been people less desirous of forming a clique . . . They were great friends – the men all hard at work in different ways, the women occupied and busy . . . It is a shock to read that one so beloved by many friends as was Lord Haldane should have doubted whether their influence was on*

---

* Clumps is described as 'a game in which questions are asked for the purpose of enabling the questioners to discover a word or thing previously selected by two persons who answer the questions'.

balance good. I do not suppose that it was a question they ever considered, for
. . . they never thought of themselves as a clique at all, nor did they ever dream
of influencing anybody. But when they are remembered as individuals it
would be hard to deny, not only the brilliance and the achievements, but the
courage and kindness and high sense of honour, the wit and gaiety and grace
and gentleness, that they shed around them into life . . .[32]

On 10 July 1889 Willy and Ettie attended a special dinner at the Batchelors'
Club in Piccadilly staged by their friend George Curzon, and discovered on
their chairs one of the rhyming panegyrics offered by their host for each
guest.[33] This dinner (prior to Curzon's departure to Switzerland for his health)
was one of the defining occasions of the Souls. Curzon staged a second dinner
on 9 July 1891 before setting off for further overseas travels (some years ahead
of his appointment as Viceroy of India in 1899, when another dinner was
organised).

Amid the candid descriptions set out in her autobiography, Margot
Asquith recalled:

> It was through Betty and Maggie Ponsonby that I first met Lady
> Desborough. Though not as good-looking as the beauties I have
> catalogued, nor more intellectual than Lady Horner or Lady Wemyss,
> Lady Desborough was the cleverest of us. Her flavour was more delicate,
> her social sensibility finer . . . I do not suppose she was ever unconscious
> in her life, but she had no self-pity and no egotism . . . she created more
> joy for other people than anybody . . . Etty Desborough was fundamen-
> tally sound and the truest friend that ever lived . . . She married Willy
> Grenfell, a man to whom I was much attached and a British gladiator
> capable of challenging the world in boating and boxing.[34]

After the family losses of her early childhood, Ettie grew up seeking the
reassurance of a close circle of women and men. Entertaining at Taplow was
organised scrupulously, as the Grenfells, though wealthy, were not hugely rich
at this time. She threw herself into the role of being a hostess (much of which
she had learned from the Cowpers).[35] As Jane Abdy and Charlotte Gere
emphasise, although she lived in a large house with staff, Ettie 'was naturally
frugal, a teetotaller, and never smoked. She ate little: a slice of pheasant and
potato sufficed, for she regarded food as sustenance, no more. This quiet and

deliberate avoidance of opulence was symptomatic of the Souls' whole way of life.'[36]

For Ettie the importance of the Souls was first as this intimate circle of trusted confidantes – which on occasions she was keen to extend – but also as an intellectual stimulus and a means to pursue her life as an individual, distinct from Willy's preoccupations with politics and sport and the management of his estate. She invited writers she admired to Taplow and the visitor books reveal occasions when Henry James, H. G. Wells and Oscar Wilde were guests. For a period, she was close with Wilde and he dedicated one of his short stories to her.[37] After 1895, when Wilde's trials made his sexuality public, Willy was perhaps more shocked than Ettie and said that Wilde wasn't to be invited to Taplow again. In 1898, after Wilde approached him for financial support, Willy wrote to Ettie: 'I enclose a letter from O.W. I shall not send him anything: he was never a friend of mine at Oxford, if one once begins one would have to go on and on, and I don't want to be mixed up with him.'[38]

A few were resistant to Ettie's charm. The social reformer Sidney Webb, after sitting next to Ettie at a luncheon, described to his wife Beatrice how he found her 'unpleasing with her artificial and insincere talk and silly trick of shutting her eyes at you'.[39] But Ettie's social skills were widely admired, whether creating house parties at Taplow or when she and Willy made use of the Cowper house at 4 St James's Square for entertaining in London. Looking back in 1937, the Duke of Portland recalled how 'The joy of Lady Desborough's parties was the brilliance of the talk, its wit, its speed, its fun . . . Even the young and timid found themselves burgeoning into wit under her particular sorcery . . . People talked of her in terms of magnetism, electricity, bright light.'[40]

After 1900 those associated with the Souls dispersed – with greater family, political or business interests – and the group no longer had the same resonance or social import. Arthur Balfour and Ettie remained close, and, typically, he wrote confidentially in November 1911 ahead of his resignation as Leader of the Opposition, following the constitutional crisis:

My dear Etty, I don't want you to learn from any lips (– or pens –) but mine that I intend to resign the leadership within a few days. I won't attempt to give reasons by letter: when we meet I will do so in full measure . . . only a few people know and I am most anxious that the matter shall not be talked about or get into the paper . . . please therefore keep a discreet silence.[41]

Some of the Souls' children, dubbed 'the Coterie', began to make their own mark in society.[42] But members of the Souls retained their friendships, albeit in a time of greater political and social turbulence, and later some of them wrote memoirs that led to further analysis of how influential they had (or hadn't) been in earlier years.[43]

A. J. Balfour with Ettie Desborough, snapshot by Lady Ottoline Morrell, 1925.

IO

Together and Apart

Overseas journeys – letters and relationships – the expense of socialising – silver wedding anniversary

Willy and Ettie's lives as a married couple in the late 1880s and '90s were energetic and complex, sometimes together, sometimes apart. Ettie was devoted to their young children and also to entertaining, her personal correspondence and local charities. Willy spent time on the Taplow estate (including developing a fine herd of Jersey cattle) and family business interests, attending to public life in Maidenhead and his necessary engagements as an MP, while allowing time for occasional writing and his extensive sporting pursuits. Ettie wrote to Margot Asquith in December 1892: 'We are here till the 12th, such a lot of things I want to do before then, don't you think 24 hours a day is a ridiculously inadequate allowance? It sometimes makes my heart sink with despair to think <u>how</u> little of the kingdoms of the world & the glories of them one could attain to even the dimmest apprehension of, even if one toiled every hour of one's life & lived every moment of it.'[1]

Nevertheless – and with the support of loyal Taplow staff – the arrival of five children doesn't appear to have diminished their social rounds or stood in the way of longer trips abroad. Their joint travels included:

The United States and Canada for several weeks in the autumn of 1888, when Willy returned to Buffalo and again swam the large basin below the upper Niagara Falls [see *Chapter 5 Exploits and Adventures*]. On this trip Ettie met Oliver Wendell Holmes, the distinguished American expert in law (and friend of her guardian, Henry Cowper) in Boston, with whom she began an extended correspondence.

Willy (back row in pith helmet) and Ettie Grenfell (seated, second from left, also wearing a hat) as part of a shooting party at Cooch Behar.

India at the end of 1891 and early 1892, when they travelled to Bombay (Mumbai) and Ettie spent January and February with Lord and Lady Wenlock in Madras (Chennai) while Willy was away hunting game, after which they were entertained by the Viceroy, Lord Lansdowne, in Calcutta (Kolkata), and travelled together to Darjeeling and Cooch Behar (Koch Bihar) and visited historic sites at Benares (Varanasi) and Agra.

The United States and Canada again, in April and May 1899, first to Florida, where Willy was intent on beating the record for the number and size of tarpon to be caught in the Gulf of Mexico [see *Chapter 8 The Great Amateur*] and then to Ottawa, where Ettie went ahead to stay with the Governor-General of Canada, Lord Minto, and his wife. Willy was excited to report on 30 April, 'Yesterday I got five [tarpon] – 172lbs. 135lbs. 111lbs. 108lbs. 101lbs – had another big one on shore when the reel broke & wouldn't turn, & I lost him. Over 160lbs at least . . . Please give my humble respects to their Excellencies, & look out for any nice short-legged bay horses with black points – your loving Willy.'[2]

Egypt and Sudan in early 1913, accompanied by Monica. They joined Lady Alice Salisbury and her daughters, and stayed with their friend Lord Kitchener (British Agent and Consul in Cairo) before Willy went on to pursue big-game hunting in the Sudan.

Tarpon caught by Willy in the Gulf of Mexico, 1899.

Ettie, Willy and Monica, Giza, 1913.

In the same years Willy made his own trips overseas, including for meetings in Paris, Brussels and Vienna; to Eichhorn (now Veveří Castle in the Czech Republic) for shooting in 1890 and 1895; to the Aegadian Islands off the north coast of Sicily in May 1901 (hoping to fish for tunny); with the British Fencing team to Athens and Paris in 1906; back to Canada in 1911 (partly to buy land in the burgeoning city of Winnipeg); and to Stockholm for an International Olympic Committee meeting in 1909 in advance of the Olympic Games in 1912.

Nicholas Mosley comments that while 'Willy occupied himself in his usual ways . . . He continued to write his careful, tender letters, in which he told her not of himself, but of his movements.'[3] This is not entirely fair, for although Willy was keen to inform Ettie about how many game birds or stags he had killed, he also commented on family matters, was solicitous about Ettie's health, shared occasional intimacies and also wrote numerous separate letters to the children.

The cycle of the years before the First World War, in addition to being welcomed by friends to their house parties and by family to Panshanger, involved Willy joining shooting parties at various houses and lodges in the autumn and spring. The many great estates to which he was regularly invited in the 1890s included: Bolton Abbey, Skipton (Duke of Devonshire); Dunrobin Castle (Dukes of Sutherland); Lochmore (Duke of Westminster, leased from the Duke of Sutherland); Holkham (Earl of Leicester); Welbeck (Duke of Portland); and Amport House (Marquess of Winchester). His letters would start with a stalking or shooting tally and then move on to personal matters. Writing in 1905 from Braemore Lodge, Dunbeath, Willy apologises for his previous 'beastly letter' caused by 'doing badly on the hill, & missing . . . I hope you will burn that epistle – there is no woman in the world like you, either as pretty or as clever, or anything else. Yr loving Willy.'[4]

In an earlier letter of 1890 addressed to Mrs Grenfell at Wrest Park (one of the Cowper family houses), he opens with 'My darling little Catts' and later in the year to St James's Square, he asks, 'And how are you? Still bilious?' before commenting on the forthcoming Henley Regatta, 'I hear Kilby is the coming champion . . . the regatta will be crowded: special trainers etc. Let us know what you intend doing by <u>wire</u> – yr aff. husband Willy G.' When they both visited India in early 1892, and separated because of his hunting exploits, he penned, 'I hope you will have a very good time but not <u>too</u> good: I wish you were here but I don't suppose you would enjoy the bullock cart tonight. Catts is a wonderful wife & there is no one in the world half as wonderful and gent loves her very much.'⁵

When separated later the same year because of election work in Hereford he confessed:

My dearest, I have only about 2 minutes having been canvassing all day – odious horrible work. You can't tell what I am going through here. However I knew exactly what it would be – I believe there is some chance of getting in. They all expect me to live here and never budge til the day of the election . . . I have been on my legs all day and haven't even seen a paper yet.' [And after being elected in July 1892, early the following year, Willy wrote slightly self-centredly,] *'I am very sad at you not being able to come to Hereford – we might have had . . . fun down here – and it will be very dull here without Catts. I shall get away as soon as I can . . . I hope that you do not feel dull . . . I hate going down to Hereford for as long without you.*⁶

What was shared in letters was, by definition, only expressed because of being apart. While Willy retained fewer of Ettie's letters to him, their correspondence gives an impression of what their everyday breakfast-time conversation might have been like. Commenting on family matters, for example, such as worrying in September 1897 about his younger brother, 'It is too sad about Charles, he is quite off his head . . . It has always been so from the time he was at school: he is very like Uncle Henry only Uncle Henry always had a pretty good mind to his own interests, especially when he was dealing with other people's money.'⁷ And in December 1904 he was pleased to report on royal assent for the future godparenting of Willy and Ettie's next child, Imogen, writing that he was 'delighted that you are better . . . Isn't it splendid about the Queen? I asked her last night & she was charming: she said she would be <u>delighted</u>.'⁸

On occasions Willy is touchingly (perhaps schoolboyishly) enthusiastic about his personal accomplishments and openly displays the highly competitive element of his character. At the start of the Boer War in 1899, he was too old for regular service (though fit and active in his forties), but still keen to serve, so signed up as a Major in the 1st Battalion of Buckinghamshire Rifle Volunteers. Writing from Shorncliffe Army Camp in Kent, in August 1900, he reported:

Inspection is over all right, & the Battalion were much complimented.' [And later the same day in a second letter,] *'I have got through my exams – 2 papers, & company and Battalion Drill, a <u>long</u> way first: I got 93 & 95 out of a possible 100 for the two papers, and the beauty of it is that I am practically just as well off as if I had passed at the school, & shall be able to go up for the Field Officer's certificate at the school, which only takes a fortnight . . .* [9]

Willy sometimes discussed meetings or potential appointments, or simply things he was hoping for: rather pointedly (and confidentially) in this case, in October 1904, when he sensed the possibility of a peerage and being appointed Governor-General of Canada (about which Ettie was very unkeen): 'My Dearest – here I am: having taken the chair at the Upper River Committee so it was a good thing I attended the Board. I suppose the exciting letter will come here tomorrow: what I long to get off is fighting the next Election, but I suppose there is no chance of that.' And the next day:

I have just got your letter and have put it away safely – I suppose the upshot is that A.J.B. [Balfour] will probably do nothing as he will leave it in the hands of others . . . there is no reason why he should from the party politics point of view. I wonder whether he put his oar in about Canada: I believe the Canadians judging from the papers would have liked us to go . . . I suppose one will have to waste £2000 & all one's time over these wretched elections for some time longer & then be where one started. [10]

As well as sharing confidences, their letters allowed Willy to confess when he was worried about himself or, occasionally, about how things were between them. In late November 1920 he wrote about an unspecified health concern: 'I went to see Dr Sequieira who gave me some different stuff which I hope may do me some good . . . I am still very wretched.'[11] And a week later:

My dearest, what a wonderful letter you have written – it makes up for all the trouble we are going through – but you must take back what you have said of yourself – it is I who am perfectly rotten & stupid – not to say boring, but all that matters is that you should be content with such as I am, when everyone adores you so. I shall see you tomorrow. Till then, your loving Willy. [12]

Letters occasionally gave Willy the opportunity to let off steam (in private), including about members of the Souls, such as the American diplomat Henry White and his wife Margaret and daughter Muriel, knowing that Ettie would be sympathetic:

> *I have had a day with the White family, but they have only now departed*
> *– Harry uttering indiscriminating, nauseating, and stentorian encomiums*
> *to the very last moment, with Muriel a good second, only beaten by the*
> *physical weakness of her sex. Since Monday I have been struggling in vain*
> *against an overwhelming sea of ceaseless platitudes & am quite prostrate . . .*
> *I hope you are enjoying your Scotch tour: I think Scotland does one more*
> *good than anything.*[13]

Their correspondence paints a picture of solicitude and confidence, rather than intense intimacy. Ettie and Willy's marriage might have been under pressure in the early 1890s, given Ettie's close relationships with various male admirers (such as John Baring and Evan Charteris). Among the Souls a certain intensity of friendships was commonplace, and some speculation has continued among historians and biographers as to how relationships played out between expressions of strong affection (which were also commonplace) and actual physical affairs (which seem to have been rare). As Jane Abdy and Charlotte Gere put it, 'Among the Souls, for the most part, the tradition of courtly love was carried on, with intensely romantic sentiments exchanged in letters and in poetry; only rarely were their carefully ordered lives seriously disrupted.'[14] There has been discussion about the degree of intimacy between various women and prominent public figures, such as between Arthur Balfour and Mary Elcho. However, the Tory politician Harry Chaplin described the Souls' creed as: 'Each woman shall have her man, but no man shall have his woman.'[15]

As Nancy Ellenberger writes, 'The extent of infidelity among the highest levels of society in Britain has proven notoriously difficult to determine . . . A good deal of discourse and anecdotal evidence from the 1880s suggests, however, that contemporaries *thought* that privileged wives were experimenting with extra-marital relationships more than had been the case with their mothers in the middle decades of the century, and that they were breaching the spirit, if not always the letter, of the Seventh commandment.'[16]

In the early 1890s, as Ettie extended her social reach, she was widely admired for her good looks, vivacious spirit and style, and although now married, she encouraged some younger men to spend time with her, flattered no doubt by their persistent attentions. Ettie's admirers, Evan Charteris and John Baring (later Lord Revelstoke), adored her all her life, and John's brother Maurice, another devotee, produced an illustrated children's book, *Forget-Me-Not and Lily of the Valley*, with Ettie as 'The lovely Pink, whom everybody was in love with'.[17]

If her close male friendships caused any concern to Willy, it isn't reflected in his letters, either earlier or later. Richard Davenport-Hines, referring to the late 1880s, observes: 'This awkward period – about which nothing clear can be traced – closed when Willie took Ettie away to India in late November 1891. "It was all so wretched (one's own little private thread of life) & I longed to escape from it all", she recalled a year later.'[18]

Some kind of a puzzle remains. Whatever was understood between Ettie and Willy (which isn't revealed in the surviving letters), it allowed her a certain independence and freedom to pursue close friendships with those – like Charteris and Baring – who wrote passionate letters to her. As Davenport-Hines puts it, 'Willie's reactions to Ettie's "spangles" remain inscrutable: doubtless he was unsettled by her moods at this time; but . . . he was confident and trusting in his marriage, and proud rather than hurt by his wife's power over other men.'[19] What proved more difficult was Ettie, in the 1900s, forming friendships with younger men not much older than her son Julian, who resented this deeply.

The Grenfells' socialising entailed considerable expense. Willy and Ettie were not as wealthy as, say, their neighbours the Astors at Cliveden, but they had sufficient income to maintain a lifestyle in keeping with the expectations of Maidenhead civic largesse and the other Souls.[*] Nicholas Mosley notes that their expenditure on housekeeping at Taplow in 1899 was £2,118.6.10½d (according to the meticulous records kept by Ettie), more than £200,000 in today's money.[20] The most expensive months were June, when there were summer parties and Ascot, and December, with extensive Christmas entertaining.

Income for Willy came principally from rentals on the Taplow estate, and he continued to hold mining shares (enthusing at one point about his investment in Gold Crushers mining equipment) and business and land holdings in

---

[*] There seem to have been occasional comments that Ettie was perceived as parsimonious: recycling her garments, for instance, into cushions or other house furnishings.

Canada [see *Chapter 18 Commerce, Empire, War and Peace*]. He clearly sought further income and experimented in new business ventures: for example, in a new disinfectant called Electrozone. In a letter to Ettie from Brussels in spring 1896, he remarks, 'I was very pleased that John Baring likes Electrozone. I have been extolling its virtues among the Foreign Bimetallists!'[21]

In pursuit of more income, the Grenfells leased Taplow Court for the summer of 1897 to the King of Siam (Thailand) in England for Queen Victoria's Diamond Jubilee celebrations. The Taplow Paper Mills were a significant source of income, but a fire in 1901 precipitated new investment and Willy expressed a characteristic mix of concern and excitement in a letter to Ettie:

> *I have got great schemes for the mill . . . I shall put in a turbine instead of the old water-wheel, and connect the pumps with the Paper mill machinery, so there will be 5 different ways of driving them, (1) my turbine, (2) Gas Engine, (3) Cail's water-wheel, (4) Cail's turbines, (5) Cail's steam engine . . . So the pumps ought to be independent, as the new ones are well above the '94 flood. I shall get a cheque for £4507–9–0 tomorrow & £365 for loss of rent, I shall put the £4,500 on deposit.*[22]

However, when Ettie's uncle Francis died in 1905, she was confirmed as a principal beneficiary of his will. And on her aunt Katie Cowper's death in 1913, she and Willy became considerably wealthier, though this also brought direct responsibility for the house and estate at Panshanger, very much larger than Taplow Court.

After 1905, with her social status further enhanced as Lady Desborough, Ettie is recognised by commentators and diarists as a notable Edwardian. Beatrice Webb observed in her diary after meeting Ettie in 1907 (a remark that might otherwise have applied to Willy), 'Great organizing capacity; ought to be head of a great institution', adding rather tartly, 'To outward appearance she is a smart, handsome, cleverish woman. Beneath it she has an iron will, excellent temper and methodical mind, but with neither wit nor reasoning power.'[23]

Willy and Ettie's socialising extended into royal circles and they were on familiar terms with the Prince of Wales and Princess Alexandra in the 1890s. Later, as King Edward and Queen Alexandra, they visited Taplow in the middle weekend of the 1908 Olympics and posed for a group photograph (Lord Haldane boasting how the King had specifically arranged him lying at the front by his feet).[24]

King Edward VII and Queen Alexandra visiting Taplow Court in July 1908.

The death of Edward VII in May 1910 effected Desborough considerably, and he noted to Ettie that he was 'very sad about the King – he was always so very kind, and a great man' and, the next day, 'I am too sad, he is somehow one of the few people one misses personally' and seven days later, 'I am miserable about the King.'[25]

Following the death, a new Court was formed, and on 2 January 1911 Queen Mary appointed Ettie, together with Lady Minto and Lady Ampthill, as a Lady of the Bedchamber. The Queen was a childhood friend whom Ettie had known as May (daughter of Princess Mary Adelaide of Teck). Imogen (Willie and Ettie's youngest, and the old Queen's goddaughter) was still only six and Ivo thirteen when Ettie commenced this extended work at Court, with fortnightly periods in residence at Buckingham Palace, Windsor or Sandringham for parts of the year. Davenport-Hines describes how, 'A few months after her Court appointment, in April 1911, the King and Queen visited Taplow with their sons. In a memorable moment of *lèse-majesté* the young Princes climbed to the gallery of the covered real tennis [stické] court, armed with tennis balls, which they pounded down on their father as hard as they could.'[26] Royal service, however, entailed more time apart from Willy.

As their silver wedding anniversary approached, Willy and Ettie's friends sought to mark it in a suitable form. George Curzon and Lady Essex invited ninety potential subscribers to pay for wrought-iron garden gates for Taplow (with a fountain and sundial). These were unveiled on 17 February 1912, a telling

Ettie, Monica and Imogen by the anniversary gates, Taplow Court, 1924.

symbol, perhaps, of the firm union comprised of two closely interlocking but separate components.

Royal connections strengthened in the inter-war years, including through sport, and King George V announced in 1928 that Willy was to be appointed a Knight of the Garter. Willy wrote to Ettie from Taplow:

> *I am sending a letter which I had to read several times before I took it in – please keep it – Do you think our poor friend has gone a little potty in the head? Or do you suppose I shall be a real K.G.? I am not at all sure that it is not a little too much of a good thing for one with simple inclinations – I think you had better not say a word to anyone, not even Mog [Imogen].*[27]

A day later he followed up by saying, 'I wrote to Mr Baldwin to thank him – one cannot indeed do less – It is most kind of him – a bit too much – and I should think many of my friends will be annoyed if it comes off which I suppose it will?' Four days later he wrote, 'The boys were what I first thought of – with tears.'[28]

Ettie's devoted royal service continued and periods of attendance at Court resulted in exchanges of letters, such as those in early 1936, when the King was gravely ill. Willy wrote on 19 January, 'you must be having a terribly anxious time at Sandringham and one can only hope for the best'. A day later, after the King's death, he expressed simply, 'How one will miss the King!' From Panshanger, two days later he wrote:

> *I got two letters from you this morning, and see that the Queen will probably want you, at which I am not surprised. I shall attend the ceremony tomorrow . . . The Primrose League Gazette wants me to write an appreciation of the King by Saturday, which I will do, & I shall see you before then . . . I see I wrote one, quite good, when King Edward died.*

On 24 January he reported, after attending the lying-in state in Westminster Hall, that, 'It was very cold . . . but very solemn and impressive . . . On Monday I go to the T. Conservancy & move a resolution of sympathy . . . I do trust you are not overdone.'[29]

II

———◦———

The Family World

The Children's Journal – growing up at Taplow Court – country-house life: Taplow and Panshanger – support and staffing – selling the Raphael

CHILDREN AND FAMILY

Early in 1888, expecting the arrival of their first child, Julian, Ettie started her own 'family journal', in which she wrote about family events and added photographs and memorabilia. It mirrored The Children's Journal kept by Willy's mother, Georgiana, and Ettie continued it in eight volumes through to the 1940s.[1] Annual holidays and larger social gatherings were given particular attention, with Ettie's pride in the children's achievements a continuous thread. The journal charted their progress in the nursery and at school (Eton rather than Harrow for the three boys), and in swimming, riding or other sporting successes (such as Monica's swimming medals at the Bath Club), and as they progressed to university and then into the army (the boys) or prepared to 'come out' and enter the world of London society (Monica and Imogen).

Childhood at Taplow was thus closely witnessed and documented: a compensation, perhaps, for the losses in Ettie's own upbringing, shuttling between the houses of her grandparents and aunts and uncles. Yet any view of Willy's and Ettie's children is necessarily coloured by the terrible tragedies of Julian's and Billy's deaths in 1915 and Ivo's following a car crash in 1926. Indeed, Ettie drew on the first three volumes, and their letters, to create an extended account of Julian's and Billy's lives, which she published in 1916 soon after they were killed in the First World War.[2]

Julian, Imogen on Patty, Ivo, Willy, Monica, Ettie and Billy, Taplow Court c. 1909.

It is difficult to summarise the particulars of their lives or to do justice to the complexities of relations between parents and children. But Willy and Ettie set certain positive elements in place, trying to ensure that however busy they were with their public and social lives, their presence was felt. The five children were raised in the privileged and supportive surroundings of Taplow Court – amid the comings and goings of guests – and with a daily schedule that gave them time with their parents, even if on a somewhat regimented basis. Unlike the more rigid social constraints of upper-class Victorian households, Ettie tried to establish an informality in their parenting, with an immediacy of affection – 'intense attentive sympathy' as Richard Davenport-Hines describes it – rather than always with physical contact.

Their second son Billy, aged only four, dictated his somewhat precocious 'History of the Family', which Ettie claimed to have taken down verbatim:

> Billy is a thin boy, but a good boy, but his Dada will never in the winter stop at home. He is a tall man. But his wife is a good mother. She reads to her boys every evening and plays with the little baby [Monica]. Sometimes she is a cross baby and what makes us laugh is when Mama calls her back and she will not come. And she is very fond of her brother named Billy – fonder than of her brother called Julian. Billy is kind to

her and lies on the cushions and cuddles with her, and at night he hides behind the curtains and when she comes after him he gallops down the passage and makes her laugh . . . And Dad, sometimes when he is not away, he reads to us the book called *Gulliver's Travels*.[3]

Both Willy and Ettie made reading to the children a particular priority, and Ettie's journal treats them all fairly equally, though competitiveness emerged early between the two elder boys, Julian (known as Max) and Billy. Monica, looking back in her memoir, *Tracery*, regarded this as a good childhood, with close bonds between her and Julian and Billy, support from their parents, from nannies, maids and staff (and their children). Writing in *Bright Armour* (her book about her time as a nurse in the First World War), Monica described in glowing terms how, 'We all had the most happy childhood, spent at our much loved home at Taplow, and made perfect for us by our parents. We were a large family and very devoted to each other . . . united by affection and laughter, and we rushed to meet all the fun. My brothers and their friends were clever and remarkable, and they added brilliance to an already happy throng.'[4]

Though devoted to her children, Ettie was quite often away visiting friends or her extended family. Willy would send her an account of the young children in the nursery (sounding rather modern): 'I have been to tea with them and they were very well and messy – quite happy smearing buttery crusts over each other's faces and sweeping everything in reach on to the floor. Max forgot to wipe his plate on his head – but otherwise they enjoyed themselves.'[5]

Willy was clearly not in charge – that was the role of Nanny Wake, who also wrote to Ettie with frequent updates on life with her charges: tears and tantrums as well as smiles and giggles.

In September 1898 Ettie was on holiday with Julian, Billy and Monica in Swanage, Dorset, and heavily pregnant with Ivo. Her labour commenced unexpectedly and Willy wrote from Scotland on the 5th to say, 'Just coming in after getting a stag here at Braemore, I got Moore's telegram, 8 o'clock, saying "Son born this afternoon both quite well. Mrs Grenfell particularly wishes you not to come south."'[6] He wrestled with the question of whether he should disobey her:

How wonderful, and how glad you must be it is over – but why produce infants with such extraordinary alacrity? I thought this one was to be a Cockney, but it is a Swanagerian. I do hope that it is all right and that you are comfortable.

How lucky Dr Moore was there, apparently more handy than at Maidenhead. I shall not stalk tomorrow, but walk straight back to Langwell, and I hope get some telegrams, good long ones, and not wretched sixpenny things that no one can understand, but a good ½ crown's worth. You say you particularly wish me not to come, but I want to come and see Catts & little quartus, a most pushing gentleman, & is he all right after all he went through in early life; I should like to know what he weighs. Just put 6 or 7 or 2½ in a telegram, without pounds or anything, & I shall know – and whether he is quite sound – and how you are . . . I am <u>so</u> glad it is all over if you are all right, & Moore says you are. I do hope it was not a bad time – I shall soon see you – but wire.

Willy didn't travel south in the end, staying in Scotland – even though nervousness about the frailty of the new-born Ivo caused Ettie to have him baptised in Swanage – and wrote again at the end of the month:

My Dearest, I got your telegram and sent mine off from the station – I am so glad that you are getting strong so quickly, after all you have been through . . . indeed there is no woman who can hold a candle to Catts in any way whatsoever, and it is not the smallest use their trying & I love her . . . Best love to the children, & the Squeaker – your loving Willy.[7]

Julian with family friend Lord Kitchener, Taplow Court, 27 July 1902.[8]

Something of father–son relations can be gleaned from the phrase 'darling dad', often used by Julian and Billy in their letters from school and university. And although Julian wrote more letters to his mother from Oxford, a typically solicitous missive from May 1910 reads:

> *My darling dad – I am so glad that your British section at the Vienna Exhibition is such a success, you must have had a tremendous lot of work and worry with it, and it must have been a great satisfaction getting it so good in the end, and being able to feel that it was so well worth it. I expect that the work devolved upon you in the end, as it always seems to do; they have found out whatever you put your hand to prospers, and they treat you accordingly.*[9]

Julian's time at Oxford, where he mixed sporting success in boxing and rowing with a bullish persona in his college life at Balliol, became complicated, however, as he increasingly rebelled against the influence of his mother, and took exception to some of her recent male friendships, a few of them from his own generation. Nicholas Mosley describes how:

> Julian Grenfell had been a product of his class and culture; he had also rebelled against these . . . When he was twenty-one Julian had written a short book that was his polemic against conventional society – a plea for individuals to be honest with themselves and by this to influence the world. It was an astonishing book for an upper-class young man in 1910 to have written. His family hated it, and it was never published. Then Julian had some sort of breakdown which was called a 'brainstorm' by his family; he would lie for hours with a loaded shot-gun by his side. Then he recovered, joined the regular army, and dutifully fitted in.[10]

By the winter of 1909–10 Julian was suffering from severe depression, exemplified by alarming accounts of him in Ettie's sitting room with a gun on his lap.[11] Taking time out from his studies, he opted for a pass degree rather than honours (as had his father), which he took in the summer of 1910 – enough to get him a place in the army, which he had determined would be his new adventure. After training, he was posted to India, and his letters home describe a boisterous time with the 1st (Royal) Dragoons, with riding and pig-sticking as favourite activities (although also writing poetry), followed by service in South Africa.

Julian, Ettie and Billy by society photographer Bassano, published in The Bystander, *5 October 1910 and later in* The Tatler, *30 July 1913.*

In the winter of 1912–13 Julian considered leaving the army and briefly contemplated becoming an artist. Monica commented later that 'Julian's great absorption that Winter . . . besides hunting, was in pictures and art; he had a very great love for them, and a really remarkable talent for drawing. He one day announced quite gravely a project of giving up the Army, and going to work at painting in Paris – but this idea was received with such irrepressible laughter by Billy and Bron [Lucas] that it was not mentioned more.'[12]

After success at Eton, winning prizes and a place at Balliol to read classics like his father, and then the prestigious Craven scholarship, Billy also had mixed fortunes at Oxford. He was sent down for unacceptable behaviour (including drunken vandalism in college), although he also won a blue in tennis. In a 2021 stage play titled *Into Battle*, about the clash of privilege and class, much was made of the contrast between the boorishness of the Grenfell boys at Oxford and their subsequent heroism on the Western Front.[13] At the time, the considerable worry for their parents was complemented by consistent support, though for the boys Willy must have seemed a very hard act to follow. Whatever the changing fortunes for the family and sometimes strained relations between children and parents, in his own letters Willy exuded love and steady backing.

Writing to Monica on 3 June 1924, the day after her wedding to Air Marshall

Jack Salmond, Willy wrote: 'My dearest love, and sincere wishes and confident hopes for your future happiness . . . The wedding was the greatest show on earth . . . Please give my love to dear Jack.'[14] But just over two years later, when the family was desperately trying to recover from the shock of Ivo's death, he wrote from France on 19 October, describing Imogen, their youngest daughter, as being 'broke down'. Then on 28 October, as they were trying to find some stability, that 'It is almost impossible to realize that we shall not see our beautiful Ivo again – yr loving Dad.' Two years later and his letters reverted to a more typical everyday mix: writing from Whiteslea on 28 September, 'Mogs [Imogen] Is getting quite good at sailing – she is now out with the Viscount in half a gale.'[15]

COUNTRY-HOUSE LIFE – TAPLOW AND PANSHANGER

Four-year old Billy Grenfell described how: 'We live at Taplow Court, that is the name of the place. Taplow is a very big house, it looks red outside and the flower beds are some in the shape of stars and others round-pieces. Taplow has also very kind gardeners. The woods are very dear, they end at the river Thames. The river Thames runs into the North Sea through Taplow and London.'[16]

Taplow Court was built on a site of ancient occupation going back at least to the Iron Age, but its modern history dates from a seventeenth-century manor house acquired and remodelled by George Hamilton, 1st Lord Orkney, in the early eighteenth century (he also owned the neighbouring estate of Cliveden). The 5th Earl and Countess of Orkney sold the house in 1852 to

Taplow Court, Buckinghamshire, photographed in the 1890s.

Willy's grandfather, Charles Pascoe Grenfell, who in 1855 employed William Burn to create the turreted and eclectically styled neo-Tudor mansion that survives to the present day and is Grade II listed.

The site is important not only for a seventh-century Anglo-Saxon burial mound (first excavated in 1883) but also for spectacular views from this spur of land towards Windsor Castle and Eton and its beautiful riverside location.[17] The ruined parish church which stood alongside the mound was taken down in 1853, and a new church of St Nicolas built in Taplow village, though the churchyard and family vault remain beside the house.[18] A cedar walk was planted in the eighteenth century by Sir Charles Barry and 'pleasure gardens' established and renewed over generations. Planting trees became a Taplow tradition, and a list survives that includes the saplings planted by Queen Alexandra and other notable visitors, right up to Winston Churchill in June 1938.[19]

In telling the story of the writers John Armstrong Chaloner and Amélie Rives, the writer Donna Lucey describes what a young American couple might have made of being invited to Taplow Court as guests of Ettie, feeling privileged perhaps to be admitted to the intellectual circle of the Souls:

> At Taplow Court Amélie witnessed the pageant of English country life – the three thousand-acre estate staffed with some twenty servants; the four-story-high arcaded entrance hall in ecclesiastical Romanesque style, with stag heads on the walls and elephants' feet as vases; the ancient Anglo-Saxon burial mound adjacent to the house that had just been unearthed six years earlier and was still a great topic of conversation.[20]

While the immediate Thames-side site at Taplow encompassed 200 acres, the Buckinghamshire and Berkshire estates that Willy inherited amounted to at least 3,000 acres and apparently yielded some £7,000 a year in the 1880s (around £900,000 today).[21] Oversight of the lands and tenancies was therefore a critical part of Willy's work: estate issues ranging from an exchange in 1887 with William Morris, writing on behalf of the Society for the Protection of Ancient Buildings, about the condition of the fifteenth-century manor house at Ockwells (which formed part of the extended Taplow holdings), a great concern about the renewal of the extensive Taplow Paper Mills after a fire in 1902, and various long-running sagas about lease arrangements, including for the Queen's Arms pub in 1905.[22]

Julian, Monica, Billy, with Ivo behind, and Mr Joel working on two of Grenfell's punts (with white painted interiors), August 1903.

Monica Grenfell mentions a big map on the wall in the harness room at Taplow, used for planning expeditions and 'there were rings on the map to show the mileage', presumably helpful for hunting or longer rides out.[23] Riding, tennis, punting and swimming were on offer to the children as they grew up in these privileged surroundings. The river was perhaps the most special element, and Monica confirmed, 'We went on the river a lot. Besides loving its beauty, I think of the Thames, and its shady backwaters, as a great influence, indeed as a strong stream through our lives. Daddy often punted us up to Odney Pool for a picnic tea, we grabbed scented rushes on the way there, restrained by Mummie from leaning over too far in order to do this.'[24]

The Thames was explored and exploited by the children, as Billy described in a letter to Julian in the spring of 1911:

We had a glorious party at Taplow . . . While Lord D., bless him was dominating the Thames from Boulter's Weir, Duff (who cannot swim) and I shot it with great éclat in the best punt. He was perfectly angelic about it, never 'grummeled' a bit, and only ran round with admirable promptitude to the Blow-hole to pick up the britten-boards . . . I then dived in from the Weir, and was at once gently pulled to the bottom by the undertow amid shouts of joy from friends on shore. However, I re-emerged 30 yds. lower, and Joel was black with rage at missing this unique chance of saving his 101st heroic life (women, children, and Thames Salmon non-compris.)[25]

Monica commented later how she 'went through some moments of terror after Billy had dived into the flooded, turbulent river from above the sluice gates of Boulter's Weir. I thought he might have hit his head on one of the wooden piles. I looked at Daddy, who was much nearer to him, he was leaning on the rail of the bridge and looking intently at the water. Billy emerged at last, a long way down stream . . . greeted with shouts of joy.' Not surprisingly, high-spirited fun on the river was something of a Taplow speciality. Ettie described how in the first of what were termed 'Eton parties' in the spring of 1904, 'There was a Water-Fight, in which Norah Lindsay was very nearly drowned, and Winston Churchill, who had just arrived from London – was flung into the River, in a great-coat, spats and a top-hat – in which he swam very composedly.'[26]

Taplow was undoubtedly an accessible, well-appointed and popular location for guests joining the Grenfells for 'Saturday to Mondays' and for lunch parties on a Sunday. Each summer Ettie (with the Taplow staff) might stage as many as ten weekend parties and several Sunday lunches, when the meal would be followed by punting or tennis. Monica gives an account of batches of guests arriving at teatime on a Saturday, the accommodation of maids and valets who came with each guest being organised by Mr Bart [Barrett Good]. All this fascinated the children: 'There were galleries all round the central hall at Taplow up to the second storey, and as the guests met before dinner in the library and then crossed the hall to the dining room, going in to dinner in the formal manner arm-in-arm, we could watch them without being seen. I often joined the throng in my dressing gown, as it was a very good spectacle.'[27]

Taplow was not above criticism, however, and Jane Abdy and Charlotte Gere describe 'one guest referring to it being like a hotel', in the sense of being very un-private.[28] For others, Ettie's taste for vivid colours was not just dominant but distracting: the cushions often being made from her discarded evening dresses. The garish decor indicated a lack of preciousness and was perfectly suited perhaps for house parties.

In January 1889 the *Lock to Lock Times* gave an enthusiastic account of their wider social patronage of the local community:

The Hall Taplow Court.

Postcard image of the Neo-Romanesque central hall at Taplow Court, hung by Willy with trophy heads and rowing oars.

In his administration of the Taplow Court Estate he sets an example which might by advantage be followed by others. He annually throws open the grounds to a large number of people, many of whom come for miles in order to attend the monster annual fête for which Taplow Court is famous, and where Mr Grenfell may be seen with his wife dancing in the arena, and patronising the roundabouts, side by side with his many humble friends. Mr Grenfell . . . spends the greater part of his time on the river, where he is one of the best-known figures, and it is but few of the frequent visitors to Maidenhead waters who have not come across a herculean form propelling a racing punt at a terrific speed – a model of good form to others, and with evident enjoyment to himself.[29]

While Ettie kept her own private dressing room on an upper floor in one of the turrets, Willy filled his study with the mementos and residues of sporting and hunting achievements, creating a stereotypically masculine space to which he could easily retreat. Unlike Ettie, a teetotaller, Willy kept a bottle in his study behind a secret panel.

The Grenfells redecorated the interiors at Taplow but didn't feel the need to initiate architectural changes (and may have had budget limitations). Seven months after their wedding, Willy had written to Ettie to say:

> When we get back we must set to work on your room. I think a good big sofa in front of the fire and plants etc. behind it would look nice and be useful which is the first consideration in furnishing a room – also you ought to have a good white screen with some of those Correggio engravings which are beautiful. I have the <u>complete</u> set, first state. I thought they would look nice panelled in a bedroom half-way up, which would be original, in white wood – not all the rooms are done up now.[30]

Willy added the indoor stické court in 1892 and elements of modernisation were considered around the turn of the century, with Willy reporting back to Ettie on the electric lighting he encountered in other houses in this period. In November 1898 he commented from Hartham Park: 'This is rather a nice place with electric light or rather electric darkness, as I cannot find a place where I can see.' However, by October 1901 he reported from Netherby that the electricity costs £350 a year and 'you have a clear and convenient light, but not a pleasant one to read by, and I expect we should always use lamps for ourselves'. His view changed by August 1905, when he proposed, 'I think we should really have a Telephone [and] Electric Light? . . . a telephone costs very little: splendid for – Fire/Doctors etc.'

Money was found in April 1906 to install electricity at Taplow, though Willy was at the time in Athens for the Intercalated Games and sent detailed instructions on where wires should run; he commended Ettie, writing somewhat patronisingly, 'I got one letter from you yesterday about the electric light, & you seem to have done splendidly.'[31]

Wiring was not fully installed at Panshanger until much later, the spring of 1937, as the priority had been to sort out heating and plumbing in this vast house. The other key marker of modernity, the motor car, came earlier, with Willy buying a Rothwell and joining the Automobile Association in 1910, writing to Ettie, 'the motor is being done green inside, & a speaking tube put in, & the crest put on: the little accessories, clock, looking glass etc. can be got in London'.[32] Built in Oldham by the Eclipse Machine Company, with a

Lord Desborough with Monica and a Taplow staff member in the Rothwell, c. 1919.

20-horsepower four-litre engine, it had a top speed of 50 mph. The firm used 'Eclipses All Others' as its slogan and Monica described learning to drive on the car in 1913, and it having 'harsh gears', but she also admitted to an early 'smash'.

The census returns for 1891 and 1901 provide a view of Taplow Court staffing, with a complement of about twenty (although at busy times there could be more than thirty) including:

Nurse
Nursery Maid (x2)
Lady's Maid
Housekeeper
Cook
Laundry Maid (x2)
House Maid (x3)
Dairy Maid
Kitchen Maid
Hall Boy
Butler
Coachman (and 2nd Coachman)
Groom
Gardener

William Henry Grenfell is described in the 1891 census as a 'Magistrate living on his own means' and in 1901 rather tersely as 'JP. MP. Landowner'. For the children, some staff were more significant than others, and Monica makes particular mention of Miss Poulton 'our strict governess' and Mr Williams the coachman, as well as nannies Matilda Wake (Nanny Wake) and Harriet Plummer (Hawa), and Mr Joel the boatman, Elizabeth Neave the cook (Nea), Mr Hunt the house carpenter, Mr Williams the head gardener, and Barrett Good the butler (Mr Bart). An extended sociability is confirmed through her passing comment that 'Mr Bart's sons and the many little Joels and Jack Williams were great cronies of ours'.[33]

A short piece appeared in the *Maidenhead Advertiser* in 1928, starting with the line 'The perfect butler has been found in the employ of Lord Desborough'. This reference to Barrett Good, who worked for the family for fifty years and as butler for forty-five, confirmed that he was an absolutely central figure in the operation of Taplow Court. After Willy's death, an obituary in the same newspaper included a sub-heading of 'Loyal Servants': 'The death of Lord D will be felt deeply by many of his old servants chief among whom is Mr Barrett Good, personal valet, butler and house steward to his Lordship for sixty-four years. Mr W. Joel, waterman for over fifty years, Mr Arthur Simmonds, gardener at Taplow Court for more than fifty years, and Mr. George Emmett, land agent for the last seventeen years . . . all will regret the passing of a kindly master.'[34]

Rosa Gwilliam, who started as a 'still-room maid' in 1900, and progressed through various roles in the kitchen to become head cook, confirmed that 'life in service in those days was great if you were lucky enough to be in a good home with good people as long as everyone knew their place. Taplow Court was such a place and the Desboroughs good people.'[35] The staff were sometimes set the challenge of supporting very large social gatherings, including international congress meetings or diplomatic visits.

In August 1897 Willy had reported (in racist terms) to Ettie after giving an account of his umpiring at the Amateur Punting Championship, 'In the evening I was introduced to the King of Siam – a little man with a bright yellow face who bawls at you. He told me it was very good of me to lend him Taplow – he will soon find the difference between letting and lending, which he doesn't yet quite understand.' This was an unusual summer rental and not a regular arrangement, and Willy was concerned (but pragmatic) about the imposition on the staff, particularly when the royal retinue was somewhat expanded:

I hear from Lodge [Mr Lodge, chief agent for the Taplow estate] that the King of Siam is going to have a great fete on the 21st – a Garden Party and illuminations of the house etc., and 120 sailors are coming from his yacht – they are going to sleep in the Tennis Court which will be heated – and this will make difficulties with the insurance company. But I have told Lodge not to make too much fuss about it, as the extra premium for a short time cannot come to very much.[36]

In January 1912 the winter entertainments were taken to another level with a large fancy-dress ball at Taplow. All the guests were photographed for an album, with Willy appearing as a Renaissance prince.

When Francis, 7th Earl Cowper, died on 18 July 1905, his death caused the break-up of the extensive Cowper estates that had placed him among the richest landowners in England, with some 38,000 acres across eight counties.[37] As he and Katie Cowper were childless, this brought great changes for his nephews and nieces, including Auberon Herbert (Bron Lucas) and Ettie, who inherited Panshanger in 1913 on her aunt's death.

Her share of the Cowper estates included the large early nineteenth-century house, the park landscaped around the River Mimram by Humphrey Repton, surrounding farms and properties, and an exceptional art collection assembled across several generations, and notably by the 3rd Earl.[*] Ettie set up a Panshanger Fund and realised that she might have to sell the smaller of the two Raphael paintings. After first being offered to the National Gallery, a sale was negotiated through Joseph Duveen for £70,000 (equivalent to around £8 million today). What later became known as the Small Cowper Madonna was

---

[*] After 1905 Desborough took a close interest in the business aspects of the estates that Ettie had inherited, including holdings in the coal fields of Nottinghamshire and Kent. After a visit to Kent in September 1912, he wrote: 'I went down to Kent yesterday as there are only 13 tenants . . . The greatest change is at Danbridge Farm – they have erected a chimney 180 ft high (250,000 bricks and 120 tons of cement) which I went to the top of being hauled up the inside of the chimney on a board: one got a splendid view from the top.' He went on to describe the workshops and machinery for two shafts 'which they sink on our land'. He sent a long account of the Wingham and Stour Valley Collieries and what a success it would be – 'employing 200 men and when working 3,000 colliers, which means a population of 10,000 . . . One really ought to go to Notts & Kent 2 or 3 times a year.' 5 September 1912, Hertfordshire Archives and Local Studies, Hertford, D/ERvC1159/600. Later that month he reported that 'I saw Ld Harding at the Carlton – he said that he had heard we were going to become Coal millionaires in Kent!' The enterprise failed and the Desboroughs sold their land.

Panshanger House near Welwyn Garden City, Hertfordshire, c. 1910.

sold on to Paul Widener, a collector in Philadelphia, and subsequently bequeathed to the National Gallery of Art, Washington. The *New York Times* claimed that the sale represented the 'largest sum ever paid for a painting'.[38]

Ettie wrote to Balfour that she didn't wish to start the new period of ownership of Panshanger 'by selling a picture, but I hope it will be our first & last Sale, & that the income of this sum will just make the difference to us of being able gradually to get this place into good order, & to live here part of each year, which we undoubtedly *could not* otherwise have done'. By the autumn of 1913, works had started on the heating and plumbing, which were completed in 1914.[39] Willy and Ettie intended to return to Panshanger for six months in October, with the King and Queen Mary invited for pheasant shooting in December, but everything changed in August with the outbreak of war.

Julian had written to Ettie from South Africa in 1913, 'It's very good getting such a lot for the Raphael, and it ought to make things easier, oughtn't it? I'm glad that the noise in the water-pipes at Panshanger is getting less. And the New Old Smoking Room sounds as if it would be awfully nice.'[40] Earlier in the same year he remarked to Willy, 'I hope your pedigree cattle will be a success at Panshanger' (following Willy's success at Taplow) but elsewhere he wrote: 'I believe the Raphael was entailed, and I am getting up a lawsuit.'[41] Even as a joke (the painting was not in fact restrained by any covenant or family trust), it revealed something of the strains of intergenerational expectation.

Politics and Public Service

12

Trusted Servant

First steps as a Member of Parliament – from Liberal to Conservative – House of Lords – civic duties – wider public service – the Police Committee

William Grenfell had a strong sense of duty, like many in his family and also many from the middle and upper classes (even if public service was linked on occasion with personal advancement). Among his forebears, Pascoe, Charles Pascoe, Charles William and Henry Riversdale Grenfell had all been Members of Parliament, although the first two continued to operate their copper smelting business at the same time. The range of his public duties was great and this chapter outlines his various roles and their impact from the 1880s to the 1940s, against a backdrop of complex domestic politics and momentous world events.

His public-facing activities (outside of sport, business and appointment to civic institutions) included becoming a special correspondent for the *Daily Telegraph* in the Sudan in 1885, serving as an MP in Salisbury (twice), and then as the MP for Hereford and for Wycombe before moving to the Lords. He served in the Liberal governments headed by the Earl of Rosebery, acting briefly as Parliamentary Private Secretary to the Chancellor of the Exchequer, Sir William Harcourt, and in the Conservative government of Stanley Baldwin as Deputy Chief Whip in the House of Lords from 1924 to 1929. Nearer to home he served as the Mayor of Maidenhead (twice) and as High Steward, as Deputy Lieutenant of Buckinghamshire and then Tower Hamlets, as a Justice of the Peace and as High Sheriff for Berkshire. At the end of the First World War, and with considerable unrest over pay and conditions in the police force, Desborough chaired an inquiry into police pay and conditions in England, Wales and Scotland – a report that is still cited today.

Grenfell remained close to the Royal Family in various roles: he was appointed a Commander of the Royal Victorian Order (CVO) in 1907 for services to the Sovereign, Knight Commander in 1908 and Knight Grand Cross (GCVO) in 1925. In 1928 he was appointed a Knight of the Garter (KG).

FIRST STEPS

Before leaving Oxford in 1879, Grenfell had enrolled as a student at the Inner Temple, presumably as the first stage towards a career in law.* However, he didn't pursue this option and in early 1880 he was invited to stand as a Liberal candidate for Salisbury (there were two seats for this constituency). Given that he was only twenty-four, Grenfell was aware of the charge that 'he was too young to enter Parliament'. However, the report of a Liberal Party meeting on Saturday 27 March, in the Hamilton Hall in Salisbury, noted Grenfell's appetite to follow in his forebears' footsteps and enter politics: 'He contended that the government of a mighty empire was an important task, and he was anxious as early in life as possible to devote his abilities to the study of political sciences.'[1]

He gave a short address, followed by his sister singing 'Hard Times Come Again No More' and later his uncle, Henry Riversdale Grenfell (serving Deputy Governor of the Bank of England), making a few observations on the questions now before the country and asking the electors of Salisbury to enable his nephew to commence his political career as representative for their ancient city.[2]

On the following Thursday, Grenfell addressed a crowded meeting of the party (with much cheering), saying, 'He wanted to make Parliamentary life the object of his study and that it was an advantage to be able to enter upon it when he was young; and as every trade and every art required a most sincere devotion, so Parliamentary life – which was much more important than any of those trades or arts, in that on it depended the very existence of hundreds and thousands of human beings – required a longer and much more difficult apprenticeship.'[3]

---

* Grenfell was admitted to the Inner Temple on 28 June 1878 but was not called to the Bar. He was still at Balliol and would simply have paid a fee and signed the register. He would then be eligible to dine in the hall and would have had to undertake the required number of dinners to be called to the Bar – as this suggests, the training was informal.

The young Grenfell then proceeded to review foreign relations as they presently stood in a witty speech that apparently caused much laughter. His ambition to be a long-serving politician was clear, though his political journey would be tortuous.

The Liberals won both seats, with Grenfell beating his Conservative opponent by 133 votes. Given that there were only 1,969 registered voters and 91.1 per cent voted, it is evident how narrow was the electoral base.[4] Grenfell arrived in Parliament on 29 April 1880 to take his seat. But, as was often the case in this period, he didn't make his maiden speech until many years later (in March 1901 when he addressed a question on the Indian Mint and silver rupees as part of his interest in bimetallism).

In late 1882, Grenfell, already the senior Liberal member in Salisbury, was appointed by Queen Victoria as a Parliamentary Groom-in-Waiting. As was customary, on being appointed to this post, Grenfell offered his resignation as an MP, thus triggering a by-election.[5] Sir William Harcourt wrote to him on 4 August 1882: 'My dear Grenfell, it is with great regret I have directed your appointment to the Chiltern Hundreds to be taken out today as requested. I wish with all my heart it had been any other office than the groom.'*

The consequent by-election took place on 21 November 1882 and Grenfell lost by 183 votes to the Conservative candidate, Coleridge Kennard. Reports at the time suggested unfair influence had been exerted to secure this outcome. Although Grenfell indicated he would renounce his position as Groom-in-Waiting, he had to wait until the 1885 General Election to try again to be MP for Salisbury.[6] Given that he was new to politics and hoped for a lengthy career in Parliament, it may come as a surprise that Grenfell should have spent part of 1884 on a trip to the Rockies and as a special correspondent for the *Daily Telegraph*, helping cover the Mahdist war in the Sudan in the spring of 1885. This may also tell us something important about his character, and if the Suakin 'interlude' enhanced his image as a man of action, it may equally, if indirectly, have served his political interests.

RETURN TO POLITICS

A General Election took place in late 1885 and Grenfell won back the now reformed single-seat constituency of Salisbury, defeating his rival by forty-five

---

* 'Taking the Chiltern Hundreds' refers to a legal fiction used to effect resignation from the House of Commons. Since MPs were not permitted to resign, they were instead appointed to an 'office of profit under the Crown', which required MPs to vacate their seats.

votes (on a 98 per cent turnout). He thus resumed his parliamentary career, serving from 24 November 1885 to 1 July 1886, in late February 1886 being appointed Parliamentary Private Secretary to Sir William Harcourt MP, Chancellor of the Exchequer. It seemed that Grenfell's political career was on the move, but this lasted less than nine months before he again lost his seat. A further General Election had been triggered by the Liberal government's defeat on the Irish Home Rule Bill, and it put the Conservatives back in power under Lord Salisbury, supported by a breakaway Unionist group of Liberals. Gladstone and the bulk of the Liberal Party supported Irish Home Rule, which proved to be deeply unpopular. Grenfell was not entirely comfortable with the party's position on Ireland but he defended Gladstone in local meetings prior to the election. He had stood as a Gladstonian Liberal, but despite his considerable local following, he lost his seat.

Grenfell was now without a parliamentary seat and tried for re-election as a Liberal for the Windsor by-election in April 1890 but lost by a substantial 550 votes in a Tory stronghold. His own doubts were clearly expressed to Ettie: 'My dearest, I don't the least know what I'm doing as I am never allowed to sit down. The way this election is being mismanaged is ridiculous – & most of my time is wasted.'[7] (Much later his *Times* obituary would describe it oddly as 'an amusing by-election at Windsor in which his rowing and punting prowess figured largely'.[8])

However, the 1892 General Election afforded him a further opportunity and he now stood as a Liberal candidate for Hereford, winning by a majority of 127 votes with a swing of +7.4 per cent to the Liberals. He served from 4 July 1892 until 4 August 1893. A *Lock to Lock Times* commentator wrote: 'Apart altogether from political considerations the news that Mr. W. H. Grenfell, the famous oarsman and punt-propellor at Taplow Court, has been elected as MP for Hereford was received in the Maidenhead district with a very great deal of pleasure and satisfaction.'[9]

In 1893 he resigned his seat over both bimetallism [see *Chapter 14 Passionate Campaigner*] and the Irish Home Rule Bill, joining with the breakaway Liberal Unionist Party wing, which by then had aligned itself with the Conservatives (the two would merge and form the Conservative and Unionist Party in 1910). In a letter to his agent in Hereford, Grenfell commented:

As the Government have decided to retain the Irish members in the fullest representation to which they are entitled and to allow them to vote on purely

English, Scottish and Welsh matters while . . . they are to have the exclusive control of their own affairs, I cannot support the policy of Home Rule under the shape which it has now assumed.[10]

He continued:

I am also out of sympathy with the present Government on another great question, which is of even wider importance, namely the Currency Question.[11] *I believe that the attitude taken by the present Government with regard to this question is ruinous to the industries and trade of this country and that it has been the chief cause of the calamities which have overwhelmed British interests in silver mining communities . . . The continuation in power of a Government which is not only barring the way to international monetary reform but is actively decreasing the money value of the world . . . that I cannot desire to see it prolonged.*

He remained a member of the Liberal Party but it was clear that he was slowly moving towards 'Toryism', influenced not least by the Conservative politician and future Prime Minister Arthur Balfour who, as noted in Chapter 9, was a frequent visitor to Taplow Court.[12] Grenfell had joined the Conservative Party by 1898 when the *Dundee Advertiser* tartly commented: 'His accession will bring no great strength to the Tory Party for Mr Grenfell, though a man of social position, has no political influence or authority. He is a bimetallist, and Mr Balfour and he will be able to condole with each other in the steady decline and approaching death of that particular form of economic heresy.'[13]

This shift of allegiance clearly damaged his political progress and it wasn't until 1900 that he regained a seat, when he was elected Conservative MP for Wycombe with a majority of 2,529 (amid a much-expanded electorate).[14]

This was a surprising result in what was seen as a safe Liberal seat, and he served from 1 October 1900 to 30 December 1905: his longest period of continuous parliamentary service.[15] The vote had centred around a 'finish the war' (Boer War) stance adopted by the Conservatives and was unlikely to be repeated. Fortunately for Grenfell, and in advance of the General Election held from 12 January to 8 February 1906, he was included in A. J. Balfour's resignation Honours List, as Baron Desborough.[16] The news broke in early December and was reported in the *Morning Post*:

Promotional postcard for William Grenfell, 1900 election.

Mr WILLIAM HENRY GRENFELL is an all-round man who has distinguished himself in the field of politics and athletics. He is a famous old 'Varsity oarsman, and as chairman of the Thames Conservancy has devoted much attention to the improvement of the great waterway . . . Mr Grenfell has been a lifelong advocate of bi-metallism and also has been prominently identified with Mr Chamberlain's Tariff Reform policy, of which he is an able exponent.[17]

In his resignation address to his constituency Grenfell commented:

Our President has referred to the position which my great-grandfather and father occupied in the House of Commons, and I, on my own part, can remind you that I have had 25 years' experience of political life, and therefore much as I feel the greatness of the honour which has been conferred upon me, I feel also that it has been conferred on one who has taken his share in political contests – I have fought seven – and political responsibility – in attempting to govern this great country as wisely and well as his lights would permit.[18]

*Caricature of William
Grenfell by F. Lynch, c. 1905,
with his prominent
carnation buttonhole.*

Amusingly, in choosing the title Baron Desborough he took the name of the ancient Chiltern Hundred through which he resigned from the Commons. *The London Gazette* recorded the official announcement conferring his new title on Friday 5 January 1906.[19]

Thus 1905 marked the end of his career as a Member of Parliament. It had been a somewhat chaotic journey and one in which events had conspired to limit his opportunities for political advancement. Alongside the political turbulence of the era is the question of aptitude and ability. Grenfell was not a 'party' man and in the somewhat febrile times he may have appeared remote and principled (fighting causes such as bimetallism) despite his political connections. He was conscious, however, of keeping up those links, writing to Ettie from Copenhagen in 1909, just as she was trying to find a suitable house as a base in London:

*I hope that we shall have a really good house . . . give one or two Political
Dinners, as I really think we ought to do something in that line: Austen –
Bonar Law, Acland, Hood, Alfred Lansdowne, Lord Cawdor, Hewins,
Ridleys, St Abinger, Cecil A. Pearson, Harmsworths, to whom I owe much,*

Londonderries, Lloyd George, Asquith, Salisburys, Alfred Milner, Crowthers,
House of Lords Whips, and many others – we may just as well go [for] it if
we have a house – and it will be great fun – & we are getting older . . . I
wonder what house you will get? Chesterfield Gardens I hope . . .[20]

HOUSE OF LORDS

Although much of what Grenfell achieved more broadly between 1905 and
1940 came after his elevation to the House of Lords, when he was in his fifties,
his contributions in the House itself were limited in his early years. After the
First World War, shorn of some of his war-related duties, he became more
active and of his 699 parliamentary contributions overall, 690 were in the
Lords. He was most active in 1911 (with fifteen contributions), 1917–20 (97)
and 1925–30 (518).

Proposals for new jobs
for members of the
House of Lords
following reform,
Punch's Almanack,
1918 .

His speech in the House of Lords on the Declaration of London deserves special mention. This was a declaration in 1909 by all the major naval powers in Europe – along with Japan, Russia and the USA – concerning the Laws of Naval War. It largely reiterated existing law but it sought to deal with such issues as blockades, contraband and prizes, and to elaborate on the rights of neutral entities at a time of war. Given this scope, it is not surprising that the London Chamber of Commerce (LCC) produced its own report on the matter in 1910, highlighting the greater reliance of Britain on seaborne trade. It took the view that the Declaration would 'impair the nation's strength in time of war' and it should not be ratified. The submission was signed by Lord Desborough, who tabled an extensive motion in the Lords in March 1911, drawing in part on the LCC response, and setting out his case:

My Lords, the Declaration of London is divided into nine chapters, and concludes with some final provisions; there are seventy-one Articles altogether . . . I shall confine my criticisms to three main points – first, the effect of the Declaration in exposing to capture or deliberate destruction of food supplies borne to this country in time of war in neutral vessels; secondly, the admission of the principle of destruction of neutral prizes; and, thirdly, the absence of any provision in the Declaration for preventing the conversion of merchant vessels into commerce destroyers on the high seas.[21]

He closed by noting, 'the concluding paragraph . . . is the one with which I am in most accord – namely, "Done at London," for that is where we have been done, and on February 26, 1909.'

He did not press for a vote on his motion and on 13 March he withdrew it, having secured agreement that the government would consider matters further. Later in 1911, at the Annual Meeting of Chambers of Commerce in London, he returned to the topic, suggesting that the Declaration of London, 'like the curate's egg, was good in parts but those parts were very few indeed'.

FURTHER APPOINTMENTS

In the middle of his career in the Lords, Desborough was considered for the Governor-Generalship of Canada. He had long taken an interest in Canada both in relation to exploration, hunting and investment.[22] He first visited Canada in 1881, travelling via New York, and was away for three months, and returned briefly to Quebec in 1884 and again in 1888, sailing with Ettie to the USA in August before travelling up to Niagara and repeating his swim across the pool at the base of the Falls [see *Chapter 5 Exploits and Adventures*]. In 1911 he returned to Canada with investment in mind, and from this trip the idea of the Governor-Generalship may have emerged, although an actual offer was not made until May 1921. [See *Chapter 18 Commerce, Empire, War and Peace.*]

On 1 December 1924, at the age of sixty-nine, Desborough was appointed as Captain of the Yeomen of the Guard.[23] This was a government appointment and typically the holder also served as Deputy Chief Whip in the House of Lords. Desborough undertook this role until 4 June 1929 and it was one of his busiest periods as a parliamentarian. When asking whether Desborough would extend his period of service, Lord Stamfordham (private secretary to George V) said that 'the King would be very glad if you found it possible', and indicated that the Prime Minister agreed, on the understanding that he should not vote or take political action against the government.[24] But Desborough replied to Stamford-ham that, 'I am afraid it would not be possible for me to undertake to abstain from political action. I am interested in several constituencies.'[25]

He agreed, however, to bridge the gap until the election of a new government.[26]

Lord Desborough, Captain of the Yeoman of the Guard, 1924.

The hung parliament of 1929 ended Desborough's period of office and although he continued to attend the Lords, his contributions waned. He gave his last speech in the Chamber on 22 July 1937 at the age of eighty-two in a debate on the Agriculture Bill. Looking back over his speeches, there are familiar themes – fisheries, wildlife, drainage, the River Thames, the date of Easter, bimetallism, the army, and the Declaration of London.[27]

CIVIC DUTIES IN THE LOCALITY OF TAPLOW COURT

In addition to his work in Parliament, Desborough held numerous, and sometimes honorific, municipal offices. These included Mayor (1895 and 1896) and High Steward (1884–1945) of Maidenhead, Justice of the Peace for Buckinghamshire, Deputy Lieutenant for Tower Hamlets, High Sheriff of Buckinghamshire (1889) and Deputy Lieutenant of Buckinghamshire (1915).[28] These were unpaid, but all required attendance at meetings and ceremonies. He finally resigned from his mayoral post because he was too busy (later being made a freeman of Maidenhead in 1918), writing to Ettie in September 1897:

> *They want me to go on being Mayor – but I think <u>no</u>, and shall give up the Council too, which has made the Town Clerk very sad . . . the Drainpipe Scheme is now complete . . . the Technical School finished, the Standing Orders passed, & the rates reduced by 1/2d. I feel I should leave with rather a halo.*[29]

As a major local landowner (the extended Taplow Court estate eventually comprised over 10,000 acres), Grenfell was a major presence in the locality. From the 1890s he became a great benefactor and President of a number of Maidenhead sports clubs, including cricket, rowing, golf, gymnastics, rifles and bowls. Indeed, he gifted the land on which some of these clubs still play and contributed a variety of cups to support local competitions, most notably the Grenfell Cup (the Challenge Cup), an eighteen-hole strokeplay competition at Maidenhead Golf Club, and the Julian Cup for limited-over club cricket at the cricket club.[30] [See *Chapter 8 The Great Amateur*]. After his death, the *Maidenhead Advertiser* pointed out: 'The name of Desborough is perpetuated in many forms in Maidenhead. His name will be revered in the town and district for many generations. By his death we lost a fine citizen and staunch friend.'[31]

There is a Grenfell Avenue, a Grenfell Place and a Grenfell Road, and Grenfell Park was created out of his donation of a former chalk pit. This was the first public park in the town, opened in October 1889 (it poured with rain), although the first major event to be held there, in June 1897, was the celebration of Queen Victoria's Diamond Jubilee.[32] However, in response to the Mayor at an evening reception following the original ceremony of dedication, Grenfell said, 'Well gentlemen we today opened the Recreation Ground under somewhat disadvantageous surroundings. It reminded me of a day on which it would have been more appropriate, perhaps, to open a swimming bath or some aquatic carnival – as you know in such duties I have not infrequently taken part.'[33]

The park was planted with a variety of trees and seeds brought back by Grenfell from his journeys overseas.[34] Though originally offered on a ninety-nine-year lease, Grenfell subsequently announced that it was a freehold gift to the town. He was President of Maidenhead Hospital (1905–36) and was often invited to officiate at the opening of new amenities such as Maidenhead Golf Club (1896), Maidenhead Railway Station (1897) and the Public Library (1904). He encouraged the installation of electric light, started subscriptions for the town clock and donated the land for All Saints Church. There is a college named after Desborough (the former Maidenhead County Boys' School) along with a sailing club, a channel of the Thames, an island and a car park!

WIDER PUBLIC-SERVICE ROLES

Grenfell took on an array of public roles, most of which came after he had been ennobled. He was made President of the London Chamber of Commerce and the British Chamber of Commerce and was on the Council of the British Imperial Council of Commerce [see *Chapter 18 Commerce, Empire, War and Peace*]. He was appointed President of the British Dairy Farmers' Association, the Central Chamber of Agriculture (1903) and Chairman of the Freshwater Fish Committee under the Board of Agriculture and Fisheries, as well as being founding Chairman of the Thames Salmon Association and President of the British Agricultural Association (1925).[35]

Desborough's family estimated that at one point he was serving on 115 committees at the same time. This is perhaps unlikely – though in Appendix 2 we set out his known roles – but there is no doubt he was always extraordinarily busy, as many of his letters to Ettie demonstrate.* Contemporary press

---

* Much turns on how this count is undertaken. For example, at the Thames Conservancy he sat on at least five committees and similarly in the House of Commons.

comments make frequent reference to Lord Desborough being unable to attend because he was otherwise engaged. However, when he had agreed on an appointment or to help an organisation, he was unstinting in the time he would devote.

As a consequence of his public roles in the later decades of his life, he became a notable (and generous) figure, such that he found it necessary to print the following card:

> Lord Desborough regrets that he cannot at present subscribe to any more Cathedrals, Chapels, Schools, Hospitals, Fire Brigades, Recreation Grounds, Associations, Boy Scouts, British Legions, Girl Guides, Athletic Clubs, Gymnastic Clubs, Boxing Clubs, Rowing Clubs, Football Clubs, Cricket Clubs, Testimonials, Regattas, Horticultural Shows, Agricultural Societies, Horse Shows, Orphanages, Cattle Shows, Salvation Armies, Bands, Hounds, Oddfellows, Freemasons, Benefit Societies, Political Funds, Choir Funds, Missions, or any other of the very numerous objects for which subscriptions and donations are daily demanded.[36]

POLICE PAY AND CONDITIONS

As the First World War was drawing to a close there was growing unrest among police officers with respect to their pay and conditions (reflecting not least much unpaid overtime and loss of leave during the war and a ban on unionisation).[37] A National Union of Police and Prison Officers (NUPPO), formed in 1913, had a somewhat clandestine existence and a move to gain official recognition by the Home Office was rejected in April 1917. On 27 August 1918 a police officer was dismissed for union activities and this triggered a strike call from midnight on 29 August. The ultimatum to meet the union's demands was ignored and by midday on 30 August most of the Metropolitan police and the City of London police were on strike. Two days later and reflecting the feverish atmosphere, the Prime Minister, Lloyd George, intervened and reached a settlement with the union. Pay was increased through a War Bonus and pensions were put in place, the dismissed officer was reinstated and in theory a union was to be recognised. Over the space of a few months the London settlement was accepted elsewhere in Britain and the union's membership rose from 10,000 in August to around 50,000; in essence most of the police in the country.

Having bought some time, the government was aware there were still significant outstanding grievances: pay was often lower than for agricultural labourers and there were considerable local variations in terms and conditions, as these were the responsibility of local authority watch committees. By the start of 1919, the government had agreed to set up an independent committee to investigate police pay, pensions and allowances. In late February, Desborough, despite difficult relations with Lloyd George as Prime Minister earlier, was appointed as Chairman and the Committee began work on 1 March. Desborough was joined by another member of the Lords and five MPs, with a civil servant from the Home Office as secretary.

The Committee moved at speed, holding a series of meetings with police personnel (including members of NUPPO), local authorities and others. It had thirty-four sittings and thirty of these included hearing evidence from 148 witnesses. Given the complexity of the police service across the whole of Britain and Ireland, it was a considerable challenge to get a full picture. In May 1919 Desborough described the inquiry to Ettie as 'a very intricate & long affair – pay, pensions, recruiting, organisation, control of the whole Police – no two counties or boroughs are the same. We ought to sit all day & every day, but the other members just come & go.'[38]

As the Committee made clear, 'we considered it essential to obtain a comprehensive presentation of the grievances, claims and aspirations in the minds of the men, as well as the views of the Police Authorities'.[39] The Committee produced a first report in July 1919, some five months later, and a second in 1920.[40] Its recommendations proved long lasting in their impact and still provide a basis for pay and conditions in the police service today.

Given the fragmented structure of policing in Britain, there was an expectation that the Committee might recommend 'nationalisation', i.e. making it a national service rather than a service overseen by local authorities. However, Desborough's Committee rejected this option, arguing that in Britain it was best as a local service where a close relationship between police and the populace could be maintained. At the same time – in terms of pay and conditions – the Committee recommended these be standardised across the country and that a further boost to pay should be made beyond what was agreed by the Prime Minister. It also stepped around the question of unionisation and the role of NUPPO by suggesting that there be a formal police body with rights to be involved on matters such as pay and conditions.

Given that the first report was published rapidly, by July 1919 the government had little choice, in the face of continuing discontent, but to accept the recommendations. A new Police Act clarified that police could not be members of a union but an alternative representative body would be established: the Police Federation.* The government took the view that if it followed the recommendations of the Desborough Committee on pay and conditions, then most police officers would be satisfied. In the Second Reading of the Bill in the House of Lords, on 5 August 1919, the Earl of Jersey commented:

> reference should be made to the very great debt of gratitude which the Government and the police owe to the Chairman and members of the Committee. Considering the difficulty of the subject and the wide range of evidence that had to be taken, their first report was issued in a remarkably short time as a result of indefatigable work, and their recommendations met generally with warm approval both from the rank and file of the police force and from the police authorities.[41]

Even if a police union was prohibited, he accepted that a policeman:

> should have an inalienable right freely to bring his grievances, if any, to the notice of the highest authority, and this is provided, and made statutory, by the creation of the Federation . . . The question of a representative body for the police was not included in the terms of reference of the Committee, but the Committee came to the conclusion that the establishment of some system for the purpose would be necessary as a corollary to the application of the principle of standardisation of pay . . .

By mid-August the Police Act 1919 was in place (referred to as the Policemen's Charter).[42] Work continued and the second part of the report was published in February 1920 (along with full minutes of the evidence considered). This focused on proposals to further reduce the role of local watch committees in borough forces (scrapping forces serving populations under 50,000) and beginning a process that saw greater central control, expanded training and better coordination between forces.

---

* This was established to represent the views of all officers up to the rank of Chief Inspector, but with no right to strike.

The Desborough report was of great significance. The work undertaken by the Committee was recognised as thorough and far-sighted, changing fundamentally the nature of policing in Britain. The report and its outcomes were not without controversy as, although the police welcomed it, local authorities which had to finance the costs were less than enamoured. Lloyd George had to work hard to persuade individual authorities that it was the right outcome.[43]

In his restrained way Desborough had triumphed and, typically of his engagement in public service, the effect was extensive and long term. He had been active in national politics as a member of both the Commons and the Lords and was ever present in terms of civic duties. He was often referred to as the 'go-to man' of his times and there is plenty of evidence to support this view. His contributions seemed genuinely focused on public service rather than self-advancement and they continued into his eighties.

Much later, in her response to the Thames Conservators after Willy had died in 1945, Ettie would note: 'I think you will like to know that our eldest grandson, Julian Salmond, aged 18, joined the RAF last Saturday, so there is no break in Grenfell "service".'[44]

13

The Lords and Socialism

The Primrose League – The Pall Mall Magazine *1895 – defence of the House of Lords – the 'wave of socialism' – constitutional checks*

With a long family history of involvement in local and national politics, William Grenfell, like his forebears, saw public engagement as part of his duty as a local dignitary – a duty attendant on his status in society. Throughout his political career there was a tension between his well-established standing as a prominent landowner and the ebb and flow of national politics. Discussion of politics was undoubtedly part of conversations between members of the Souls, even if it wasn't central (given the wide range of political affiliations). Indeed for some, their conversations were an escape from the exchanges at Westminster.

The changing political landscape of the 1880s and '90s saw the development of the Primrose League. Established in 1883 by Lord Randolph Churchill and others to continue the work of Benjamin Disraeli (who had died in 1881), it offered a popular and 'modern' form of conservatism, aiming to broaden political engagement as the franchise was enlarged. Although formally independent of any political party, it was linked to the Conservatives and the breakaway Liberal Unionists and its members took a pledge of allegiance to the Empire and the Sovereign (this was later extended to free enterprise and more) – its Latin motto was *Imperium et Libertas, Empire and Liberty.*[*]

Grenfell became an active member of the League in the 1890s at a time

---

[*] The Primrose League declined in significance after the First World War but lingered on as a social organisation before being wound up in 2004 and merged into the Conservative Party.

when he had lost faith in the Liberals and later served as its Chancellor.[1] It was the first political organisation to give equal status to women and was hugely successful at a regional and district level, acquiring more than 2 million members by 1910, half of whom were women.[2] During Grenfell's period of association it became apparent that where the League was most active, Unionists were more likely to be elected to Parliament.

In the same period, Grenfell published what appears to have been his most detailed (albeit somewhat scholarly) political statement. This was an article written in 1895 for the *Pall Mall Magazine* (published 1893–1914), launched by Lord Astor as an offshoot of the *Pall Mall Gazette*.[3] 'Concerning the question of the House of Lords and Socialism' offers a strident rejection of the policies being pursued by Lord Rosebery and his Liberal government.[4] Rosebery had succeeded Gladstone as Prime Minister in March 1894 and led the government until June 1895. Rosebery then lost the General Election and was replaced by Lord Salisbury and the Conservatives, to which Grenfell affiliated himself, having already stood down in 1893 as a Liberal MP.

After his periods as a Liberal, Grenfell's resignation letter to the Liberal agent in Hereford set out a notably progressive agenda, including universal suffrage, land reform, rebalancing local rates between tenants and landlords, the provision of better homes for the working classes, leasehold enfranchisement and the provision of allotments and smallholdings, along with a reform of taxation.[5] The *Yorkshire Gazette* described him as 'a Liberal of considerable courage, and his action in tearing himself away from his party . . . stamps his political conduct with sterling independence'.[6]

Upon resigning, Grenfell made clear that he was *not* retiring from public life and hoped to find a constituency in Lancashire or Yorkshire, where the currency question (one of his greatest concerns) was better understood. By 1894 he was campaigning on behalf of Unionist candidates, and when he returned to Parliament in 1900 it was as a Conservative MP for Wycombe, replacing Lord Curzon, who had stood down on the death of his father, Earl Howe.[7] While Curzon had been the Unionist candidate, Grenfell suggested that a Liberal Unionist was a Conservative, 'only he did not like to call himself so . . . He would prefer to call himself what he was and what he felt himself [to be] and therefore he called himself a Conservative.'[8]

His political journey had been somewhat complicated and the article for the *Pall Mall Magazine* marks his shift from Liberal to Conservative. Written ten years before Grenfell was elevated to the Lords, it captures key themes that were central to his thinking about the nature of government. He begins by reaching back into history to chart the arguments for a second chamber, not least those assuming the benefit of its collective experience and wisdom. He argues for the hereditary principle while recognising that nothing is guaranteed (in contrast to the more certain bloodlines supposedly found in horses). He then turns to Lord Rosebery's proposal to reform the House of Lords, mocking its lack of specificity, for example: 'I will not say now the exact course we shall pursue because we must have our hands free.' As Grenfell put it: 'In other words, "We are going to have a great revolution, but I cannot exactly tell you now what we ask you to rebel about, partly because we have not made up our minds ourselves, and partly because, if we told you, you might not approve of it."'

Grenfell claims this to be a repeat of the 'Great Confidence Trick' played over the Home Rule Bill (on which he resigned) but suggesting that 'the cases are rare in which the same person is taken in twice'. He elaborates on the role of the second chamber as a check or balance, citing Cromwell's restoration of it in 1657 and Napoleon's favourable description of it as a 'great bulwark of the British Constitution'. He considers the 'present position a most complicated one: we have sixteen cabinet ministers, with apparently sixteen different plans of dealing with the Second Chamber, contradicting each other, and a prime minister who spends much time in contradicting himself'.[9]

He attacks the current House of Lords for its failure to oppose the introduction (in the Finance Act 1894) of a new estate duty that replaced a patchwork of probate duty, account duty, certain additional succession duties and the temporary 1889 estate duty. He points to the contrast between the Home Rule Bill of 1886, which he voted for, and the Home Rule Bill of 1892 that, as he believes, the Lords rightly opposed, and also the amendments to the Employers' Liability Bill. He continues: 'On these two counts, which are the head and front of the offending of the House of Lords against the present Government, I can think no great case can be made out for a Revolution against the House of Lords . . . The fact is we want a much stronger second chamber. We have no written Constitution, we have no Supreme Court, we have no Presidential Veto.'[10]

Grenfell comments that 'there is a wave of socialism passing over civilisation, which, though we may say lightly we are all Socialists now, is a much graver danger than is generally realised.' With a rhetorical flourish he sets out how:

No one is justified in saying one word against honest men who, struck to the heart by the intolerable misery which they see around them, devote their lives to finding some cure for that misery – on the contrary, they should be honoured; but at the same time their schemes should be carefully examined in the light of history and of the labours of economists, and if they are founded on wrong principles, which instead of diminishing misery they seek to cure, are likely to increase it, they should be strenuously opposed. On the other hand, if Socialism is sound in theory, and would in practice dispel poverty, by all means let us become Socialists.[11]

He notes that the Trades Union Congress argued that 'it is essential to the maintenance of British industries to nationalise the land', and he acknowledges that at present there was much 'undeserved and most lamentable suffering, when there is a fear of an inevitable reduction in wages in agriculture and many great industries' and that 'one could hardly blame the long-suffering poor if they turned to those means', even if they might regret it in the longer term.[12] He therefore sees the dividing line between the two great parties as having been obliterated and that the fight in years to come would be between individualism and socialism.

He devotes the last five pages of his article to arguing that the Liberal Party had now become a home for socialism, before discussing the merits and failings of this in theory and practice.[13] Perhaps inevitably, he touches on the destruction of private property and supposed suppression of individualism, quoting from *The Spectator* that 'free trade and free enterprise, of individualism and independence, will produce far more than the Socialistic system'.[14] He finishes by reasserting the link between resisting reform of the Lords and defending the country against socialism, and asserts:

But if there is any truth in the contentions which I have raised above as to the direction in which we are moving at an ever-increasing pace, it is to be hoped that, until it is definitely stated what constitutional checks are to be placed on the power, or rather the tyranny, of a 'log rolling' majority in the House of Commons, a large majority of the people in this country will think once, twice and thrice before they follow Lord Rosebery into his 'tremendous' but vague revolution.[15]

The article is in effect a manifesto, covering issues about which Grenfell felt deeply. Although he was on the right wing of the Liberal Party before moving across to the Conservatives, he was liberal-minded in a wider social sense.[16] Many, however, would have seen him simply as a member of the Establishment, closely linked with the Royal Family. Yet, while being paternalistic and elitist at times, he was in favour of one-nation politics and was more aware than others may have perceived of the diversity of late-nineteenth-century society.[*]

---

[*] As a very active sportsman, he was constantly engaged in clubs and committee work that involved crossing divides and making compromises. He was adept at spotting talent and getting the best out of teams, however they were formed and whoever they included.

14

Passionate Campaigner

What was bimetallism? – the advantages of silver – a fixed date for Easter – 1928, an Act is passed but never implemented

It was a core part of Grenfell's character that he pursued campaigns doggedly across decades, including bimetallism and the promotion of a fixed date for Easter. He had a lifelong interest in bimetallism: he was active in the Bimetallic League, wrote papers and gave numerous speeches on it, including in Parliament.

BIMETALLISM

What is bimetallism? At its simplest, it involves having both a gold and silver standard (linked by a fixed exchange ratio between them) against which individual national currencies are 'pegged'. A number of countries, including England (from 1717), France and the United States, adopted a bimetallic standard when they established a central bank. Yet in 1816 England officially abandoned bimetallism and by 1844 had adopted the monometallic gold standard, with Bank of England banknotes becoming the standard legal tender, fully backed by gold. Both in the run-up to this decision and in its aftermath there was considerable controversy regarding the advantages and disadvantages of bimetallism, its advocates arguing that it increased the supply of money, helped stabilise prices and aided the setting of exchange rates. Britain abandoned its gold standard in 1931 (supposedly on a temporary basis but never re-established), though it has continued to hold gold bullion reserves in the Bank of England for the UK and other governments.

Grenfell's family had long been advocates of bimetallism [see *Chapter 2*

Early Years]. His great-grandfather Pascoe Grenfell had argued in its favour in the early 1800s and his uncle Henry Riversdale Grenfell was a founding member of the Bimetallic League, formed in 1882, and an active Chairman of its General Council. Grenfell became a Vice President of the League, serving on its Executive Council and its committees for Parliament and the City of London.

During the 1880s and '90s there was growing pressure to reopen the issue and challenge the retention solely of the gold standard.[1] This was both a national and an international cause, with some in France and the United States also arguing strongly for reform, albeit as part of wider struggles with the British Empire and amid a failing global economy. In Britain there was a Royal Commission on Gold and Silver in 1886 and an Indian Currency Commission in 1893.

Grenfell was thus part of a movement gathering considerable momentum, but there were frustrations along the way, as he expressed to Ettie in 1890:

> *I have been in correspondence with Frank Harris who has offered to put a Bimetallism supplement every week in the Sat. Review of which the League will distribute 1,500 copies. I* __must__ *get this done: most important – much better than spending time over a paper which the League intend doing – but they are* _idiots_. *I cannot get them to wake up, they go muddling along, it is merely winking in the dark.*[2]

There were a good number of British parliamentarians supporting the cause (in 1895 A. J. Balfour, leader of the Conservative Party in the Commons and a Minister in Lord Salisbury's government, was in favour), and numerous conferences and international congresses were held. Grenfell spoke on the topic at the British Association meeting in 1893 and at the 1894 International Bimetallic Conference in London, having just resigned his seat in Parliament over this issue. He attended the International Bimetallic Conference in Brussels in April 1896 and was described by an American associate as the 'greatest Silverite'.[3]

The bimetallists were taking a wider view of the functioning of the economy rather than focusing on financial markets alone. They were concerned about the impact that fluctuations in the price of gold had on agriculture and trade. The Grenfell family were at heart miners, merchants and businessmen. They understood the markets for minerals and metals and the vulnerability of single commodities such as gold. They were also internationalists, imperialist in outlook and determined to see Britain retain its global trading dominance. The currency question was central to that. Desborough, who became President of the British Imperial Chamber of Commerce in 1913, recognised that a considerable portion of British trade was with 'silver-using' countries and that England would be the 'greatest sufferer' as the process of demonetising silver continued.[4]

In addition to his reported speeches, Grenfell published several pamphlets on the topic. His first was titled 'Mr Gladstone and the Currency' in *The Fortnightly Review* in 1893 and focused on a stable measure of value as part of a concerted case for bimetallism: 'I believe no Government since the time of George III has done so much harm to England and the world outside England, or has been the cause of so much human misery as have Her Majesty's present advisers owing to the attitude they have taken up on this all-important matter.'

When he described this to Ettie, he said, 'I have been bimetalizing with moderate success, it is such a grind writing it all: I don't know whether I hadn't better spit it out just as it comes.'[5] He castigated the government's interventions and obstructions in the recent International Monetary Conference, held in Brussels in late 1892, where it had effectively blocked any progress towards re-establishing the role of silver. He then challenged Gladstone's speech in a Commons debate on the currency question in 1893, treading carefully because he recognised that Gladstone was both popular and a great orator.

Grenfell works through a number of case studies – Indian cotton, the price of wheat, the cost of labour and the price of silver and gold – in this nineteen-page article arguing the case for a bimetallic standard. He closes the text with two final remarks:

That England is the great creditor country cannot be gainsaid; that England has debts owed to her in every portion of the globe cannot be denied; but I am happy to think that there are many in England, and I should number the Prime Minister first among them, to whom the honour of England is at least as sacred as her debts, and who blush to see England playing the part not merely of a Shylock, for Shylock only asked for his due, but of a Shylock who uses false weights and measures, and strenuously resists all attempts to have them rectified. And again, perhaps to use a more convincing argument, is this war upon silver wise in her own interests? Are not many of the debts owed to her by Silver-using countries . . . ?

In April 1896 he attended a major bimetallism conference in Brussels, commenting to Ettie, 'The Bimetallic delegates went to the King's Garden Party today, and he was most gracious to me and we had a drink together which I hope will be put down to the credit of Bimetallism . . . If the United States can only be induced to open their minds to Silver with certain concessions from Europe we should get Bimetallism very soon. That was my motion and I think it is the only thing that amounts to anything.'[6]

In 1904 he explored similar issues to his 1893 text in further detail, in a privately published pamphlet (reprinted in 1928 and 1933).[7] In 1909 he followed this up with his article 'The Real Yellow Peril', which, as readers now appreciate, is about the failings of the gold standard.[8] His much-delayed maiden speech in the House of Commons (really a question) – coming many years after he was first elected, which was not unusual in this period – was on the topic of Indian silver coinage in March 1901; and in 1932, persistent as ever, he returned to the issue of bimetallism in a House of Lords debate on the advantage of a gradual return to the bimetallic system of currency that existed in the world before 1873.

Cartoon of 'Bimetallists to the Rescue' – silver versus gold and raising the banner for Free Coinage – by Lady Rolleston, published in a pamphlet titled 'Silver Money – the Case for its Restoration', 1934.[9]

Grenfell's efforts were, frustratingly, to no avail, though there were moments when it may have felt otherwise. Despite this, he remained a committed bimetallist throughout his life. Although the topic has long been off the political agenda, it is not entirely forgotten and resurfaces periodically.[10]

FIXED DATE FOR EASTER

In a short debate in the House of Lords in 1920, Desborough argued that there was considerable 'inconvenience arising from Easter being a moveable Feast and from an antiquated calendar'. He moved to resolve that His Majesty's Government be requested to summon a conference at the earliest possibility to consider the advisability of (1) the establishment of a fixed date for the celebration of Easter and (2) the reform of the calendar.[11]

He emphasised that he was acting as a 'mouthpiece of a very large number of Chambers of Commerce who for many years past have been carrying resolutions in favour of a fixed date for the celebration of Easter'. He highlighted the current potential for the date of Easter to vary by up to thirty-five days and the negative consequences this had for commerce, schools, universities and holidays. The government made clear its opposition, primarily on procedural timing but also to the approach Desborough had taken, and he withdrew the motion. But a month later, in August 1920, Desborough reported to Ettie that:

> *The Archbishop of C.[Canterbury] summoned me yesterday, and told me that he had addressed the 252 Bishops on the question of a fixed date for Easter, and not one of them had raised any objections. He asked them to send any remarks they might have to make on the subject in writing. In the meantime he told me to go ahead, so I suppose I shall prepare a Bill and introduce it next session. I shall also get the Chambers of Commerce of the Empire to pass a resolution in favour of it at Toronto. The Archbishop said that such a resolution would help matters a good deal.*[12]

Desborough was encouraged and by 1921 was back in the Lords proposing a Fixed Easter Bill, in part derived from his recent visit to Toronto for the Imperial Chambers of Commerce. He laid out a scholarly assessment of the arguments, to which the Archbishop of Canterbury replied:

> the care he has bestowed on this subject and of the perseverance with which he again and again returns to a task in which I think he has

received quite unfair discouragement, or lack of adequate encouragement. He has also given evidence of a power of exposition in an exceedingly technical, and rather learned and far off controversy . . . on which
I congratulate him most heartily.[13]

The government was sympathetic but felt this was an issue on which the
churches and commerce should rally support. In November 1921 Desborough
questioned the government on communications with the Holy See.[14] In reply
it was clear the Holy See saw no case for change. But his international lobby-
ing continued and in March 1923 he wrote to Ettie from Rome. After noting
that Mussolini, the fascist leader of Italy, had opened the International
Chamber of Commerce meeting, he explained: 'Today my Easter resolution
was passed: they all cheered me, and cheered the passing of the Resolution!
Marvellous. Yesterday I saw Cardinal Gasquet, who was very pleasant, but I
have got to see Cardinal Gasparri [the Pope's Secretary] to make arrangements
about the Pope.'[15]
     And the next day he described how:

> *Today I dine with Theo Russell [British Minister Plenipotentiary to the Holy*
> *See]. He took me to see Cardinal Gasparri at the Vatican: I have seen the*
> *two Cardinals & am by way of seeing the Pope this morning.*
>   *I spoke again on Easter & the Resolution was carried at the <u>Plenary</u>*
> *Congress, so that is done.*
>   *I don't know what Gasparri will do; he is a wily old fox – & was very*
> *non-committal but asked for the papers which I gave him – However I don't*
> *expect 20 centuries to be upset in 5 minutes.*[16]

In 1928 Desborough came back proposing a Second Reading of the Easter Bill,
offering further evidence for support, including from within the worldwide
Anglican community.[17] In reply to Desborough's speech, the Secretary of State
for India, the Earl of Birkenhead, remarked: 'If the matter is carried through
now it will, I think, be impossible to resist the conclusion that the credit is
largely due to the pertinacity with which the noble Lord has pursued this
topic for so long a period of time . . . The Government are entirely favourable
to the proposals.'[18]

'The Inconstant Nymph', Punch *by Bernard Partridge, 11 April 1928.*
Mr Punch (to Easter), 'YOU'RE ALWAYS WELCOME MY DEAR: BUT IT WOULD
BE A GREAT CONVENIENCE IF YOU COULD CONTRIVE TO COME AT THE
SAME TIME EVERY YEAR.'

Although the Easter Act received Royal Assent in February 1928, the central provisions of the Act have never been brought into effect. The commencement clause (the Statutory Instrument) gave discretion to the government as to when to introduce it. It chose not to do so and because the Act has never been replaced by another piece of legislation, it remains on the Statute Book – the longest-running example in the UK legislature.[19] Members of Parliament have successively sought to have it introduced but governments have continued to duck the issue (partly because it requires international consensus). The current Archbishop of Canterbury, Justin Welby, has taken this up with Catholic and Orthodox representatives and suggested (in 2016) that he hoped it would be enacted within ten years.

In 1928 Desborough wrote the preface for a book by David Fotheringham offering a detailed historical account of the date of Easter and exploring the evidence on the baptism and crucifixion of Christ, a key underpinning of the issue.[20] In 1930 Hansard records how Desborough reminded the House that:

> I have taken an interest in this subject for many years, and since putting this Question on the Notice Paper I have received a somewhat lengthy letter from the Home Office asking me to postpone it, at all events for the present. As I understand that negotiations are now proceeding under the ægis of the Government with other Powers, that the Government are anxious to secure agreement on this matter so that the Act can be put into operation, that the subject is also coming before a Committee of the League of Nations at an early date, and that the present juncture is not, for many reasons, a Convenient time for instituting a debate upon it in your Lordships' House, I will, with your Lordships' permission, postpone my Question indefinitely.[21]

In 1932 he raised the issue once again and a government spokesperson noted:

> While there can be no question of an indefinite postponement of the decision to be taken by the Government in regard to the application of the Easter Act, it seems obviously desirable to await the result of the communications to be made by the League to the religious authorities. I do not think there is any further information that I can give my noble friend, but I do assure him that, the Government are very anxious that this Easter Act should be put into force.[22]

Desborough returned to the question in 1936 for the last time (relating to reform of the Calendar); clearly it was still too difficult for the government to implement the Act. It must have been a bitter blow for Desborough, who had succeeded against the odds in getting the Act passed, only to fall at this last hurdle after more than sixteen years.

15

Bringing the Games to Fruition

From Athens to London – the British Olympic Council –
international rules – Imre Kiralfy and the Franco-British Exhibition
– a new stadium – the Games and disputes – the Marathon

The creation of the modern Olympic Games in Athens in 1896 was the achievement of Baron Pierre de Coubertin, who was passionate about rekindling and
promoting 'Olympic' ideals of sportsmanship and international cooperation. As
colonial rivalries at the end of the nineteenth century overflowed into serious
international conflicts, such an aim resonated with many. Desborough, in his
summary report at the end of the 1908 Games, confirmed that these ideals were
the core purpose – well beyond the scope of any regular athletics meeting:

> a dominant idea of the old Hellenic games was peace, and that although
> the superb physical efficiency they fostered naturally produced a citizen
> qualified in all respects to serve his state against a foreign enemy, the
> Olympic Games were the expression of good-fellowship as between
> Greek and Greek, the one institution, indeed, which united the Hellenic
> race during a history which was marred throughout by internal conflict
> . . . The same idea of peace and unity in connection with international
> athleticism is capable of a modern application.[1]

Desborough shared this aspiration along with de Coubertin's ambition to
create an international event that would attract large numbers of participants
and spectators. The British Olympic Association (BOA) was founded in
London in May 1905 at a meeting at the House of Commons presided over by

the MP Sir Howard Vincent, who had recently been appointed as a British representative on the International Olympic Committee (IOC). William Grenfell (who became Lord Desborough at the end of the year) was appointed as Chairman and the Association gained an energetic and well-connected sporting figure who would give it considerable momentum.[2] A Council member at the time remarked that Desborough possessed 'the skill of a D'Artagnan, the strength of a Porthos, the heart of an Athos, and the body of an Englishman'.[3] And a later commentator noted how 'With his rowing and swimming and fencing and tennis, his Lordship was, as Gilbert and Sullivan might have had it, the very model of a modern English Olympian.'[4]

In Athens in 1906, Desborough enjoyed the Intercalated Games, despite being nervous about his own fencing bouts, given that he was now over fifty and finding himself thrown into discussions about an Olympics for London in 1908. On 24 April he reported to Ettie the fights that he relished, with a 'rib-roaster' against the Captain of the German team, as well as the whole experience of the Games: 'I spent the evening watching the illuminations between the two Queens – so you can see how regal I have been.'[5]

However, a key issue that would prove disruptive in London – fair adjudication – was forced on him directly in Athens. Two days later he complained how 'we fought the French and made a tie, & were finally beaten by 3 points: we really won but the judges treated us most unfairly, especially me which they all allow – I hit three straight off & was not allowed one. It was quite ridiculous, and I am frightfully annoyed.'[6]

Competing was the primary reason for being in Athens but, as we have seen, finding a way to bring the Games to London became the larger objective. Desborough, having now obtained a positive royal response vital to his enterprise, wrote to Baron de Coubertin, President of the IOC in Paris, and described his final festive day in Athens:

Yesterday I put on my gorgeous new uniform & had lunch with the King [of Greece] – a very big affair, and then we were given prizes in the Stadium – bunches of olive [leaves] from the top of Olympia, & medals – very good ones – amid the cheers of the populace. We got these as second prize, & the Belgians got third. We really won without a doubt, and I am very sad about it . . . If the Games really come off in England in 1908 I shall have a very great deal to do being President of the Olympic Committee – but I do not know if we should be able to raise the money: one ought to have £10,000 guaranteed.[7]

Lord Desborough descends from the platform as British fencers receive their medals, Athens 1906.

As he travelled back from Athens on the steam yacht *Branwen*, with Theodore Cook and Cosmo Duff-Gordon, Desborough took the opportunity to discuss the complexities of staging a London Games. He was heading for Paris, where he would fence competitively and hoped to gain outline agreement with de Coubertin on London as the best option. He confirmed his determination in a letter to Ettie from Venice: 'I want to see Coubertin & Brunetta d'Usseaux [a keen sportsman and fellow member of the IOC] about 1908; it will be a great business & one doesn't quite see how to get the money – However if the King helped, as I believe he would, it would go all right.'[8] Grenfell was a determined fixer and arranged to visit Rome, en route from Venice to Paris, so that he could discuss with Italian sporting officials their views on what were innocently termed 'the rules for several sports'.[9]

After the fencing team's return to Britain in the late spring of 1906, even more pressing than the need to confirm royal approval was engaging the British sporting associations. Letters of consultation were sent out seeking support for a London Games. The response was positive. This was important, as many in 'society' and those holding senior sporting positions thought Royal Ascot, the Henley Royal Regatta and the Wimbledon Tennis Championships were the important set-pieces of the summer season, while adding a whole clutch of sports wrapped into an expensive international event would be distracting and superfluous. Given modest audiences for the Paris and St Louis Games in 1900 and 1904 and the work required for a London Games, the enthusiastic endorsement of sporting associations was a crucial if by no means certain outcome. That they agreed to take part was an indication of trust in Lord Desborough and an acceptance of his personal authority.

Two other British figures made crucial commitments to creating an Olympics for London. The Reverend Robert de Courcy Laffan had known de Coubertin since 1897, and was a former headmaster of Cheltenham College who became vicar of St Stephen Walbrook and was Secretary of the new BOA. Laffan emerged as the busiest figure at the centre of the British Olympic organisation and was joined on the IOC by the equally determined Theodore Cook, an Oxford rowing blue, sportsman and writer (and later editor of *The Field*) who had assembled the fencing team for Athens in 1906.

Some may have hoped that Britain might make recompense for the sparse results in Athens. As Olympic historian Matthew Llewellyn puts it, 'For a nation accustomed to claiming the laurels of victory and effortless superiority, Britain's twenty-four medal (eight gold, eleven silver, and five bronze) Olympic campaign was viewed as a source of national embarrassment.'[10] However, if Britain claimed to have originated so many sports, now adopted elsewhere, decline might inevitably lie ahead. As Theodore Cook put it, 'England no longer stands alone, as she once did, as the apostle of "hard exercise" . . . We have had to see our best pupils beat us.'[11]

Desborough and the BOA moved quickly to create a British Olympic Council (BOC) specifically to organise the Games, and by the autumn of 1906 were in close deliberation about which events and venues would be needed and what monies required. Reflecting his determination to push on, several critical decisions were taken early. The BOC proposed that each sporting association should take charge of organising their events within the Games, that each country taking part would send a designated team (rather than allow athletes to nominate themselves) and that rules for each sport should be properly codified and agreed internationally, a hugely important step in terms of Olympic managerial development. As Desborough put it:

Less than two years is a brief space in which to organise an international meeting for which . . . the ordinary period of four years has been found none too long . . . The work has been enormous, as . . . there are more than twenty separate competitions, and that for each of these separate books of rules have been drawn up, translated into French and German, and circulated in each of the competing countries. The organisation of the games themselves, the definition of the amateur qualification, the framing of the programme, the fixing of the number of competitors for each event, were all matters which have involved great thought and labour. The definition of the word 'country' also presented questions of no small difficulty.[12]

The newly formed Olympic committees (in those countries wanting to participate in London) took responsibility for liaising with their own sporting associations in the selection of the best athletes, and this essentially set the pattern for future Olympiads. A later estimate of the scale of the administrative correspondence and management required stated that a 'total of the more important letters exceeds ten thousand . . . and 800 officials [were] needed [for the Games]'.[13] There was also the critical matter of raising sufficient funds.

Herbert Asquith, as Chancellor of the Exchequer, had already clarified the British government's unhelpful and unbending position when he announced in March 1906: 'I see no reason for granting any subsidy from public funds.'[14] This applied to Athens, and didn't bode well for government interest in the Olympic enterprise as a whole. The forty-strong British contingent for Athens had had to cover its own costs, and this favoured wealthy individuals. Although Lord Desborough was selected for the British fencing team because in Theodore Cook's opinion he was 'at the top of his game', he also had the resources to travel. Cook couldn't have known that Desborough's presence in Athens would prove critical to bringing the Olympics to London for 1908.[15] Asquith later referred to Desborough approvingly as having the 'tranquil consciousness of an effortless superiority'.[16]

Following his masterly networking in Athens in 1906 Desborough benefited from another unplanned opportunity that proved critical in staging the 1908 London Olympics. In 1904 a treaty of friendship had been signed between Great Britain and France. The Entente Cordiale set out arrangements for matters of colonial control (Britain would have 'freedom of action' in Egypt, and France in Morocco) and provided reinforcement of France's strategic position in Europe, countering the alliances being made by Germany and its evident militarisation. A 'Franco-British' exhibition was proposed for London (on a 140-acre site at Shepherd's Bush), to be organised and promoted by the exceptionally creative theatrical entrepreneur Imre Kiralfy.

Within the conception of the 'White City', Kiralfy and Lord Desborough came rapidly to an ingenious agreement: that the Franco-British Exhibition Company would construct a stadium and track to the specifications of the BOC and at their own cost, in return for a proportion of the ticket revenue.[17] This was a vital breakthrough for Desborough. At a BOC meeting on 20 December 1906, Kiralfy pledged to 'underwrite total advertising and construction costs, including a 110,000-capacity stadium, running and cycling tracks, lawn tennis courts, a swimming pool, dressing rooms, and convenience stands. In addition, the exhibition authorities would advance . . . £2,000 towards preliminary expenses, as well as guaranteeing one-fourth of total gross profits from the games.'[18] Given the Council had almost no funds of its own, this was a hugely advantageous arrangement which effectively made the London Games viable.

In the provision of new, large-scale sporting facilities and internationally agreed rule-setting, Desborough was breaking new ground in London. Metric measurements were adopted (other than for the marathon and the rowing course at Henley) and more events for women were planned than previously, with archery eventually producing a field of twenty-five British female entrants.

The Shepherd's Bush site was extensive and Kiralfy closely controlled the design of buildings, erected as large, modern halls, with architects commissioned simply to embellish them with ornate facades. Historian Paul Greenhalgh describes how the exhibition included:

> twenty palaces, seven huge pavilions (each 70 by 400 feet) and the largest machine hall ever built (at 300,000 sq feet it bulked larger than the legendary Galerie des Machines at the Paris Expositions of 1889 and 1900) . . . the site landscaped with ornamental gardens, courts, vistas and an artificial lake containing five-eighths of a mile of navigable water . . . 150,000 electric globes and arclamps and 7,000 gas lamps . . .

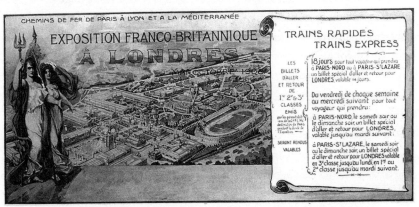

A 1907 French poster promoting rail travel to the Franco-British Exhibition.

A view of the elaborate architecture of the 1908 Franco-British Exhibition,
referred to as the White City.

Amusements including Irish and Senegalese Villages, a Ceylon Teahouse,
a scenic railway, a Canadian toboggan run, a Pathé News Cinematograph
. . . and the Flip-flap, a 'two armed pincer-like construction that lifted
groups of visitors across the site'.[19]

Arrangements were rapidly made: a contract was signed on 14 January 1907
and Lord and Lady Desborough took part in a ceremony to position the first
stanchion by main contractors George Wimpey on 31 July 1907. More than
5,000 tons of steel would be required to create what was then the largest
stadium in the world.

Both a running track (24 feet wide with a lap of 586 yards 2 feet, or exactly
one-third of a mile), and one for cycling (35 feet wide and 660 yards in
circumference, making a banked lap of three-eighths of a mile) were included,
plus wrestling platforms and a 100-metre swimming pool (very much better
than Highgate Ponds) with a dramatic demountable diving tower, and the
central area inside the track able to be used for Olympic field events later in
the year. Compared to the cramped stadium in Athens, the London running
track – laid out and tested by the Amateur Athletic Association – was superb.

Aerial view of the Olympic Stadium before the completion of more covered stands, but with the 100-metre swimming pool visible inside the running track and banked cycle track, with the White City exhibition pavilions behind.

By early May 1908 Desborough was working on arrangements for the ceremonial events, and writing to Ettie, 'I am off now to see the P of Wales about opening the Exhibition & then Lord Knollys[*] – the King is apparently consulting him about <u>his</u> opening it.'[20] Before the official opening of the Franco-British Exhibition, Desborough had been supervising test events in the new stadium and spent time at the displays, as he reported to Ettie on 17 May:

> *Dearest, The Exhibition was quite a different place yesterday. I was there all day, & lunched & dined & saw the fireworks (French) in the Stadium, very good. Roads quite dry, and the white buildings lit up by 500,000 electric lights, the finest thing I have seen of the sort. The Indian Court is really remarkable when lit up. I found Harry Stonor [who worked in the royal household] and others and took them to see the Lady's diving & some sports, & gave them tea at the Garden Club – quite first rate – and showed them the Pictures all hung, quite superb, they beat the French hollow. There were 100,000 people there yesterday.*[21]

---

[*] Francis, Lord Knollys was Private Secretary to the King.

In the same letter he mentions 'old Kiralfy' and refers to him as a 'champion muddler' but confirmed that 'without him there would have been no exhibition & no stadium'. He described the stadium as 'A.1. for running, cycling, swimming etc.'.

The official opening of the Franco-British Exhibition took place on 26 May 1908 with King Edward VII and the President of France, Armand Fallières, officiating, and Lord Desborough and Imre Kiralfy in attendance, watching a procession of clubs, tableaux and athletics displays and demonstration running and cycle races. In *The First London Olympics 1908*, Rebecca Jenkins emphasises the important point that with Pathé News based at the exhibition and considerable circulation rivalry between newspapers and magazines, this was a moment when photographic and film coverage became significant, and to some extent part of the event.[22] Huge numbers of picture postcards were circulated, some of the images for which were photographed from a balloon.[23]

In seeking extended international participation, based on official national teams, the 1908 London Games inevitably became subject to rabid bouts of partisan nationalism, though not always at the level that caused George Orwell later to describe international sport as 'war minus the shooting'.[24] Having applied his formidable organisational and diplomatic talents to finding a site, creating the first custom-built stadium, raising the necessary funds, overseeing a system of rule-setting sport by sport, there were still, for Desborough, once the Games started, extensive disruptions, including accusations of unfair judging and differing viewpoints about professional and amateur status. He estimated after the Games that he gave 139 speeches at lunches, banquets and other social functions linked with the Olympics.[25] However, as Chairman, he was ultimately responsible for this great sporting festival taking place at what was a time of fractious domestic politics.*

Desborough shared de Coubertin's overriding ambition to create an international event that would attract more participants than any previous occasion. At the start of the Games, he experienced pressure from all sides but held fast to the larger picture and what would be seen in today's terms as the 'values' of the event. At an inaugural Olympic banquet he encouraged officials and competitors to work together in a spirit of international harmony and mutual respect.[26] As reported in *The Times*, he declared that 'many points must arise on which

---

* The suffrage demonstrations included the 'Mud March' of 9 February 1907 and 'Women's Sunday' on 21 June 1908, which half a million protestors attended in Hyde Park.

British women archers taking part in the 1908 Olympic Games.

there would be strong difference of opinion . . . But as sportsmen we must be willing to give as well as take.'[27] This wasn't just about the ambitions of the athletes and enjoyment of spectators but a determination to promote international fellowship to counter evident and growing hostilities in the world.

Despite the arrangements for ticket revenue from spectators, expenses arising from hospitality for athletes and officials needed to be covered. Desborough made a last-minute appeal to Lord Northcliffe, owner of the *Daily Mail*, with the bold claim that 'Perhaps, indeed, through these Olympic Games good feeling between nation and nation – the good feeling which helps prevent the outbreak of war – may be at least as well promoted as by diplomatists sitting round a board.'[28] After a successful *Daily Mail* campaign, more than £10,000 was subscribed, with the largest single donation of £1,500 being offered by the popular German bodybuilder Eugen Sandow.[29]

Out of the 3,000 entries, nearly 2,000 athletes arrived in London. The British team was, not surprisingly, 'the largest with 736 men and 39 women, France entering 208 athletes, and Sweden with 168 and America 122'.[30] Unlike the British government, which offered no support to organisers or athletes, the French, German and Canadian governments provided funds for their teams. Despite the funding constraints – and heavy rain at the start – it was 'much the greatest athletic gathering on record'. Hopes were high and, as Desborough stated: 'In the Games of London were assembled . . . representatives of the generation into whose hands the destinies of most of the nations of the world are passing . . . We hope that their meeting . . . may have a beneficial effect hereafter on the cause of international peace.'[31]

By the time the King arrived at the White City Stadium on 13 July 1908 for the inauguration of the Games themselves, the royal box boasted a fascia proclaiming 'Edward VII, Rex et Imperator'. On a very wet west-London afternoon, with various princes, dukes, officials and competitors in attendance, Lord Desborough stepped forward and announced, '"May it please your Majesty to declare the Olympic Games of London open." The King, in a loud voice, replied immediately: "I declare the Olympic Games of London open." Whereupon six Royal trumpeters of the Household Cavalry blew a fanfare, the band played "God Save the King," and the international competitors gave three cheers for His Majesty.'[32]

In words that have resounded across the generations, IOC President Pierre de Coubertin pronounced, 'The importance of these Olympiads is not so much to win as to take part'; in 1908, however, few participants, if they were honest, would have agreed with this statement, and the London Olympics tested the notion almost to destruction.[33]*

Spectators at the Olympic stadium, with cycle track, running track and swimming pool visible.

---

* De Coubertin's phrase derived from a sermon preached in St Paul's Cathedral on the first Sunday after the start of the Games, when Ethelbert Talbot, the Episcopalian Bishop of Pennsylvania, referred to 'the lesson of the real Olympia – that the Games themselves are better than the race and the prize. St Paul tells how insignificant is the prize. Our prize is not corruptible, but incorruptible'.[34]

On the opening day the *Daily Telegraph* caught something of the symbolic importance of the occasion, stating: 'We are on our trial, not only before the . . . athletes who have trusted us sufficiently to come over here, but before the trained observers who represent the twenty different nations competing, and the trial is not merely concerned with athletic matters; it will be affected by a hundred different details of character, of conduct, of organisation; and it will have a widespread and enduring influence upon the political and social future of the world.'[35]

However, even the opening ceremony created opportunities for offence to be taken: the American and Swedish flags were carelessly omitted from the international line-up and in the procession of national teams the shot-putter Ralph Rose apparently failed to dip the American flag as he passed the King. His team Captain, Martin Sheridan, is said to have observed provocatively, 'This flag dips to no earthly king.'[36] Differences of view about national representation were evident: the Irish not wanting to be part of the British team; Finland unhappy under the Russian flag; New Zealand athletes having to compete as part of Australasia; Austria objecting to Bohemia being allowed its own delegation; and Danish athletes trying to block the Icelanders from entering the stadium.

There were differences of opinion about the line between 'professional' and 'amateur', and the decision by the BOC to have British officials umpiring all events failed to win universal trust or acceptance. James E. Sullivan, the senior official American delegate to the Games, was openly critical of arrangements for the athletes, as well as the organising and judging. He stoked Anglo-American rivalries and used media interest to ensure that his negative comments were published in US newspapers. He accused the British of blatant partisanship – 'They taunted us in every conceivable way. They ridiculed our flag . . . Their conduct was cruel, unsportsmanlike, and absolutely unfair' – thus reinforcing the British view of Sullivan as a firebrand.[37] And, despite international consultation on the newly established rules undertaken by each sporting association, there were several official complaints in the first days of the Games. Some questions seem fairly trivial – whether a pole-vaulter might create a small indent in the ground to give better purchase for the base of his pole or the question of what boots could be worn in the tug-of-war: everyday footwear or specially prepared? – but they mattered tremendously to those who had travelled long distances to compete.

After heavy downpours and poor attendance in the first week of the Games, *The Sketch* suggested remedying this with a women's marathon race in fairly scanty traditional Greek dresses.[38] Warmer, drier weather and discounted ticket prices produced a larger public response in the second. But on Thursday 23 July the 400-metre running event resulted in a major dispute. Lieutenant Wyndham Halswelle, a Scottish runner (who won silver in the 400 metres and bronze in the 800 metres at the Games in Athens in 1906) posted the fastest qualifying time and was up against three Americans: John Taylor of Cornell, William Robbins of Harvard, and John Carpenter representing the Irish-American Athletic Club. The race wasn't run in lanes, and on the final bend Halswelle attempted to overtake Carpenter, who ran wide and appeared to use his right elbow to prevent his competitor coming past. The British judge, Dr Arthur Roscoe Badger, immediately flagged a foul, and officials ruled Carpenter to be disqualified and the race to be rerun two days later. American commentators thought this a flagrantly biased judgement, and Robbins and Taylor refused to take part, so Halswelle reran the final on his own: the only such occasion in Olympic history. At the next Olympics there would be lanes.

The British magazine *Academy* claimed that 'A more disgraceful exhibition of foul running has never been seen on an English track, and it is becoming increasingly obvious that in future American "Amateurs" will have to be debarred from taking part in athletic contests in this country, which are supposed to be reserved for gentlemen.'[39] No doubt all Desborough's diplomatic skills were deployed to keep the squabbles in check. At the final dinner for officials and competitors he spoke about needing to accept some differences of view: 'There must be, owing to the variations in the manner of conducting sports in various countries, differences of opinion, but when those did arise the BOC endeavoured to settle them according to a policy of "fair field and no favour".'[40] The Americans were not present at the dinner to hear these soothing words. But although their trainer Mike Murphy had argued that they should abandon the Games entirely, the fact that they stayed to the end of the summer events was later acknowledged by James Sullivan to be due to 'the courtesy and diplomacy of Lord Desborough'.[41]

On the following day, Friday 24th, the marathon was run from the East Terrace of Windsor Castle to the Olympic Stadium, extended to the Terrace so that the Princess of Wales and her children could be involved, thereby establishing 26 miles and 385 yards (42.195 kilometres) as the Olympic distance ever since.

Start of the 1908 Olympic Marathon, East Terrace, Windsor Castle, 24 July 1908, with Lord Desborough standing on the seat of a car holding one of the starting pistols.

The Princess recorded that she 'pressed a button on the table, which by means of an electric cable communicated with Lord Desborough's motor-car. Lord Desborough (who was standing on the front seat of his car) and Mr Jack M Andrew each fired a pistol, while the Crown Prince of Sweden gave them the word to go.'[42]

Seventy-five runners had entered and fifty-five set off on the day, representing sixteen nations, the hot weather resulting in only twenty-seven making it to the finish. The first runner into the stadium was the Italian Dorando Pietri. Over the next dramatic minutes it became clear he was suffering from severe exhaustion. He turned the wrong way inside the stadium, was redirected

Dorando Pietri being helped across the marathon finishing line by Jack Andrew, the clerk of the course, and Dr Michael Bulger of the Irish Amateur Athletic Association and chief medical officer for the day.

around the track, but stumbled and fell, only to be picked up by officials, who hoped he could finish the race. He collapsed across the finish line. Although Pietri was declared the winner, American protests ensued and, after debate among the umpires, the decision was reversed and Pietri was disqualified for having received assistance. The American runner Johnny Hayes was confirmed as the winner, achieving a new Olympic record of 2 hours, 55 minutes and 18.4 seconds.

Overnight, however, Dorando Pietri became an international sensation. Desborough sent flowers and a note, 'with every wish for your speedy and complete recovery', referring to his 'splendid achievement, which has the sincere sympathy of every man and woman in the vast crowd at the Stadium'.[43] At the Olympic prize-giving, widespread public sentiment was expressed when Queen Alexandra presented him with a special silver-gilt trophy – arranged, one assumes, behind the scenes by Desborough. Arthur Conan Doyle, who was beside the track both as a medical officer and a correspondent for the *Daily Mail*, spoke for many when he remarked, 'The Italian's great performance can never be effaced from our records of sport, be the decision of the judges what they may.'[44]

Queen Alexandra with Lord Desborough presenting her personal trophy to Dorando Pietri.

16

Olympic Dreams and Reality

American complaints – amateur versus professional – Olympic Regatta Henley – Stockholm and beyond

The disputes at the 1908 Olympics exposed both prejudices and shifting expectations of what an Olympic Games should be. The differences between British and American athletes were in part about training, with American athletes often employing professional coaches to increase their chances of winning. Although self-evident today (particularly in a sporting world of 'marginal gains'), this approach was still anathema to some. G. K. Chesterton insisted that:

> We in England make sport prominent, we make it pervasive; but we do not in our souls make it important . . . We must look into [the American sportsman] not for the light vices of vain or sensual loungers, but for the solid vices of statesmen or fanatics, for the sins of men inflamed by patriotism or religion. He cannot shake hands after the fight . . . We should condemn him not only as a cad but as a fool . . . What can be the fun of being a winner if one is not admired for one's way of winning? What is the pleasure of gaining glory if one loses honour?[1]

This was an extreme view, and one countered, for example, by Conan Doyle, who argued that Americans should be admired, not least for their passion for victory and their 'remarkable appearance of all-round excellence'.[2]

The range and depth of American complaints about the London Games continued – despite supportive opinions from some of the US sporting establishment, and successes of other kinds such as John Taylor being the first black American athlete to win Olympic gold in the medley relay – so that Theodore Cook felt obliged to publish an extended response, separate from the official report he submitted to the IOC:

> We are very well aware that many shortcomings were apparent in the organization of the most complicated international meeting that has ever taken place. But it is curious that, alone among our thousands of visitors, Mr Sullivan and his friends should have left us not merely without a word of thanks, but with the accusations of discourtesy, inhospitality, and deliberate dishonesty . . . [He] and his friends continually protested against everything while the Games were in progress, and continued to misrepresent the facts after they were over.[3]

Other Americans went out of their way to work with Lord Desborough after the Games to heal wounds and re-establish international sporting relations. The American Olympic Council President, Casper Whitney, praised Desborough as BOC Chairman for his 'individual effort' and 'unswerving sportsmanship' and conceded that 'We have here in America the same fault-finding, suspicious and bickering classes that you have in England.'[4] In reply to being offered an honorary Olympic medal at the end of the summer Games (but at the same time as conducting a robust correspondence with Theodore Cook in which he refuted the accusations against the US team), President Roosevelt, himself a keen sportsman, wrote to Desborough to say, 'Indeed you have had about as difficult and complicated a time as any one could have, but you have won golden opinions; the American athletes are a unit in singing your praises. I congratulate you on what was really a great feat.'[5]

The 1908 Games brought renewed focus on the amateur/professional issue. The key figure of James Sullivan had risen to seniority in American athletics very much on a platform of promoting untainted amateur sport. He had no desire to be dictated to by the British. Also, as Rebecca Jenkins puts it, 'Whereas to sportsmen like Lord Desborough or to Baron de Coubertin the concept was about perpetuating the spirit of a gentlemanly code, Sullivan's evangelical determination to root out sham amateurs – athletes who performed for money – was about a battle to distinguish socially valuable sport from the "sinful" world of seedy gambling parlours and rigged boxing matches that flourished in the big city. Sullivan was fired by an almost religious belief in sport as a mechanism for the betterment of society.'[6] This last point, however, did chime with Desborough's own convictions.

In the background were issues of social distinction and class. When, in the 1890s, Desborough (as Willy Grenfell) had accepted the position of President of the newly formed Bartitsu Club, created by Edward Barton-Wright, it extended his interest in fencing as a combat sport. But we've seen how, although appearing participative and open – including for women – Grenfell patronisingly referred to this new martial art as establishing 'an athletic class for people of good standing'.[7]

The modern Olympic movement openly promoted a myth that the ancient Greek games were contested among 'amateurs' when the evidence suggests that monetary prizes were both normal and significant for participants. The Greeks had no notion of amateurism, and it was a deliberate obfuscation to suggest otherwise. However, as Lincoln Allison clarifies, it was crucial to make the Olympic ideal one of universal values and nobility – it was no longer pagan or professional – as a contribution to global peace and well-being.[8]

'In these terms the appeal to an ancient, arguably universal, lineage has proved immensely successful, even if it was based on an historical myth.'[9]

Allison writes, 'The classical-amateur myth was an extrapolation backwards of a set of values whose real home was among the European aristocracy and English public schools of the nineteenth century.'[10] The myth reinforced the concept of a moral framework for amateur sport, with the emphasis on developing skills and relishing the pleasures of playing the game: the innate value of participation.[11] [See *Chapter 3 Manhood and Morals*.]

Why did the amateur/professional issue matter so much? First, because so much of the enlargement of sporting activity in the second half of the nineteenth century, whether linked to schools or through the development of local clubs, emphasised a separation between newly codified sports (in which Britain played a prominent role in devising and promoting the rules) and wager-linked activities such as horse-racing, boxing, road-running or professional sculling.

Secondly, in the context of the Olympics, there was a simple argument of fairness: those who participated in sport in their spare time could never easily compete with those whose daily work involved similar physical activity, whether as trainers or (in the case of rowing) as watermen. Thirdly, these anxieties were heightened in the context of international competition. It was well known that different sports had differing definitions of who was professional and who amateur; indeed, that these definitions varied in different countries. IOC members had hoped to forestall future disputes at the Olympics and in 1905 came to a view about how to define an amateur.

> An amateur is a person who has never taken part in a professional race or at a meeting open to all comers, nor has raced for any form of monetary prize or for money, or for any part of money provided by the admission fees to the ground, or against professionals, and who has never at any period of his life been a professor or teacher for a salary of physical exercise.[12]

For the 1908 Games the IOC recognised that the BOC had no choice but to accept the interpretations of amateurism from each of the sporting associations.[13] As Chairman, Lord Desborough reasserted in his official report, 'The Olympic Games are exclusively for amateurs . . . the underlying principle being that an athlete is no longer an amateur if he makes money out of the sport in which he engages.'[14]

Fourthly, there was a wider concern about over-specialisation. The all-rounder, like Desborough himself, could for many in Britain be seen as an ideal model: preventing sportspeople from having unbalanced lives and promoting fitness and a healthier lifestyle more broadly.

However, the promotion of all-round sporting ability was likely to clash with the innate specialisation of open international contests gathered together in the Olympic Games. As they evolved, despite adding multi-sport events such as pentathlon and heptathlon, each successive edition attracted athletes seeking to be the best in the world – not just the best in their region or country – and thus tightly focused on highly specific skills. This contradiction wasn't easily recognised by those organising the 1908 Games. The continuing debates about professional and amateur transmuted in the later twentieth century into revised practices which recognise that most sportspeople at the level of world competition expect to train full time and therefore need financial support, while not competing directly for monetary reward.

The 1908 Olympic Regatta followed in the week after the athletics and took place at Henley-on-Thames, over a slightly lengthened Regatta course of one and a half miles, with eighty-one athletes from eight nations participating. The town was decorated with flags and Chinese lanterns, an open-air concert

The 1908 Olympic Regatta course at Henley-on-Thames.

was staged at the Phyllis Court private members' club, competitors and officials were offered lunch at Desborough's home, Taplow Court, on Sunday 26 July, and special events were staged in the town.

On 31 July, the last day, Lady Desborough presented the medals – including to Leander Club, representing Britain in the eights, which defeated Belgium in the final by two lengths – followed by a municipal banquet and ball in Henley Town Hall. On the following day, George A. Kessler, the 'Champagne King', gave a banquet and fête for 300 guests at Bourne End, with re-creations of Athenian temples, and illuminations and fireworks, which Desborough attended.

The motorboat races and sailing events took place in the Solent: with 6-, 7- and 8-metre yacht classes off Ryde, Isle of Wight, between 27 and 29 July, and 12-metre yacht class races on the Clyde, involving *Hera* versus *Mouchette* (with *Hera* the winner) on 11 and 12 August. For the first time in the Olympics, speedboats were raced on Southampton Water, with France winning gold with *Camille* driven by Emil Thubron, and silver for Britain with the 400hp *Wolseley-Siddeley*, driven by the Duke of Westminster (even though it ran aground).

*Lady Desborough, with
Lord Desborough, presenting
the Olympic gold medal to
H. T. Blackstaff, winner of
the single sculls, Henley-on-
Thames, 31 July 1908.*

In the autumn, various Olympic events were staged, including football, with eight teams taking part, and rugby, with two, in the central area of the stadium at White City. The Games concluded with hockey on 31 October, after which a farewell banquet was of fered in Holborn, at which Lord Desborough spoke as Chairman (before loud cheers and a rendering of 'Auld Lang Syne'): 'Whatever nationality we may belong to, we can all say tonight that both the Summer and the Autumn Games of 1908 have been a success. I will also say that we were able to extend to that great body of athletes a hospitality which will show them that we are not unmindful of the way we have been treated when we have gone abroad.'[15]

Over the summer there had been much debate in the press, covering specific disputes, the overall value of the Games, and prospects for the future. *Vanity Fair* published its own summary on 29 July:

Great Britain has done very well, having easily kept her pride of place with twenty-three firsts in the Stadium, as against eighteen firsts won by the United States; Sweden being a bad third with five firsts. A good many of us regret the fact that British representatives were beaten in running and jumping; but there can be no doubt that we shall be beaten in these contests until our amateurs submit to a severer system of training. Every British competitor carried several pounds of superfluous flesh, whereas the Americans had almost as little flesh on their ribs as on their teeth; and when races are won by fractions of a second the man who cherishes flank fat is sure to be beaten . . . Our teams must put themselves under trainers if they would win the next Olympic games.[16]

On balance, whatever the controversies, the 1908 London Games both rescued and greatly re-energised Baron de Coubertin's vision. There was widespread agreement that the unprecedented scale and complexity of these Olympic Games had been handled – without any government assistance and at very short notice – with remarkable efficiency and success. This was very much to the credit of the team of Robert de Courcy Laffan, Theodore Cook and Lord Desborough. The organising in 1908 was not made easier by continuing disruption in domestic affairs, with large-scale suffrage demonstrations, extensive political divisions over Home Rule for Ireland, and widespread protests and strikes over pay and conditions in various industries.[17] However, this reinforced for Desborough the value of the Olympics as a non-political event of international importance. Olympic historian Keith Baker quotes *The Empire* magazine's summary that Desborough was 'utterly devoid of arrogance, or side, which frequently causes Englishmen to be detested by the foreigner'.[18] Baker's own conclusion is that 'He emerged from the Games . . . with Laffan, [as] truly one of the two great pillars on which the British Olympic movement has been built.'[19]

Desborough supervised Britain's participation in the 1912 Games in Stockholm, and attended as a personal guest of King Gustav V. The Games did not go well for the British. Given the very limited financial support the BOA could offer towards the costs for British sporting associations to send their best competitors, this was not surprising. Britain managed to send 210 men and ten women athletes to Stockholm (compared to the 736 men and thirty-nine women at the 'home' games of 1908) but came third after America and Sweden, which was condemned by the British press as a tremendous failure.[20] Blame was laid on the lack of funding or adequate training, and for some this was further proof of the poor physical state of the nation and, for others, the decadence of British society.

In August 1912 Arthur Conan Doyle, looking towards the next Olympics – planned for Berlin in 1916 – contributed to a correspondence in *The Times*, in which he advocated widespread reforms for British participation. Theodore Cook (as editor of *The Field*) revived the concept of creating an Empire team as a means of extending the pool of amateur talent that Britain might draw on, a prospect bolstered by various 'Empire' contests and that had been raised at a Council meeting of the BOA in July 1911.[21] Over that summer Desborough was involved in the Inter-Empire sports championship staged as part of the Festival of Empire at Crystal Palace. In August 1912 he chaired a special meeting to discuss potential reforms. This produced several suggestions, including, as Matthew Llewellyn puts it, that 'a significant portion of the money raised would be used to support national governing bodies of sport to develop schemes for effectively finding, training and preparing future British Olympic champions'.[22]

By this stage Desborough was ready to stand down as Chairman of the British Olympic Association. When he resigned, it seemed, in Llewellyn's words, that 'the loss of such a well-respected and influential leader came as a devastating blow to the BOA, particularly during a period of proposed reform'.[23] Pierre de Coubertin expressed his 'deep regret' on hearing the news and thanked him for 'the great services which you have rendered to the Olympic cause'. In seeking a replacement he turned to another tall and athletic aristocrat, Algernon St Maur, the 15th Duke of Somerset.

What was planned for Berlin in 1916 could not, of course, take place. After the First World War, the Olympic programme was resumed in Antwerp in 1920, but Germany did not take part again until 1928. In London, the White City Stadium resumed a rather multifarious life as the home for greyhound racing from 1927, with occasional athletics, rugby and football matches as well as speedway racing and rock concerts.[24] It was demolished in 1985.

Public Gain, Private Loss

17

The Thames Remade

The River Thames – Thames Conservancy – new investment – Boulter's Lock elevator – Desborough Channel – the Thames in his life

The *Derby Daily Telegraph* reflected that, 'Nobody had a closer connection with the Thames than Lord Desborough. He had swum in it, rowed on it, represented it in Parliament, lived by the side of it, spent hours fishing in it, administered it and measured it.'[1]

The Thames was indeed central to Grenfell's life: in some ways the river created him as much as he changed the river. It is on the Thames that his life and contributions are most evidently celebrated by the landmarks with which he is linked.[2] He was appointed as a conservator of the River Thames in 1895 and Chairman of the Board of the Thames Conservancy (TC) in 1905, at the age of fifty, a post he retained until his retirement in 1937, a combined service of some forty-two years: remarkable by today's standards.[3]

After his death, when the Conservators were mourning the loss of such a great figure, the remarks of Sir Jocelyn Bray, Conservancy Chairman, were sent to Ettie Desborough, and she responded by saying, 'Yes, his "best love was the Thames", man and boy, and what pleasure he drew from its sources, every labour a joy.'[4]

THE RIVER THAMES

Willy Grenfell joined the TC at the age of forty-one and served on it until he was eighty-two, a period during which both the Thames and the Conservancy underwent considerable change. It is easy to take rivers for granted as part of the natural order of things, but in reality they can alter fundamentally over

Lord Desborough, Conservator from 1895 and Chairman of the Thames Conservancy, 1905–37, detail of illustration by Philip 'Pip' Mendoza for Mayfair *magazine, 4 July 1914.*[5]

time, as the Thames was modified in Grenfell's lifetime from 1855 to 1945.[6] The Thames was transformed during this period from being a means of transport with associated trades to a river focused on sport and leisure in its upper reaches, at the same time being crucial to the expansion of London as the national and imperial capital: during the nineteenth century the London docks were developed as the very heart of the British Empire. The Thames was always a crucial supplier of drinking water to the capital.

The Thames shifted from being an important source of water, food and work within a largely rural setting over its 215-mile length to becoming ever more urban and commercial. In his 1906 book *The Silvery Thames*, Walter Jerrold writes, 'From the Nore to London it is the Highway of Commerce, from London to Oxford it is the Stream of Pleasure and from Oxford to the Cotswolds it is the River of Quiet,' while acknowledging that 'the Stream of Pleasure takes up the burden of commerce some time before it becomes the great highway'.[7]

Large towns along its banks, such as Oxford, Reading, Maidenhead,

Kingston and Richmond, developed as centres of substantial population and business. As it flowed into the suburbs of the metropolis, through the Cities of Westminster and London and onwards to the Thames estuary, so commercial forces were magnified. Over time, polluting industries grew up, including brewing, tanning, printing and paper-making, chemical processing and metal-working, along with suppliers of essential services such as power and water. And as populations and industries expanded, so did the scale of human effluent and industrial waste. The health of the Thames, simultaneously the source of drinking water that enabled such expansion to take place, was, even by the 1850s, fighting a losing battle against economic 'progress', and the river became ever more polluted. Fish stocks were declining – and the railways enabled fish from the sea to be widely distributed – and river fishermen had to find new sources of work, many on the land and some as boatbuilders.

Edwin Chadwick's great work *The Report on the Sanitary Conditions of the Labouring Population of Great Britain* was published in 1842 and charted the dreadful living conditions of the majority of the population. This was published a few years after the first cholera outbreak in 1831-2, but before its reoccurrence in 1848-9, 1853-4 and 1866-7, causing in total the deaths of around 150,000 people. Ultimately the source of the cholera outbreaks was traced back to contaminated water supplies. This precipitated the construction of sewers, though many simply drained back into another part of a river (including those constructed in London by Joseph Bazalgette from the 1850s).

In 1866 the Royal Commission on the Pollution of Rivers commented:

> Throughout the whole course of the river [Thames] from Cricklade to the point where the Metropolitan Sewage commences, fouling of the water by sewage from cities, towns, villages and single houses generally prevails. The refuse from paper mills, tanneries etc. passes into the stream. There is no form of scavenging practised for the surface waters of the Thames, but carcasses float down the stream until wasted by corruption. The river receives unchecked the whole of the pollution, solid and fluid, of the district; and this same water, after it has been so polluted, is abstracted, sand filtered and pumped into the Metropolis for domestic use.[8]

The Thames Conservancy Board was established in 1857 shortly before the 'Great Stink' in July and August 1858, when the hot weather in central London exacerbated the stench of untreated human waste and industrial effluent on the banks of the Thames. The outcry that followed led in part to the building by the Metropolitan Board of Works (MBW) of an extensive network for sewage treatment that had its outfall east of the capital.[9] Anthony Wohl suggests that the 'new Board did little to hold the MBW or industrialists to account nor was it active in seeking improvements'. However, he makes no mention of the very limited resources at its disposal nor the fact that the incumbent Lord Mayor of London was the Chairman by right under the Thames Conservancy Act of 1857 up until 1894.[10]

What is evident is that although the Conservancy was itself responsible for the full length of the Thames, the Board's work was made possible only through working with local district and parish authorities, landowners and industries where the river flowed. This caused an unrelenting struggle between competing interests, and finding common ground was hard. If it was difficult everywhere else, it was doubly difficult in the London metropolis.

Having control of the river that passed through the capital was a challenge compounded by London having the Port of London, the premier port in Britain, central to the growth of the economy. The port was itself made up of various private dock companies with limited capacity to upgrade their facilities in line with expanding trade. A Royal Commission on the Port of London argued in 1902 that the facilities were outdated due to a lack of investment, with the river too shallow for ships to reach the upper docks and wharves. The blame for this was placed at the door of the Thames Conservancy. The Commission highlighted divisions that obstructed improvement of the port, the slow turn-around times for loading and unloading ships, and poor railway connections.

In its recommendations, the Commission argued that a single public authority should be created to manage both the docks and the tidal river, from Teddington to the sea. This was not universally welcomed and was opposed not just by the Conservancy but also by the private dock companies. However, the government moved, in effect, to nationalise London's docks with a new Port of London Authority proposed in the King's Speech at the Opening of Parliament in November 1903.

Given the complexity of the undertaking, there was considerable delay as different parties sought to establish whether and how a Port of London Authority might come into being. The strength of opposition was such that an early Bill was abandoned by the Conservative government and alternative Bills were promoted by different interests, including the TC and the London County

Council. There was a degree of confusion and tension in the TC Board. Sir Fredrick Dixon-Hartland, the Chairman since 1895, opposed any plan to pass control of the Lower Thames to a new authority. Grenfell, however, was in favour of dividing the Conservancy, as the two sections of the river were so different. He criticised the TC for putting up its own Bill, suggesting that 'to have attempted to carry a private bill through Parliament giving them powers to initiate the suggested reforms' was misconceived and that they would be 'wise to spend their money in doing what dredging they could instead of wasting it in Parliamentary expenses'. At the same time, he defended the TC against any charge of neglecting the Port of London, pointing out that 'it has no power to raise money for the purpose of dredging to the extent required to admit the larger steamers'.[11] In 1905 Dixon-Hartland resigned as Chairman and was replaced by Grenfell.

At the first meeting in early January 1906, following the resignation but prior to his appointment, Grenfell was reminded by fellow Conservator Admiral Bosanquet that Grenfell himself had planned to oppose the Conservators' own Port of London Bill (which had been somewhat amended) – and this would place the Board in an anomalous position. Bosanquet suggested it might be better if the Board withdrew the Bill since, 'if the Bill went forward but with the opposition of the chairman the board would lay itself open to contempt and derision of the House of Commons and the public'.[12] But Grenfell said he would support the Bill even if it contained substantially the same terms as it had when it left the Board. A pragmatic Grenfell was elected unanimously!

In the summer of 1906 Lloyd George, President of the Board of Trade in the new Liberal government, concluded that a single nationalised port authority was indeed the best solution. Structural improvements were seen to be essential to improve the port's position against its leading European rivals. A Bill was introduced by him in April 1908, although guiding it through the House fell to his successor, Winston Churchill, and it received Royal Assent as the Port of London Act in December 1908. The following March the Port of London Authority came into being – taking on management of the tidal River Thames and its docks. It was a non-profit, self-governing trust in which excess revenues were used to improve the river and port facilities or to reduce charges. The Authority was responsible for maintenance of the river channels, provision of moorings, regulation of river traffic, the licensing of wharves, the removal of wrecks and the prevention of pollution. It took over the duties of the TC on sixty-nine miles of the tidal Lower Thames from Teddington to the Thames Estuary. The TC was thus left with responsibility solely for the upper, non-tidal river.

GRENFELL AND THE CONSERVANCY

When Grenfell was appointed a Conservator, the majority of Conservators were members of the City of London Corporation, with a minority as nominees of the government. He was himself nominated by the Board of Trade, and his long period of service included the First World War, when many staff were conscripted and maintenance was greatly reduced.[13]

Once he took over as Chairman in 1905, he oversaw reorganisation following the loss of the Lower Thames. He then had the considerable task of rebuilding the confidence and capability of the TC before being thrust into leading it through the war and then through the Great Depression.

The Conservancy had limited powers and resources. It could levy merchandise tolls on freight traffic, licence fees on pleasure craft, tolls on boats passing through locks, and charges for the extraction of water, but it received no government grant funding before the 1930s. It also had limited staffing – in 1914 there were 435 staff and twenty-eight appointed Conservators. Although the tidal Thames passed to the control of the Port of London Authority in 1908, the responsibilities of the Conservancy remained considerable, with increasing urbanisation, industrialisation and pollution beyond London itself. It frequently operated at a deficit and was reliant on borrowing, which in turn required debt servicing. Money was a constant problem, added to the weight of its statutory duties, ranging from navigation to environmental monitoring. Similarly, the TC was short of physical resources and most notably dredging equipment capable of dealing with the significant scale of operational activity along the Thames.

What is evident from the minute books and other records is the scale of Desborough's engagement in the Conservancy, and equally the direct involvement of the Conservators in week-by-week decision-making: about everything from large issues of capital expenditure to the levying of fines or the regulation of bathing. At one time or another he was a member of the following committees: Finance and General Purposes, Works, Navigation and Regulation of Water, Conservators, Parliamentary and finally Freshwater Fish.[14] Meetings were frequent (weekly in some cases) and complex, given the different interests represented (those of landowners, water boards, local councils and parish authorities, drainage boards and so on).

An Inter-Departmental Committee report of 1923 noted that 'there was no evidence of wasteful or inappropriate expenditure by the Conservators and . . . they were impressed with the efficiency, foresight and economy with which the Conservators carried out their public duties.'[15] Desborough's annual statement on the work of the Conservators attracted considerable media attention – it was regularly printed and circulated – usually given at the first meeting of the New Year. In it, Desborough would set out what the Conservancy had accomplished over the past year and what it was planning in the future, commenting on rainfall or flooding, and reflecting on the staff undertaking all the work.

He was not afraid to express a view. For instance, in 1915, after the floods of the previous years, there was a campaign for a Royal Commission. Desborough made it clear he agreed with the government that such a request should be refused. He perceived it as a waste of money not least because the Conservancy knew more about the problem than a commission could ascertain. In his 1928 report he was outspoken (and considerably far-sighted) about the real problem created by houses being built on land subject to flooding and he expressed the view that there should be more forceful ways of preventing this.

Desborough's detailed knowledge of the river and his commitment to it, as a user (both competitor and leisure boater) and administrator, was impressive.[16] Indeed, in some quarters he was known as 'Father Thames', and J. E. Vincent in his 1909 book *The Story of the Thames* commented that 'All users of the Thames owe an immense debt of gratitude.'[17]

He often emphasised the critical matter of the water supply and in his 1935 annual statement, as it was called, wrote that 'the greatest benefit performed by the Thames is the supply of 7,000,000 people with water. Without the Thames London would be impossible.'[18]

Flooding at Chertsey in 1926.

As well as promoting the river's vital role in supplying drinking water and draining the land, he was active in seeking to improve the Thames as a habitat for fish, being well aware of the depredations caused by population growth and pollution. He was the founding Chairman of the Thames Salmon Association, set up to help ensure the salmon population was sustained, and was active in building fish ladders and placing elvers in the Thames to help sustain the eel population. In 1921, as President of the Salmon and Trout Association, he urged the government to pass legislation to tackle river pollution. He was also Chairman of the government's Freshwater Fish Committee, which sent out questionnaires to fifty local boards of Conservators on the Thames: of the thirty-six that replied, only six reported their district free of pollution.

Of the major building projects undertaken during Desborough's period of office, the transformation of Boulter's Lock at Maidenhead was one of the most significant. The lock had been at the centre of the boating craze in the period from 1880 to 1920, as portrayed in the famous 1897 painting by Edward John Gregory.[19] The lock was a popular place to visit, not least on the Sunday after Royal Ascot week, when the rich and famous congregated in skiffs, punts and steam launches. Congestion was a serious problem on many weekends, and on starting the major rebuild of the lock (through the purchase of Ray Mill Island in 1909), the Conservancy removed a cumbersome trolley system by which small boats were hauled from one end of the lock to the other.[20]

A busy Boulter's Lock c. 1895 with tracks of the original trolley system behind.

Two 'elevators' were created instead: mechanical conveyor belts to speed the flow of unpowered craft and their passengers around the lock. They were driven by an electric motor and each consisted of a rotating belt of wooden slats with chocks attached to prevent rowing boats from tipping over while the occupants remained seated in their boats. The boat conveyors opened in 1912 on Ray Mill Island, but the rebuilding of the lock was not completed until later in the year.[21] The conveyor belts no longer exist and there is no record of when they were removed, but this was a brilliant piece of creative innovation.[22]

In 1924 Desborough presided over the opening of the rebuilt Iffley Lock, south of Oxford – so that its weirs could discharge more water and thus reduce flooding risk in Oxford – as well as installing boat rollers and a new lock house. On the landing to the east of the bridge above the rollers is a bronze plaque set into the wall. This was a donation by Desborough, modelled on the head of his own shorthorn bull named Red Michael, sculpted by Charles Wheeler (later President of the Royal Academy). The ring through the bull's nose functions as the starting point for the last eight in the processional university Eights Week bumping races that occur in May each year.

Lord Desborough with the Mayor of Maidenhead at the opening of the electric boat conveyor at Boulter's Lock, Maidenhead, 29 June 1912.

*Willy demonstrating the mechanical boat conveyor to delegates attending an
International Navigation Conference, 8 July 1923.*

Red Michael *by Charles Wheeler, Iffley Lock, Oxford.*

Flooding along the Thames was a serious problem, with major floods in 1894, 1903–4, 1912, 1914–15, 1928–29 and 1947. Desborough had commented in his annual statement after the 1912 floods: 'The cost of taking any effective steps would be far beyond the resources of the Conservancy itself. The whole course of the river from its source to Teddington Lock, where the jurisdiction of the Conservancy ends, requires dredging and deepening. There are many corners in the stream which require to be cut off and the river straightened. In some places side channels are wanted to take away the flood water.'[23]

The frequency and scale of flooding meant it remained a high priority for the Conservancy, and Desborough often spoke on the subject. Indeed, it was suggested that in 1928 when he was 'lying ill with influenza at his beautiful Thameside home . . . and for several days there were two charts in his room, one at the head of the bed and the other at the foot of the bed. The one at the head . . . registered the ups and downs of the patient's temperature. The other at the foot was for Lord Desborough to record hour by hour the rise and fall of the water levels at various points of the Thames.'[24]

In May that year, the seventy-two-year-old Desborough laid the commemoration stone to mark the reconstruction of Godstow Lock and the improvement to navigation of a twenty-eight-mile stretch of the Thames north of Oxford. Many of the old flash weirs (with removable boards allowing a surge of water to pour through, carrying boats as well) were removed and new pound locks and weirs put in place, along with significant dredging. As Desborough noted in his speech, 'the work would improve navigation and water supplies and reduce flood risk'.

In welcoming Sir Christopher Musgrave as Chairman of the Metropolitan Water Board, he observed, 'We are friends now but when we have to discuss the question of money we do not always agree with such mutual enthusiasm,' touching on enduring tensions between the underfunded Conservancy and those organisations and authorities that benefited from its work. In asking Lord Desborough to lay the stone, Alderman M. J. Greenwood, Chairman of the Conservancy's Finance Committee, commented, 'During the long time that he had the privilege of presiding over the deliberations of the Finance Committee they had only one thought, and that was to do everything they could for their Chairman, because while in some bodies there might be some doubt as to the rulings of the Chair, they never had that doubt in the Thames Conservancy.'[25]

Over a number of years with successive Thames Conservancy Acts (1921, 1924, 1932), the Conservancy extended its powers. The most significant project during Desborough's time in office was undertaken between Weybridge and Teddington – the Thames Improvement Scheme – at an estimated cost of £300,000 – at least £30 million today.[26] It aimed to reduce the incidence of flooding by increasing the flow of the river. It included greatly enlarging Teddington Weir and putting in roller sluices, widening the river at Hampton Court, enlarging Molesey Weir and Sunbury Weir, widening the river above Walton Bridge and constructing the Desborough Channel between Shepperton and Walton Bridge, to widen and deepen the river there.[27]

These extensive works were carried out through the use of direct labour under the Public Works Facilities Scheme (Thames Conservancy River Improvement) Confirmation Act, aimed at increasing employment, and instituted two years ahead of the Works Progress Administration programme in the United States. The work on the Channel commenced on 23 January 1934 and was completed in seventeen months. However, the complete programme of works took some five and a half years, with around 200 men employed: 'a large number being specially transferred from the distressed areas'.[28]

The Desborough Channel was broken through on 30 June 1935 and Desborough attended in a launch with other TC officials. At three-quarters of a mile long and 100 feet wide, the Channel now enabled users to avoid three miles of winding river. At a TC Board meeting in 1936–7, Desborough remarked: 'It was partly an unemployment scheme and I must say that the unemployed we engaged behaved splendidly. They worked hard and cheerfully under cold and wet conditions and their behaviour was such that I believe a good many of them obtained employment in the locality.'[29]

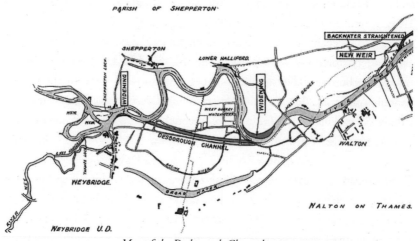

Map of the Desborough Channel, 1934.

Lord Desborough exchanging salutes with workers from the bows of the Conservancy launch
Donola, *as the Desborough Channel is broken through in 1935.*

The scale and complexity of the work undertaken during Desborough's
tenure was significant when one considers the numerous bodies that had to be
consulted and brought onside. The Centenary report catalogues the Conservancy's
work under four headings – Constitution and Administration; Navigation
and General; Land Drainage; and River Purification – which indicates
the span of the Conservancy's activities.[30]

Desborough's appetite and understanding of all things Thames led him to
become an early proponent of a Thames Barrage. The catastrophic flood of
January 1928, triggered by heavy rain upstream and a tidal surge in the
Thames, resulted in the collapse of the Thames embankment, causing fourteen
deaths and extensive property damage, including to the art collection of the
Tate Gallery stored below ground at Millbank. Commenting in the *Richmond
Herald*, Desborough said: 'Not even the Thames Conservancy, or the Port of
London Authority, can stop the water coming in from the North Sea. The
only way I can see is the one that was suggested, and which I recommended
21 years ago. That is, to put a barrage from Tilbury to Gravesend, with locks
in it.'[31]

He argued that 'the removal of the tides from the London Reaches is, in
my opinion, the greatest single measure that can be taken for the benefit of
London as a whole'.[32] In 1943, in the context of the potential for post-war
reconstruction, Desborough wrote the foreword to a book entitled *Tideless*

Thames in Future London by J. H. O. Bunge, which summarised the engineering studies and arguments for a barrier.[33] It was ahead of its time, and the Thames Flood Barrier was eventually constructed at Silvertown in east London, opening in 1982 to prevent surges from the sea rather than creating a tideless Lower Thames.[34]

At the Conservators' meeting on 11 May 1936, J. D. Gilbert drew attention to Desborough's forty years of service since attending his first meeting on 11 May 1896. In reply, Desborough reflected that the Secretary, F. W. Geary, had joined at the same time and had also completed forty years, while the chief engineer, G. J. Griffiths, had undertaken thirty-five years and the solicitor, Mr Corble, the same. It highlighted his ability to form and hold a loyal team.

Desborough had been absent from the first meeting in 1937, and at the February meeting Lieutenant Colonel F. G. Barker congratulated the Chairman on his return and his restoration to health: 'may he long be spared to preside over us'. However, in April, Desborough, now eighty-one, advised the Conservators that he would not be seeking reappointment. They implored him to stay, but he was adamant. As Sir Jocelyn Bray set out in his speech after Lord Desborough's death:

> Can any of us who were present at the Board Meeting when Lord Desborough told us he was not going to seek re-appointment ever forget that scene when Member after Member rose and begged him and implored him to stop with us, but he was quite adamant and so we lost our great leader. But what we haven't lost and please God, we shall never lose, is the tradition he created, the esteem in which the public hold the services we render them and the high position we undoubtedly occupy among the various Government Departments with which we come into contact. All this he created since we started struggling to get on our feet after the River below Teddington had been taken from us. Truly he ordered our way aright . . .[35]

On leaving office, Desborough was presented with an illuminated address signed by all the Conservators and senior staff, on which were engraved in its four corners Iffley Lock, Boulter's Lock, the Desborough Channel and Teddington Weir – the major works completed during his time in office.[36] He was also presented with a bronze sword, said to date from 800 BC, recovered from the bed of his beloved Thames.[37]

Thames Conservancy Valedictory Address 1937; clockwise from top left: Iffley Lock, Boulter's Lock, Teddington Weir and the Desborough Channel.

Desborough was recognised as having outstanding leadership skills, showing great consideration to those who worked with him and working tirelessly to secure 'the welfare of the River Thames with which your name will ever be associated'. Over his long tenure as Chairman he supervised the transfer of the tidal parts of the Thames to the Port of London Authority; the passing in 1930 of the Land Drainage Act, which made the Conservancy the supervising authority for a river catchment of some 3,845 square miles, including 2,393 miles of tributaries; and the carrying out of the Thames Improvement Scheme, the largest works conducted at that time, widening the river between Shepperton and Teddington and almost doubling the flow over Teddington Weir. The Conservancy continued to be active in policing river purification, building new locks and rebuilding others, and Desborough oversaw a reorganisation of its work with an updating of its byelaws.

This chapter has focused on Grenfell's engagement with the River Thames, which was deeply personal and expressed in his active participation in river-based sports (whether rowing, punting or fishing, as discussed earlier) and in the management and conservation of the river itself through his extensive

Willy punting participants in the Wakefield Cup swimming competition at Taplow, June 1936.

contribution to the Thames Conservancy. These interests were sustained over a lifetime. His sense of stability and order – reflected in many sections of this book – and the values that underpinned it might suggest a wealthy landed gentleman, conservative and backward-looking. But as the electric boat elevator at Boulter's Lock demonstrates, or his innovative thinking around a Thames Barrage, he was a man with an eye for the future. Regardless of which hat he was wearing, he was utterly committed to the Thames.

18

Commerce, Empire, War and Peace

London Chamber of Commerce – British Imperial Chamber of Commerce – Empire and Canada – Tariff Commission – First World War and the Volunteer Training Corps – air power – the Pilgrims

Grenfell was an imperialist, and much of this book highlights his belief that British oversight of large parts of the world was in the interests of the ruled as well as the ruling. Whatever presumptions (and oversights) underpinned such a view, it was paternalistic rather than aggressive or militaristic at heart. He was also an internationalist and recognised the benefits of cooperation around the world, not least as a means of underpinning global trade. Europe was riven with conflict through much of his life, and while the British Empire might have its own priorities, he recognised the growing importance of transatlantic alignment with the United States, both as a country that had established its own independence and one that was powerful enough to promote world peace.

COMMERCE

Desborough was often referred to as a businessman – rather than simply a titled landowner – and he appears to have bridged these two identities with ease. This may have stemmed from his experience of the Taplow estate or from his family background in mining and metals, as he was active in the stock market while staying close to developments in the mining industry.

In 1910 he was appointed President of the London Chamber of Commerce.[1] The records suggest that his role was largely titular, although, as noted earlier, he was closely involved in the debates on the Declaration of London [see

Chapter 12 Trusted Servant]. The LCC had been central to the work of organising the first Congress of the Chambers of Commerce in the Empire in London in 1886.[2] As President of the LCC, Desborough attended an inaugural meeting of the British Imperial Chamber of Commerce (BICC) held on 5 July 1911.* He proposed the motion that the existing Congress should take on the title of the British Imperial Chamber of Commerce and he became a member of the new council to lead the organisation.

The LCC met the costs of setting it up and staff were effectively seconded from the LCC to the BICC. At the 8th Congress of BICC in 1912, the following year, Desborough was the Chairman and gave several speeches, including one at an evening reception and dinner at which he reminded delegates that 'the businessmen coming from every portion of the Empire . . . looked to Parliaments to carry out legislation which would, as far as possible, assimilate in the various Parliaments of the Countries the continuity of legal enactment highlighting commercial law, trade-marks and company law striving to make one law current throughout the great Empire'.[3] Desborough's ambition for the Empire to become a single trading area is clear and he went on to suggest that one day there would be a great Senate established for the British Empire; in effect a parliament of parliaments.

He took the opportunity to reflect on the recent passing of the Parliament Act 1911, which abolished the power of the House of Lords to veto public Bills introduced in the House of Commons. This flowed from the recent clashes between the two houses in relation to the so-called People's Budget, introduced by Lloyd George, as Chancellor of the Exchequer, in 1909, and specifically around the contentious issue of a land tax. Nicholas Mosley, biographer of Julian Grenfell, reflected on Desborough's view of the 1909 Budget, observing that he was strongly opposed to the land tax proposals, declaring that 'if the Bill is passed we will emigrate to Canada. We simply cannot bear to live here.'[4] He subsequently went to Canada to search for property in which to invest (or live) and established a family trust aimed at limiting the tax liabilities that might arise.[5]

The Lords voted down the proposed reform, and both elections in 1910 (January and December) were in effect fought on the Liberal government's proposals to reduce the powers of the upper house. On the death of Edward

---

* The BICC was intended to bring together the interests of commerce across the Empire and provide a means of strengthening it. This meeting followed the Imperial Conference held in late May and June, and came after the Coronation of George V on 22 June 1911.

VII, the new King, George V, indicated in 1911 that he would create more Liberal peers in order for the necessary legislation to be passed.[6] As discussed earlier, Grenfell's interest in constitutional matters had been evident in his 1895 article 'Concerning the question of the House of Lords and Socialism', arguing against the Liberal Party's stated desire to introduce as yet unspecified reforms to the House of Lords.[7] [See *Chapter 13 The Lords and Socialism*.]

In his 1912 BICC speech, Desborough referred to the time when 'the two Houses of Parliament worked together co-ordinately and with equal power'. He went on to draw a parallel with the two sons who had been left an elephant and who couldn't agree as to its future. The younger son resolved to shoot his half of the elephant and Desborough explained that 'from some points of view the junior branch of the legislature had adopted the attitude of the younger son; they had not only shot at their part of the elephant but they had hit it'.[8] Much merriment ensued and the elephant metaphor subsequently reappeared in other speeches.

In 1913 Desborough became the President of the BICC, a position he retained until 1921.[9] With the outbreak of the First World War, BICC congresses were postponed and smaller annual meetings were held instead. At the first of these in 1915, Desborough remarked, 'I very much regret to say that I shall not be able to stay throughout the whole of these proceedings. A memorial service is shortly going to be held for two relatives of mine who fell in the war – one got the first VC in this war – and I should be very sorry not to show them my last respects.'[10]

As Lord Desborough withdrew from the meeting, the replacement Chair, Stanley Machin, commented: 'Lord Desborough's presence here today, almost straight, one might say, from the deathbed of his eldest son, is an example of how Englishmen know how to do their duty. I think everyone here knows what a magnificent specimen of an Englishman Lord Desborough is.' Desborough was indeed understated and dutiful at a time of great anguish. His son Julian had died on 26 May and Julian's cousin, Francis, had been killed two days earlier. Given that the Annual Meeting was held on 2 June, it was extraordinary that Desborough had attended any part of it. [See *Chapter 19 Great Losses*.]

Desborough frequently argued the case for building imperial commerce as a necessary adjunct to military might. He gave the opening address at the Business Conference in 1916 and was an active Chairman. The Canadian Trade Commission commented, 'there were no three names from which men engaged in trade and commerce throughout the Empire drew greater inspiration than [those of] Lord Desborough, Stanley Machin and Sir Algernon Firth'. The Toronto Congress was postponed to 1920, when it was chaired by Desborough, who sailed to Canada, arriving on 11 September. He attended the Congress until the 28th and went hunting until 11 October. Although he combined business with personal pleasure, these visits took up a considerable amount of time and were central to his personal commitment to empire.[11] In the official report of the Congress he quoted an extract from Alfred, Lord Tennyson's poem written at the request of the Prince of Wales for the opening of the Indian and Colonial Exhibition by Queen Victoria in 1886:

> Britain's myriad voices call,
> 'Sons, be welded each and all
> Into one imperial whole,
> One with Britain, heart and soul!
> One life, one flag, one fleet, one throne!'
> Britons, hold your own!

EMPIRE AND CANADA

In an earlier phase of his life Grenfell had taken an interest in Canada, first as a place of adventure and later for investment. In 1888, after his second swim below the Niagara Falls, he travelled to Kamloops in British Columbia for a hunting trip and on to Vancouver Island, before returning by train across Canada to sail home. He clearly loved what he saw, and, having started from Kamloops, he described how they came to 'a most ripping river, woods & mountains on both sides and lovely clearwater; a splendid place for bathing or punting as it had a glorious hard white sand bottom . . . then on in a stage here 30 miles . . . It will take a week from here to get into Caribou Country with pack train and a week back so I shall not have much hunting and I <u>must</u> get something if possible.'[12]

In 1899 he and Ettie visited and stayed with Lord Minto, Governor-General (Ettie revealing how bored she was by this).[13] Minto retired in 1905 and Richard Davenport-Hines suggests that 'Willie had greatly desired this post', though, as he also points out, Grenfell was not (yet) a peer, which may have limited his chances.[14]

However, the pattern of combining exploration, sport and business continued, and in 1911 he returned to Canada, travelling first to New York with the Duke of Sutherland (known as 'Strath') on the RMS *Olympic*. From New York the party embarked on the Duke's steam yacht *Catania* and sailed up the US coast before entering the St Lawrence River. They continued to Fort William and then took a special train (presumably reserved for his party) all the way to the Pacific coast, stopping at various towns to assess potential investments. The party returned to England on the RMS *Lusitania* in early November – a trip of some four months. Hunting was definitely secondary this time, and he recorded in his diary that he was entertained grandly and played cricket on board ship.[15] Back home, Ettie received a letter dated 15 August 1911 asking where to send the title deeds related to the purchase of an island in Little Georgian Bay in Lake Huron, Canada. Desborough had clearly begun investing.[16]

The *New York Times* of 13 August 1911 ran the following headline:

ENGLISH LANDLORDS COMING TO START TENANT FARMS

The article noted that the Duke of Sutherland and Lord Desborough would visit Canada, where they would explore the merits of creating tenant-farming settlements based around migrants from the Duke's estates in Scotland. The Duke already owned land in various parts of Canada, and Desborough and others would apparently join him as potential investors. Desborough was also thinking of living in Canada, concerned like many wealthy people about increasing rates of taxation in Britain.

In 1888 Desborough had already expressed to Ettie his desire to invest in Canada: 'I believe it would pay to invest in some land out here if one could get it fairly cheap as it is sure to go tremendously . . . The Canadians are much better chaps than the Yanks . . . I am very glad I have seen this country – it is much better than I expected and I believe there is lots of money to be made in it: the climate is splendid and so is the soil and I should like to put some money in it.'[17]

The letters to Ettie from 1911, against a backdrop of strikes and industrial unrest in Britain, and threats of increases to the taxation of estates, explain his plans, linked to the Duke of Sutherland's new venture:

10 August: There are 3 Land Development Camps to visit, & with that & Calgary, & Revelstoke [location of the Dominion Sawmills]; there will be no time for sport.

3 September: I have met with Johnston and Mead Taylor: they have been carefully through the Dominion Sawmills property and accounts. Their report is good and bad: the timber is there all right and the Mills, and there is they compute £100,000 of timber cut and ready to sell, but there will be charges in the selling department, and more money spent in 'yards' all over the country to dispose of the timber before it can be profitably sold.

5 September: I have done a great deal of business here with the Trust [and it] is doing very well – but the Dominion Sawmills will have to be re-organised as regards the selling end which is not well managed. The timber is there but they are not selling it properly.[18]

The party made their way to Brooks, Alberta, a town sponsored by the Canadian Pacific Railway Company (CPR), which built an elaborate irrigation scheme to help expand agricultural production. He continued:

7 September: This country is marvellous & it is to be hoped they will not spoil it. Wonderfully fertile – miles of corn, & then trees and little lakes . . . It is a good thing I came out here: I shall get a grip of the Dominion Sawmills business. The Trust is doing splendidly: we shall work up a big & sound business, through two first rate men here.[19]

8 September: Enormous irrigation works going on – I am going to try to let the C.P.R. reserve me a farm at Strath's price – it is scheduled for double the amount next year. It will be broken up and farmed by contract: Strath's man will look after it. I can sell out some of my Canadian things which have gone up a good deal & pay for it in instalments. The C.P.R. want to make this settlement a success.[20]

J. F. Gilpin's Ph.D. thesis on 'The Canadian Agency and British Investment in Western Canadian Land 1905–1915' argues that British investment in Canada really began in 1911 – the year of Desborough's visit – with the creation of Dominion Sawmills and Lumber Limited, a company incorporated in British Columbia but with a London board of directors, including Willy.[21]

Desborough's letters are full of enthusiasm for the vast lumber resources available and for investing. And his references to the Trust appear to be to an investment trust that backed the sawmills, as government rules forbade ordinary banks from investing in resource projects. It is evident from a list of securities deposited with Lloyds Bank in August 1912 in his name that Desborough was actively buying shares in railways, investment companies and utilities in Western Canada.[22]

The *New York Times* article mentioned above described Desborough as 'very rich' and in its profile of him it commented that he 'has been repeatedly mentioned as the one man of all other best qualified as British Ambassador to the United States owing to his pronounced American sympathies and his celebrity as an all-round athlete'.

It did not come to pass, but his standing in North America remained strong. In 1912 a photographic portrait of Desborough was featured in an extravagantly titled six-volume book by Basil Hansard, *Leaders of the Empire: A Roll of Fame, including Politicians, Ecclesiastics, Lawyers, Sailors, Soldiers, Scientists, Artists, Authors, Musicians, and others who are Men of the Century*.[23] And later, in 1921, a year after Willy had attended the Toronto Congress, names were canvassed for the post of Governor-General of Canada. These included the Prince of Wales, Lord Byng and Lord Desborough.[24] This list was whittled down and a note from the Colonial Office to Lord Stamfordham, the King's Private Secretary, on 11 May 1921 reported on news back from Canada that 'Lord Desborough would be acceptable in every way as Governor-General. I am therefore ascertaining informally whether he would be willing to allow me to submit his name to the King. In the event of his being willing I will have a formal submission.'[25]

On the same day, following an official letter to the King from Winston Churchill, Secretary of State for the Colonies, Stamfordham replied that 'His Majesty will be glad to approve of Lord Desborough as Governor-General of Canada if he is prepared to undertake the office, as to the probability of which the King feels a little doubtful.'[26] But the next day the Colonial Office wrote to Stamfordham clarifying that the matter was ended: 'The King may wish to know at once that Lord Desborough has written today that on private grounds he does not wish his name to be submitted for the Governor-Generalship.'[27] It seems that Ettie was entirely opposed, but Willy may have hoped that as discussion continued, she would change her view. Clearly she didn't.

THE TARIFF COMMISSION

In the early 1900s there had been sustained pressure, not least from the Tariff Reform League, to repurpose the British Empire as a single trading bloc: the so-called Imperial Preference, promoted most notably by Joseph Chamberlain. Inevitably this was opposed by those who favoured free trade and Chamberlain attempted to find a way through the impasse by creating an unofficial Tariff Commission to undertake detailed sectoral analysis and come up with an evidence-led set of proposals. Some fifty-nine 'businessmen' were tasked with carrying out the work, Desborough among them (he was on the agricultural-sector committee). Seven volumes on different industries were assembled over a period of five years, though the report was never published. Desborough was recorded as saying that it would actually have been possible to produce a specific scheme of duties within a month, which could then have been authorised by the Commission.[28]

FIRST WORLD WAR

As Germany's growing military and naval power caused widespread alarm, Desborough joined others in arguing for greater reinforcement of national and imperial defences. Asquith's Liberal government had hoped to salvage some remnants from the failures of the International Peace Conferences at The Hague in 1899 and 1907, which had sought to establish cooperation over the rules and restrictions on the conduct of war. While opposition to the Declaration of London related to a specific concern about the question of seizure of enemy goods carried on neutral ships, the debate highlighted the increasing alarm about growing militarisation.

In the spring of 1914 Desborough was also prominent in a new round of opposition to Irish Home Rule. A so-called British Covenant was signed by those opposing the delayed third Bill by which the government hoped to establish a degree of self-rule for Ireland. On 5 March the *Westminster Gazette* published a 'Ballade of the New Covenant', a poem and 'Who's Who' of the New Covenanters, prominent supporters of the cause, including Willy, listed as: 'Lord Desborough, KCVO. A famous athlete. Represented his University, rowing and running. Twice swam Niagara.' One verse ran:

> Lords Roberts, Lovat, Milner – three
> Determined Diehards in a row,
> All covenanting hard leave me
> Just caring not a tinker's-blow.
> George Hayter Chubb (who lunches so)
> With me alas will cut no ice,
> But think of Desborough, oho
> The man who swam Niagara twice.

Three more verses end with a Desborough line. On 26 March Julian wrote to his father from Potchefstroom in South Africa, where he was serving with the 1st (Royal) Dragoons, 'I *love* the "Westminster" verses about the Covenanters, and it makes me prouder than ever of having you for my father; but it always makes me terribly jealous and envious too, and it is strictly contrary to the Christian religion to be jealous of one's father.'[29]

As the threat of war increased through the summer of 1914, Ettie and Willy were close to key figures in government. Davenport-Hines describes how 'Throughout the escalating crisis Ettie was privileged to hear the most authoritative assessments from the principal actors.'[30] After the assassination of Archduke Ferdinand in Sarajevo on 28 June led to Austria's declaration of war against Serbia, and the bombing of Belgrade a month later was followed by mobilisation in Russia and Germany, it wasn't clear initially whether Britain would be drawn into the conflict. Willy and Ettie had lunch at Downing Street on 30 July with Prime Minister Asquith and his wife Margot, Sir Edward Grey, the Foreign Secretary, Lord Knollys and Waldorf Astor, and that evening Willy dined alone with Lord Kitchener.

Ettie, staying the next weekend at Grimsthorpe Castle in Lincolnshire, wrote on 2 August to Monica: 'Darlingest, the news looks very bad, we have no papers today but lots of telegrams – how it twists one's heart,' and on the next day: 'Nothing could look worse than the news . . . One can only try to keep quiet & calm . . . One longs to do something instead of thinking & thinking.'[31] After the invasion of Belgium by Germany on 4 August, and the expiry of an ultimatum, war was declared (and Kitchener immediately appointed Secretary of State for War).

PROTECTING THE REALM

Grenfell had first engaged with military service as a member of the Harrow Cadet Force, reaching the rank of Sergeant in 1871.[32] In adult life he joined the Buckinghamshire Rifle Volunteers and was a Major in the 1st Battalion from 1900 to 1914, but he never became a regular soldier.[33] Such volunteer forces were created in 1859, but they remained largely localised, with leadership from Lord Lieutenants in each county. Their focus was on home defence, and membership was dominated by middle-class recruits, in part because equipment (both uniforms and weapons) had to be paid for by individuals. By the later part of the nineteenth century, central control over these volunteer forces had grown, and some volunteers saw active service in the Boer War.

In August 1914 a London County Councillor wrote to *The Times* suggesting that a London Defence Force should be set up, and three days later Desborough, now fifty-eight and too old for active service, agreed to become President of an organising committee: the Central Committee of the London Defence Force. As fears of invasion grew and more local forces were mobilising, the War Office became increasingly concerned that this process was out of control. With its priorities understandably elsewhere, in September the War Office authorised the creation of the Volunteer Training Corps (VTC) and in November the London committee was transformed into the Central Association of Volunteer Training Corps with Desborough as its President. A military adviser was appointed, and it became the body to which individual defence forces could affiliate and was responsible on a national basis for the rules and regulations by which they could operate.

In March 1915 Desborough wrote to the King:

> *I am glad to be able to report that from 20 to 40 corps are being affiliated weekly to the Central Association. Some counties such as Surrey and Cheshire will have ten battalions each organised under a county committee under the patronage of the Lieutenant of the County. The fact that your Majesty has taken an interest in the VT Corps has already proved an enormous stimulus to the movement which I hope may prove of some practical utility even beyond the fact that drill and training is of itself a great advantage to the population and might prove of service should there be civil commotion in the country as the Corps understand they are to act with the Civil as well as the Military authorities should the occasion arise.*[34]

The VTC was not allowed to interfere with recruitment into the Regular Army; there were to be no uniforms other than an armband and there was no state funding. By 2 June 2015 there were some 2,000 individual corps, encompassing around 600,000 volunteers, and increasingly the VTC was being drawn upon to guard installations, protect railways and equally to help bring in the harvest.

In October 1915 a private member's Bill, the Volunteer Bill, was introduced in the House of Lords by the Marquess of Lincolnshire. In his opening speech on the Second Reading he set out how:

> Your Lordships will remember that fifteen months ago, at the outbreak of the war, a great flame of patriotism burst out all over the country: young

men flocked to the Colours, and everybody, whatever his age or the position he occupied, was anxious to do what is called 'his bit.' In consequence of that a large number of Volunteer corps, comprising men who had passed military age, were started all over the country, but it was thought at the time – I suppose wisely – by the military authorities that these independent corps might in some way interfere with the recruiting of the new Armies, a million men having been called for to meet the then emergency.

It was necessary that something should be done in the matter, and, as always happens in England, the right man came forward exactly at the right moment to do what was wanted, and that man was Lord Desborough.[35]

Desborough followed by setting out the challenge (and opportunity) for the VTC:

In the first place I should like to say that it has been the one aim and object of the Central Association of Volunteer Training Corps . . . not to add anything to the great burdens which now rest upon the over-worked War Office. In fact, the object of recognising the Central Association of Volunteer Training Corps was to relieve the War Office of the enormous correspondence which arose from the remarkable outburst of patriotism to which the noble Marquess alluded.

When war broke out there rose up in almost every hamlet throughout the country men who were longing to employ their spare time at any rate in preparing themselves to the best of their ability for the duty which might fall upon them of defending their country . . . [So] by a Letter dated November 19, 1914, [the War Office] appointed us as the association which should have the power of affiliating corps, and decreed that these corps, if they did affiliate, should be recognised and given the power to fight for their country.

Since that recognition there was a Letter . . . issued by the Home Office to certain Lords Lieutenant, in which it was plainly stated that it was the duty of every man at this crisis in his country's history, if he was of military age and not otherwise debarred, to enlist in the Army, but that if he was not of military age or otherwise debarred it was his duty to join the nearest Volunteer corps . . . If he did that, he would be allowed to take up arms in case of invasion for the defence of his country; but if he did not do it, such arms as he might have in his possession would be taken away from him and he would be set to perform such menial tasks as might be allotted to him.

In most of the counties of England and Wales there is now a large body of Volunteers officered and drilled without any aid from public funds. Whatever merits we may have, the only article we have received from the Government up to the present time is a small piece of ornamental red flannel with the letters 'G.R.' upon it; but seeing that every man who wears it has the right to bear arms for his country the mark is, I venture to say, one of distinction.[*]

Having got so far in the organisation, there came to the Central Association from all over the country, from those who were entrusted with the defence of the various military districts, requests for the services of these men . . . [and] there are a large number of places where Volunteers, having been asked to do so, are carrying out important duties, in some cases guarding railways, in others protecting aeroplanes and places where munitions are stored.

What became a difficulty was the fact that volunteers had been given the right to carry out these duties, but their 'status' – given they were not soldiers – was not sufficiently clear. Arrangements needed to be formalised so that the VTC could properly dovetail with the requirements of the military and that meant having an appropriately defined status.

In a further debate on the Bill in November 1915, Desborough offered a vivid picture of the VTC's work:

The Sunday before last, I went down to the very large ordnance works at Didcot. I did not go alone, because from various parts of Oxfordshire and Berkshire 900 Volunteers in uniform marched in sections and squads from their various localities to special trains which took them to those ordnance

---

[*] This led to them being called George's Wrecks and Genuine Relics. Desborough described how 'The War Office Letter of November 19 was loyally accepted throughout the country, and we proceeded to organise these corps. The Volunteers in the different hamlets were formed into platoons, the platoons into companies, and the companies into battalions; and finally, when appealed to, the Lords Lieutenant of no less than thirty-eight counties came forward and consented to start what were practically county Volunteer corps.'

Cover of The Volunteer Training Corps Gazette, *1 January 1916.*

stores; and only yesterday morning I heard the colonel in charge there say that it would have been absolutely impossible for him, without the help of those Volunteers, to have despatched the enormous number of trains which there were in Didcot siding on that particular Sunday.

This movement has been largely extended at Oxford. I happened last Sunday to have the honour of shoving a truck in company with the Professor of Political Economy, the Public Orator, the Professor of Geology, and the Professor of Anthropology at Oxford; and these gentlemen and many more Volunteers are going to turn up next Sunday, when we hope to have 1,500 men assisting in this work. What we want to secure is that these men, when working at a place like an ordnance store, should be ipso facto under military law for the time being.[36]

The Volunteer Act only finally came into law in December 1916, but at the start of that year a Military Service Act had imposed conscription on all single men aged between eighteen and forty-one (subsequently up to age fifty-one). It exempted the medically unfit, clergymen, teachers and certain classes of industrial worker. A second Act was passed in May 1916 which extended conscription to married men.

*Lord Desborough overseeing First World War volunteers, Didcot, 1917,
from a press cutting pasted into a family album.*

Conscription caused the creation of Military Service Tribunals that adjudicated as to whether men could be exempted from conscription. If they were exempted, the Tribunal could require them to join the VTC.* In 1917 the War Office claimed that some 100,000 of the volunteers should be doing military service and it was agreed to slim down the VTC, though in early 1918 there were still some 285,000 volunteers. The force then began to wither away and it was suspended in December 1918, before being formally disbanded in January 1920. However, 18,500 men in the motorised corps were kept on until 1921, potentially for use in strikebreaking.[37]

Between 1915 and 1916 Desborough also served as a Representative in France for Lloyd George (as Minister of Munitions), helping boost the output of armaments by retrieving from the Western Front those men whose skills were much needed back in Britain. It was Lloyd George's effectiveness in this post that bolstered his successful bid to become Prime Minister in late 1916.

---

* After the Volunteer Act of December 1916, those exempted from conscription were required to serve the VTC for the duration of the war and undertake a required number of drills on an annual basis.

AIR POWER

Willy Grenfell had his first exposure to the potential of aerial warfare while observing the use of balloons (used for reconnaissance) in the Suakin campaign in the 1880s, and by 1908 he and many others believed that the airship would become a key weapon. However, that was the year that the Wright brothers exhibited their machine in Europe, and the following year Blériot flew across the English Channel. David Cannadine describes the involvement of various aristocrats in the early days of aviation as 'adventure and propaganda, augmented by a little politicking', which helped a number of entities to emerge to promote the development of military aviation.[38] Lord Desborough spoke at a meeting of the Aerial Defence Committee of the Navy League in the Mansion House on 5 May 1913. Supporting the motion of creating an air-defence capacity in Britain, as he was, he noted the scale of voluntary subscription in Germany for raising an air fleet and asked, 'Could we not do the same, including the Dominions in our appeal?' If the thing was to be done, it had to be on a large scale. He suggested going to the Committee of Imperial Defence and argued that 'we can raise an enormous sum to be put at your discretion – it may be for aeroplanes, for dirigibles, for stations around the coast or for schools of flying'.

Later in 1913 an Imperial Air Fleet Committee was created with Desborough as Chairman, to undertake exactly what he had suggested. The aim was to raise awareness of air defence across the Empire and find funds to give each dominion an aeroplane, as the basis for starting its own fleet.[39]

On 17 April 1913 the pioneer British aviator Gustav Hamel had made a 230-mile flight from Dover to Cologne, the first from Britain to Germany. Sponsored by the *London Standard* newspaper and carrying one of its reporters, Frank Duprée, it was arranged in concert with this newly formed Committee.[40] Gustav Hamel, son of Edward VII's Royal Physician, was a debonair young flyer who learned to pilot Blériot planes in France in his early twenties.[41] He helped to convince the government of the military potential of planes by participating in a demonstration to a parliamentary committee at Hendon Aerodrome on 11 May 1911. And on 9 September he delivered the first item of air mail to Windsor Castle, landing on the East Terrace, after making fourteen loop-the-loops in front of King George V and Queen Mary.

With the threat of war imminent, the Committee presented Hamel's plane *Britannia* to the people of New Zealand (it was shipped out at the end of the year but was returned for European war work in 1915). After the formal

Lord and Lady Desborough with Gustav Havel (in cloth cap) for the presentation of the
aeroplane Britannia *to the people of New Zealand, 22 May 1913.*

presentation, Ettie reported, 'Willie went up in the "Britannia", and the
engine broke down, but Hamel landed with great skill.'[42] On the back of this,
Desborough appealed through the press for £10,000 to enable the Committee
to pursue its objectives.[43] He later summarised the Committee's key aims as
being to: 'Rouse the nation to a realisation of the threatening peril from
aeroplanes and airships and the pressing need of the organisation of adequate
means of aerial defence by giving a striking practical object lesson of the
powers of the modern aeroplane.'[44]

Hamel became a friend of the Desboroughs – he landed a plane at Taplow
on 14 July 1913 – and was soon close with Monica.[45] Writing to his mother
from South Africa on 4 December, Julian remonstrated, 'She is <u>not</u> to marry
Hamel, or any blue-blooded idiot.'[46] Tragically, however, on 23 May 1914,
Gustav Hamel crashed his plane in the English Channel and died: lost even
before the war had started.

The Committee even inspired a musical performance, 'Britannia Must Rule
the Air', dedicated to Lord Desborough as President and published in 1913.
Desborough was energetic in leading appeals for funding and attending
widely publicised events. He argued for the military potential of planes, while
using his London Chamber of Commerce connections to raise money. For

Music published for 'Britannia Must Rule the Air', 1913, featuring the young flyer Gustav Hamel and the London Standard *reporter Frank Duprée.*

example, he was in Oxford in early June 1914 for a flying exhibition arranged by the Air Fleet Committee.[47] The event aimed to secure funds to present an 'Oxford' aeroplane to Australia. Although Desborough had gathered some support from the university, it was evident from a subsequent appeal letter of 15 July that trying to raise the necessary £2,000 was quite a challenge.

In these early days of aviation, a flying display by Gustav Hamel was the principal attraction for the Oxford event, which took place just after his fatal crash. His replacement at Oxford was Lord Carbery, who managed to crash his plane while practising, just prior to the exhibition, although he did return to loop the loop and carry passengers for short flights. Despite such risks, Desborough remarked in his speech that he had had the pleasure of going up in the very machine used by Hamel in his flight from Dover to Cologne.

The Imperial Air Fleet Committee's efforts to raise funds to buy planes were only modestly successful – they tried getting loyal citizens and businesses to support the purchase of planes for specific dominions. London gave a plane to South Africa and other machines were donated by Liverpool, Leicester, Leeds, Sheffield, Huddersfield, Manchester, Hull, Birmingham and Glasgow.

Towards the end of the war a piece of Pathé News footage shows a typically smiling Willy in Kingston-upon-Hull leading the ceremonial presentation of a new Sopwith Camel (serial D3388) being offered to the people of Australia.[48] The thousands who attended the ceremony that day would have felt part of an exciting moment, in which the new technologies of flight and the great expanse of Empire could connect for common purpose.[49] The Committee's work did not, however, immediately trigger the creation of air forces in the dominions. On balance, the larger impact seems to have been in raising awareness of the contribution of aeroplanes in modern warfare, Desborough being convinced that any war would now be won in the air.

During the First World War, Desborough balanced his work with the VTC and the Air Fleet Committee, including pairing up visits, given that military uniform was effective for public occasions. He also found time to be Superintendent of the Queen Mary's Royal Naval Hospital in Southend-on-Sea and allowed Taplow Court to be used as a rest home for 'nurses who have suffered in health from the strain of war work and to American officers on leave' and 'open air entertainment is the rule' (including punting trips with Lord Desborough) as described in *The Times*.[50]

After the war, creating such new opportunities across the Empire, whether commercial or sporting, was a Desborough theme and he continued his interest in flight, including through his leadership of the Chamber of Commerce. In January 1919, at the Connaught Hotel, the LCC hosted a meeting chaired by Desborough to discuss 'Commercial aviation in the light of war experiences'.[51] Major General Sir F. H. Sykes, Chief of the Air Staff, speculated in his address on the emergence of transatlantic passenger flights and the role aviation could play in civil society. As with the Thames Barrage project, Desborough was quick to embrace modern developments, albeit driven by a firm commitment to Empire, tradition and British interests.

THE PILGRIMS

In the inter-war years Desborough was engaged with the Pilgrims, a body established to 'promote goodwill, good fellowship and everlasting peace' between Britain and the United States. It was a high-level networking organisation with presidents and prime ministers as members, alongside ambassadors and some of the Royal Family, working to promote connections between politicians, business leaders and those with influence in civil society. He was Chairman from 1919 to 1929, in succession to the founder Sir Harry Brittain.[52]

Lord Desborough hosting the Pilgrims' farewell dinner for Ambassador Kellogg, with the Prince of Wales and Winston Churchill at top table, 30 January 1925.

In January 1924 he reported to Ettie (who was in Cairo), 'The Strike is still on, & I am in London . . . We shall have a great Dinner [in honour of the American Ambassador Frank Kellogg] . . . Socialists, Ambassadors, Lord Chancellors, one Speaker, the P. of Wales.'[53]

Time magazine in 1929 reported on a dinner of the Society in London in June and noted (accurately or not) that 'it is as Chairman of the Pilgrims he [Desborough] is now best known to the world'.[54] The article referred to him slightly disparagingly as the present Yeoman of the Guard and to his tendency to embroider his speeches with 'quips and quiddities'. Desborough had high regard for America, but wasn't above making cryptic comments about Americans, at least when it came to sport. In 1933 he observed (or perhaps quipped), in relation to the America's Cup yacht racing, that 'Britannia may rule the waves but America waves the rules', before adding 'why do they bother to race at sea? Why not just fight it out with barristers on land?'[55]

The Pilgrims operated through social occasions, mostly formal, but its purpose wasn't socialising and it had parallels for Desborough with the Olympic movement, which he believed was a force for good. In his own retirement speech in 1930, Desborough reminded everyone at dinner about the objective of the Pilgrims:

to promote peace and goodwill among all the nations of the World and more especially between our nation and the United States of America. The last two functions given by the Pilgrims during my Chairmanship were one in which forty nations took part in celebration of the signing of the Peace Pact and the other a dinner at which I presided to Mr Kellogg, the author of the Peace Pact . . . and it does emphasize something towards that universal peace which we are all working for.[56]

19

———

Great Losses

Julian Grenfell in the army – the Western Front – wounded and death – 'Into Battle' – death of Billy Grenfell

In previous chapters we have examined the public roles that Lord Desborough pursued during the First World War. Yet the experience of the war had infinitely more impact for him in relation to his family. By 1914 Julian Grenfell was already serving as a regular soldier, and his sister Monica soon decided to become a nursing probationer. Julian's younger brother Billy, who had been working towards the examination for postgraduate study at All Souls, Oxford, applied for an army commission in August 1914.

In the years before 1914, while serving in India and South Africa, Julian expressed his personal enthusiasm for fighting, almost as if it were a particular kind of sport, even if he disliked the army as an institution. After the declaration of war, his regiment, the 1st (Royal) Dragoons, left South Africa on 25 August and arrived in England on 10 September. They spent time in camp on Salisbury Plain before setting off to France on 6 October. By the 11th he recorded his first reactions in a letter to his mother:

We've got within 15 miles of them Germans now, and hope to be at them tomorrow. It's all the best fun one ever dreamed of, and up to now it has only wanted a few shells and a little noise to supply the necessary element of excitement. The uncertainty of it is so good, like a picnic when you don't know where you're going to; and the rush and the hustle of trying to settle things in the whole confusion, unpacking & packing up again, and dumping down men and horses in strange fields or houses or towns, and fighting to get water

*& food and beds for the horses and water and food and beds for the men and
oneself, when one knows that probably another start will be made before
anything is got . . . The roads are chock a block with troops and guns and
supplies and transport and wounded; and aeroplanes in the air.*[1]

This was written from the French side of the border near the Belgian town of
Ypres and included a list of supplies he hoped his mother would send, headed
by a Burberry mackintosh and including a map case, matches, pipe-lighter,
sou'wester, prismatic compass, batteries for his electric torch and new field
glasses. Exchanges of letters were frequent and on the 15th he reported:

*Darling Mother, I've just got your letter of Oct 8. I hope the Burberry will
arrive soon, because it rains like cats and dogs every day, and an ordinary
coat just gets and remains sodden . . . We've been fighting the German
cavalry patrols for the last day or two, but not much damage to either side.
We downed one of their aeroplanes yesterday, which was good; and exciting
– a sudden tremendous burst of fire, maxims and all . . . Only the Christian
virtue of Faith emerges triumphant. It is all the most <u>wonderful</u> fun; better
fun than one could ever imagine.*[2]

As Nicholas Mosley points out, his 'love of war is shocking to modern taste
. . . Julian had no illusions about war: he was not surprised when killing was
killing.'[3] However, when Julian wrote to his mother saying, 'I adore war. It is
like a big picnic without the objectlessness of a picnic. I've never been so well,
or so happy', one senses an expression of fierce bravado in the face of the grim
reality of trench-fighting and worsening physical conditions. While deliberately assertive in tone to Ettie, he was despondent at the difficulties of using
their horses, the raison d'être of a cavalry regiment.[4] Some descriptions,
however, were more nuanced:

*I <u>was</u> pleased with my troop, under bad fire; they used the most filthy
language, talking quite quietly, and laughing, all the time; even after the men
were knocked over within a yard of them. I longed to be able to say that I liked
it, after all one has heard of being under fire the first time. But it's bloody. I
pretended to myself for a bit I liked it; but it was no good; it only made one
careless and unwatchful and self-absorbed. But when one acknowledged to
oneself that it was bloody, one became alright again, and cool.*[5]

Captain Julian Grenfell DSO
photographed by Maull & Fox.

The letters contain frequent expressions of gratitude for supplies sent by Willy and Ettie, interspersed with requests for both basics and extras for his men and himself. On 28 October 1914 he wrote: 'Yes, you are a really great War Mother.' But within two weeks his letters return to his response to the fighting, intended perhaps to lessen his parents' worries (repeating how happy he is), but no doubt stoking further alarm:

> *It is all the best fun; I've never felt so well or happy, or enjoyed anything so much. It just suits my stolid health and stolid nerves and barbaric disposition. The fighting excitement vitalises everything – every sight and word and action. One loves one's fellow man so much more when one is bent on killing him . . . I went to sleep the other day when we were lying low in the trenches, with the shrapnel bursting within 50 yds all the time, and a din like nothing on earth! The noise is continual and indescribable.*[6]

In November, Julian sent a particularly vivid description of his solo effort to combat German snipers by moving yard by yard towards the enemy and how:

I crawled on again very slowly to the parapet of their trench. It was very excit-
ing. I was not <u>sure</u> that there might not have been someone there – or a little
further along the trench. Then the German behind put his head up again. He
was laughing and talking. I saw his teeth glisten against my foresight, and I
pulled the trigger very steady. He just gave a grunt and crumpled up.[7]

That afternoon, Julian crept again towards the German trench but found it empty, so the next morning he returned, killed two soldiers and made a crucial report on the movement of troops. Julian won the Distinguished Service Order (DSO) for this exploit, but in his 'game book' he simply added two entries: 'November 16th: 1 Pomeranian' and 'November 17th: 2 Pomeranians'.[8]

At the end of November, Julian had three days' leave back at Taplow, but by early December had returned to France and offered thanks for more supplies: a stove had arrived, 'a most glorious thing', and a pair of 'hawking gauntlets. I retract everything I said against them. They are perfect . . . Your cake will be glorious for the mess.'[9] Writing to 'My darling Dad' on 22 November, Julian thanked Willy for his letters, teased him that he hoped that 'Germany is getting no more copper', and after offering an update on the German military position, explained that 'Your Canadian coat is the admiration of all beholders, and does me very well.'[10]

By early 1915 Willy had started the Taplow Volunteers and been appointed to his role of President of the Central Association of Volunteer Training Corps, while Ettie was organising with the Maidenhead Red Cross, Billy was serving with the 8th Rifle Brigade and Monica had completed her training at the London Hospital. Letters through the spring of 1915 include Julian's descriptions of virtual stalemate at the Front and his time in and out of the trenches. However busy, the family, like so many others, were constantly worried. In early March he wrote: 'My dear Dad . . . You must be having a tremendous lot of work with the Volunteers. It is a good thing that they are taking over the bridges, etc., and it will relieve a lot of men for other things. But it must be a great undertaking to have to deal with so many of them. They certainly ought to make you a general. Why haven't they?' And with further sniping at the Germans in mind, he asked if he could now have Willy's .303 rifle with telescopic sights – 'I would be awfully glad to have it, and to have it soon.' Julian had previously asked if the Taplow butler could send out a supply of spirit every fortnight, and noted, 'I have also written to Mr Bart to send out my little Colt repeating pistol, and some extra ammunition for it.'[11]

Julian was offered leave in April 1915 and visited Paris for the first time. On 5 May he wrote: 'My darling Dad – Thank you very much for your letters, also for the Port wine . . . Will you please thank Mother for electric torches, chocolate, cigarettes, and pipe-lighters, for the men, and the gas respirators, which all arrived quite safely. We are all tremendously fit and well.'[12] Monica was now working at the military hospital at Wimereux near Boulogne (having been chaperoned out by Ettie at the end of 1914) and Willy and Ettie planned what would have been an exceptional visit to France.

On Tuesday 12 May Ettie wrote to Monica:

One line to say that after simply unspeakable difficulties, which at one time seemed final, that angel Lord K [Kitchener] has got us permission to go to Boulogne . . . I expect you will have got my letter asking you to engage us rooms at the Hotel Folkestone, unless you can find anything decent at Wimereux. Two small bedrooms for Daddy and me, and a room for Gaston . . . I don't believe there is the faintest chance of our getting up to the Front with this heavy fighting going on, but I do hope that Julian will get down to us . . . ps I am bringing out such a lovely poem of Julian's to show you.[13]

At 4 a.m. on Wednesday 13 May the Germans started a heavy bombardment of a hill and trenches near to the second line occupied by Julian's Dragoons. At midday Julian walked up the hill to check if German troops were advancing, and on seeing that they were, took a message to the Somerset Yeomanry in the trench in front. He went back up the hill with the General in charge of his Brigade and a shell landed close; both were wounded but a shell splinter hit Julian's head. As Nicholas Mosley describes, 'He was so cheerful that people did not think his wound was serious. He said "I think I shall die". And when a friend remonstrated with him he said "You see if I don't!"'[14]

After being treated in a nearby dressing station, he was moved to No. 10 Casualty Clearing Station with the presumption that he would be sent back to England to recover. A pencilled note from Julian dated 14 May reached Taplow on the 16th:

Darling Mother, Isn't it wonderful and glorious that at last after long waiting the Cavalry have put it across the Boches on their flat feet and have pulled the frying pan out of the fire for the second time . . . We are practically wiped out, but we charged and took the Hun trenches yesterday. I stopped a Jack Johnson with my head, and my skull is slightly cracked. But I'm getting on splendidly. I did awfully well. Today I go down to Wimereux, to hospital. Shall you be there? All all love Julian of the 'Ard 'Ead. Longing to see you and talk!! Bless you![15]

'Jack Johnson' was slang, derived from the American heavyweight boxing champion, to describe the impact of a heavy German 15 cm artillery shell. The upbeat tone was typical of Julian's bravado. Monica visited him the next day, and in a telegram home she relayed that, despite his wound, there was no need for anxiety. As Ettie recounts, 'Billy came to Taplow from Aldershot at 12 that Sunday morning, and Ivo from Eton to say goodbye to him [Billy]. It was a lovely day; they were happy.' Willy and Ettie anticipated that another telegram would tell them on which ship Julian would arrive back in England, but instead a message came from the Commandant of the Boulogne Hospital with worrying news: 'Your son here wounded in head. Better come. Use this as permit.' Ettie commented that 'Billy, Ivo and Imogen were most brave and calm; the thought of their faces was often a help in the hours to come. That was Billy's last day at Taplow.'[16]

Billy, as planned, set off to join his regiment, but in a harrowing scramble Willy and Ettie – with special permission from the Admiralty – crossed the Channel that night on an ammunition boat. Monica recalled how 'My parents walked into my room just as I was washing my face and doing my hair, a little after 5 o'clock the next morning: it seemed like a miracle.'[17] An X-ray indicated that the splinter had penetrated one and a half inches through Julian's skull and into his brain; he was operated on, it was thought success-fully, but it would take some days to confirm this. Ettie's account (in her journal) of the following days is agonising, recalling her conversations with Julian and the day-by-day, hour-by-hour hope of recovery. The family tried to comfort each other, with Monica frequently present and Billy visiting on Wednesday the 20th (after his Rifle Brigade Battalion was rested near Boulogne following deployment at the Front). Five days later, Billy wrote to his father in a more fatalistic tone:

My dear Daddy – I got your second letter to-day with the less good account of dear Ju. The issue lies with God alone, & He will decide it for the best. I pray to Him to be with you all in these days, and to uphold the splendid courage that you have shown through all . . . I thank Him too for having allowed the dear boy to show his glorious valour to all the world before he was struck down.[18]

PEERESS'S ANXIETY.

Captain the Hon. Julian Grenfell, D.S.O.
—(Maull and Fox.)

Lady Desborough.—(Val L'Estrange.)

Captain the Hon. Julian Grenfell has been wounded at the front. His mother, Lady Desborough, has gone over to help to nurse him.

News report of Julian Grenfell's injury in the Maidenhead Advertiser, *May 1915.*

That the great war is now being pushed forward in grim earnest is too manifest by the long list of casualties pub-
War Victims. lished daily. Officers as well as men are falling. Captain Gledstanes, of Taplow, is, alas! among the killed, while Captain Julian Grenfell, D.S.O., eldest son of Lord and Lady Desborough, when leading his company of Dragoons in an attack on the enemy was seriously wounded in the head, and is now in a military hospital at Boulogne. Not only will the sympathies of my readers go out to the relatives of these officers, but to those of the rank and file who have fallen in battle. Meanwhile, the depleted ranks must be filled up. Lord Kitchener asks for 300,000 men. He must have them. How many from Maidenhead? A goodly number, I hope—and single men should be the first to volunteer. It is not fair that married men should join the colours while so many young fellows with no ties or encumbrances hang back, content to see others don the khaki and shoulder the rifle to fight for them.

While the prospects for recovery diminished, Willy and Ettie remained steadfast in their hopes, even as Julian underwent a second operation. Monica commented later that 'The nurses looking after Julian were so excellent and wonderful, especially Sister Knight. During the last days of Julian's illness, she once told me to take Daddy out and away from the hospital for a short time on some pretext – she said the long waiting was harder to bear for a man.'[19] On Tuesday the 25th Willy wrote to Lord Kitchener, who was especially fond of Julian, to say that he was 'very bad: there is little or no hope now'.[20] That morning his condition had worsened, and Ettie describes how Julian said:

'Hold my hand until I go'. A shaft of sunlight fell across his feet; he smiled at his mother, and said 'Phoebus Apollo'. After that he did not speak again, except once, about 2.30, to say his father's name. He snapped his fingers for a cigarette, but could not smoke it . . . At 7.30

on Wednesday morning, May 26th, they thought that he was dying, but he lived on till 20 minutes to 4 in the afternoon. He knew them till the very end, and moved his mother's hand to his lips. At the moment that he died, he opened his eyes a little, with the most radiant smile that they had ever seen on his face.[21]

Ettie had already forwarded Julian's poem 'Into Battle' to *The Times* and it was published on Friday 28 May, with Julian's death announced the same day. The final lines of 'Into Battle' read:

> Through joy and blindness he shall know,
> Not caring much to know, that still
> Nor lead nor steel shall reach him, so
> That it be not the Destined Will.
>
> The thundering line of battle stands,
> And in the air Death moans and sings;
> But Day shall clasp him with strong hands,
> And Night shall fold him in soft wings.

The poem captured some defiant elements of the national mood (even if somewhat religiose and sentimental) and attracted wide interest. Henry James referred to 'those extraordinarily living and breathing, ringing and stinging, verses . . . out of which, round his sublime young image, a noble and exquisite legend will flower'.[22]

Willy wrote to Kitchener again on the 28th: 'Dear Julian is to be buried today: his end was quite peaceful & he looked very happy.'[23] After the service Willy, Ettie and Monica retreated to recuperate for a few days at a house nearby in the Hardelot Forest, and Billy joined them for a precious afternoon. This was the last time they saw him. On 1 June Billy wrote to his mother: 'The more I think of Darling J, the more I seem to realise the nothingness of death. He has just passed on, outsoared the darkness of our night . . . How beautiful his poem is. It perfectly expresses the unity & continuity of all created things in their Nature. I pray that one tenth of his gay spirit may descend on me.'[24]

In a four-page letter to the King, written from France on 30 May in response to a telegram, Willy explained: 'Our beloved son's end came very peacefully and we were thankful to be with him for the last days of his life, although the alternatives of hope and fear were hard to bear. He gave his life very gladly for his King and Country.'[25]

Mary Wemyss visited Willy and Ettie, a fortnight after Julian's death, and described Ettie as: 'Quite wonderfully calm, and upheld by a sense of Julian's continued presence and love . . . I had tea with Willy; my heart aches for him, he looked so crushed, so seared, so patient and so brave.'[26]

In her journal, Ettie later included a piece by the poet, author and critic Edmund Gosse from the *Edinburgh Review* in October 1917, entitled 'Some Soldier Poets', in which he referred to a question asked by a fellow officer: 'Could any other man in the British army have knocked out a heavyweight champion one week and written that poem the next?' and Gosse went on to comment:

'Into Battle' remains, and will probably continue to remain, the cleverest lyrical expression of the fighting spirit of England in which the war has found words. It is a poem for soldiers, and it gives noble form to their most splendid aspirations. Julian Grenfell wrote, as he boxed and rode, as he fought in the mud of Flanders, as the ideal sporting Englishman of our old, heroic type.[27]

Billy exchanged letters with his parents through June and July. He asked for his .275 Mannlicher rifle to be sent out, together with ammunition, and commented to Willy that 'The National Volunteers are appreciated at last at their true value. I do wish they would send you out with an Army Corps. Our Generalissimos have not all got that iron nerve or that push-and-go which is requisite.'[28] Ettie had written with Taplow news, including: 'Poor Daddy is so very unwell too, with a dreadfully bad knee, sprained, I suppose . . . He is really quite crippled and of course it is so bad for him getting no exercise.'

Billy wrote to Ettie, and thanked her for jam and for a book of poems by Rupert Brooke (who had died on 23 April), which caused him to comment disconsolately, 'God, how he felt. I am glad not to be in England now. What a sad, disgraceful, unennobled, burglarious huckster among nations we are; and we are not doing much out here to right it, whether because we cannot or because they won't let us.'

He wrote about their immediate loss: 'Darling Julian is so constantly beside me, and laughs so debonairly at my qualms and hesitations. I pray for one-tenth of his courage.'[29]

*Newspaper image of Second Lieutenant
Billy Grenfell with the 8th Rifle Brigade at the
Western Front, 1915.*

Ettie wrote to Billy on Monday 2 August expressing her great concern about the Battle of Hooge, and wanting to know where he was.[30] Queen Mary's diary for the same day includes the entry: 'Rained all day, detestable . . . After luncheon drove to Taplow to see poor Ettie Desborough, I had not seen her since her son was killed. I stayed with her an hour, she was wonderful . . . half an hour after I had left they received the news of the death of their second son "Billy". It is too sad.'[31]

It was the most dreadful news, no less appalling for having been so much feared. On 30 July Billy had been leading his platoon in a charge and was killed less than a mile from where Julian had been wounded. Though buried by fellow soldiers where he fell, subsequent shelling caused his body to be lost. 'He is lying there now,' Willy wrote to Nancy Astor on 6 August, 'in front of all.'[32]

The losses and grieving of others, with sons of friends also gone, added to the ghastly common tragedy unfolding in these months.[33] Julian and Billy's cousins Riversdale and Francis Grenfell had been killed: Riversdale in September 1914 and Francis (having been awarded the Victoria Cross in August 1914) in May 1915, two days before Julian. Ettie's Christian faith helped sustain her, but the impact on the family was immense. The thought, which Ettie expressed, that the two boys would not now miss each other – united in heaven – can only have offered limited comfort. She wrote to Lord Kitchener on 9 August: 'They envisaged death very clearly, and went gaily to meet it, and how could we wish it otherwise, or wish to bring them back from joy and freedom. They always thought of death as a gateway, not a barrier, and the path to new life and work.'[34]

The shock rippled widely; commiserations on the second Grenfell loss and tributes to Julian and Billy flowed in. Margot Asquith wrote in her *Autobiography*:

In less than six months Lord and Lady Desborough had lost their two sons; young men of 25 and 28, who combined all that life can give of courage, brains and good feeling and I could hardly think of them without tears. . . . While discussing the Grenfell brothers with Lord Kitchener at dinner that night, I said with impulse that I thought faith should be rewarded in this world by more knowledge, and that I longed for one glimpse of God's purpose – if only a gleam of hope as to our sure immortality. The expression on Lord Kitchener's face was one of puzzled kindness, and he handed me the port. To hide my emotion he turned abruptly to the table and, changing the subject, said we had only ourselves to thank for the failures of war.[35]

20

---·---

Dynastic Tragedy

*Ettie's 'stubborn gospel of joy' – Pages from a Family Journal –
memorials – the death of Ivo*

With heavy casualties on the Western Front through 1915, and large-scale
clashes the following year, including the naval Battle of Jutland in June, there
were many more British and German deaths. A generation of young men was
torn apart, decimating families across Britain, Europe and the British Empire.
In June 1916 Lord Kitchener was on a diplomatic mission to Russia, on board
the armed battleship HMS *Hastings*, when it hit a mine off Orkney and more
than 700 men were drowned, including Kitchener himself. Kitchener's friends
at Taplow were much affected by his death. Among the children of the Souls
– known by some as 'the Coterie' – the deaths of Hugo and Yvo Charteris,
Charles Lister, Bron Lucas, John Manners, Edward Horner and Raymond
Asquith (son of the Prime Minister) were bitter losses. The death of the poet
Patrick Shaw-Stewart in particular, on Christmas Eve 1917, was a huge blow
for Ettie.

A predictable response was to seek solace by trying to make contact with
the dead. Spiritualism already had a growing following through the nineteenth
century and Godfrey Webb, an older writer and one of the Souls, had a strong
interest, shared by A. J. Balfour and others. The physicist Sir Oliver Lodge
published a book after his own son was killed in 1915, titled *Raymond, Or Life
and Death: With Examples of the Evidence for the Survival of Memory and Affection After Death*. Under Lodge's influence some of Willy's and Ettie's friends
attended seances, as they did themselves, believing that they might be in
touch with Julian and Billy.

Ettie apparently refused to wear mourning clothes and continued to see friends, to chat and make jokes, and her courage – her 'stubborn gospel of joy' – was perceived by friends as an inspiration. Cynthia Asquith commented, 'It is the end of one's youth, all this. Ettie and poor Willy. How can they face such utter desolation, such extinction of joy, glamour and hope.'[1]

It was Lord Rosebery who suggested to Ettie that she might create a book as a memorial for Julian and Billy. In March 1916 Ettie wrote to her friend, the scholar Walter Raleigh, that 'I want to make their own writings & sayings tell the short story, with a very sifted few of the letters about them, & hardly a word besides. It will of course be only a little private record, for closest friends.'[2] In the event, Ettie worked tirelessly to compile an extensive selection of letters from school and college, interspersed with her commentary on their childhood (drawn from the pages of her journal and scrapbooks) as well as letters from Julian in his early days in the army, from him and Billy at the Front, letters between the children and some of the many letters of condolence received by her and Willy after their deaths.

Julian, Ettie and Billy in The Tatler, *11 August 1915, based on the 1910 photograph; headed with a quotation from Kipling: 'If blood be the price of admiralty / Lord God, we ha' paid in full.'*

In June 1916 Ettie sent the manuscript of *Pages from a Family Journal 1888–1915* to the printers (Spottiswoode, Ballantyne & Co Ltd. in Eton High Street). While working on the proofs she told Lord Kilbracken that she had 'cut out every single criticism, even the mildest, of people, & discussion of people, except words of light passing praise, & hoped so to defend the book a little from within, if it *did* ever slip into non-intimate hands'.[3] Ettie's close editing evidently ensured that Julian's phase of instability (when he was fiercely critical of his mother) wouldn't be visible, and she selected – and occasionally enhanced – the key events and scenery of their lives to make them appear as attractive as she recalled them. It was, however, a great enterprise, extending to 660 pages. Although Ettie originally planned to print only fifty copies, 250 were despatched that summer to family and selected friends, together with brief covering notes from Ettie.

Willy wrote a short preface:

The following pages have been compiled by my wife from the Journal which she kept for our children from their earliest years. The book is privately printed, and is intended for Julian and Billy's brother and sisters, and for their most intimate friends.

The boys wrote freely, and their letters were often too personal to be printed in full, although they have not been cut down without a sense of loss . . .

It is hoped that the few great friends who see the book will be reminded of the happy times with which Julian and Billy will always be associated.

Desborough, Taplow Court, June 22, 1916[4]

Friends responded with sympathetic warmth. Ettie's women friends relayed how touched they were – Diana Manners telling Duff Cooper that it left her 'sobbing as though her heart would break' and Margot Asquith referring to it as 'full of vast sketches of love'. Rudyard Kipling (whose son John had been killed in September 1915) called it 'a most wonderful volume quite apart from its record of those two splendid boys and the home life that gave them their strength. We have read it . . . aloud and have laughed and cried together.' John Buchan described it as a 'an extraordinarily *rich* book' while Maurice Baring said it was 'much more than a record of Billy & Julian. It is like an emblem, a banner and microcosm . . . of all we are fighting for. It is a reflection of the soul & spirit & the *core* of the heart of England.'[5]

Ettie had poured into the book her intense love for her sons, fired by her emotional desolation at their loss. She may not have intended it to have a wider symbolic role, but given the response to Julian's poem 'Into Battle', she cannot have been surprised. Nor is it clear how much she planned that her extensive and sometimes coy portrayal of an almost too perfect well-to-do family life would clash with accounts in their last letters of the brutal horrors of the Western Front.

Julian and Billy were part of the 'Lost Generation', a 'legendary cohort of heroes' as Davenport-Hines puts it.[6] Various collective efforts started to emerge to create memorials for those killed in the war. They ranged from the unrealised project for a Hall of Remembrance, proposed by Lord Beaverbrook as Minister of Information, for which the British War Memorials Committee (formed in February 1918) commissioned works from prominent artists, to the Cenotaph in Whitehall, the Tomb of the Unknown Soldier in Westminster Abbey, the many local memorials across British towns and villages and the larger-scale structures in France and Belgium.[7] These included the Menin Gate in Ypres (one of the sites for commemoration for those whose bodies were never recovered), on which Billy's name is carved.

During the war, the painter William Rothenstein produced his own response, inspired by seeing a degree ceremony in Oxford and being reminded of processional frescoes from Renaissance Italy. He imagined a presentation of degrees when some of those killed would be brought together, including Julian and Billy, pictured with gowns over their military uniforms.

Julian and Billy Grenfell on the left and right of Rupert Brooke; detail from William Rothenstein's unfinished cartoon for a mural, 1916.

Rothenstein went as far as seeking advice from Winston Churchill and Edward Marsh (himself a patron of the arts) on who should be included, consulting their parents and requesting photographs from which he could paint. He exhibited the panels, poignantly unfinished, in October 1916, at the Eleventh Arts and Crafts Exhibition at the Royal Academy. They were not well received, with P. G. Konody, art critic of the *Observer*, suggesting, 'Mr Rothenstein has set himself an impossible task; but even if due allowance is made for the insuperable difficulties he has scarcely done himself justice.'[8] Edward Marsh, however, wrote to say, 'I think it very beautiful. You have given a beautiful vision of Billy Grenfell, and in essence it's very like what he was when I first knew him.'[9]

Pain for Willy may have been relieved in part through his continued hard work on the volunteer force during the war. However, he spent the second half of October 1915 receiving treatment at the spa in Harrogate, staying at the Hotel Majestic. He described to Ettie how 'at 8am I take 10 ounces of strong warm sulphur, & 10 ounces at 8.15 and 10 ounces magnesia water at 5pm . . . and Vichy, massage, douche, needle bath on alternate days'.[10] Part of the treatment was for one of his knees – now aged sixty, he complained that he could not run – but he was also 'in a very low state all round when I came'. He recovered sufficiently to travel to France in December 1915, to lead a team from the Labour Supply Department investigating which skilled men could be released from the Front, given the need for key workers to help increase munitions production in Britain (from ship joiners and furnace builders to pipe fitters and brass finishers).[11] While there, he took advantage of the opportunity to speak with those who served alongside Billy. Writing to Ettie on 14 December, he described how:

Charles Lister, John Manners, Julian Grenfell, Rupert Brooke, Billy Grenfell, Hugo Charteris and Edward Horner in one of three panels of William Rothenstein's unfinished but remarkable cartoon of 1916 for a memorial mural of the fallen sons of the Souls, on display at Taplow Court.

Yesterday we went . . . up towards Ypres. I saw the 8 Batt. R.B. in mud up to their knees in a so called rest-camp. Gladstone I had a long talk with, and Billy's Platoon sergeant who came back with 5 men only of that platoon – He said Billy's last words were 'Remember you are Englishmen' & then 'Charge – Platoon.' [12]

And two days later:

I saw Col Machlachlan & Sheepshanks and was with them an hour & saw Billy's servant – We had long talks about Billy, and I gave them both photos – Col M was so affectionate about Billy, and full of his quaint doings which are quite a tradition in the Battalion. [13]

Willy had hoped to see where Billy had been killed as, although there had been a temporary grave, his body had not been recovered. But on the 20th he told Ettie that 'it was impossible to get along the road to Ypres – shells were dropping all along the road'. [14]

Few of Willy's feelings are recorded from this period, but on the anniversary of Julian's death in May 1916 he wrote to Ettie (who was staying by the sea): 'This time last year comes back to one very vividly, and I am glad that you are away in peace and quiet – but it is never very far from one's thoughts at any time.' [15] And the following year he noted how 'one thinks of this week two years ago – more and more as time goes on, and of dear old Bill'. [16] Life for all of them was fundamentally changed, and Cynthia Asquith commented in her diary, after a visit to Panshanger in January 1917, that 'Poor Desborough is most piteous . . . He looks like some great animal who has been struck on the brow, neither wanting nor expecting conversation.' [17]

Amid their continuing grief, though with ongoing support from family and friends, the question of a possible memorial began to form. The writer and poet Hilaire Belloc was among those who, when writing to Ettie in August 1915, had expressed a view about memory and immortality:

We should not deny the fact of separation, nor deceive ourselves with imaginary things, because any falsehood or illusion is a drug, and unworthy of human majesty. We should accept the full burden of what is plainly true, absence and separation, but we should not make our final conclusion upon that, or let the mind stop there in its judgment . . . There is no great love

that believes itself capable of ending, or that does in fact end. It is of the very
stuff of immortality.[18]

A poignant photograph of Desborough standing with Ivo and Imogen was
published in *The Tatler* in 1919 under the title 'Whose Privilege It Is – To Have
Suffered Irreparable Loss for his Country and for Freedom', exemplifying the
very public nature of their losses. Just after the end of the war, Ettie recorded in
her journal that 'We went to see Mr Bertram Mackennal's new model for the
Phoebus Apollo (the other model most unfortunately got broken, in the clay)'.[19]
This was a sculptural memorial planned for the south terrace at Taplow Court,
not far from the old walled burial ground that contains the family vault built by
Pascoe Grenfell, situated in a leafy corner a short distance from the Saxon
tumulus. When Willy and Ettie commissioned the Australian artist Mackennal
– who had designed the Olympic medals in 1908 – to create a representation of
Apollo in his horse-drawn chariot (with Julian's last words in mind), they
wanted the text of Julian's 'Into Battle' to be carved on the back.

In the immediate post-war period the Desboroughs' lives returned to a mix

Period photograph of the Grenfell memorial by Sir Bertram Mackennal, Taplow Court,
unveiled 1920.

of Willy's busy public service, dominated by the Police Committee and the Thames Conservancy, with a less ostentatious version of the country-house social round that Ettie had previously organised (though with many notable guests still invited to Taplow Court), along with visits to Scotland and her continued service at Court.[20] But Pathé News footage showing Willy in uniform unveiling the new War Memorial in Maidenhead on 5 December 1920 demonstrates how every memorial event must have reinforced their grief.[21]

Death was unexpectedly in the air on Thursday 2 December 1920 when Willy found out that his own death had been mistakenly reported in the previous day's edition of the *Birmingham Gazette* while supposedly visiting that city, and his obituary then published in *The Times*.[22] He had been at home on the Wednesday night (rather than in Birmingham) but came into the Bath Club to escape the flood of messages of condolence that were pouring in to his wife. When he arrived around noon he was given an especially 'hearty welcome'. In fact, it was the 8th Earl of Bessborough (Chairman of the engineering company Guest, Keen and Nettlefolds) who had collapsed and died while speaking at a dinner in Birmingham.

The mistaken obituary prompted this possibly apocryphal telephone exchange between Desborough and the editor of *The Times*: 'Look here you've published my obituary this morning.' To which the editor replied, 'I'm sorry my Lord – where did you say you were calling from?'[23]

Ettie's journal for these years is taken up with Ivo's progress and Monica's and Imogen's social connections and marriages. Ivo had finished at Eton in 1916, entered Sandhurst and joined the Grenadier Guards, with every intent of following his brothers into active service, but Willy and Ettie discussed with the military authorities how he might be kept away from danger. Willy hoped that Ivo's poor eyesight might ensure that he didn't serve, and described to Ettie in August 1916 how Ivo had a medical examination at the War Office and was declared 'unfit', as even with glasses his sight was not thought good enough. There might still be an appeal, but he described how: 'Ivo was very dejected, but after all you cannot get into the Army if they won't have you, and he will have done everything possible. I think the next Board may pass him . . . It would be a great relief if they would not have Ivo, but I am doing all that can be done. I do not think the war can last long enough for him to go out.'[24]

In the event, Ivo wasn't on active service before the end of the war. In 1920 he went up to Christ Church, Oxford, to study agriculture but, although he won a blue in boxing (and spent whatever money he could, despite his father's complaints), he didn't complete his degree and took up estate management, training with Lord Bledisloe at Lydney in Gloucestershire. After Lydney, Ivo went to farm near Hawkhurst in Kent with Stanley 'Joe' Clarke – in a joint enterprise for which he received some modest support from his parents. Davenport-Hines comments that 'Like Julian in the army or Monica in the Whitechapel hospital wards, Ivo was reacting against the de-luxe sophistication of Taplow, and needed earthier companions than his mother's manicured, perfumed and pomaded guests.'[25]

Before long Monica was engaged to the dashing figure of Air Marshal Sir John (Jack) Salmond, who had a distinguished record of flying and command from the First World War and continued in senior posts in the air force through the inter-war years. His first wife, Helen Lumsden, had died in childbirth in 1916, and he and Monica were married at St Margaret's Westminster in June 1924. In due course they had two children, Julian and Rosemary. Following Imogen's introduction to London society in 1923, and having disentangled herself from a potential engagement to Tyrone Waterford, she met Henry Rainald, 6th Viscount Gage (known as George). They married at St Nicolas' Church, Taplow, on 26 February 1931. A fragment of British Pathé footage shows the bride holding white lilies and stepping out from a large automobile amid a busy throng outside the church. George Gage had served in the war as a Captain in the Coldstream Guards and as a Lord-in-Waiting at Court, but having inherited Firle Place in Sussex in 1912, he became immersed in managing the house and estate. He and Imogen had three children: George, Nicolas and Camilla.

George, Camilla and Nicolas Gage, photographed by Bassano at Taplow Court, 27 July 1939.

In January 1925 Willy wrote to Ettie (in Switzerland) with news of Ivo's two-seater car:

Please give my very best love to Mog [Imogen] and tell her that I have just had a letter from Ivo who is delighted with his 'Lucky Five'. . . He also says that he went into the garage at full speed, and forgot how to stop, and smashed a pet box of the Major's, but he thinks that his 'Lucky Five' is going to save him from these adventures in future.[26]

Sadly, this wasn't the case. He was driving near Hawkhurst in late September 1926 when the steering wheel broke, he collided with a wall and a heavy stone fell on the front of his head. He was taken to Hawkhurst Hospital and a message reached Willy and Ettie who were staying in Bath (where Willy was being treated for rheumatism). Ivo remained in a coma after emergency surgery, with Willy and Ettie at his bedside, and Imogen in support. (Monica, meanwhile, was seven months pregnant.) Despite initial improvement Ivo died, on 8 October, after exactly the same number of days during which Julian had been treated in Boulogne eleven years before. Tucked into her journal for these years is an envelope with a handwritten account by Ettie, laying out in terrible detail every moment of her hopes, fears and distress.

Ettie's friend Maurice Baring wrote a poem, titled 'Ivo Grenfell, October 8, 1926':

'What have they done to you, where have they taken you?
Answer us, Ivo, my son.'
'I have sailed far away on a marvellous voyage,
With Julian and Billy and Bron.'
'Shall there not come to us, news of you, word from you,
Sign of you, Ivo, my son?'
'I am nearer to you than the closest of whispers,
With Julian and Billy and Bron.'
'The Autumn wind blows and the leaves are deserting us,
Summer leaves, Ivo, my son.'
'The same wind came blowing in Springtide and Autumn,
For Julian and Billy and Bron.'
'Breathe but a message to say all is well with you,
Just a word, Ivo, my son.'
'Our word to you is: "Let God have His way with you":
Ivo and Julian and Billy and Bron.'[27]

This was a further family disaster, unexpected and ghastly. According to Jane Abdy and Charlotte Gere, 'those who knew [Ettie] well said that this useless tragedy saddened her far more than the deaths of Julian and Billy in the glory of battle'.[28] Writing to Monica on 28 October, Willy wrote: 'Dearest Mon . . . It is almost impossible to realize that we shall not see our beautiful Ivo again . . . yr loving Dad.'[29] Two days earlier Ettie had emphasised to Monica how much Willy had adored Ivo: 'Only you & I & Mogsie know what this was to him – the cumulative anguish.'[30] Family life would continue, but diminished from what it had been, and the Desborough title would die out.*

Willy, Sir Theodore Cook and Ivo, Taplow Court, early 1920s.

---

* Ettie exerted whatever influence she could to have the Desborough title preserved – by skipping a generation, potentially to Monica's son Julian – but to no avail.

21

—◆—

Last Years

Whiteslea Lodge, Panshanger and Taplow – an autobiography? – Oxford oration – health in decline – death on 8 January 1945 – tributes and honour – Walter de la Mare's 'The Rapids'

After Ivo's death in 1926, Whiteslea Lodge passed to Willy and became a special place of retreat and renewal for the family. A section of the Norfolk Broads had been purchased in 1908 by Bron Lucas, (Ettie's cousin, Auberon Herbert, 8th Baron Lucas) Edward Grey and Edwin Montagu – politicians and members, later, of the same Cabinet – with the intention of creating a bird sanctuary. This was a few years after the fledgling National Trust had founded the country's first nature reserve at Wicken Fen in 1899, ninety miles south and east. Bron Lucas also bought Heigham Sound, Horsey Mere and Hickling Broad, which had with it a small thatched cottage, Whiteslea Lodge, built around 1870.[1] He extended the cottage in 1909, and decided to leave the property and his share of the Broad to Ivo Grenfell. So, when Bron died in 1916 of wounds sustained while serving in the Royal Flying Corps in northern France, it was Ivo who took on the mix of responsibilities for nature and birdlife that came with the 3,000-acre estate.

Willy and Ettie made further improvements, including putting the house on a concrete raft to stop it sinking. In the later 1920s and '30s they would stay each summer, with children and grandchildren visiting, while in the winter Willy enjoyed a mix of wildfowl shooting with the care of the marshes. Around 1929, as part of the renovations, Willy and Ettie commissioned four large murals representing the birdlife of the marshes from the wildlife artist Roland Green, who lived nearby on the Broad. They added further paintings by Green over a number of years.

Roland Green working on the larger panels for Whiteslea Lodge.

The harvesting of reeds and sedge and the nurturing of endangered species, such as bittern and marsh harrier, were overseen by Jim Vincent, the long-standing bailiff and head keeper.* Writing to Monica from Whiteslea in September 1928, Willy remarked how 'Here we have been flighting and partridge shooting with neighbours and ourselves & have got a good few . . . three days of 40 brace and the teal are coming in.'² An article in *The Illustrated Sporting and Dramatic News* of August 1934 referred to the broad and marsh at Whiteslea as having 'judicious preservation and keepering' which have made it 'probably the best all-round wildfowl shoot in England'. It noted that 'An average of a thousand duck and between two and three thousand coot are killed each year at Hickling', so the mix of conservation and culling continued.³ [See *Chapter 7 Outstanding Sportsman.*]

In his Whiteslea diary Willy gives a detailed daily account of the weather and the shooting and fishing – often for pike. A typical entry (Sunday 4 March 1934) records: 'My knee was bad. I fished in the afternoon and got 5 pike: 17lbs – 8lbs – 5lbs – 6lbs – 2½ lbs.'⁴ In April 1936 a 'Mr Seth from the Zoo' brought eight ruffs and two reeves [males and females of a particular type of sandpiper] to be introduced, but they 'didn't do well'.⁵ In September, Willy noted how he 'bought a beautiful new little Austin in Norwich which goes like a bird, the Rolls is having a thorough refit at Derby, & the car I hired

---

* This also involved guarding against egg thieves, and Willy was involved in a campaign to expose a notorious couple in pursuit of rare eggs. He wrote a 'Foreword' to Eric Parker, *Ethics of Egg-Collecting – its uses and abuses*, The Field, London, 1935.

Whiteslea Lodge, Hickling Broad, in 2021.

here was no good . . . There are lots of ducks and we have had some very good flights – and there is the usual number of partridges. The Baldwins were coming over today from Blickling but he has been smitten with very bad lumbago – so they have put off their visit.'[6]

In 1937 Willy visited a mink farm nearby: 'I came away with the conviction that I had no desire to be a Mink farmer.'[7]

Between the wars, the great Cowper mansion of Panshanger complemented Taplow as a part-year residence for the Desboroughs, with guests joining them for entertainment in the house, shooting on the estate or boating on the River Mimram. This was the last phase for such grandeur, and David Cannadine describes how 'the rise of the cult of the country house has taken place in the same century which has witnessed the decline and fall of the aristocracy as a self-conscious, self-confident elite of wealth, power and status'.[8]

It was only in 1937 that electric lighting was fully installed in Panshanger, and Ettie made further sales to support the future viability of the estate. In May 1919 she and Willy put 2,817 acres of the outlying estate up for auction and Ebeneezer Howard (who had created the first garden city at Letchworth before the war) raised the funds required to acquire 1,500 acres, which allowed him to start creating Welwyn Garden City.[9] In 1928, following bidding from various dealers, Ettie sold, with regret, a second Raphael, dated 1508 and known as the Niccolini-Cowper Madonna, to Andrew Mellon for $875,000 (just over $13 million today), who donated it to the National Gallery of Art in Washington DC. It was, once again, the highest price paid at that date for a single painting.[10] When news of the sale spread, *The Bystander* magazine made the philistine comment that 'Something representing close upon £9,000 a year hanging upon your walls is a prodigious price to pay for the pleasure of possessing a picture you seldom see, and in these days of heavy estate burdens and taxation that income going into your bank account is certainly more satisfactory than the possession of a Raphael.'[11]

The custodianship of Panshanger included the care of the exceptional collection of paintings and decorative arts assembled over several generations, from the 1st Earl to the 7th, including outstanding works acquired in Florence by the 3rd Earl Cowper (many works are now part of the collections at Firle Place, Sussex).[12] While Ettie was at Sandringham, in the period of King George V's final illness and death, Willy sent her an account (dated 27 January 1936) of one of the largest and grandest paintings going out on loan:

> *Mrs Bruce will probably have written to you, but I have heard from her. That the Van Dyke was very heavy, and took two hours to get it off the wall. With the help of the very efficient man, two van men, Peter Williams and the gardeners, they got it down without mishap, and out of the house through the ante-room door on to the terrace, as I suggested to Mrs Bruce,* who says that Panshanger is very quiet now, and she misses everyone very much.*[13]

The Picture Gallery at Panshanger, photographed in 1939.

---

* Mrs Bruce was housekeeper at Panshanger. She went on to become housekeeper at Windsor Castle for George VI.

During the Second World War, Taplow Court was offered by the Desboroughs to St Stephen's College girls' school in 1940, which was regarded as vulnerable to bombing, being located in Folkestone. Sister Jean Marian and a colleague inspected Taplow (as other sites had been offered) and their first reaction was that it was unsuitable.[14] It was hard to black out, rambling, full of collectables, including the Old Masters (various paintings including Dutch School works, referred to as the 'Desborough collection'), and a ballroom with full-length portraits of Ettie and Willy (the pastels by Ellis Roberts). They were shown the indoor stické court, a sports hall, the grounds and the burial mound. They worried about all the furniture the Desboroughs had left behind – including four-poster beds – and the huge open hall with its animal trophies. They resolved, nevertheless, to move the school there, following its use for three months to host evacuated London families.[15] With help from women in Taplow village it was cleaned up and usefully occupied by the school through the war.

St Stephen's College pupils among Willy's trophy heads in the gym at Taplow Court.

Once Taplow Court had been taken over by St Stephen's College, the Desboroughs occupied a part of Panshanger, which was offered as a temporary reception centre for families evacuated to Hertfordshire villages. For a period, it also housed young mothers and babies escaping the Blitz.[16] In January 1941 Willy reported to Ettie:

> *Something has happened since your departure . . . Yesterday I was rung up by the C.Council to know if we could take in for a short time some children who had been evacuated, and whose quarters were unsatisfactory . . . So I said all right, as I know you wanted the house to be used. I saw matron just now, & she proposes to use rooms not set aside for the mothers in case of infection of any sort, so I hope all will be well, and when you get back you will find 13 little darlings.*[17]

Towards the end of his life, in 1944, Willy offered to sell the Whiteslea Lodge and estate to Christopher Cadbury, a conservationist and regular visitor, but the sale was not concluded before his death in 1945. It was subsequently sold to the Cadbury family and the Norfolk Naturalists Trust, and, with additional funds, held for public benefit through the Norfolk Wildlife Trust. As conservationist Nick Acheson writes on the Trust's website: 'In the early years of the twentieth century the Whiteslea estate at Hickling Broad was the private preserve of ministers, aristocrats and royalty, with dedicated and forward-looking keepers protecting its rare birds. Since 1945, as a Norfolk Wildlife Trust reserve, it has been loved by the whole of Norfolk.'[18]

After Willy's death, at the end of the war, Taplow Court was sold to British Telecommunications Research, a subsidiary of Plessey Electronics. The Soka Gakkai International organisation acquired the house in 1988, restored it (though Ettie's original decorative schemes have not survived) and have operated it since as a national Buddhist centre, opening it on occasion to the public, and organising fascinating exhibitions about the Grenfell family.

Ettie lived out her last years in just a few of the rooms at Panshanger, often writing under a tent on the lawn with a view across the lake.[19] Nicholas Mosley recalled how, soon after the Second World War, he met Monica's daughter Rosemary at Oxford and fell 'madly in love' within a fortnight. Rosemary invited him for a drive to visit her grandmother but he knew nothing of where they were going or who she was. They passed a gatehouse at the edge of an estate and at first he presumed this must be the place. Having passed this point he saw the huge house – 'a bit like a battleship' – but was taken by Rosemary through the servants' entrance to a little sitting room in which an old lady was sitting in a bath chair, who he, at first, thought was the housekeeper. Ettie, however, held out her hand to Nicholas and said simply, 'I was a friend of your grandfather, Lord Curzon,' and all was explained.

Ettie died on 28 May 1952, the thirty-seventh anniversary of when she and Willy had buried Julian. As Richard Davenport-Hines concludes, 'She never forgot her dead: her choices always were controlled: she did nothing by accident.'[20] Henry 'Chips' Channon summed her up in his diary, in his inimitable waspish manner, as 'one of the most baffling, intoxicating and strangest of characters that I have ever come across. Hard, shiny, insinuating, determined, ruthless, gay, witty, and amusing, she had a genius for life, for friendship, for society . . . a cynical wife, a great lady, *une grande amoureuse*, a brilliant letter-writer, and the greatest conversationalist of the age, she played with people's lives, loves and destinies in high-handed Renaissance style.'[21]

The Panshanger estate was put up for sale and bought by a developer, who decided to demolish the house while exploiting the estate for gravel. Nothing of the house remains but for the brick skeleton of the orangery (or melon house); the extraction of gravel continues, although the park is open to the public.[22]

When, in 1920, *The Times* had mistakenly published an obituary of Lord

The Orangery at Panshanger, 2018.

Lord Desborough by the pond at Taplow Court by Stanley Ballance c. 1934.

Desborough, twenty-five years ahead of his death, it was a marker of his public reputation, as his importance was widely acknowledged. In later life, Willy was approached by publishers and agents proposing that he write an autobiography and seeking his agreement. Methuen was interested in a book about Whiteslea, and Eric Turrell wrote from Hutchins and Co. on 3 December 1939 to ask about a memoir; Willy answered, characteristically, that he always seemed too busy.[23]

Ettie's biographer refers to Lytton Strachey's account of staying at Taplow Court in 1930, when the guests including a 'knot of dowagers and [J. M.] Barrie', and 'Lord Desborough himself was really the best of the crew – a huge old rock of an athlete'.[24] Harry Mount claims that his own grandmother remembered Desborough in 'old age, casting a mournful fly across Taplow's Norman baronial hall while Ettie's guests chattered away in the dining room next door'.[25]

Desborough celebrated his seventy-fifth birthday in October 1930 by making an innovative form of benefaction: taking out a £10,000 insurance policy in favour of St Dunstan's – now known as Blind Veterans UK – a charity established in 1915 to offer support to ex-servicemen and -women with visual impairments.[26] He had often been referred to as the 'go-to man' of his times, focused on public service rather than self-advancement, and he continued with advisory and charitable work and oversight of the Taplow estate into his eighties. He once suggested that 'he had been so busy all his life he had not had time to grow old', and this was despite the various intermittent ailments that caused him to seek treatment or rest cures.

From the mid-1930s, longevity (and experience) increased his status, enhanced perhaps by his ability to recall a completely different era of mid-Victorian Britain. The 1938 BBC sound recording of Desborough's account of the 1877 dead-heat Boat Race (in his wonderful courtly tones) is a vivid example of such a shift in time.[27] Recalling the Oxford crew's disappointment, he would have been acutely aware of just how much the world of sport and the world itself had changed.

When Cyril Bailey, Public Orator for Oxford University, introduced Lord Desborough for the presentation of an Honorary Degree on 22 June 1938, he spoke (in Latin), with suitable flourish:

Next is a venerable Oxford Old Boy who – more than anyone else – has been for his entire life closely connected with the Thames. Imagine if you will Old Father Thames, rising up from his very own waters, cloaked in a blueish-grey garment, addressing our hero in these words:

'In Eights in youth you cleft with
rapid oar
My sacred streams and conquered
Cam's keen crews;
And thrusting punt with pole, you
vanquished all
Who came against you; then, in
later years
Your care it was my waters to
preserve,
Remove the mud and stem the
falling banks;
Gladly your task you plied and
made me clean,
Fit channel for my boats to travel
down.
Come then and let me wreath your
hoary head.'

'Tu puer octonos inter
mea flumina sancta
remo sulcabas rapido,
Camique sequaces
vicisti iuvenes; tu conto
trudere cymbam
callidus aequales superasti
non semel omnes.
mox ubi cura data est mea
conservere fluenta,
et purgare lutum et ripas
stabilire caducas,
sedulous imposito
gaudebas munere functus,
me purumque simul
reddens et navibus aptum.
laetus adi, lauro sine
tempora cana coronem.'

He (Desborough) has not just stood out for his sporting achievements and for his conservation of the river, but has . . . provided a shining example of a life lived honourably, zealously and dutifully.[28]

By now Desborough was an observer rather than a participant in political life. Following the ill-fated Munich Agreement, he wrote to *The Times* on 7 October 1938: 'Our gratitude goes out to the Prime Minister for the wonderful part he played in saving the world from the horrors of war by a few hours, and I think that the gratitude of Czechoslovakia should go out to him as well, for what he did to preserve what could be preserved of their recently formed State by an international guarantee.'[29]

If briefly on the wrong side of history, as peace negotiations failed in 1939 and war approached, Ettie wrote that 'Willie has been so steady & calm all through: I said to him, after the gleam of hope on Wednesday, "What shall we do if it breaks down again now?" He said, "Go through the war as well as we can."'[30]

Now eighty-eight, Willy's health deteriorated in 1943. He succumbed in July to an attack of jaundice and was confined to bed for nearly four months. Ettie referred to him as having 'terrible depression'.[31] Yet, typically of Desborough's attention to detail, in April 1944 he took the time to write to Mr Birt, Secretary of the Dittons Skiff and Punting Club, to promise that 'I shall be very pleased to be Patron of your Club for another year, and I am enclosing a cheque for one guinea.'[32] Willy had a serious heart attack in October 1944, though by early 1945 his health had improved. On the evening of 8 January 1945 he confided to Ettie, 'I should like to live two more years.' Instead, he died peacefully the next day, from myocardial degeneration, arterio-sclerosis and oedema.[33] Ettie wrote to the Queen about 'The relief of knowing that his pain and wretchedness are over for ever and there can never have been a more perfect peace than in those last few hours and the look on his face afterwards.'[34]

Richard Davenport-Hines describes this as the end of a marriage that was 'a confederacy with a secret history that only the two of them knew' – the end of fifty-eight years of common memory.[35] At a distance from that intimacy, Desborough's death was a public event, with Ettie receiving up to fifty letters of condolence a day. Amid the many glowing tributes, Lord Crawford described how Willy had 'ennobled everyone around him' and how he was 'an example and symbol of England – England of the past . . . calm, strong, good, courageous, wise, tolerant & great'.[36] Less flattering was a note in Chips Channon's diary: 'Lord Desborough, "Old Man River" as I nicknamed him, is dead at last at the age of 89. A kindly man, anecdotal, gentlemanly, a bore, broken-hearted, and always over-shadowed by his intriguing, gracious, brilliant dominating wife, he seemed little more than a heavy shadow at her great political, social parties . . . He loved his three sons, like princes they were.'[37]

The poet Walter de la Mare sent a poem to Ettie and wrote: 'It seems all but incredible that so many triumphs – & what they implied – could be achievable in one lifetime, especially as he so frequently must nearly have lost his life in attaining them. He would not have cared for many things in the world as it seems to be tending now; & he must have been tired. But I have lost a friend for whom I had a great affection, & admiration.'[38]

When Desborough's real obituary was published in *The Times*, on 10 January 1945, it focused on his practical achievements: 'With his union of social gifts, personal charm and administrative ability, he was known as a man who could get things done . . . The multiplicity of his interests was indeed only matched by his industry and sense of duty.'

On the same day her son-in-law, George Gage, wrote to Ettie:

My dear Lady Desborough
I suppose this is the most inevitable of all the losses you have had & in a sense the least unhappy considering the wonderful life Lord Desborough has had.

But the strain of the last two years must have been great & now it is all over & you have your own illness & all the other troubles of these times to think about, you must feel almost inclined to give up trying any more as it were. So I hope that you will remember how devoted we all are to you down to the youngest & how much we hope you will go on being what you always have been to the family.

I feel I saw quite a lot of Lord Desborough during the last few years & I was awfully impressed with his memory & clear mind and wisdom right up to the end. I often thought when he was talking to me about the past & about the people he had known, that he himself represented as much as any of them, the ideas of this country. And apart from that he was perfectly charming to us all & we shall miss him frightfully.

My best love, George[39]

The *Maidenhead Advertiser* ran tributes across two editions. On 24 January 1945 the paper described the complexity of local bonds in Taplow and Maidenhead, making reference to his many sporting connections, before emphasising:

> even this extraordinary record of interests and activities gives no idea of how personal and intimate was the connection between the Borough and the High Steward. In spite of his many and varied duties elsewhere, Lord Desborough always seemed to have time to spare – till his giant powers began to fail – to give personal attention, not only to the offices he held in the Borough, but to the problems and importunities of individual citizens. And the townsfolk, in their turn treated as personal events, the occasions of joy and sorrow at Taplow Court, the welcoming of the bride, the coming of age of the heir, the loss of the three sons. Surely the relationship was a unique one and should not be forgotten in an age of changing values.

The poem that Walter de la Mare sent to Ettie was titled 'The Rapids':

> Grieve must my heart. Age hastens by.
> No longing can stay Time's torrent now.
> Once would the sun in eastern sky
> Pause on the solemn mountain's brow.
> Rare flowers he still to bloom may bring,
> But day approaches evening;
> But ah, how swift their withering!
>
> The birds, that used to sing, sang then
> As if in an eternal day;
> Ev'n sweeter yet their grace-notes, when
> Farewell . . . farewell is theirs to say,
> Yet as a thorn its drop of dew
> Treasures in shadow, crystal clear
> All that I loved I love anew
> Now parting draweth near.[40]

Lord Desborough punting on the sidestream at Taplow in the 1930s.

APPENDIX I

Chronology of the Life of
William Henry Grenfell, 1st Baron Desborough

Year & date

1855: 30 October   William Henry Grenfell born; second child of six, to Charles William Grenfell MP and Georgiana Lascelles.

1861: 4 May   Father, Charles William, dies aged thirty-eight.

1863–8   Attends preparatory school in Malvern.

1867: 21 March   Grandfather, Charles Pascoe Grenfell, dies; inherits Taplow Court.

1868–74   Attends Harrow School in Rendalls House; school cricket eleven 1873–4; achieves record for running the mile in 4 minutes 37 seconds.

1874–9   Reads classics at Balliol College, Oxford. Because of illness takes time out, and transfers to a pass degree in the summer of 1879. Continues to run, and rows for Balliol College VIII from 1876.

1875: 23 February   Becomes a freemason and is initiated into the Apollo University Lodge, No.357, Oxford, the same day as Oscar Wilde; resigns in December, but joins other lodges throughout his life.

1876–7   Takes up climbing in summer vacations: ascends the Matterhorn by three different routes; climbs the Little Matterhorn, the Matterhorn, Monte Rosa and the Weisshorn within eight days.

1876: 30 October   On the day of his 'majority' a certificate is presented to his mother and Uncle Henry, at Taplow Court. Willy unexpectedly arrives and joins the ceremony.

1877: 24 March   Rows in the Oxford v. Cambridge Boat Race: the only dead heat.

1878: 13 April   Rows in winning Boat Race crew, defeating Cambridge by seven lengths. Elected President of Oxford University Boat Club.

1878   Becomes Master of the Oxford University Drag Hounds. Elected President of Oxford University Athletic Club and wins three-mile race against Cambridge.

1879: 19 June   Awarded a pass degree (BA) at Oxford.

1879   Following the formation of Maidenhead Rowing Club in 1876, Grenfell is appointed Captain in 1879.

1880: 31 March   Elected MP for Salisbury, as a Liberal, serves until 22 November 1882.

1882   Appointed Parliamentary Groom-in-Waiting.

1884   Appointed High Steward of Maidenhead, and every year to 1939 organises a High Steward's Banquet at Taplow Court.

1884   Travels to America and Canada; swims across pool at base of Niagara Falls; travels on to Rocky Mountains to go hunting.

1885   Elected a Steward of Henley Royal Regatta.

1885: March–April   Travels to the Sudan as a special correspondent for the *Daily Telegraph* covering the second Suakin campaign; reports on the Battle of Tofrek.

1885: 24 November   Re-elected MP for Salisbury, serving until 1 July 1886; Private Secretary for the Chancellor of the Exchequer, Sir William Harcourt.

1885   Rows as stroke across the Channel in a clinker eight.

1887: 17 February   Marries Ethel (Ettie) Priscilla Fane (born 27 June 1867) at St George's Church, Hanover Square; honeymoon trip to Paris, Cannes and Monte Carlo; then without servants to Rome, Brindisi and Cairo.

1888: 30 March   Birth of Julian Henry Francis Grenfell.

1888–94   Running Mr W. H. Grenfell's Harriers, formerly titled as Prince of Wales's.

1888–90   Wins Amateur Punting Championship for three years. Appointed Chairman of Thames Punting Club in 1890, and President from 1899.

1888: September   Travels with Ettie to Boston; second swim across the pool at Niagara Falls; hunting expedition in the Rocky Mountains; meets with Ettie in San Francisco.

1889   Appointed High Sheriff of Buckinghamshire.

	Rows, in team of three, from Oxford to Putney: 105 miles in 22 hours.
1889: 26 October	Ceremony and dinner of dedication for the Recreation Ground, land donated by Grenfell to the Borough of Maidenhead.
1890: 29 March	Birth of Gerald William (Billy) Grenfell.
1890: 2 April	Defeat in Windsor by-election.
1891: March	Full-length portraits in pastel of Willy and Ettie by Ellis Roberts.
1891–2	Winter trip to India with Ettie to Bombay (Mumbai); Ettie spends January and February with Lord and Lady Wenlock in Madras (Chennai) while Willy away hunting game; entertained by the Viceroy, Lord Lansdowne, in Calcutta (Kolkata); travels with Ettie to Agra, Benares, Cooch Behar (Koch Bihar) and Darjeeling.
1892: 4 July	Elected MP for Hereford, as a Liberal, serving until 4 August 1893, when he resigns over Gladstone's Second Home Rule Bill.
1893	Builds stické (indoor tennis) court at Taplow Court.
1893: 29 March	Birth of Monica Margaret Grenfell.
1894	Appointed as founding Chairman and later President of the Bath Club at 34 Dover Street, London W1.
1895–6	Elected Mayor of Maidenhead.
1895: December	Attends international bimetallism conference in Paris.
1895: April	Publishes article, 'Concerning the question of the House of Lords and Socialism', in the *Pall Mall Magazine*.
1896	Appointed as a Conservator to the Board of the Thames Conservancy, becoming Chairman in 1905.
1896: April	Attends international bimetallism conference in Brussels.
1896–7	Re-elected as Mayor of Maidenhead.
1897: July and August	In the summer of Queen Victoria's Diamond Jubilee year, Taplow is leased to King Chulalongkorn of Siam. Ettie and the children spend two months in Saint-Pierre-en-Port, Normandy.
1897	Diamond Jubilee celebration in Grenfell Park, Maidenhead, now planted with seeds and trees from Grenfell's overseas trips.
1898	Birth of Ivo George Winfred Grenfell.
1899: May	Trip to the USA and Canada; first visit to the Gulf of

	Mexico for tarpon fishing – Grenfell catches 100, Ettie seven; in Ottawa, stays with Lord and Lady Minto, Governor-General of Canada.
1900: 1 October	Elected MP for Wycombe, as a Conservative and Unionist, serving until 30 December 1905.
1900: February	Becomes a Major in 1st Battalion of Buckinghamshire Rifle Volunteers.
1902	Formation of Amateur Fencing Association; Grenfell appointed as President.
1902: 17 December	Grenfell switches on the current to electric-light cables at the new Maidenhead Corporation generating station.
1903	Leads opposition to Tariff Reform as President of the Central Chamber of Agriculture.
1904–6	Wins épée prize at the Military Fencing Tournaments.
1904: 27 October	Opens the Carnegie-funded Public Library in Maidenhead.
1905: 11 February	Birth of Alexandra Imogen (Mogs) Grenfell.
1905	Formation of the British Olympic Association; Grenfell appointed Chairman.
	Appointed as President of the Maidenhead Hospital, with a ward named after him.
1905: December	Appointed to the House of Lords as the 1st Baron Desborough.
1906: April–May	Represents Britain at Intercalated Olympic Games in Athens in épée; carries flag for Britain in the opening ceremony. Appointed as a member of the International Olympic Committee.
	Appointed Commander of the Royal Victorian Order (CVO).
1907	Appointed President of the Lawn Tennis Association.
1907: 23 February	Founder of Lord Desborough Masonic Lodge, No.3200, Maidenhead.
1908	Oversees Olympic Games taking place in west London, linked to the Franco-British Exhibition, referred to as the White City.
1908: 18 July	King Edward VII stays at Taplow Court.
1908	Appointed Knight Commander of the Royal Victorian Order (KCVO).
	Vice President of the Maidenhead and District Rifle Club,

and fires the first shot on the opening of the Gullet rifle range.

1909   Appointed Chancellor of the Primrose League.

1910: 22 February   Gives lecture, 'The Story of the Oar', at the Philosophical Institution in Edinburgh.

1910: April   Acquires first family motor car: a Rothwell built by the Eclipse Machine Company in Oldham, with a 20hp four-litre engine.

1910   Appointed President of the British Dairy Farmers' Association; offers the Desborough Cup to the champion butter maker.

1910–13; 1916–19   Serves as President of the London Chamber of Commerce; in 1911 chairs a special committee to oppose the Declaration of London.

1911: 2 February   Death of Georgiana Grenfell, Willy's mother.

1911   Appointed President of the Epée Club.

1911: August–November   Travels to Canada with the Duke of Sutherland, appraising business and investment opportunities; time spent hunting.

1912   Appointed President of Marylebone Cricket Club.

Attends Stockholm Olympic Games as Chairman of the British Olympic Association.

Chairman of the British Imperial Chamber of Commerce for the 8th Congress, held in London.

1913–18   Serves as Chairman of the Imperial Air Fleet Committee promoting aerial defence of Britain.

1913: 13 May   Names the *Britannia* aeroplane at Hendon Airfield.

1913   As President of the Lawn Tennis Association inaugurates the Desborough Cup, a gold challenge cup for tennis playing golfers.

1913: March–April   Visits Egypt with Ettie and Monica, staying with Lord Kitchener in Cairo; travels on to the Sudan for big-game hunting.

1914: November   Appointed President of the Central Association of Volunteer Training Corps.

1915: 26 May   Julian Grenfell dies of wounds in France, with Willy and Ettie beside him at the Wimereux Military Hospital, just north of Boulogne.

1915   Taplow Court adapted to become a rest home for ten nurses.

1915: 30 July	Billy Grenfell killed in action at Hooge, West Flanders.
1915	Represents the Minister of Munitions in France, overseeing the selection and recall of workmen for key positions in war production in Britain.
	Becomes Superintendent for the Queen Mary's Royal Naval Hospital, Southend-on-Sea.
1916	Ettie compiles and edits (principally from letters from Julian and Billy) *Pages from a Family Journal*; privately published and circulated to family and friends.
1916: 3 June	Presents aircraft donated to Canada by the Leicester Chamber of Commerce, through the Imperial Air Fleet Committee.
1916 and 1917	Continues to shoot in Scotland, supporting the efforts of the Venison Supply Committee (formed July 1916) to increase the supply of meat in Britain.
1917	Presents aircraft for India, donated by the people of Leeds through the Imperial Air Fleet Committee.
1919–29	Serves as Chairman of the Pilgrims of Great Britain.
1919	Appointed Chairman of the Home Office Committee on the Police Service of England, Wales and Scotland.
1920: 2 December	A mistaken obituary of Lord Desborough published in *The Times*, after the death of Lord Bessborough.
1920: 4 December	Inaugurates the Maidenhead War Memorial outside the Public Library.
1920	Appointed founding President of the Achilles Club, combining athletes from Oxford and Cambridge.
1920: September–October	Visits Toronto as President of the London Chamber of Commerce and of the British Imperial Council of Commerce; attends 9th Congress of the Chambers of Commerce of the British Empire; follows with a hunting trip to the Yukon.
1920	Memorial for Julian and Billy erected next to the old churchyard at Taplow Court, sculpted by Sir Bertram Mackennal.
1921: May	Offered the post of Governor-General of Canada; declines the appointment.
1923	President of the International Navigation Congress in London.
	Desborough's shorthorn, 'Denton Betty', wins female champion of all breeds at the Royal Show; successfully breeding shorthorns at Panshanger.

1924	Opens new Iffley Lock, Oxford; part of sequence of improvements to the Upper Thames.
1924–9	Serves as Captain of the Yeomen of the Guard.
1925	Appointed Government Deputy Chief Whip in the House of Lords.
	Appointed Knight of the Royal Victorian Order (KCVO).
	Appointed President of the Royal Agricultural Society.
1926: 8 October	Ivo Grenfell dies in hospital following a car crash in Kent.
1927	Keeps diary of visits to Whiteslea Lodge, Hickling Broad, Norfolk, inherited by Willy from Ivo.
1928	Appointed Knight of the Order of the Garter.
1928: February	Easter Act, fixing the date for Easter, receives Royal Assent, but is never enacted.
1928	Elected Honorary Fellow, Balliol College, Oxford.
1930	Appointed President of the Amateur Athletic Association.
1933: February	Republishes 'On Money', advocating bimetallism, in the *Empire Review*.
1935: March	Presents prizes at the annual boys' boxing championships run by London Federation of Boys' Clubs at the Royal Albert Hall.
1935: 30 June	Breaking through of the Desborough Channel, the extensive Thames flood-relief scheme for Shepperton; Desborough Island established.
1935: August	Welcomes athletes at the 4th International Games for the Deaf at White City.
1937	Retires as Chairman of the Thames Conservancy after thirty-two years.
1937: 26 May	Speaks in the House of Lords on the subject of the Thames Barrier.
1937: 22 July	Last speech in Lords on the subject of Thames drainage.
1938: 22 June	Awarded Honorary Doctorate by the University of Oxford.
1940	St Stephen's College girls' school occupies Taplow Court and Willy and Ettie move to Panshanger House for the duration of the Second World War.
1944	Writes introduction to *A Tideless Thames* by E. O. Bunge, arguing for a Thames Barrier.
1945: 9 January	Death of Lord Desborough at Panshanger House.
1952: 28 May	Death of Ettie Desborough at Panshanger House.

APPENDIX 2

Appointments, Honours, Military Record, Cups and Medals

Appointments

Organisation	Year	Role
Alpine Club	1876–1945	Member, then Senior Member
Leander	1877–1945	Member and Member of the Committee, 1882–92
Oxford University Boat Club	1878	President
Oxford University Drag Hounds	1878	Master
Oxford University Athletic Club	1878	President
Maidenhead Rowing Club	1879–1936	Captain, then President
Vincent's Club, Oxford	1879	President
Constituency of Salisbury	1880–82 then 1885–6	Member of Parliament (Liberal)
Royal Household	1882	Parliamentary Groom-in-Waiting to Her Majesty
Borough of Maidenhead	1884–1945	High Steward
Henley Royal Regatta	1885–1939	Steward, Committee of Management, 1885–6 and 1908–39, Chairman, 1934
HM Government	1885	Private Secretary to the Chancellor of the Exchequer
W. H. Grenfell's Harriers	1888–94	Master
County of Buckinghamshire	1889	High Sheriff
Thames Punting Club	1890	Chairman, then President from 1899
Queen's Club	1891–2	President
Constituency of Hereford City	1892–3 (resigned)	Member of Parliament (Liberal)
Bath Club	1894–1942	President
Borough of Maidenhead	1895–7	Mayor
Thames Conservancy Board	1896–1937	Conservator, then Chairman (sometimes known as President) from 1909
Maidenhead Golf Club	1898–1903	President

Thames Salmon Association	1898–1907	Chairman
Bartitsu Club	1899	President
Constituency of Wycombe Division, Buckinghamshire	1900–5	Member of Parliament (Unionist)
Royal Life Saving Society	1901–44	President
Amateur Fencing Association	1902, 1911–26	President
Central Chamber of Agriculture	1903	President
Grenfell Lodge No.3077	1904	Senior Warden, then First Master
Coaching Club	1905–3	President
British Olympic Association	1905–13	Chairman
Maidenhead Hospital	1905–36	President
House of Lords	1905–45	Baron Desborough
Intercalated Olympic Games, Athens	1906	British Fencing Team (Silver Medallist)
Lawn Tennis Association	1907–26	President
Desborough Bowling Club, Maidenhead	1907–36	President
Lord Desborough Lodge No.3200	1907	Immediate Past Master
Olympic Games, London	1908	President
Buckinghamshire County Cricket Club	1908	President
Croquet Association	1908–33	President
Maidenhead and District Rifle Club	1908	Vice President
British Sea Anglers' Society	1909	President
Royal Life Saving Lodge	1909	1st Immediate Past Master
The Primrose League	1909–11	Chancellor
South Bucks Conservative Association	1910–34	President
British Dairy Farmers' Association	1910	President
London Chamber of Commerce	1910–13, 1916–19	President
Festival of Empire	1911	President
Epée Club	1911–26	President
Marylebone Cricket Club	1911–12	President
All England Lawn Tennis Club	1912–15	President, then Vice President to 1945
Four-in-Hand Driving Club	1912–26	President
British Imperial Chamber of Commerce	1913–21	President
Imperial Air Fleet Committee	1913–18	Chairman
Salmon and Trout Association	1913–45	President

Central Association of Volunteer Training Corps	1914–20	President
Queen Mary's Royal Naval Hospital, Southend-on-Sea	1914–19	Superintendent
HM Government	1915–20	Minister of Munitions' Representative in France
County of Buckinghamshire	1915	Deputy Lieutenant
Board of Agriculture and Fisheries Freshwater Fish Committee	1917	Chairman
Home Office Committee on the Police Service	1919, 1924	Chairman
Pilgrims of Great Britain	1919–29	Chairman of Executive Committee
Achilles Club	1920–45	President
Amateur Wrestling Association	1920–33	President
Flyfishers' Club	1922	President
International Navigation Congress	1923	President
Shorthorn Society of Great Britain	1923–24	President
Dittons Skiff and Punting Club	1923–45	Patron
Yeomen of the Guard	1924–9	Captain
Royal Agricultural Society	1925	President
Taplow Cricket Club	1925	President
HM Government	1925–9	Deputy Chief Whip in House of Lords
The Stadium Club (sports club linked to White City)	1926	President
Channel Swimming Association	1928–45	President
Amateur Athletic Association	1930–36	President
London Federation of Boys' Clubs	1936–8	President

There are references without dates or corroboration to Lord Desborough serving as President of the Maidenhead Horticultural Society and on the committee of the Land Union, and as a member of the Lord Mayor's Committee for the Distribution of the Titanic Fund.

Honours

Order of the Redeemer, Greece	1905	Member
Royal Victorian Order	1907	Commander
Royal Victorian Order	1908	Knight Commander

Royal Borough of Maidenhead	1918	Freeman
Royal Victorian Order	1925	Knight Grand Cross
Order of the Garter	1928	Knight
Balliol College	1928	Honorary Fellow
Oxford University	1938	Honorary Doctorate of Civil Law

Military Record (Voluntary Service)

Regiment	Date	Rank	Notes and Sources
Harrow Volunteers. This may have been the 18th Middlesex (Harrow) Corps, one of the Volunteer units formed in 1859 and after	?.	Captain	*London Gazette* entry in 1900 refers to him as formerly serving as a Captain in the Harrow Volunteers. B. Rose, 'The Volunteers of 1859', in the *Journal of the Society for Army Historical Research*, September 1959, vol.37, no.151, pp.97–110
Harrow School Cadet Force	1871	Sergeant	Harrow School Archives
Royal Buckinghamshire Militia	1873	Sub-lieutenant	Applied but did not join. Emma Thoyts, *History of the Royal Bucks*
		Presumably joined subsequently.	*Militia*, 1897
Royal Buckinghamshire Militia	1876 (11 Nov.)	Resigned commission as Sub-lieutenant	*London Gazette*
1st Battalion, Buckinghamshire Rifle Volunteers	1900 (Jan)	Major	*London Gazette*
1st Battalion, Buckinghamshire Rifle Volunteers	1906 (Nov)	Resigned his commission as Major	*London Gazette*
Central Association of Volunteer Training Corps	1914–20	President	Entry in *Oxford Dictionary of National Biography* and Wikipedia
Royal Army Service Corps, Motor Transport (Volunteers)	1918 (Nov)	Hon. Lieutenant Colonel	*London Gazette*
Home Guard	1939	Private	No official source

Cups and Medals donated by Lord Desborough or established in his name

The Challenge Cup (Grenfell Cup)	1905–	The Challenge Cup (Grenfell Cup) was one of the first trophies established at Maidenhead Golf Club,

presented by W. H. Grenfell. The
Challenge Cup is an eighteen-hole
strokeplay competition, for players
having a Handicap Index below 15.5. It
was first won in 1898 by E. M. Fletcher,
before Grenfell made his donation.

The Desborough Cup   1913–   Donated by the Lawn Tennis Association,
the Desborough Cup is for county level
or higher tennis players competing in a
handicap golf match – www.desborough-
cup.co.uk. There is also a Desborough
Bowl competition, open to all members of
an ITF- or LTA-affiliated] tennis club.

The Julian Cup   1924–   Presented by Lord Desborough in
memory of his eldest son, Julian Grenfell;
for cricket clubs in the Maidenhead
area playing evening games with a fixed
number of overs.

Desborough Perpetual   1925–   The Women's Amateur Athletic
Challenge Cup   Association Championship Desborough
Perpetual Challenge Cup, presented
by Lord Desborough GCVO. It was
awarded to winners of the WAAA Long
Jump Championship between 1925 to
1995, and since 2010, the trophy has been
awarded to the winner of the England
Senior Championships Long Jump.

Desborough Cup   Later 1920s–2018   Donated by Lord Desborough to the
National Amateur Rowing Association
(which included manual labourers and
working-class rowers in local clubs) for
Championship Eights. It was competed
for until 2018.

London Fencing Club Challenge   1928–   Desborough presented the London
Trophy and Desborough   Fencing Club with an 18-inch-high
Foil Medal   silver statuette by Felix Joubert of
the club's recently retired foil coach,
Jean-Baptiste Mimiague, as a challenge
trophy. In addition, each year the
Desborough foil medal (2½ inch diameter
in silver) has been awarded annually to the
club's most promising foilist.

Desborough Annual Challenge Cup for Boxing	1932	A cup for the armed services, NCOS and other ranks, and organised by the Chevron Club; Desborough was chair of the Committee.
Desborough Perpetual Challenge Trophy	1947–	Donated to the Thames Punting Club by Lady Desborough; a cup that Desborough had himself won in 1888.
Desborough Medal	1953–mid-1960s?	To honour Lord Desborough's chairmanship of the Thames Conservancy, 1905–36. River and Rowing Museum entry states: 'Instituted by the Thames Conservators to commemorate the coronation and perpetuate the memory of Lord Desborough. Keith Osbourne was one of the first to receive the medal, which was presented annually.'

APPENDIX 3

Sources, Publications and Select Bibliography

Sources

Lord Desborough kept journals when he was travelling, and these and his letters to his wife Ettie, to whom he wrote regularly when he was away from home, and to his children have survived. He didn't, however, leave any personal diaries nor any extensive correspondence with friends, and descriptions appear only occasionally in memoirs from the period. We worked to trace his life from surviving letters and journals, from the journal kept by his mother Georgiana, the many albums and journals compiled by Ettie, and by the accounts titled *Tracery* written by their daughter Monica. We also gleaned material from the records of the many organisations he contributed to, together with numerous press reports of his sporting and other activities, and speeches in the House of Lords and contributions to parliamentary committees.

In addition to various Grenfell family records and albums, the key holdings we drew on included the records of various sports clubs, including the Alpine Club, Dittons Skiff and Punting Club, the Epée Club, the Flyfishers' Club, the Lawn Tennis Association, Leander Club, Maidenhead Golf Club, Maidenhead Rowing Club and the Thames Punting Club.

Papers relating to Lord Desborough and the Grenfell family include those at:
Balliol College, Oxford
Berkshire Record Office, Thames Conservancy Records, Reading
Bodleian Library, Oxford
British Library, Library and Sound Archive
British Newspaper Archive
British Olympic Archive, University of East London
Buckinghamshire Archives, Aylesbury
Firle Place, Sussex
Hertfordshire Archives and Local Studies (including Hertfordshire Library), Hertford
Houses of Parliament Records and Archives

London Metropolitan Archives
Maidenhead Library
Oxford History Centre
River and Rowing Museum, Henley-on-Thames
Royal Archives, Windsor Castle
Taplow Court

Publications by William Grenfell, Lord Desborough (in chronological order)

Early in life William Grenfell imagined he might become a writer, and although he didn't pursue this, he wrote short pieces and longer articles throughout his life, including those related to his favourite sports and various campaigns.

Grenfell, William Henry, 'Rowing at Oxford', *English Illustrated Magazine*, vol.7, pp.495–506, London, 1889/90.

—, 'Lost in the Rockies', *The Nineteenth Century Magazine*, vol.XXXI, no.183, May, pp.839–49, London 1892.

—, 'Mr Gladstone and the Currency', *The Fortnightly Review*, No.CCCXXI, vol.LIV, 1 September, pp.297–316, New Series, London, 1893.

—, 'Concerning the question of the House of Lords and Socialism', *Pall Mall Magazine*, vol.V, April, pp.671–83, London, 1895.

—, *An address on bimetallism: delivered at the Junior Constitutional Club on November 22nd, 1895*, pamphlet, McCorquodale, London, 1895.

—, 'Punting and Punts', in the Earl of Suffolk and Berkshire, Peek, Hedley and Aflalo, F. G., eds, *Encyclopedia of Sport*, vol.2, Lawrence and Bullen, London, 1898.

—, McLean, D. H. and W. H. Grenfell, *Rowing, Punting and Punts*, no.IX in the Suffolk Sporting Series, Lawrence and Bullen, London, 1898.

—, 'Punting', in Aflalo, F. G, ed., *The Cost of Sport*, John Murray, London, 1899.

—, 'The Mediterranean Tunny', *The Nineteenth Century Magazine*, October, pp.639–49, London, 1901.

—, 'Masters of Their Arts III: Rowing', *The Badminton Magazine*, vol.XIV, pp.237–47, March 1902.

—, 'Rowing' in Watson, A. E. T., editor, *English Sport*, Macmillan, London, 1903.

—, *On Money*, William Lea, London, 1904 (and also 1928 and 1933).

Desborough, Lord, *Official Report for the London Olympic Games*, British Olympic Council, Summer 1908.

—, 'The Real Yellow Peril', *The Financial Review of Reviews*, Westminster Gazette, September, London, 1909.

—, 'The Story of the Oar', *The Field, The Country Gentleman's Newspaper*, vol.115, London, 19 March 1910.

—, 'Introduction', *Catalogue of exhibits in the British section of the International Shooting and Fields Sports Exhibition, Vienna, 1910*, His Majesty's Stationery Office, London, 1911.

—, 'Tarpon fishing in the Pass', in Aflalo, F. G., editor, *A Book of Fishing Stories*, pp.143–60, J. M. Dent, London, 1913.

—, *Fifty Years of Sport at Oxford, Cambridge and the Great Public Schools: Eton, Harrow and Winchester*, arranged by Lord Desborough and edited by Croome, A. C. N., Lyttelton, Hon. R. H., Page, Arthur, and Noel, Evan B., Walter Southwood, London, three volumes, 1913, 1913 and 1922.

—, *Lord Kitchener As I Knew Him, an address delivered at a Memorial Service to Lord Kitchener at the Canadian War Memorial Hospital, Cliveden, on Sunday 11th 1916*, reprinted from the *Empire Review*, pamphlet privately published, 1916.

—, 'Introduction', Winstanley, H. M., *Punting*, Methuen, London, 1922.

—, 'Foreword', Eliott-Lynn, Sophie. C., *Athletics for Women and Girls: How to be an Athlete and Why*, Robert Scott, London, 1925.

—, 'Preface', Fotheringham, D. R., *The Date of Easter and other Christian Festivals*, Society for Promoting Christian Knowledge, London, 1928.

—, 'An article on a fixed date for Easter', *World Trade, Journal of the International Chamber of Commerce*, 1929 [referred to in a letter to Ettie, 30 November 1929, Hertfordshire Archives and Local Studies, Hertford, D/ERvC1159/1102].

—, 'Foreword', Pash, H., editor, *Fifty Years of Progress 1880–1930. The Jubilee Souvenir of the Amateur Athletic Association*, Amateur Athletic Association, London, 1930.

—, 'Sport of Many Kinds', in *Fifty Years, Memories and Contrasts, A Composite Picture of the Period 1882–1932*, by twenty-seven contributors to *The Times*, pp.196–201, Thornton Butterworth, London, 1932.

—, 'Foreword' in Howel, E. B., Stén, H. and Duelle Alling, N., Banco Hipotecario, Argentina, *Silver Money, the case for its restoration: being a precis of some of the world's most authoritative opinion*, Headley Bros, London and Bankers Publishing Company, USA, 1934.

—, 'Preface', Gravé, Félix, *Fencing Comprehensive*, Hutchinson, London, 1934.

—, 'Foreword', Parker, Eric, *Ethics of Egg-Collecting*, The Field, London, 1935.

—, 'Foreword' in Bunge, J. H. T., *Tideless Thames in Future London*, Thames Barrage Association, London, 1944.

Parliamentary speeches and reports

William Grenfell was a Member of Parliament for three constituencies (Salisbury, Hereford and Wycombe), serving in total around eight and a half years (twice in the 1880s, once in the 1890s and his longest period from late 1900 to 1905). He then served in the House of Lords for forty years, being particularly active between 1925 and 1928.

He is recorded as having made 699 contributions in Parliament, though some of these are very brief. His first contribution was in 1901 and his last in 1937. Full details are available at: api.parliament.uk/historic-hansard/people/mr-william-grenfell/index.html

One significant contribution involved chairing the post-First World War committee on the Police Service, known as the Desborough Committee, its output being the Desborough Reports. See *Report of the Committee on the Police Service of England, Wales and Scotland. Part I*, Cmnd 253, 1919; *Part II*, Cmnd 574, 1920; further Committee Report, Cmnd 2086, 1924.

Selected texts about William Grenfell, Lord Desborough

Interview in *Lock to Lock Times*, No.32, 12 January 1889.

'Mr. William Henry Grenfell', *Baily's Magazine of Sports and Pastimes*, No.365, vol.LIV, July 1890, pp.1–3.

Feature in *Mayfair and County Society*, 4 July 1914.

Lord Desborough, obituary, *The Times*, 10 January 1945.

Lord Desborough, obituary, *Maidenhead Advertiser*, 17 January 1945.

'All Rounder from an Amateur Age', *Country Life*, 2 June 1983, p.1485.

Entry in *Oxford Dictionary of National Biography*, Ian F. W. Beckett, Oxford University Press, Oxford, May 2012.

Grenfell Family History entry, grenfellhistory.co.uk/biographies/william_henry_grenfell.php

Wikipedia entry, en.wikipedia.org/wiki/William_Grenfell,_1st_Baron_Desborough

Select bibliography

Abdy, Jane and Gere, Charlotte, *The Souls*, Sidgwick & Jackson, London, 1984.

Ackroyd, Peter, *Thames: Sacred River*, Chatto & Windus, London, 2007.

Allison, Lincoln, *The Politics of Sport*, Manchester University Press, Manchester, 1986.

—, *Amateurism in Sport, An Analysis and a Defence*, Frank Cass, London, 2001.

Asquith, Margot, *The Autobiography of Margot Asquith*, 1962; originally published in two volumes in 1920 and 1922, edited by Mark Bonham Carter, Weidenfeld & Nicolson, London, 1995.

Baker, Keith, *The 1908 Olympics: The First London Games*, Sportsbooks, Cheltenham, 2008.

Balfour, Arthur J, *Chapters of Autobiography*, Cassell, London, 1930.

Balston, Jenny, *The Story of St Stephen's College*, published by the Old St Stephenites Society, 1994.

Barker, Philip, 'The story of the first Lord of the London Olympic Rings', 3 June 2012, www.insidethegames.biz/articles/17153/lord-desborough-the-niagara-falls-swimmer-who-helped-save-the-london-1908-games-

Birley, Derek, *Sport and the Making of Britain*, Manchester University Press, Manchester, 1993.

Bolger, Angela, *The changing face of Taplow Court*, catalogue for an SGI-UK exhibition at Taplow Court, 1997.

Brassard, Nigel à, *The Rise and Fall of Stické Tennis 1874–1939*, Ronaldson Publications, Oxford, 2017.

Bruce, James, *The Neptune Book of Tennis & Rackets*, James Bruce, 2015.

Burnell, R. D., *The Oxford and Cambridge Boat Race 1821–1953*, Oxford University Press, Oxford, 1954.

Burstall, Patricia, *The Golden Age of the Thames*, David and Charles, Newton Abbot, 1981.

Campbell, John, *Haldane: The Forgotten Statesman who Shaped Modern Britain*, Hurst & Company, London, 2020.

Cannadine, David, *The Decline and Fall of the British Aristocracy*, Yale University Press, New Haven, 1990.

—, *Aspects of Aristocracy: Grandeur and Decline in Modern Britain*, Yale University Press, New Haven, 1994.

—, *Ornamentalism: How the British Saw Their Empire*, Allen Lane, The Penguin Press, London, 2001, paperback edition, 2002.

Channon, Henry 'Chips', *The Diaries (Volume 3): 1943–57*, edited by Simon Heffer, Hutchinson, London, 2022.

Cooch Behar, Maharajah of, *Thirty-seven Years of Big Game Shooting in Cooch Behar, the Duars, and Assam. A rough diary*, Rowland Ward, London and Bennett, Coleman & Co., Bombay, 1908.

Cook, Theodore Andrea, *The Cruise of the Branwen*, privately published, London, 1908.

—, *The Sunlit Hours, A Record of Sport and Life*, Nisbet, London, 1925.

—, *Character and Sportsmanship*, Williams and Norgate, London, 1927.

Davenport-Hines, Richard, *Ettie: The Intimate Life and Dauntless Spirit of Lady Desborough*, Weidenfeld & Nicolson, London, 2008.

Deford, Frank, 'The Little-Known History of How the Modern Olympics Got Their Start', *Smithsonian Magazine*, July 2012.

Defty, Andrew, 'What happened to the Easter Act, 1928?', Who Runs Britain?, April 2017, whorunsbritain.blogs.lincoln.ac.uk/2017/04/17/what-happened-to-the-easter-act/

Desborough, Ettie, *Pages from a Family Journal 1888–1915*, private press, 1916.

—, *Flotsam and Jetsam*, occasional pieces including letters to *The Times*, private press, 1949.

Dodd, Christopher, *Henley Royal Regatta*, Stanley Paul, London, 1981.

—, *The Oxford and Cambridge Boat Race*, Stanley Paul, London, 1983.

Eade, Brian, *Along the Thames: Britain in Old Photographs*, Sutton, Stroud, 1997.

Eade, John, Thames website, Where Thames Smooth Waters Glide, thames.me.uk

Egremont, Max, *Balfour: A Life of Arthur James Balfour*, William Collins, London, 1980.

Ellenberger, Nancy W., *Balfour's World: Aristocracy and Political Culture at the Fin de Siècle*, The Boydell Press, Woodbridge, 2015.

Evans, David, *A history of the Julian Cup, 1924–2004, 80 years of local limited overs cricket*, Denwal Press, Maidenhead, 2004.

Fare, Malcolm, Fildes, Luke and Gray, Edmund, *The Epee Club – 100 Years*, The Epée Club, 2000.

Ferriday, Patrick, *Before the Lights Went Out: The 1912 Triangular Tournament*, Von Krumm Publishing, Brighton, 2011.

Fotheringham, Rev. David R., *The Date of Easter and other Christian Essays*, Society for Promoting Christian Knowledge, Macmillan, London, 1928.

Francis, J. M. and Urwin, A. C. B., 'Francis Francis 1822–1886; Angling and Fish Culture in Twickenham, Teddington and Hampton', Borough of Twickenham Local History Society Paper, no.65, 1991.

Gage, Nicolas, *My Life So Far, Memoirs of Nicolas Gage*, Dynasty Press, London, 2020.

Gilpin, J. F., 'The Canadian Agency and British Investment in Western Canadian Land, 1905–1915', thesis submitted for the degree of Doctor of Philosophy at the University of Leicester, June 1992.

Greenhalgh, Paul, 'Art, Politics and Society at the Franco-British Exhibition of 1908', *Art History*, vol.8, no.4, pp.433–52, December 1985.

Grenfell, Julian, *Julian Grenfell, soldier and poet: letters and diaries*, ed. Kate Thompson, Hertfordshire Record Society, Hertford, 2004.

Hansard, Basil, *Leaders of the Empire*, vol.iv, with photographs by Reginald Haines, Virtue and Co., London, 1912.

Hardyment, Christina, *Writing the Thames*, Bodleian Library, Oxford, 2016.

Harris, Luke J., *Britain and the Olympic Games, 1908–1920*, Palgrave Studies in Sport and Politics, 2015.

Herd, Andrew, *The Flyfishers – A History of the Flyfishers' Club*, Medlar Press, Ellesmere, 2019.

Jenkins, Rebecca, *The First London Olympics 1908: The definitive story of London's most sensational Olympics to date*, Piatkus, London, 2008.

Jerrold, Walter, *The Silvery Thames*, Alf Cooke, Leeds, 1906.

Kent, Graeme, *London's Olympic Follies: The Madness and Mayhem of the 1908 London Games, A Cautionary Tale*, The Robson Press, London, 2012.

Lambert, Angela, *Unquiet Souls: The Indian Summer of the British Aristocracy 1880–1918*, Macmillan, London, 1984.

Lee, Simon, *Vincent's 1863–2013*, Third Millennium Publishing, London, 2014.

Lion, Paul, *It's a Load of Rowlocks: A Potted History of Maidenhead Rowing Club*, Maidenhead Rowing Club, 2020.

Llewellyn, Matthew P., *Rule Britannia: Nationalism, Identity and the Modern Olympic Games*, Routledge, Abingdon, 2012.

Lovesey, Peter, *The Official Centenary History of the Amateur Athletic Association*, Guinness Superlatives, London, 1979.

Mackenzie, Jeanne, *The Children of the Souls: A Tragedy of the First World War*, Chatto & Windus, London, 1986.

Mangan, J. A., *Athleticism in the Victorian and Edwardian Public School: The Mergence and Consolidation of an Educational Ideology*, Cambridge University Press, Cambridge, 1981.

—, *The Games Ethic and Imperialism: Aspects of the Diffusion of an Ideal*, Frank Cass, London, 1998.

Mangan, J. A. and Walvin, James, eds, *Manliness and Morality: Middle-class Masculinity in Britain and America, 1800–1940*, Manchester University Press, Manchester, 1987.

McManus, Mary Kathleen, 'The End of Imperial Diplomatic Unity, 1919–1928: Anglo-Canadian Relations from the British Perspective', thesis submitted for the degree of Doctor of Philosophy, University of London, March 1992.

Meynell, Violet, *Julian Grenfell*, Burns & Oates Ltd., London, 1917.

Mosley, Nicholas, *Julian Grenfell: His Life and the Times of His Death, 1888–1915*, Weidenfeld & Nicolson, 1976.

—, *Efforts at Truth: An Autobiography*, Secker & Warburg, London, 1994.

Parry, Major E. Gambier, *Suakin, 1885 by an Officer who was there*, Kegan Paul, London, 1885.

Rice, Jonathan, *Presidents of the MCC*, Methuen, London, 2006.

Ridley, Jane, 'The Souls', Oxford Dictionary of National Biography entry, published online, 22 September 2005.

Rivington, Robert, *Punting: Its History and Techniques*, R. T. Rivington, Oxford, 1983.

Robinson, John Martin, *Felling the Ancient Oaks: How England Lost its Great Estates*, Aurum History, London, 2011.

Rogers, G. *A Century of Bowling in Berkshire 1910 to 2010*, Royal County of Berkshire Bowling Association, 2010.

Rose, William and Penelope, *So Many Boats, So Little Time*, catalogue of the Rose Collection, private press, 2019.

Salmond, Monica, *Bright Armour*, Faber and Faber, London, 1935.

Smales, Nigel, *Taplow Moments: A Unique History*, Words by Design, Oxfordshire, 2015.

Solomon, David J., *A history of fish and fisheries of the River Thames*, Fluvial Books, United Kingdom, 2021.

Tickner, Lisa, 'Messing about in Boats: E. J. Gregory's "Boulter's Lock: Sunday Afternoon" (R.A. 1897)', *Oxford Art Journal*, vol. 25, no. 2, pp.1–28, December 2002.

Tinniswood, Adrian, *The Long Weekend: Life in the English Country House Between the Wars*, Vintage, London, 2018.

—, *Noble Ambitions: The Fall and Rise of the English Country House after World War II*, Basic Books, New York, 2021.

Thames Conservancy, The, *Centenary Report, 1857–1957*, Thames Conservancy, London, 1957.

Tranter, Neil, *Sport, Economy and Society in Britain, 1750–1914*, Cambridge University Press, Cambridge, 1998.

Vurpillat, J. T., 'The Other Cross of Gold: The United States and the Search for Global Monetary Stability, 1867–1900', Ph.D. Dissertation, Graduate School of the University of Texas at Austin, 2014.

Watts-Russell, Penny, 'Coal, Copper, Copperopolis . . . a tale of smelting copper at Middle and Upper Bank works, Swansea', *The Journal of the Trevithick Society*, no.46, 2019.

—, 'The Grenfells of Marazion', *Old Cornwall*, vol.16, no.2, Autumn 2022.

—, 'The Grenfells of St Just & the Grenvilles of Kilkhampton: of the same Cornish stock, fact or fiction?', *Journal of Cornwall Association of Local Historians*, no.75, pp.50–57, Spring 2023.

Wenham, Simon, *Pleasure Boating on the Thames: A History of Salter Bros, 1858–Present Day*, The History Press, Stroud, 2014.

Wilcock, Bob, *The 1908 Olympic Games, the Great Stadium and the Marathon: A Pictorial Record*, The Society of Olympic Collectors, London, 2008.

Wilton, Iain, *C. B. Fry: King of Sport*, Metro Publishing, London, 2002.

Wohl, Anthony S., *Endangered Lives: Public Health in Victorian Britain*, Dent, London, 1983.

APPENDIX 4

Acknowledgements and Picture Credits

We want first to acknowledge the great encouragement and energetic support we received from Deborah Gage, as a knowledgeable member of the Grenfell family and curator of the collections at Firle Place, Sussex. We are also grateful for the enthusiastic collaboration of Paul Mainds, founding director of the River and Rowing Museum in Henley-on-Thames, who has been a fount of knowledge on all things relating to rowing, the Thames, Leander Club and Lord Desborough.

The help of other members of the Grenfell family has been invaluable and, in particular, Ivo Mosley and Penny Watts-Russell: in locating records and photographic materials, guiding us in thinking about the diversity of Desborough's achievements, and reviewing draft chapters. We are also grateful to Lord Nicolas Gage and Lady Camilla Cazalet, Lord Desborough's surviving grandchildren, for sharing memories and providing access to family albums. Others in the family, including Richard Aylmer, David Cazalet, Hal Cazalet, Viscountess Alicia Head, David Salmond, Lady Verity Ravensdale, Caroline Vance and members of the Mosley family – Amanda, Clare, Matthew, Robert and Teresa – have also been helpful with offering encouragement and access to photographs and albums. Additionally, we have benefited from using the Grenfell Family website, www.grenfellhistory.co.uk, maintained previously by Arthur Coomb, and are grateful to Peter Grenfell Coomb. Sanda McWilliam and Angela Bolger of SGI-UK encouraged us to spend time at the Desborough family home, Taplow Court, while Jonathan Reekie and Lavinia Greenlaw generously invited us to visit Whiteslea Lodge on Hickling Broad.

In our early explorations we were greatly encouraged by advice from Richard Davenport-Hines, whose full biography of Ettie Desborough brilliantly evokes the world of Taplow Court. We were also pleased to talk with Nicholas Mosley, whose biography of Julian Grenfell offers many insights into the dynamics of the earlier generations of the Grenfell family.

There are many with Thames connections who have shared their knowledge and we are grateful to them, including Graham Bartholomew (Thames Sailing Club); Mark

Blandford-Baker (Balliol rowing); Peter Bowell (chronicler of Abel Beesley); John Carpenter (Island history, Shepperton); Göran R. Buckhorn and Tim Koch (Hear the Boat Sing website); Tom Christie (Thames Conservancy history); Simon Davis; Chris Dodd (history of rowing); Diana Douglas (early Thames Punting Club history); John Eade (Where Thames Smooth Waters Glide website); Mark Edwards (Richmond Bridge Boathouse); Christina Hardyment; Jeff Manning (Henley Sailing Club); Nick Pollard (Sunbury and Shepperton Local History Society); Penny Rose (Rose Collection); Dr David Solomon (Thames Fishery); Simon Wenham (Thames historian); Thomas Weil (rowing historian); Mike Sweeney, Tony Gordon, Geoffrey Leggett, Timma Marett and colleagues at Leander Club, Henley-on-Thames; Catherine Neale, Katherine Robson, Cate Tren and David Worthington, River and Rowing Museum, Henley-on-Thames; Way's Bookshop, Henley-on-Thames; as well as Daniel and Sarah Teuten, Matthew Gordon, Mike Hart, Simon Leifer, Natalie Maclean, Christopher Nairne, Mark Vellacott and members of the Thames Punting Club and colleagues at City Barge, Dittons Skiff and Punting Club and the Thames Traditional Boat Society.

Lord Desborough's rich and varied participation in sport means that we are indebted to many colleagues who generously shared their knowledge and contacts, including Chris Paris and David McCulloch (angling); John Knott (Flyfishers' Club); Kevin Beaumont (Buckinghamshire County Cricket Club); Paul Smee (cricket and the Triangular Tournament); Adrian and Marion Coles (cricket and Wisden); David Partridge (Epée Club); Malcolm Fare (National Fencing Museum); Mike Williams (game hunting in India); James Bruce and Nigel à Brassard (stické tennis); and Neil Howitt and Robert McNicol (All England Lawn Tennis Club). We particularly appreciate the detailed research on the 1908 Olympics undertaken by Matthew P. Llewellyn of California State University, Fullerton, and the Latin translation of Lord Desborough's Oxford University encomium undertaken by Bernadette and Roger Hurcombe.

We have explored papers in various public collections, including during the complex period of lockdown restrictions, and would like to acknowledge particular help from various specialists, including Nigel Buckley and Naomi Tiley, Balliol College Library, Oxford; Lara Garrett, Berkshire Record Office (Thames Conservancy Records); Dr Kate Thompson, former county archivist for Hertfordshire, and cataloguer of Panshanger and Desborough family papers, and Chris Bennett, current archivist, and colleagues, Hertfordshire Archives and Local Studies, Hertford; Richard Ward, archivist, House of Lords Archives; Chris Atkins, former librarian, and Barbara Story, local studies librarian, Maidenhead Library; Ann Marie Linnabery, History Center of Niagara; Rick Berketa, Niagara History; Nancy Lang, Ojibway Heritage Society, Ontario; Alice Millea, University Archives, University of Oxford; and Jenny

Balston and Veronica Colin of the Old St Stephen's Society. We are also grateful for help from staff at the Bodleian Library, Oxford; British Library; British Newspaper Archive; British Olympic Archive, University of East London; Buckinghamshire Archives, Aylesbury; London Metropolitan Archives; Olympic Foundation for Culture and Heritage, Lausanne; Oxford History Centre; and the Rifles Berkshire and Wiltshire Museum, Salisbury.

There are many individuals who have given advice and support in relation to our research and writing, and in tracing materials and images, who we should like to thank, including Kevin Batchelor; Tim Boon; John Campbell; David Cannadine; Andrew Dilley, University of Aberdeen; Keith Dugmore; Phil Dutton, formerly Imperial War Museum; Angela Evans; Richard Faithfull; Tace Fox, Harrow School; Charlotte Gere; Tim Gerrard; Helen Ghosh, Balliol College; Brett Holman, University of Melbourne; Andrew Jacob; Martin Maclean (patents); Richard McLauchlan; Stephen Marfleet; Stephanie Marsh; Bill Morris; Eleanor Nairne; Javier Pes; Mark Pessell (The London Wanderer); Anthony Quinn, Magforum.com; Hugh Salmon, author of *Into Battle*; Adrian Tinniswood; Mike Williams; and Pam Turner.

We are specially grateful to all those who made advance pledges in support of *Titan of the Thames* (with Andrew Hall, Alan Lovell, Randy Lerner and Leander Club generously becoming patrons), which has made the book possible. Special thanks go to Katherine Grainger for contributing so enthusiastically to the book, and to colleagues at Unbound for their commitment to spreading the word about Lord Desborough, and in particular to Mathew Clayton and DeAndra Lupu, and to Imogen Denny for managing the editing of the book so sympathetically, Richard Collins and Tamsin Shelton for their attentive work on the text, Rina Gill and Suzanne Azzopardi for their publicity and marketing expertise, Lisa Fiske for the production, and to Mark Ecob for his design work.

Our very special thanks go to Lisa Tickner and Esther Williams, who have offered constant encouragement and helpful critical advice, over many years, for which we are tremendously grateful.

*

We gratefully acknowledge permission to quote from letters and diaries, particularly from the Gage, Grenfell and Mosley families, and from Hertfordshire Archives and Local Studies and Buckinghamshire Archives. We appreciate the help given by many in locating images and advising on them, particularly Bernard Horrocks at Tate. Images are reproduced in the book by kind permission and courtesy of the Grenfell Collections at Firle Place, Sussex, for paintings and albums (p.39, p.43, p.67, p.81, p.90, p.91, p.112, p.116, p.117, p.132, p.218, p.270, p.274, p.279); members of the

Grenfell and Mosley families for images in additional family albums (p.13, p.27, p.33, p.35, p.34, p.62, p.64, p.70, p.84, p.100, p.115, p.125, p.133, p.138, p.143, p.147, p.159, p.162, p.180, p.238, p.251, p.266); Buckinghamshire Archives (p.15, p.18, p.37, p.45, p.49, p.54, p.82, p.136, p.141, p.145, p.158, p.237, p.241, p.262); Olympic Foundation for Culture and Heritage (p.187, p.188, p.189, p.191, p.192, p.196, p.197, p.202); National Portrait Gallery (p.122, p.247, p.257, p.264); Thames Conservancy images courtesy the Environment Agency (p.215, p.220, p.221); Hertfordshire Archives and Local Studies (p.18, p.195, p.203); the University of Southampton courtesy SGI-UK, Taplow Court (p.259, p.260); Maidenhead Rowing Club (p.40); Christie's (p.2); Matthews-Northrup Map courtesy Boston Public Library (p.51); Rifles Berkshire and Wiltshire Museum (p.55); St Paul's Cathedral (p.56); Rose Collection (p.66); River and Rowing Museum, Henley-on-Thames (p.68); Diana Douglas (p.69); Jonathan Reekie (p.177, p.268); Tony Quinn at Mag-forum.com (p.210); Alamy (p.74, p.78); Topfoto Images (p.75, p.224, p.243); Malcolm Fare and Museum of Fencing (p.79); Flyfishers' Club (p.94); Getty Images (p.98); kind permission of Baylis Media Ltd. (p.104); Lost Heritage – www.lostheritage.org.uk – courtesy of Matthew Beckett (p.150); Maidenhead Library (p.217); Berkshire Record Office (p.223); Mary Evans Picture Library (p.240); Old St Stephenites courtesy Jenny Balston (p.271).

September 2023

Notes

Chapter 1: The Importance of Athens

1. Desborough to Ettie Desborough, 14 April 1906, on board SS *Ortona*, en route to Naples, Hertfordshire Archives and Local Studies, Hertford, D/ERvC1159/365.

2. Desborough to Ettie Desborough, 15 April 1906, on board SS *Ortona*, Hertfordshire Archives and Local Studies, Hertford, D/ERvC1159/366; Steam Yacht *Branwen* was launched in 1905, 135' length overall, and the first vessel built at the John I. Thornycroft & Company's Woolston yard.

3. Desborough to Ettie Desborough, 18 April 1906, Messina, Hertfordshire Archives and Local Studies, Hertford, D/ERvC1159/368.

4. The other representative was Robert Bosanquet, archaeologist and director of the British School at Athens; he offered Desborough and the team a tour of the Parthenon and some of the ancient sites during their stay.

5. Desborough to Ettie Desborough, 22 April 1906, Hotel Imperial, Athens, Hertfordshire Archives and Local Studies, Hertford, D/ERvC1159/369.

6. See comment on royal connections to fencing: www.leonpaul.com/wordpress/fencings-royal-connection/

7. Desborough to Ettie Desborough, 23 April 1906, Hotel Imperial, Athens, Hertfordshire Archives and Local Studies, Hertford, D/ERvC1159/376.

8. Ibid.

9. Theodore Cook gives a full account of the trip made by the Olympic fencing team to Athens and the discussions about a London Olympics for 1908 in Theodore Andrea Cook, *The Cruise of the Branwen*, privately published, London, 1908.

10. Lord Desborough, obituary in *The Times*, 10 January 1945.

Chapter 2: Early Years

1. The certificate is now in the collection of the Hertfordshire Archives and Local Studies, Hertford; the event was reported in the *Maidenhead Advertiser*, 1 November 1876, with the press cutting pasted into Georgiana Grenfell, The Children's Journal, Buckinghamshire Archives, Aylesbury, D-X_1174/1.

2. *Maidenhead Advertiser*, 1 November 1876.

3. Georgiana Grenfell, press cuttings from the *Maidenhead Advertiser*, 1876/77 in The Children's Journal, Buckinghamshire Archives, Aylesbury, D-X_1174/1.

4. For an assessment of broader changes in terms of 'political and social promotion' and upwards mobility in the nineteenth century, see Leonore Davidoff, *The Best Circles*, originally published by Croom Helm, 1973, republished the Cresset Library, London, 1986, p.60.

5. Pascoe Grenfell (1636–65) was the son of Hercules Grenfield (*sic*) and Jane Busvargus. Although there is no resolved view as to whether the Grenfell family is a branch of the Grenville family, when made a peer in 1905, Lord Desborough was granted a coat of arms emblazoned with devices used in the seventeenh century by the Grenville family. The issue is explored by Penny Watts-Russell in 'The Grenfells of St Just & the Grenvilles of Kilkhampton: of the same Cornish stock, fact or fiction?', *Journal of Cornwall Association of Local Historians*, no.75, Spring 2023, pp.50–57.

6. We are very grateful to Penny Watts-Russell for sharing articles, published since 2005, in *The Journal of the Trevithick Society*, on the earlier history of the Grenfell family and their connections with Cornish mining, copper and tin. See also the family history website: www.grenfellhistory.co.uk/. Grenfell was certainly aware of his early forebears, writing to Ettie, who was staying in Cornwall in 1907: 'I am delighted that Newquay is such a success: I wonder whether you will see St Just . . . Vide Three Clarions [is] over my Great-Great Grandfather's seat in the South Aisle in St Just Church (in the window, painted glass).' Desborough to Ettie Desborough, Taplow, 20 May 1907, Hertfordshire Archives and Local Studies, Hertford, D/ERvC1157/389.

7. For a biographical summary see www.historyofparliamentonline.org/volume/1790-1820/member/grenfell-pascoe-1761-1838. The business interests of Thomas Williams stretched from making copper trinkets traded for enslaved people in West Africa to the copper sheeting for the protection of ships' hulls. A full account of the business partnership between Pascoe Grenfell and Thomas and Owen Williams is offered by Penny Watts-Russell in 'Coal, Copper, Copperopolis . . . a tale of smelting copper at Middle and Upper Bank works, Swansea', *The Journal of the Trevithick Society*, no.46, 2019. Grenfell shipped copper ores from Cornwall to Swansea, where they could be smelted using nearby Welsh coal to produce copper ingots.

8. For records of the Williams and Grenfell businesses in South Wales, see the Richard Burton Archives, Swansea University Libraries and Archives: archives.swan.ac.uk/Record.aspx?src=CalmView.Catalog&id=LAC%2f45

9. Pascoe Grenfell and Thomas Williams differed on the question of the abolition of slavery, as Williams was an anti-abolitionist. A study of Grenfell family business interests in the 1830s reveals, however, investments in copper mining in Cuba, in which slave labour was employed; see Chris Evans, *Slave Wales: The Welsh and Atlantic Slavery, 1660–1850*, University of Wales Press, Cardiff, 2020. An account of Pascoe Grenfell's conversion to parliamentary reform is offered by Penny Watts-Russell in

'Pascoe Grenfell's long & winding road...', *The Cornish Banner*, November 2014, February and May 2015.

10. The purchase price is given by Angela Bolger, *The changing face of Taplow Court*, catalogue for an SGI-UK exhibition at Taplow Court, 1997, p.9.

11. Penny Watts-Russell in her article 'The Grenfells of Marazion', *Old Cornwall*, vol.16, no.2, Autumn 2022, goes on to note that 'Pascoe had embarked on the road to gentrification when he had had his portrait painted in the late 1760s; the acquisition of a coat of arms, seals and accoutrements of fine living indicate a family advancing socially and materially'. Strictly speaking the word 'gentrification' refers to a locality, but is sometimes used, as here, to refer to a family acquiring higher social status.

12. Such was Pascoe Grenfell's accumulation of land after his arrival in Taplow in 1794 that in 1835, in the run-up to the coming of the Great Western Railway, some twenty-one parcels of land owned by him were listed as touched by its proposed route on the Maidenhead side of the Thames. Information from Penny Watts-Russell. The enlargement of the Taplow estate included adding Iver (1800), Shoppenhangars (1801), the Manors of Bray (1818), Ockwells and Kimbers (1846), Taplow Court from Lord Orkney (1852), Lowbrooks (1856), Cresswells (1860), Philberts (1863), Foxleys (1864) and various other properties including the Orkney Arms (Skindles) and the Taplow Paper Mill. When the estate was dissolved in 1953, after Ettie Desborough's death, it comprised 12,000 acres. See Tom Middleton, *The Book of Maidenhead*, Barracuda Books, Chesham, 1975.

13. 'By the end of his life, in respect of his land-owning credentials, Pascoe had nothing to prove. His Taplow estate, by the time his great-grandson William Henry inherited it in the 1870s, enlarged with additions made by his son, was 3000 acres.' Penny Watts-Russell, 'The Grenfells of Marazion, continued', *Old Cornwall*, vol.16, no.3, Spring 2023.

14. Hertfordshire Archives and Local Studies, Hertford, D/ERvF127.

15. See Skindles Hotel Taplow, Historic Building Record Level 2, Built Heritage Consultancy, London, August 2015.

16. Georgiana Grenfell, The Children's Journal, Buckinghamshire Archives, Aylesbury, D-X_1174/1.

17. Ibid., 13 September 1864, Buckinghamshire Archives, Aylesbury, D-X_1174/1.

18. Grenfell to Georgiana Grenfell, 1873, undated, Hertfordshire Archives and Local Studies, D/ERv/C1157/21; uncertainties about his health recur throughout Willy's life, seemingly a mix of badly timed illness, strains from excessive exertion, and the effects of stress.

19. Arnold Lunn, *The Harrovians: A Tale of Public School Life*, Methuen & Co., London, 1914; republished by Methuen, 1926, and by Viewforth Press, California, 2010.

20. Ibid., p.276.

21. Ibid., p.269.

22. Grenfell to his mother, Georgiana, late October 1873[?], Hertfordshire Archives and Local Studies, Hertford, D/ERvC1157/24.

23. Dr Benjamin Jowett was Master of Balliol from 1870 to 1893; Hertfordshire Archives and Local Studies, Hertford, D/ERvC1442/1.

24. Grenfell to his mother, Georgiana, Sunday 23 November 1873[?], Hertfordshire Archives and Local Studies, Hertford, D/ERvC1157/31.

25. Grenfell to Benjamin Jowett, December 1873; a first draft before sending fair copy to Jowett, Hertfordshire Archives and Local Studies, Hertford, D/ERvC1168/1.

26. Benjamin Jowett to William Grenfell, Balliol College, 12 December 1873, Hertfordshire Archives and Local Studies, Hertford, D/ERvC1442/1.

27. Grenfell to Georgiana, Vincent's Club paper, 1877[?], Hertfordshire Archives and Local Studies, Hertford, D/ERvC1157/60.

Chapter 3: Manhood and Morals

1. Thomas Hughes, *Tom Brown's School Days*, originally published in 1857, Chapter VI, 'After the Match', hughes.thefreelibrary.com/Tom-Browns-Schooldays/6-1

2. A very useful overview of the extensive literature on 'muscular Christianity' is offered in a paper by Andrew Parker and Nick J. Watson, titled 'Muscular Christianity and Sports Ministry', accessible at: www.researchgate.net/profile/Nick-Watson-2/publication/318214265_Muscular_Christianity_and_Sports_Ministry/links/595d0aa8458515246872a5674/Muscular-Christianity-and-Sports-Ministry.pdf?origin=publication_detail. They give a definition: 'In short, the ideology of Victorian muscular Christianity proffers the notion that sport and physical education has the potential to build manly and virtuous character, which is typically characterised by ". . . fair play, respect (both for oneself and others), strength (physical and emotional), perseverance, deference, subordination, obedience, discipline, loyalty, co-operation, self-control, self-sacrifice [and], endurance" (Collins and Parker, 2009:194).'

3. J. A. Mangan, *Athleticism in the Victorian and Edwardian Public School: The Emergence and Consolidation of an Educational Ideology*, Cambridge University Press, Cambridge, 1981, p.9.

4. See British History Online: www.british-history.ac.uk/vch/middx/vol1/pp299-302

5. Mangan, *Athleticism in the Victorian and Edwardian Public School*, p.31.

6. Ibid., p.80.

7. Ibid., p.84.

8. A Royal Commission of 1864, headed by Lord Clarendon, led to the Public Schools Act of 1868, which made changes to the governance and management of seven boarding schools. The text is available at: www.educationengland.org.uk/documents/clarendon1864/clarendon1.html

9. Clarendon Commission, 1864, Recommendations for Harrow School, no.15, p.228.

10. Ibid., p.223.

11. Ibid., p.56.

12. Theodore Andrea Cook, *Character and Sportsmanship*, Williams and Norgate Ltd.,

London, 1927, p.xiv; also referred to in Mangan, *Athleticism in the Victorian and Edwardian Public School*, p.203.

13. Mangan, *Athleticism in the Victorian and Edwardian Public School*, p.203.

14. Another commentator associated with the philosophy of muscular Christianity was the American jurist and writer Oliver Wendell Holmes Jr, whom Ettie Grenfell befriended in the 1880s, and with whom she maintained a correspondence.

15. J. A. Mangan and James Walvin, eds, *Manliness and Morality: Middle-class Masculinity in Britain and America, 1800–1940*, Manchester University Press, Manchester, 1987, p.2.

16. Derek Birley identifies the phrase 'not cricket' as originating from 1867. He mentions how, after the disarray around the Eton v. Harrow match of 1873, in which William Grenfell played, the MCC issued a manifesto which said, 'Such scenes . . . would not occur if the partisans of both schools were to assist the authorities in checking the immoderate expression of feeling at the conclusion of the match'; Derek Birley, *Sport and the Making of Britain*, Manchester University Press, Manchester, 1993, p.329.

17. Mangan, *Athleticism in the Victorian and Edwardian Public School*, p.200.

18. A pocket book, *The Old Country*, edited by Ernest Rhys, J. M. Dent, London, 1917, was issued for the benefit of troops on the Western Front in 1917. An anthology of highly nostalgic poems and articles, it includes a short essay by G. A. Paternoster Brown titled 'Play the Game' which ends with the comment that 'the love of strenuous recreation and friendly rivalry . . . [engenders] a comradeship which stands fast . . . in the real and terrible game of warfare.' As part of a spoofing line in *Beyond the Fringe* in 1961, Alan Bennett misattributed Grantland Rice's lines to W. E. Henley.

19. Lincoln Allison, *Amateurism in Sport: An Analysis and a Defence*, Frank Cass, London, 2001, p.51.

20. J. A. Mangan makes a telling point about ritual as the 'idiom of conformity', *Athleticism in the Victorian and Edwardian Public School*, p.142.

21. Leslie Stephen, 'Thoughts of an outsider: public schools', *Cornhill Magazine*, vol.27, iss.159, March 1873, p.283; quoted in J. A. Mangan, 'Social Darwinism and upper-class education in late Victorian and Edwardian England' in Mangan and Walvin, eds, *Manliness and Morality*, p.146.

22. David Cannadine, *Ornamentalism: How the British Saw Their Empire*, Allen Lane, The Penguin Press, London, 2001, paperback edition, 2002, p.30.

23. An excellent overview of the issues of sporting links with empire is provided by J. A. Mangan, *The Games Ethic and Imperialism: Aspects of the Diffusion of an Ideal*, Frank Cass, London, 1998.

24. See Chapter 2, 'Concepts of Duty and Prospects of Adventure', in Mangan, *The Games Ethic and Imperialism*; and Tony Money, *Manly and Muscular Diversions: Public Schools and the Nineteenth Century Sporting Revival*, Duckworth, London, 1997.

25. Roberta J. Park, 'Biological thought, athletics and the formation of a "man of character"', Mangan and Walvin, eds, *Manliness and Morality*, p.7.

26. See Matthew P. Llewellyn, *Rule Britannia: Nationalism, Identity and the Modern Olympic Games*, Routledge, Abingdon, 2012, pp.3–4, thesis; the connection continues, as the William Brookes School in Much Wenlock is a 'Coubertin School' and part of a European network of schools that promote the idea of educating the body and mind together, and 'where Olympian values and themes infuse every aspect of school life'; see www.williambrookes.com/about-us/

27. Luke J. Harris, *Britain and the Olympic Games, 1908–1920*, Palgrave Studies in Sport and Politics, 2015, p.5.

28. Thomas Hughes, *Tom Brown at Oxford*, Cambridge, London, 1861, was dedicated to Revd F. D. Maurice, one of the founders of Christian socialism. The narrative of a young freshman at Oxford getting caught up in rowing has similarities with Willy Grenfell's own experience at Balliol in the 1870s, and is mirrored in the fictionalised account he wrote later in 'Rowing at Oxford', *English Illustrated Magazine*, 1889/90, vol.7, pp.495–506.

29. Hughes completes his remarks by writing, 'Indeed, I am not aware that any authorized articles of belief have been sanctioned or published by the sect, Church, or whatever they may be.' In the paragraphs that follow he makes a significant distinction between muscular Christians and sporting 'musclemen'.

Chapter 4: Rowing and the Boat Race

1. See *Baily's Magazine of Sports and Pastimes*, vol.54, July–December 1890; see also *Chapter 7 Outstanding Sportsman*.

2. W. H. Grenfell, 'Rowing at Oxford'; a detailed description of bumps racing, which fed into the article, is in the Buckinghamshire Archives, D86/18/13-26. Part of Grenfell's own college, Balliol, is at the junction between St Giles' and Magdalen Street East, which appears to be a source for the fictional St Giles College.

3. Ibid., p.499.

4. Grenfell's arrival coincided with the conclusion of Asquith's time at Balliol as a student, but he then became a fellow there from 1874 to 1882. He also started at the Bar as an undergraduate, went on to join chambers and was called to the Bar in June 1876.

5. The Balliol record notes 'of new and powerful oars there was an abundance amongst whom was Mr. W. H. Grenfell'. The Leander scrapbook for 1877 notes the Oxford University Boat Club President was not idle, taking promising oarsmen out in a tub pair – Grenfell among them. His position at No.4 seems to have become consolidated by February 1877, though on 27 February the comment was made: 'No 4 who is better known on the running path and in the cricket field than on the river, rows hard and well, but is rather faulty in time, from his dropping his hands at the commencement of the stroke.' By 15 March *The Country* noted that 'undoubtedly the strongest man in the ship is Mr Grenfell, no.4'.

6. Grenfell to his mother, Georgiana, 1876, undated, Hertfordshire Archives and Local Studies, Hertford, D/ERv/C1157/91.

7. The *Balliol Boat Club Journal* noted that 'Our prospects were somewhat gloomy as we had lost a captain who had rowed in the winning Oxford boat against Cambridge in 78 & was president of the varsity BC and it seemed difficult to find anyone to fill his place.'

8. However, his surviving oar is inscribed with his weight as slightly lighter at 12 stone 8lbs.

9. Patrick Robinson, Foreword, p.9, in Daniel Topolski with Patrick Robinson, *True Blue*, Doubleday, London, 1989.

10. *Standard*, 26 March 1877.

11. This BBC sound archives recording, *From Putney to Mortlake*, May 1938, BBC Library, no.2707, with a running time of 3 mins and 52 seconds, is available through the British Library. John Snagge was the doyen of BBC outside broadcast presenters. He commented on the Boat Race from 1931 to 1980. This was the first televised boat race, though a live image was only relayed from the finish at Mortlake, with most of the race conveyed by moving coloured markers on a chart.

12. Accounts vary as to the broken-oar incident – seemingly the oar fractured under the leather, but light pressure could still be applied to a very limited degree; see archives. balliol.ox.ac.uk/Exhibitions/exhib18boatclub.asp

13. A full account of the day has been compiled by his relative Maurice Phelps in *The Phelps Dynasty: The Story of a Riverside Family*, Words by Design, London, 2012; see also Tim Koch, heartheboatsing.com/2014/04/17/lies-damned-lies-and-the-1877-boat-race/. The *University Boat Club Journal* notes there was little doubt that Oxford had won and stated somewhat dismissively that 'The judge is a very old man & perhaps equally stupid'. See also Michael Underhill, 'Centenary of a Dead Heat', *Country Life*, 17 March 1977, p.645.

14. Record of the 1877 University Boat Race, p.144.

15. Grenfell to his mother, Georgiana, 14 February 1878, Hertfordshire Archives and Local Studies, Hertford, D/ERv/C1157/113.

16. The Oxford University Boat Club records mention that, 'Grenfell would not do for 6, a very hard worker but no waterman and always out before it', vol.3., 1870–1880.

17. The Oxford University Boat Club records note that 'the President being stopped by many distinguished members of the medical faculty. He consulted Drs Acland and Walsh and Sir William Gull and finally Dr Simmonds hoping to find a supporter; on the latter's forbidding him he was obliged to give in and wished to retire, not relishing the prospect of 3 months coaching a not promising crew.'

18. He coached in 1881, 1883, 1884, 1889 and 1890, recording three wins and three defeats.

19. Grenfell, 'Rowing at Oxford', p.506.

20. Maidenhead Rowing Club mistakenly refers to him as the first Captain. In fact that was D. H. Skrine in 1876, and he was followed by K. Morgan in 1878, who then passed the mantle to Grenfell in 1879. Grenfell had a Deputy Captain who ran the club.

21. As reported in the *Maidenhead Advertiser*, Wednesday 30 April 1879.

22. He was also on the Committee of Management in 1885–6 and again from 1908 to 1939.

23. Colin Clifford, *The Asquiths*, John Murray, London, 2003, p.29.

24. His other written pieces include his contribution to the *Encyclopedia of Sport*, vol. II, edited by the Earl of Suffolk and Berkshire, Hedley Peek and F. G. Aflalo, Lawrence and Bullen, London, 1898, and a chapter on punting in F. G. Aflalo, ed., *The Cost of Sport*, John Murray, London, 1899.

25. We are grateful to Paul Mainds for pointing this out.

26. The trophy that Desborough presented to the NARA was its most important.

27. Published in *The Field,* 19 March 1910, p.210; subsequently printed as a pamphlet.

28. Though largely descriptive, the lecture highlights Desborough's curiosity and his desire to promote his own interest to a wider audience. He acknowledged that the detail in his 'Story of the Oar' lecture made it quite hard work, writing to Ettie on 4 October 1910 from Dunrobin that 'Millie arrived here yesterday and read us her lecture [which] will rather surprise the Edinburgh Philosophers: she lectures to the same people I nearly killed with the Story of the Oar.' Hertfordshire Archives and Local Studies, Hertford, D/ERvC1159/489; the advertisement for a pamphlet version of the lecture comments that 'the whole lecture is a valuable study of ancient documents, written in an easy and popular style'.

29. Again, we are indebted to Paul Mainds for this point.

Chapter 5: Exploits and Expeditions

1. Lord Desborough, 'Tarpon fishing in the Pass', in F. G. Aflalo, ed., *A Book of Fishing Stories*, J. M. Dent, London, 1913, pp.143–60.

2. W. H. Grenfell, 'Lost in the Rockies', *The Nineteenth Century Magazine*, May 1892, pp.839–49; see references below for accounts of Niagara and Suakin. *The Nineteenth Century* has recently been critically referenced by Stefan Collini, who wrote: 'Appearance in the pages of a journal like *The Nineteenth Century* was a form of consecration because it enacted the fiction that there was just one conversation and only a small number of contributors to it who mattered,' in *London Review of Books*, 8 September 2022, p.12.

3. Grenfell, 'Lost in the Rockies', pp.839–49.

4. M. E. Leigh Child-Villiers, Countess of Jersey, *Fifty-One Years of Victorian Life*, John Murray, London, 1922.

5. In 1873 Webb became the recipient of a gold medal from the Royal Humane Society of Great Britain for life-saving. He obtained this when he jumped off the Cunard steamer *Russia* to save a sailor who had been washed overboard.

6. As described in the *Illustrated London News*, 4 August 1883.

7. The exact chronology of the trip is not entirely clear as he was also in Canada and the US later in 1884. Buckinghamshire Archives, Aylesbury, D/86/1, America/Canada – Desborough Travel Diary no.2, 11 October to 17 December 1884.

8. There is a connection between Webb and Grenfell through the Humane Society and life-saving. Grenfell ensured life-saving was promoted at the Bath Club and was the first President of the Life Saving Society formed in 1891. In addition, Abel Beesley, Desborough's punting coach in the 1880s, worked as an 'officer' for the Oxfordshire Humane Society and the University Humane Society, which aimed to help prevent people from drowning (given the increased leisure use of the Thames in the late nineteenth century). Later in life Desborough promoted the importance of life-saving through his work at the Thames Conservancy.

9. As reported in *Sporting Life,* Thursday 9 June 1910, p.2.

10. We are grateful to Ann Marie Linnabery, Assistant Director/Education Coordinator, History Center of Niagara, for making this point.

11. Lord Frederick Hamilton, *The Days Before Yesterday*, Hodder & Stoughton, London, 1920, www.gutenberg.org/files/3827/3827-h/3827-h.htm#chap09

12. *Coleraine Telegraph*, 26 September 1884.

13. Millburn is John G. Milburn, an Englishman who emigrated and lived in Buffalo (see en.wikipedia.org/wiki/John_G._Milburn). Grenfell stayed with him for a night prior to the swim. Milburn was noted for entertaining prominent Americans as well as international celebrities (see https://www.wnyheritage.org/content/the_milburns_and_their_famous_home_1168_delaware_avenue/index.html). President McKinley died in Milburn's house after the assassination attempt. Milburn was a well-known bimetallist and this might have been a particular link between Milburn and Grenfell. In a letter from Grenfell of 10 October 1901, from Taplow, there is reference to Theodore Roosevelt becoming President – 'too strong for poor McKinley, who was bound to die' – and refers to enclosing a letter: 'you remember the man who said you [one] couldn't swim across Niagara: that he had lived near Niagara for 20 years & never heard of it: I stayed a night with him at Buffalo & then swam across the next day in a frightful hailstorm – and I believe McKinley died in his house.' Hertfordshire Archives and Local Studies, Hertford, D/ERvC1159/277. See also www.digitalcommonwealth.org/search/commonwealth:4m90f1763

14. Grenfell to Ettie Grenfell, 7 September 1888, Hertfordshire Archives and Local Studies, Hertford, D/ERvC1159/33.

15. Grenfell to Ettie Grenfell, 8 September 1888, Hertfordshire Archives and Local Studies, Hertford, D/ERvC1159/34.

16. Letter describing the 1888 swim which took place on Saturday morning, 8 September 1888. In a further letter from Milburn to Grenfell, the former noted he had left 'word in Niagara to send me any papers referring to the swim --- nothing appeared or my request neglected', Buckinghamshire Archives, Aylesbury, D86/3A/2.

17. Excerpts from William Grenfell, Diary America/Canada No.2, 1884, Buckinghamshire Archives, Aylesbury, D86/1.

18. In Grenfell's letter of appointment, dated 15 February 1885, John M. le Sage of the *Daily Telegraph* confirmed that he had 'head office sanction for your proceeding to Suakin as a

Chief Correspondent for the paper. You will be authorized to draw rations for yourself, servant and one horse'; he seems to have been regarded by others simply as a 'special correspondent'. Letter courtesy of Paul Mainds. However, Grenfell's licence, as issued by the Commander-in-Chief of the army in the field on 21 March 1885, refers to him as an assistant correspondent. Grenfell had tried to travel with the mounted infantry but could not get a berth, so he went as a civilian, using his connections at the *Daily Telegraph* as a way of securing a place.

19. Grenfell's diary lists the correspondents working there from *Reuters, Daily News, Standard, Morning Post, Chronicle, The Times, Times of Egypt, Illustrated London News* and *Graphic*.

20. W. H. Grenfell, Suakin Diary, Buckinghamshire Archives, Aylesbury, D86/2. This is both a detailed and neglected account of Suakin, although only covering a short period, but it includes maps and a summary commentary on the campaign. It also includes rough notes made each day before writing up in the diary.

21. Major E. Gambier Parry, *Suakin, 1885 by an Officer who was there*, Kegan Paul & Co., London.

22. *The Naval and Military Gazette*, 29 July 1885.

23. A bronze plaque in St Paul's Cathedral crypt commemorates seven of the 'special correspondents' who lost their lives in the Sudan between 1883 and 1885.

24. A news clipping in the Buckinghamshire Archives, dated only as April 1885.

25. In his diary Grenfell describes himself, in the language of the times, as 'running like an ostrich from the Fuzzies – quite unarmed and pretty dry – past various parties – two or three on a camel etc. – wish I had something to stick into a chap who took shots at me – but all's well that ends well'. Buckinghamshire Archives, Aylesbury, D86/2/31.

26. The *Oxfordshire Weekly News*, 9 May 1917, was one of many papers that over time have cited incidents relating to Grenfell and Suakin. This one some thirty-two years after the event reported that Lord Desborough's horse had been shot from under him and he found himself obliged to try his sprinting powers against a horde of 'dervishes' mounted on fleet Arab horses. His pursuers were less than 100 yards in the rear and it was only after a run of half a mile, which brought him within sight of the British camp, that the dervishes gave up the chase. Other accounts have him fighting off the enemy armed with an umbrella. These all seem to be embellished views of the diary records we have cited.

27. As reported in the *Fishing Gazette*, 2 May 1885, on the meeting the previous week. There is widespread confusion as to the dates of Grenfell's time in Suakin and not least because in a subsequent campaign in 1888 (a date commonly referred to) the British force was led by General Francis Grenfell.

28. The cost of the second field force was given as £2,127,762. This was the cost over and above the normal costs of those military units and did not include the costs of getting them to and from Suakin.

Chapter 6: Racing Punting

1. The *Maidenhead Advertiser* noted on 17 January 1945, 'The death of Lord D will be felt deeply by many of his old servants, chief among whom is Mr Barrett Good, personal valet, butler and house steward to his Lordship for sixty-four years. Mr W. Joel, waterman for over fifty years, Mr Arthur Simmonds, gardener at Taplow Court for more than fifty years, and Mr George Emmett, land agent for the last seventeen years . . . all will regret the passing of a kindly master.'

2. Lord Desborough, obituary in the *Maidenhead Advertiser*, 17 January 1945.

3. Robert Rivington, *Punting: Its History and Techniques*, R. T. Rivington, Oxford, 1983, is the definitive exposition of the development of racing punting.

4. William Grenfell, from his chapter in D. H. McLean and W. H. Grenfell, *Rowing, Punting and Punts*, Suffolk Sporting Series, 1898, pp.71–2.

5. See Simon Wenham, *Salters in Oxford*, The History Press, Cheltenham, 2014.

6. Ibid., p.105.

7. Lisa Tickner's article about Boulter's Lock captures the sense of the boating craze, 'Messing about in Boats: E. J. Gregory's "Boulter's Lock: Sunday Afternoon" (R.A. 1897)', *Oxford Art Journal*, vol.25, no.2, 2002, pp.1–28; the popular cliché of men and women getting into difficulties with punting was well established, reflected, for example, in the numerous cartoons in *Punch* magazine, see J. A. Hammerton, ed., *Mr Punch Afloat: Punch Library of Humour*, Educational Press, 1907.

8. See Bertram Symons-Jeune, *The Art of Punting*, n.p., 1907.

9. *Lock to Lock Times*, 12 January 1889; Grenfell won the Amateur Punting Championship three years in succession, 1888, 1889, 1890.

10. *Lock to Lock Times*, 4 August 1888.

11. William Grenfell, from his chapter in McLean and Grenfell, *Rowing, Punting and Punts*, pp.70–81.

12. He later referred somewhat disparagingly to those using the running method: 'The vagaries of the old punting circumnavigators are much more rarely to be met with: the numbers of those who can stand still and keep a straight and speedy course has multiplied indefinitely.' From his chapter in McLean and Grenfell, *Rowing, Punting and Punts*, p.73.

13. Gardner was clearly serious opposition, as Willy wrote to Ettie in August 1887: 'I have just heard that Gardner has got a punt 2 inches smaller than mine! So he means winning if he can.' Hertfordshire Archives and Local Studies, Hertford, D/ERvC1159/11.

14. *Surrey Express and Thameside Chronicle*, Saturday 13 August 1887. The previous week Grenfell lost to Gardner at the Maidenhead Regatta, *Berkshire Chronicle*, Saturday 13 August 1887.

15. Kilby had beaten N. M. Cohen in his heat. Cohen was the Champion in 1891 and Kilby in 1892, so both were top quality punters.

16. A quote from the *Maidenhead Advertiser*, 7 August 1889, makes the point that in winning a race by a margin 'Grenfell's punt was much the lighter'.

17. *The Times*, 1 August 1891, Buckinghamshire Archives, Aylesbury, D86/4A/2.

18. A collection of fine Thames wooden craft, boating artefacts and ephemera built up over many years by William and Penny Rose and catalogued in their book, *So Many Boats, So Little Time*, published privately in 2019.

19. From *Lock to Lock Times*, reprinted in the *South Bucks Standard*, 5 September 1890.

20. Reported in *Lock to Lock Times*, no.252, 19 August 1890, p.11.

21. *Lock to Lock Times*, no.251, 12 August 1893.

22. Based on a photograph taken by Marsh Brothers in the late 1880s; for a period, championship medals were produced by Garrard, renowned silversmiths and appointed first Crown Jeweller in 1843.

23. One of the five racing punting clubs established on the Thames.

24. This standard dimension became 28' by 2' 3". As the 1894 Report noted, this solved the problem of equality in races. In 1898 two more regulation punts were built, measuring 30' long by 2' wide at the centre and 196 lbs in weight. They were made of white pine with h ends decked in and a floor of gratings fitted between treads – the 2' racing punt as used today. An author, most likely Grenfell, styled as 'Old Blue', writing in a 1900 review of punting titled 'Retrospect of the Season', observed how the improvement in the craft reflected the rise in popularity of punting. He commented how 'marvellous changes have especially been made in best and best punts of recent years.' He offered a table of the measurement of the punts used by winners of the Amateur Championship since 1890. In 1893 the boats were 27' long and 22" wide, but by 1897 they were 31' long and only 14.5" wide.

25. Faija was praised as 'one of the original founders of the Club and one of the chief movers in the Club's reconstruction and extension. His riverside home at Sunbury was a very popular resort, with which the early history of this Club is largely associated. He was an able and enthusiastic member and his loss is felt severely by all his friends.' Thames Punting Club Report, Annual General Meeting, October 1894, pp.5–6.

26. A. Collard was the Hon. Treasurer alongside Squire, and went on to design the TPC medal with Grenfell as model, struck for the first time in 1891 and reported in the TPC Report. Faija, in commenting on the medal, said, 'a very handsome medal, oblong in shape with the figure of a puntsman on one side and the flag of the TPC on the other'. He rather pointedly does not say it is Grenfell. Henry Faija in *Lock to Lock Times*, No.22. Peter Squire's substantial and detailed chapters on punting in the volume on 'Rowing' in the *Badminton Library of Sports and Pastimes* (edited by the Duke of Beaufort, President of the TPC to 1900), 1898, reveal his great knowledge of the sport. His five chapters (on Punts and Poles, the Punting Stroke, Punt Racing, Courses, and Professional and Amateur Punters) total some fifty-four pages and include photographs to illustrate his advice using W. Haines, the Professional Champion, as his model.

27. *Maidenhead Advertiser*, 7 August 1901.

28. Prior to the opening of this boathouse, racing had started opposite The Range at Shepperton, but by 1902 this had moved to The Ryepeck and the boathouse.

29. These included: a co-authored book with D. H. McLean on *Rowing, Punting and Punts* in the Suffolk Sporting Series, 1898; a chapter on Punting, in Aflalo, ed., *The Cost of Sport*, 1899; the Introduction to H. M. Winstanley's book on *Punting*, 1922.

30. Sara Wheeler, *Cherry: A Life of Apsley Cherry-Garrard*, Vintage Books, London, 2002, p.267.

31. Obituary of Lord Desborough by Winthrop Young in the *Alpine Journal*, 1950, p.395.

Chapter 7: Outstanding Sportsman

1. The 'Caps and Bells' column in the popular magazine *Tit-Bits*, interviewing him just ahead of the opening of the Olympic Games in July 1908, referred to Lord Desborough as that 'all-round sportsman'. An article in *Country Life*, 2 June 1983, p.1485, adds to the 'All Rounder' title the caveat 'from an amateur age'.

2. He played cricket for Balliol but for reasons unknown didn't continue with cricket at university level.

3. A list of his victories at school, university and elsewhere exists in sufficient detail to suggest he had a hand in compiling it. He was clearly a very successful athlete for his school house, competing in high jump, steeplechase and the hammer, and in the 100 yards, hurdles, the mile and the long jump for the school. This carried through to Balliol College and for Oxford, though mainly competing in distance running.

4. A. C. M. Croome, ed., *50 Years of Sport at Oxford and Cambridge and the Great Public Schools*, Walter Southwood & Co., Ltd., London, 1913, pp.21–2.

5. Also Oxford University Boat Club, with Grenfell President of both clubs in the same year (1878). He was also successively Secretary, Treasurer and President (1879) of Vincent's Club.

6. J. Fowler-Dixon, ed., *Fifty Years of Progress 1880–1930*, Amateur Athletic Association, 1930. 'Shamateurism' is generally defined as the pretence that an athlete has the status of an amateur, when he or she is in fact a full-time or professional player in a particular sport.

7. It was the custom for this match for the elite to travel out to Lord's by carriage, and the MCC had specific 'carriage arrangements', with over 430 carriages being accommodated in 1874. For the 1873 Eton v. Harrow match, Wisden recorded that 40,000 were present during the two days. As Wisden commented, 'Eton v. Harrow still holds its own as the great cricket attraction of the London fashionable season . . . The attendance was as rich in rank and it was great in numbers.' It noted the Four-in-Hand Club at the West End of the pavilion and the Coaching Club at the SE corner of the ground, 'mustered in full force and fine form, every drag being superbly freighted'. John Wisden, *Cricketers' Almanack for 1874*, London, 1874.

8. The 1873 game was notable in another respect. Over-enthusiastic Harrow supporters were chairing their Captain in and out of the pavilion and a fight broke out with

Eton supporters. When the police stepped in the two groups attacked the police and other ordinary spectators who supported neither Eton nor Harrow. In a report in the *Manchester Evening News*, 14 July 1873, the headline was: 'Disgraceful Proceedings'. Grenfell also played in the 1874 match but took no wickets, though press comment suggested he was suffering from quinsy, an ulcerated tonsil.

9. The I Zingari club had been formed in 1845 and by Grenfell's nemesis, Frederick Ponsonby, whose death, as Lord Bessborough, caused confusion at *The Times* (see *Chapter 20 Dynastic Tragedy*).

10. *Athletic News*, 8 May 1911; in his book *Presidents of the MCC*, Jonathan Rice picks up this theme: 'It is hard to imagine that a more versatile man has ever been a member of the MCC let alone occupied the Presidential Chair'; see Jonathan Rice, *Presidents of the MCC*, Methuen Publishing, London, 2006, p.132.

11. In August 1911 Desborough was taken aback by the cricketer C. B. Fry's request to the MCC that it should cable the Australian Board of Control asking them to contribute a fixed sum or a percentage of their net profits on the upcoming England tour as a donation to help support the Training Ship *Mercury* of which Fry was General Manager (though it seems his wife, Beatrice Sumner, who was close to the founder of the school, Charles Hoare, was the driving force). Desborough thought this was 'infra dig' (as recorded in the MCC files for 1912). Desborough then found that others in the Committee didn't agree, and was willing to waive his objection.

12. The Imperial Cricket Conference was the forerunner of today's International Cricket Council.

13. Warner, due to illness, stood aside as Captain for the series and was replaced by Jonny Douglas; see Patrick Ferriday, *Before the Lights Went Out: The 1912 Triangular Tournament*, Von Krumm Publishing, Brighton, 2011.

14. The MCC Secretary also replied to Baillieu, saying that the 'Committee today considered your telegram but felt it was quite impossible for MCC to interfere in any way in the selection of a team to represent Australia'. *The Advertiser* newspaper in Adelaide argued on 14 March that the message Mr Baillieu received had to be read in conjunction with that sent by Lord Desborough to Mr Warner, confirming its view that 'There is not the slightest doubt that the Marylebone Club expected the Board of Control to take official notice of that cablegram.'

15. Patrick Ferriday, *Before the Lights Went Out*, p.158.

16. See *The Sportsman*, 12 February 1912.

17. As cited in *Sporting Life*, 4 May 1911; *The Sphere*, Saturday 12 May 1912. The South African magnate behind the idea, Sir Abe Bailey, argued that it would be good for cricket and imperial interests. He accepted that 'it was merely a trial' and 'if the idea was a distinct success, all well and good. If not, it can do no harm.' It was described in *The Sphere* as the feature of the 1912 cricket season.

18. *Illustrated Sporting and Dramatic News*, Saturday 10 August 1912.

19. *Sporting Life*, 23 August 1912.

20. On a visit to Toronto (for a conference of the British Imperial Chamber of Commerce) in September 1920, Desborough spoke at the Empire Club of Canada on the topic of 'Empire Sport', and emphasised that 'you want not only to be proficient at your games, but you really want to have that true spirit of the sportsman, a consideration for others, which you can learn better, I believe, through the discipline of games than you can by any other means that I know of'. See speeches.empireclub.org/details.asp?ID=62165&n=1

21. In 1928 Desborough presented the London Fencing Club with an 18" silver statuette by Felix Joubert of the club's recently retired foil coach, Jean-Baptiste Mimiague, as a challenge trophy. In addition, each year the Desborough foil medal (2½" diameter in silver) has been awarded annually to the club's most promising foilist.

22. The Epée and Sword Club was founded in 1900, with Grenfell made President in 1904. See Malcolm Fare, Luke Fildes and Edmund Gray, *The Epee Club – 100 Years*, The Epée Club, 2000, p.28.

23. *The Times*, 2 June 1902.

24. Covering International Fencing Week, *The Times*, 4 May 1903, p.10.

25. Grenfell to Ettie Grenfell, 5 May 1903, Hertfordshire Archives and Local Studies, Hertford, D/ERvC1159/301.

26. Grenfell to Ettie Grenfell, 6 May 1903, Hertfordshire Archives and Local Studies, Hertford, D/ERvC1159/302.

27. Grenfell to Ettie Grenfell, Hotel du Louvre, Marseilles, 13 April 1906, Hertfordshire Archives and Local Studies, Hertford, D/ERvC1159/363.

28. Grenfell to Ettie Grenfell, Hotel Imperial, Athens, 24 April 1906, Hertfordshire Archives and Local Studies, Hertford, D/ERvC1159/370.

29. Grenfell to Ettie Grenfell, Hotel Imperial, Athens, 26 April 1906, Hertfordshire Archives and Local Studies, Hertford, D/ERvC1159/374.

30. The original had been displayed in the entrance hall of the Imperial Sports Club at the Franco-British Exhibition. In 2019 one of these two bronze statuettes of Desborough, signed by Bonanni and 27" high, dated 1908, sold at auction for £1,500.

31. Desborough continued with occasional exhibition matches but understandably after 1909, by now in his mid-fifties, drew his competitive events to a close while continuing to fence on a recreational basis. He wrote the Preface to Professor Félix Gravé's book *Fencing Comprehensive*, Hutchinson, London, 1934.

32. 'Sport of Many Kinds' in *Fifty Years: Memories and Contrasts, A Composite Picture of the Period 1882–1932*, by twenty-seven contributors to *The Times*, Thornton Butterworth, London, p.196.

33. He wrote this up in an article for the *Nineteenth Century Magazine*, vol.XXXI, no.183, 1892, pp.839–49; see *Chapter 5 Exploits and Adventures*.

34. Writing to his sons from India, Grenfell described how 'In this camp here there is a

nasty tiger who has eaten eight people quite lately – he came into their huts and takes them away when they are asleep – The huts are made of bamboo and leaves so the tiger easily gets in. And another nasty tiger has just killed eight bullocks and I have been to see them, as the tiger may sometimes come back and if you climb up a tree near one of the dead bullocks and it is a moonlight night you may see him & then shoot fire bang and you get him which would be a very good thing, but there is no moon tonight so it is no use . . . The elephants have been very naughty too – they pulled down our huts three times in the night and it was very difficult to drive them away – It is great fun seeing the elephants crashing through the jungle: they look very big and it is a fine thing to see them fighting – One of them would have squashed your dear dad the other day but he had a big gun which went bang and knocked it over . . . and the bison here are very big.' Grenfell to Julian and Billy Grenfell, 25 January 1892, Government House, Delhi, Hertfordshire Archives and Local Studies, Hertford, D/ERvC1161.

35. His entry in the 1934 *Dictionary of National Biography* summarised: 'He loved "the hill" and stalking in Scotland, fishing in many countries, big game hunting in the Rockies, in India, and in Africa.'

36. Ettie Grenfell to Grenfell, Government House, Delhi, 10 January 1892, Hertfordshire Archives and Local Studies, Hertford, D/ERvC1070/10.

37. Lord Desborough, 'Sport of Many Kinds', in *Fifty Years: Memories and Contrasts*, p.198.

38. Ibid., p.198.

39. Undated press cuttings from *The Field* in Grenfell family albums.

40. Letter to Ettie from Lochmore, September 1895, Hertfordshire Archives and Local Studies, Hertford, D/ERvC1159/109; Willy wrote letters when he and Ettie were apart, so this was often when he was away hunting. There is no other mention of Grenfell suffering from typhoid fever.

41. Grenfell to Ettie Grenfell (with the children in Saint-Pierre-en-Port), Holkham Hall, August 1897, Hertfordshire Archives and Local Studies, Hertford, D/ERvC1159/139.

42. Grenfell to Ettie Grenfell, December 1904, Hertfordshire Archives and Local Studies, Hertford, D/ERvC1159/323; 324/5 and 327.

43. *Country Life*, 2 June 1983.

44. Desborough to Ettie Desborough, Loch Merkland, 17 October 1917, Hertfordshire Archives and Local Studies, Hertford, D/ERvC1159/768 and 769.

45. *Illustrated Sporting and Dramatic News*, 31 August 1934.

46. From Jon Edgar's account, 'A Balliol Broadland Story', jonedgar.wordpress.com/2014/08/22/a-pulborough-sculpture-a-balliol-broadland-story/

47. An article in *Country Life* titled 'With the Harriers in Broadland – the tragedy of the Marsh Harrier', by Walter E. Higham, focuses on the efforts at Whiteslea to nurture the rare marsh harrier. *Country Life*, 19 December 1931, pp.687–9.

48. See *Alpine Journal*, vol.56, no.276, May 1948.

49. Edward Whymper in *Ascent of the Matterhorn*, John Murray, London, 1880, lists

Grenfell along with J. H. A. Peebles climbing the Matterhorn on 19 August 1877 with Imseng as a guide and taking the Breil route.

50. *Sporting Life*, 4 January 1896.

51. Panshanger was requisitioned for use by mothers and babies from the East End of London; and the Grenfell family moved for a period to Whiteslea.

52. Grenfell pre-dated Fry by nearly twenty years, but died only eleven years before him. While Grenfell was born in 1855 into a relatively wealthy family of businessmen and bankers, Fry was born in 1872 of good Sussex gentry stock who traced their family back over several centuries. Comparison was made between the two of them shortly after Desborough's death in a column titled 'The All-Rounder', in *The Times*, 12 January 1945, p.5.

53. Desborough, as President of the MCC, was involved in the planning for the 1911/12 England tour of Australia. As noted in endnote 11, one suspects Desborough had a low opinion of Fry. However, the spread of Fry's reputation can be measured in his appearance in C. L. R. James's famous cricketing memoir, *Beyond a Boundary*, 1963, where Fry is referred to as one of the 'great cricketers of the day'; available at: files. libcom.org/files/c-l-r-james-beyond-a-boundary-2.pdf, p.16.

Chapter 8: The Great Amateur

1. Grenfell wrote to his sister Lina that 'I have agreed to take the mastership of the Varsity Hounds next term: it can be done for about £150 – but there are a lot of farmers to see, and some hounds to get – I shall make night and day hideous at Taplow by unholy efforts to blow a horn.' 15 May 1876, Hertfordshire Archives and Local Studies, Hertford, D/ERv C1158/3.

2. Described in Croome, ed., *Fifty Years of Sport at Oxford, Cambridge and the Great Public Schools*.

3. Ibid., vol.2, p.176. On leaving Oxford the hounds were sold to the Pau Hunt in France, which had a well-established 'Cercle Anglais' of expatriate enthusiasts. The Pau Hunt has been in existence since 1840 (for details see www.thefield.co.uk/ hunting/the-pau-hunt-26878). It seems that drag hunting was not a great success.

4. As was evident from cards advertising meetings as seen in the Buckinghamshire Archives, Aylesbury, D86/4A/5. The Archives also hold a complete book of press cuttings on his harrier pack, D86/4.

5. *Illustrated Sporting and Dramatic News*, no.IV, 14 April 1923, p.236.

6. Grenfell had been a regular user of coaches for some years. In 1899 it was reported that he won a court case (Grenfell v Hipperson) following a collision between the Stanhope Phaeton being driven by Grenfell along with Ettie, who were travelling back from Ascot, and a heavily laden waggonette being driven by Hipperson. The phaeton was cut in half and the Grenfells were thrown into the road among the debris. Willy was left stunned for a while. The Lord Chief Justice awarded the Grenfells £75 for this case of negligent driving by Hipperson. In its earlier days the Coaching Club had a wider

selection of routes and venues, and these included Sandown Park and Kempton Park.

7. Members of both clubs would also take their coaches to Lord's and to Ascot. There were also annual shows at the Ranelagh Club, where coaches and teams would be judged on the correct turnout.

8. Each club had its own uniform – brown coats for the FIHDC and blue coats with buff waistcoats for the CC.

9. The Four-In-Hand Club met in the summer on the 1st and 3rd Thursday of each May and June.

10. See Andrew Herd, *The Flyfishers – A History of The Flyfishers' Club*, Medlar Press, Ellesmere, 2019, p.415.

11. In 1917 the Board of Agriculture and Fisheries set up a Freshwater Fish Committee with specific reference to eels under the chairmanship of Lord Desborough. It issued two 'admirable' reports with the recommendations being largely implemented by the Board; see President of the Board of Agriculture and Fisheries, Hansard, House of Commons Debates 18 July 1918, vol.108, pp.1264–336.

12. In *Punch*, 29 August 1917, p.164.

13. He was also active as the Thames Salmon Association's Executive Committee Chairman, and a regular writer to the press on the subject of fishing.

14. Reported in *The Field*, 1 June 1907.

15. Desborough ordered specially made reels from Hardy for his big-game fishing with nickel-plated brass bodies and a custom ivorine handle that could be elongated when the user was in 'fish-fighting' mode. The video *Silver King: The Birth of Big Game Fishing* gives a lengthy account of the history of this sport in the USA: flylordsmag.com/silver-king-birth-of-big-game/

16. Desborough's records noted 100 tarpon scales in a frame with the date and weight on each scale for the fish caught. See also Lord Desborough, 'Tarpon fishing in the Pass', in Aflalo, ed., *A Book of Fishing Stories*, pp.143–60.

17. Grenfell to Ettie Grenfell, Yacht Decoy, Florida, 30 April 1899, Hertfordshire Archives and Local Studies, Hertford, D/ERvC1159/209; Ettie, having spent some days fishing with Willy in Florida, had gone ahead to stay with Lord and Lady Minto in Ottawa.

18. Grenfell to Ettie Grenfell, Yacht *Decoy*, Florida, 3 and 6 May 1899, Hertfordshire Archives and Local Studies, Hertford, D/ERvC1159/2010 and 211.

19. From 'Tarpon Fishing in the Pass' in Aflalo, ed., *A Book of Fishing Stories*, pp.145–60.

20. *Maidenhead Advertiser*, Wednesday 22 March 1905, p.7. A very useful analysis of tarpon fishing and 'tarpon tourism' is provided by Kevin Kokomoor, '"In The Land of the Tarpon": The Silver King, Sport, and the Development of Southwest Florida, 1885–1915', *The Journal of the Gilded Age and Progressive Era*, vol.11, no.2, April 2012.

21. Another short article (without source or date) pasted into Georgiana Grenfell's journal for 1899 records that Grenfell's record for catching the largest tarpon was with a fish weighing 182 lbs and 7' 2" in length.

22. Grenfell to Ettie Grenfell, Favignana, Aegadian Islands, 31 May 1901, Hertfordshire Archives and Local Studies, Hertford, D/ERvC1159/257; Willy met with Ignazio Florio Jnr who had an extensive business empire in Sicily.

23. *Nineteenth Century Magazine*, October 1901, pp.639–49; in the article he also makes mention of his tarpon fishing in Florida. This was penned at some speed because on 20 September he mentioned in a letter to Ettie that he was already working on the page proofs; see Grenfell to Ettie Grenfell, Glendoe Lodge, Fort Augustus, 20 September 1901, Hertfordshire Archives and Local Studies, Hertford, D/ERvC1159/266.

24. Webb had in effect become a professional swimmer, earning a living by taking up challenges and giving demonstrations. He was, however, passionate about people learning to swim, a cause close to Desborough's heart through the Royal Life Saving Society. It was no surprise that Grenfell, the great amateur, would still support such a cause.

25. Captain Webb's widow, Mrs England, laid the wreath at the foot of the memorial, and their daughter, Helen, also attended.

26. According to the historian Mark Pessell, who writes the blog the London Wanderer, the fire started in the gym and then spread by means of the lift shaft. There were no air raids that night but there was one fatality.

27. And supposedly the basis for the Drones Club of Bertie Wooster fame.

28. Grenfell to Ettie Grenfell, Lochmore, 3 October 1897, Hertfordshire Archives and Local Studies, Hertford, D/ERvC1159/169.

29. As was the Bath Cup, a relay race for public schools initiated by the club (see www.londonaquaticscentre.org/newsitems/3638 for more details).

30. As reported in *The Sphere*, 18 July 1903.

31. The society acquiring royal patronage in 1904 through Edward VII. In a speech given in Toronto in September 1920, Desborough told his audience that 'we were getting on very well with the Royal Life Saving Society. It has now spread its branches all through the British Empire. In Australasia and New Zealand and in various other parts of the Empire it is flourishing to the last degree; and it rather amused me that on the last occasion we had a communication, from Iceland asking if they could translate our hand-book into their own language.' Speech on 23 September 1920 at the Empire Club of Canada; see speeches.empireclub.org/details.asp?ID=62165&n=1

32. There was a strong Harrovian connection with Queen's in this period. For the history of the Queen's Club, see Roy McKelvie, *The Queen's Club Story 1886–1986*, Hutchinson, London, 1986.

33. See *Sporting Life*, Wednesday 29 November 1911.

34. Frank Riseley wrote: 'I recognise what you have done since you have been good enough to take an active interest in Lawn Tennis and especially since you have acted as our President'. Letter to Lord Desborough, 21 August 1925, Buckinghamshire Archives, Aylesbury, D86/18/11.

35. A search of the Patents Register held by the British Library indicates that it was never

fully patented. It was common during this era to refer to one's own design as patented even though it hadn't been through the official process.

36. See uscourttennis.org/2015/sticke-tennis/; and James Bruce, *The Neptune Book of Tennis & Rackets*, James Bruce, 2015; and Nigel à Brassard, *The Rise and Fall of Stické Tennis 1874–1939*, Ronaldson Publications, Oxford, 2017.

37. Kevin A. Batchelor, boxing historian, has been researching the participation of Willy's sons, Julian and Billy, both of whom were enthusiastic boxers.

38. At this event there were also demonstrations of Elizabethan swordplay with Grenfell performing with a rapier and dagger. There were also exhibitions of boxing and 'ornamental and scientific' swimming.

39. As reported in the *South Bucks Standard*, 16 June 1899.

40. Wikipedia has a good entry on the sport: en.wikipedia.org/wiki/Bartitsu

41. Given this is cricket, this is of course a point of dispute! This section draws heavily on David Evans's book *A History of the Julian Cup, 1924–2004 – 80 years of Local Limited Overs Cricket*, Denwal Press, Maidenhead, 2004, and available from the author.

42. There were two concrete segments at either end of the wicket with the names of Julian and Gerald (Billy) picked out in stones embedded in the concrete. These pitches no longer exist. Brooks, however, kept Desborough informed of his plans and waited for his reaction to the idea of this new format for cricket. According to David Evans in his history of the Julian Cup, Desborough wrote back and confirmed he would present a trophy. Potentially confusingly, Richard Woolmer in his *History of Holyport and Local Cricket*, privately printed, 1994, recounts a conversation he had had with Mr Brooks's son Eric, who remembered standing with his father and Lord Desborough in the 1920s when they were discussing the new competition. Desborough's daughter Imogen, who was with them, suddenly piped up, 'I think Mr Brooks deserves a cup. Why don't you give him one?' To which Desborough apparently replied, 'What a good idea.' A replica of the Julian Cup was duly presented to Mr Brooks.

43. See Evans, *A History of the Julian Cup*.

44. He apparently lobbied the MCC to adopt the Julian Rule as a way of encouraging amateur cricket. In addition to the Julian Cup, Desborough is associated with a number of cups and trophies for sporting excellence which are still awarded today. See Appendix 2 for a list.

45. See also Evans, *A History of the Julian Cup*.

46. As reported in the *Sportsman*, 16 February 1912, p.8, in a cutting made by Lord Desborough.

47. In an obituary in the *Belfast Evening Telegraph* he was quoted as saying, 'Life is just an adventure, play the game and young and old, you will be a winner.' *Belfast Evening Telegraph*, Wednesday 10 January 1945.

Chapter 9: Ettie and the Souls

1. Arthur J. Balfour, *Chapters of Autobiography*, Cassell, London, 1930, p.226.

2. For an encompassing and critical view of the British aristocracy in this period see David Cannadine, *The Decline and Fall of the British Aristocracy*, Yale University Press, New Haven, 1990, and also *Aspects of Aristocracy: Grandeur and Decline in Modern Britain*, Yale University Press, New Haven, 1994.

3. Matilda Wake (1821–1906); see Richard Davenport-Hines, *Ettie: The Intimate Life and Dauntless Spirit of Lady Desborough*, Weidenfeld & Nicolson, London, 2008, p.16.

4. Ibid., pp.29–34.

5. Ibid., pp.32–3.

6. Monica Salmond, *Tracery*, undated typescript (1960s?), Book III, Part I (1909 to December 1911), p.81. Grenfell family copy at the Hertfordshire Archives and Local Studies, Hertford.

7. Nicholas Mosley, *Julian Grenfell: His life and the times of his death, 1888–1915*, Weidenfeld & Nicolson, 1976, p.8.

8. Ibid., p.9, 7 December 1886, written from Taplow Court.

9. Ibid.

10. Grenfell to Sir William Harcourt, 4 St James's Square, 13 December 1886. Bodleian Library, Oxford, Harcourt papers: 215 fol.214.

11. Georgiana Grenfell, *The Children's Journal*, 10 December 1886 and 30 January 1887, Buckinghamshire Archives, Aylesbury, D-X 1174/1.

12. Constance Aylmer (Grenfell) to Ettie Grenfell, Taplow Court, no date, (December 1886?), Hertfordshire Archives and Local Studies, Hertford, DE/Rv/C94/1.

13. Report in *Hertfordshire Mercury*, Saturday 19 February 1887, p.3; this may well have led to the burglary at Taplow Court in January 1888, when Ettie's jewellery was the target for thieves.

14. Jane Abdy and Charlotte Gere, *The Souls*, Sidgwick & Jackson, London, 1984, p.56.

15. Davenport-Hines, *Ettie*, p.37.

16. Newspaper cutting in Georgiana Grenfell's Journal, without source but most likely the *Maidenhead Advertiser*, Georgiana Grenfell, *The Children's Journal*, 9 April 1887.

17. Ibid., April 1887.

18. In the Visitors' Book of Willy's sister Constance an entry for 24 April 1887 has signatures from Willy and from Ettie, who appears to be trying out her new name: Ethel Priscilla Grenfell. Buckinghamshire Archives, Aylesbury, D-X 1174/3.

19. Buckinghamshire Archives, Aylesbury, Linen and Crockery, D/GR/18/5.

20. Davenport-Hines, *Ettie*, p.89; and an account in *Wilts and Gloucestershire Standard*, 21 January 1888, p.2.

21. Nicolas Gage and Camilla Cazalet in conversation with the authors, Firle Place, 14 July 2016.

22. Arthur Balfour, *Chapters of Autobiography*, p.232. Ettie and her friends sometimes referred to themselves as 'the gang'.

23. She added about Balfour, 'I do not think he had any intention of flattering

me; nevertheless, it was his own amazing charm and intelligence that brought us and kept us together.' Margot Asquith, *Off the Record*, Frederick Muller, London, 1943, p.51.

24. Max Egremont, *Balfour: A Life of Arthur James Balfour*, William Collins, London, 1980, p.109.

25. Salmond, *Tracery*, Book II, p.6. Grenfell family copy at the Hertfordshire Archives and Local Studies, Hertford.

26. Ibid., Book II, p.138. Grenfell family copy at the Hertfordshire Archives and Local Studies, Hertford.

27. Ibid., Book III, Part 2, p.164. Grenfell family copy at the Hertfordshire Archives and Local Studies, Hertford.

28. Nancy W. Ellenberger, *Balfour's World: Aristocracy and Political Culture at the Fin de Siècle*, The Boydell Press, Woodbridge, 2015, p.143.

29. Ibid., p.145.

30. Abdy and Gere, *The Souls*, p.173.

31. Richard Burdon Haldane, *An Autobiography*, Hodder & Stoughton, London, 1929, p.120; see also Abdy and Gere, *The Souls*, p.128, and John Campbell, *Haldane: The Forgotten Statesman who Shaped Modern Britain*, Hurst & Company, London, 2020.

32. Letter to *The Times*, 21 January 1929, following the publication of extracts from Lord Haldane's *An Autobiography*; reprinted in Lady Desborough, *Flotsam and Jetsam*, privately printed, 1949, pp.37–40; and in Abdy and Gere, *The Souls*, p.16.

33. The rhymes for each of the guests were published by Margot Asquith in 1920 (without Curzon's permission); see Margot Asquith, *The Autobiography of Margot Asquith*, 1962; originally published in two volumes in 1920 and 1922, edited by Mark Bonham Carter, Weidenfeld & Nicolson, London, 1995. Willy and Ettie's ran as follows:

> Very dear are the pair
> He so strong, she so fair
> Renowned as the *Taplowvite Winnies*
> Ah! He roamed far and wide,
> Till in Etty he spied
> A treasure more golden than guineas

34. Asquith, *The Autobiography*, pp.131–2; Willy certainly boxed (see *Chapter 7 Outstanding Sportsman*) but when Margot Asquith wrote this she may have mentioned boxing with Julian Grenfell in mind, who was active as a boxer. Boxing historian Kevin Batchelor confirms in correspondence with the authors that there is no evidence to show that Willy boxed in later life.

35. Angela Lambert describes Ettie as having 'refined the art of entertaining at Taplow Court to a dazzling confection of mutual admiration'. Angela Lambert, *Unquiet Souls: The Indian Summer of the British Aristocracy 1880–1918*, Macmillan, London, 1984, p.140.

36. Abdy and Gere, *The Souls*, p.65.

37. Oscar Wilde, 'The Birthday of the Infanta', 1891; see Mosley, *Julian Grenfell*, pp.20–1. In a letter dated 12 November 1891 to Ettie, Wilde explained that his primary inspiration for 'The Birthday of the Infanta' came from the Spanish visual arts: 'it is about the little pale Infanta whom Velasquez painted'; see Oscar Wilde, *The Complete Letters*, p.493; referenced in Leire Barrera-Medrano, 'Spain and British Decadence, 1880–1920: Aesthetics of Extremes', thesis submitted for the degree of Doctor of Philosophy, Birkbeck College, University of London, January 2018.

38. Grenfell to Ettie Grenfell, Amport St Mary's, Andover, 2 December 1898, Hertfordshire Archives and Local Studies, Hertford, D/ErvC1159/207. As students, Oscar Wilde and Willy Grenfell were admitted to the Mason's Lodge in Oxford on the same day.

39. Beatrice Webb, *Our Partnership*, Longmans, Green and Co., London, 1948, p.9.

40. Reference to the Duke of Portland's 1937 memoir in Abdy and Gere, *The Souls*, p.55.

41. Arthur Balfour to Ettie Desborough, 3 November 1911, Hertfordshire Archives and Local Studies, Hertford, DE/Rv/C132/24.

42. See Jeanne Mackenzie, *The Children of the Souls: A Tragedy of the First World War*, Chatto & Windus, London, 1986.

43. There are various assessments of the legacy of the Souls, including a harsh view by Angela Lambert that 'Their glamour and wit and charm were constantly remarked on – spitefully by outsiders, admiringly by themselves of one another. Yet in the end nothing tangible remains . . . it is all atmosphere, and fantasy, and myth, and the froth of varnished talk', *Unquiet Souls*, p.102; a more nuanced view is offered by Nancy W. Ellenberger, *Balfour's World*, and in an earlier article, 'The Souls and London "Society" at the End of the Nineteenth Century', *Victorian Studies*, vol. 25, no.2, Winter 1982; see also Abdy and Gere, *The Souls*; and a more recent academic study by Anne-Noëlle Pinnegar, '"The Souls" and their problematic receptions, past and present: a rediscovered late Victorian "Intellectual Aristocracy,"' dissertation submitted for Master of Studies degree, University of Oxford, September 2015.

Chapter 10: Together and Apart

1. Margot Asquith papers, Bodleian Library, Oxford, c6715.

2. Grenfell to Ettie Grenfell, 30 April 1899, Yacht *Decoy*, Florida, Hertfordshire Archives and Local Studies, Hertford, D/ErvC1159/209.

3. Mosley described how Willy, when he was out of Parliament, 'climbed in the Alps, he took up fencing again, he became President of the Four-in-Hand Driving Club, he travelled as British delegate to international conferences on Bimetallism'. Nicholas Mosley, *Julian Grenfell: His life and the times of his death, 1888–1915*, Weidenfeld & Nicolson, 1976 p.78.

4. Grenfell to Ettie Grenfell, 1905, undated, Braemore Lodge, Dunbeath, Hertfordshire Archives and Local Studies, Hertford, D/ErvC1159/147.

5. Grenfell to Ettie Grenfell, 8 January 1892, Palghat, India, Hertfordshire Archives and Local Studies, Hertford, D/ErvC1159/63.

6. Grenfell to Ettie Grenfell, 9 January 1893, Hereford, Hertfordshire Archives and Local Studies, Hertford, D/ErvC1159/82.

7. Referred to here is Willy's younger brother, Charles Molyneux Grenfell (1857–1915), who married Mabel Blanche Mills, known as Moppy. They married just ahead of Willy and Ettie in early 1887. Grenfell to Ettie Grenfell, 29 September 1897, Lochmore, Hertfordshire Archives and Local Studies, Hertford, D/ErvC1159/166. Charles served in the 10th Hussars in Egypt, in 1884 and 1886.

8. Grenfell to Ettie Grenfell, December 1904, Culford Hall, Bury St Edmunds, Hertfordshire Archives and Local Studies, Hertford, D/ErvC1159/327.

9. Grenfell to Ettie Grenfell, 17 August 1900, Shorncliffe Camp, Hertfordshire Archives and Local Studies, Hertford, D/ErvC1159/238 and 239.

10. Grenfell to Ettie Grenfell, 10 October 1904, Elveden Hall, Suffolk, Hertfordshire Archives and Local Studies, Hertford, D/ErvC1159/319 and 320. The request for Willy to consider being Governor-General was explored again in May 1921 by Winston Churchill, as Colonial Secretary, though it was politely declined by Willy; see *Chapter 12 Trusted Servant.*

11. Desborough to Ettie Desborough, Bath Club, 25 November 1920, Hertfordshire Archives and Local Studies, Hertford, D/ErvC1159/872.

12. Desborough to Ettie Desborough, Taplow, 5 December 1920, Hertfordshire Archives and Local Studies, Hertford, D/ErvC1159/873.

13. Grenfell to Ettie Grenfell, Netherby, 3 October 1901, Hertfordshire Archives and Local Studies, Hertford, D/ErvC1159/273.

14. Jane Abdy and Charlotte Gere, *The Souls*, Sidgwick & Jackson, London, 1984, p.173.

15. Quoted by Max Egremont, *Balfour: A Life of Arthur James Balfour*, William Collins, London, 1980, p.115.

16. Ellenberger, *Balfour's World*, p.197.

17. Maurice Baring, *Forget-Me-Not and Lily of the Valley*, Heinemann, London, 1909; the description runs: 'The lovely Pink, whom everybody was in love with, sat in a corner under a mushroom and whispered to all the Tulips and the Hyacinths one after another, and the Rose looked at her and frowned, and said it wasn't fair on the Rosebuds and that she ought to be turned out.'

18. Richard Davenport-Hines, *Ettie: The Intimate Life and Dauntless Spirit of Lady Desborough*, Weidenfeld & Nicolson, London, 2008, p.73.

19. Ibid., p.73; the term 'spangle' was used among the Souls to refer to an admirer.

20. Mosley, *Julian Grenfell*, p.79.

21. Grenfell to Ettie Grenfell, 23 April 1896, Brussels, Hertfordshire Archives and Local Studies, Hertford, D/ErvC1159/131.

22. Mr Cail was the business tenant for the Taplow Paper Mill in this period; Grenfell to Ettie Grenfell, 27 August 1902, Hertfordshire Archives and Local Studies, Hertford, D/ErvC1159/295. On the next day Willy writes about putting mill matters in the hands of lawyers, threatening that 'if I can I shall take possession & get rid of Cail, he has treated me very badly, perhaps because he is mad – poor chap'. Drawings for the proposed renewal of the mill building were reproduced in the Taplow Heritage Assessment, 2014.

23. Noted in Davenport-Hines, *Ettie*, p.131.

24. Richard Burdon Haldane wrote to his mother on 20 July 1908: 'I spent yesterday with the King at Taplow. He & I really get on well. He was affectionate – took me out in his motor to make a call – had a photograph taken of himself & others on the lawn in which he insisted that I should be lying on the grass talking to him. He arranged the position of my feet so that my boots might not come out of focus & appear big. In the afternoon he took me for a walk alone. I did my best to smooth over ruffles with the others'; quoted in John Campbell, *Haldane: The Forgotten Statesman who Shaped Modern Britain*, Hurst & Company, London, 2020, p.32.

25. Desborough to Ettie Desborough, Vienna, 8, 9 and 15 May 1910, where he was setting up the British section of the International Sporting Exhibition. Hertfordshire Archives and Local Studies, Hertford, D/ErvC1159/469, 470 and 475.

26. Davenport-Hines, *Ettie*, p.154.

27. Desborough to Ettie Desborough, Taplow, 7 April 1924, Hertfordshire Archives and Local Studies, Hertford, D/ERvC1159/1035.

28. Desborough to Ettie Desborough, Le Chanet, Neuchatel, 8 and 12 April 1924, Hertfordshire Archives and Local Studies, Hertford, D/ERvC1159/1036A and 1038.

29. Desborough to Ettie Desborough, January 1936, Ivo Mosley family archive, Hertfordshire Archives and Local Studies, Hertford.

Chapter 11: The Family World

1. Not all eight volumes seem to have survived; two of them are among the Grenfell family papers at the Hertfordshire Archives and Local Studies. Ettie also created separate scrapbooks, photograph albums and kept visitors' books for Taplow Court, and her daughters, Monica and Imogen, assembled their own albums. In 1895 she assembled a bound manuscript volume filled with quotations from various sources, titled 'Heart's Delight', inscribed for Julian from Ettie.

2. Ettie Desborough, *Pages From a Family Journal 1888–1915*, private press, 1916.

3. Reprinted in Nicholas Mosley, *Julian Grenfell: His life and the times of his death, 1888–1915*, Weidenfeld & Nicolson, 1976, p.36.

4. Monica Salmond, *Bright Armour*, Faber and Faber, London, 1935, p.17.

5. Grenfell to Ettie Grenfell, Taplow, 2 August 1891, Hertfordshire Archives and Local Studies, Hertford, D/ERvC1159/60.

6. Grenfell to Ettie Grenfell in Swanage, 6 September 1898, Langwell, Berridale, Hertfordshire Archives and Local Studies, Hertford, D/ERvC1159/186.

7. Grenfell to Ettie Grenfell in Swanage, 27 September 1898, Dunrobin Castle, Hertfordshire Archives and Local Studies, Hertford, D/ERvC1159/188.

8. Penny Watts-Russell has pointed out that in the autumn of 1885 Willy had invited Kitchener to Taplow Court, and in his biography of Kitchener John Pollock writes: 'They had first met two years earlier when Grenfell had visited his younger brother Charles, serving in Egypt with the 10th Hussars. More than thirty years later Willy Grenfell (Lord Desborough) recalled the Kitchener of that time, before the Sinai Desert ride had affected his eyes, as "a most striking figure, tall and spare, with the most wonderful piercing bright blue eyes, set very far apart".' John Pollock, *Kitchener: The Road to Omdurman and Saviour of the Nation*, Constable, London, 2001.

9. Written from his lodgings at 8 Long Wall Street (as it was then called), Oxford, in Ettie Desborough, *Pages from a Family Journal*, p.177; Willy was President of the British section of an international exhibition of sporting trophies in Vienna in 1910.

10. Nicholas Mosley, *Efforts at Truth*, Secker & Warburg, London, 1994, pp.265–6. As well as writing the essays critical of his parents' generation – with titles such as 'On Conventionalism' and 'Divided Ideals' – Julian wrote a book of poems and sketches, seemingly of himself, titled *The Buff Book*, with scenes such as 'Buff in bed', 'Buff goes to Paris' and 'Buff winning the Elcho Shield'.

11. His worsening relationship with his mother seems to have been the principal cause, but Violet Meynell, in her memoir of Julian, writes that 'sometimes Julian was ill and depressed, the result of his great growth, and because he never spared his body the rigorous training necessary to the athlete. The worst form depression could take with him was when he felt himself separated from God.' Violet Meynell, *Julian Grenfell*, Burns & Oates Ltd., London, 1917, pp.9–10; reprinted from *The Dublin Review*.

12. Auberon (Bron) Herbert, who became Lord Lucas, was Ettie's cousin, born in 1976; Salmond, *Tracery*, Book III, Part 2, p.151. In conversation in 2016, Nicolas, Lord Gage, commented that he felt Julian really could have become an artist, and he wasn't clear why he allowed the family to hold him back.

13. Billy's bad behaviour at Balliol was a central element of *Into Battle* by Hugh Salmon, staged at the Greenwich Theatre in October 2021; see www.hughsalmon.com/theatre/

14. John (Jack) Salmond was by this time a senior figure in the leadership of the Royal Air Force, after service in the First World War in which he received numerous medals and honours.

15. Desborough to Monica Salmond, 1924–26, Grenfell family papers, Hertfordshire Archives and Local Studies, Hertford.

16. Reprinted in Mosley, *Julian Grenfell*, p.37.

17. For a detailed account of Taplow Court and the Grenfell family, see Nigel Smales, *Taplow Moments: A Unique History*, Words by Design, 2015, p.130.

18. Penny Watts-Russell notes that 'An 1872 petition by Charles Pascoe Grenfell's executors, trying to get the burial ground closed to all burials other than those families with vaults there, states 1826 for the demolition of the old church, but I have seen 1853 stated elsewhere and I can see that in 1872 memories might be purposefully clouded.' Email to the authors, 12 March 2021.

19. List of those planting trees at Taplow Court, Buckinghamshire Archives, Aylesbury, D86/24,25,29.

20. Donna M. Lucey, *Archie and Amélie: Love and Madness in the Gilded Age*, Harmony Books, New York, 2006.

21. Richard Davenport-Hines, *Ettie: The Intimate Life and Dauntless Spirit of Lady Desborough*, Weidenfeld & Nicolson, London, 2008, p.88.

22. Letter from William Morris, from the Society for the Protection of Ancient Buildings, August 1887, Buckinghamshire Archives, Aylesbury, D86/4A. In a published response to Morris, Grenfell wrote that he didn't 'want to destroy it', *Pall Mall Gazette*, 27, 1887, Buckinghamshire Archives, Aylesbury, D86/4A/1; see also Ann Darracott, *Ockwells Manor – A history of the house and its occupants*, Maidenhead Civic Society, 2023.

23. Salmond, *Tracery*, Book II, p.82.

24. Ibid., p.31.

25. Letter included in ibid., Book III, Part I, p.70; a 'britten-board' is a nineteenth-century term for a grating in the well of a punt. Willy was President of the Royal Life Saving Society, which offered medals for saving people from drowning, and had done much to encourage all those who worked on the Thames to be trained.

26. Ettie Desborough, *Pages from a Family Journal*, p.74.

27. Salmond, *Tracery*, Book I, p.45.

28. Jane Abdy and Charlotte Gere, *The Souls*, Sidgwick & Jackson, London, 1984,, p.61.

29. *Lock to Lock Times*, 12 January 1889, p.22.

30. Grenfell to Ettie Grenfell, Lochmore, 9 September 1887, Hertfordshire Archives and Local Studies, Hertford, D/ERvC1159/15.

31. Grenfell to Ettie Grenfell, 1898–1906, Hertfordshire Archives and Local Studies, Hertford, D/ERvC1159/202 and 272 and 343 and 368.

32. Desborough to Ettie Desborough, 23 April 1910, Taplow, Hertfordshire Archives and Local Studies, Hertford, D/ERvC1159/464; he also marked the end of an era by adding, 'I shall drive the team to London & try to sell the lot, coach, harness, rugs etc.'

33. Salmond, *Tracery*, Book I, pp.15 and 29.

34. Obituary in the *Maidenhead Advertiser*, 17 January 1945.

35. Rose Gwilliam, 'Memories of Taplow Court', printed in *SSC [St Stephen's College] Newsletter*, 2011.

36. Grenfell to Ettie Grenfell, 12 September 1897, Stack, Reay Forest, Lairg, Hertfordshire Archives and Local Studies, Hertford, D/ERvC1159/156.

37. See 'Panshanger, Hertfordshire', in John Martin Robinson, *Felling the Ancient Oaks:*

How England Lost its Great Estates, Aurum History, London, 2011, pp.156–69; see also Lost Heritage website: www.lostheritage.org.uk/about-lostheritage.html

38. 'More than $500,000 paid for a Raphael', *New York Times*, 26 November 1913.

39. Davenport-Hines, *Ettie*, p.169.

40. Julian Grenfell to Ettie Grenfell, 18 December 1913, in Ettie Desborough, *Pages from a Family Journal*, p.369.

41. Julian Grenfell to Lord Desborough, 18 November 1913, in Kate Thompson, ed., *Julian Grenfell, soldier and poet: letters and diaries*, Hertfordshire Record Society, Hertford, 2004, p.161; Mosley, *Julian Grenfell*, p.225.

Chapter 12: Trusted Servant

1. Cited in the *Salisbury and Winchester Journal and General Advertiser*, Saturday 27 March 1880.

2. Deputy Governor from 1879 to 1881 and Governor to 1883.

3. Also reported in the *Salisbury and Winchester Journal and General Advertiser*, Saturday 27 March 1880.

4. The Reform Act of 1867 enfranchised parts of the urban male working class, including 'heads of households'. Although it doubled the number of men who could vote from 1 to 2 million, out of 7 million in England and Wales, the franchise was still very narrow. The Third Reform Act of 1884 allowed men in counties to vote on the same basis as those in towns, with house-owning as the principal qualification.

5. His first period in Parliament was therefore very short, lasting from 31 March 1880 to 21 November 1882.

6. The Parliamentary Groom-in-Waiting was expected to be in attendance on the Queen along with other Grooms. The office ceased to exist in 1891.

7. Grenfell to Ettie Grenfell, 28 March 1890, Hertfordshire Archives and Local Studies, Hertford, D/ERvC1159/47.

8. *The Times*, 10 January 1945.

9. *Lock to Lock Times*, 9 July 1892, no.217, p.9.

10. *Western Daily Press*, Thursday 3 August 1893.

11. Grenfell was an active campaigner: e.g, his speech at the Bimetallist League meeting on 7 June 1894.

12. This was something he was criticised for: sometimes not being able to make up his mind.

13. *Chapter 15 Passionate Campaigner* gives more detail, but its proponents argued for a gold and silver standard in Britain, thus going back to before 1819 when a single gold standard was imposed. After the banking crisis of 1847, a bimetallist movement argued in favour of a dual standard. In the last quarter of the century it gathered strength but was ultimately unsuccessful in challenging the gold standard. In 1904 Grenfell published a monograph titled *On Money* where he took up the issue of

bimetallism (this ran to nine editions, the last in 1933). In 1893 the *Northern Daily Telegraph* noted, 'He first fell victim to bimetallism and now while shaving himself, his razor fell upon and severely cut his big toe.' In 1893 the *Dundee Advertiser* commented that 'Mr Grenfell is the third Liberal Unionist who has openly gone over to Conservatism, his predecessors being Mr Coghill and Lord Farquhar', *Dundee Advertiser*, 13 December 1898, p.3. By 1909, when he published an article, 'The Real Yellow Peril', about the gold standard, it was seen as an eccentric cause.

14. The printed 1900 election card for Grenfell in the Buckinghamshire Archives has the heading 'Good Government and National Prosperity' with a head shot of Grenfell against an imperial backdrop and on the obverse statistics comparing the Gladstone administration of 1894 with that of Salisbury in 1899. It includes the promotional lines: 'Secure Continued Prosperity in Trade and Poll Early for Grenfell. The Popular Candidate & Working Man's Friend.' Buckinghamshire Archives, Aylesbury, D86/14/19.

15. His supporters must have been pleased, as he wrote to Ettie on 17 October from Netherby (where he had gone for the shooting): 'I wrote 52 letters on the train: I think I must have had 200 letters and telegrams. I have kept all the telegrams and you can see them.' Hertfordshire Archives and Local Studies, Hertford, D/ERvC1159/245.

16. In the previous year, 1904, Willy and Ettie had some idea that a baronetcy might be a possibility and Ettie almost certainly lobbied A. J. Balfour as a close friend; see *Chapter 10 Together and Apart*; Grenfell to Ettie Grenfell, Elveden Hall, 11 October 1904, Hertfordshire Archives and Local Studies, Hertford, D/ERvC1159/320.

17. *The Morning Post*, Saturday 9 December, 1905.

18. *South Bucks Standard*, Friday 15 December 1905.

19. 'The KING has been pleased, by Letters Patent under the Great Seal of the United Kingdom of Great Britain and Ireland, to confer the dignity of a Baron of the said United Kingdom, upon William Henry Grenfell, Esquire, and the heirs male of his body lawfully begotten, by the name, style and title of Baron Desborough of Taplow, in the county of Buckingham' in the *London Gazette*, Friday 5 January 1906, no.27871, p.107.

20. Desborough to Ettie Desborough, Hotel Bristol, Copenhagen, 5 February 1909, Hertfordshire Archives and Local Studies, Hertford, D/ERvC1159/430.

21. Desborough gave a long exposition on the subject: The Declaration of London, a tabled motion by Lord Desborough, House of Lords, 8 March, 1911, Hansard, vol.7, cc325-338.

22. Buckinghamshire County Archives, Aylesbury, AR7/70: D86/1.

23. In November 1924 Lord Curzon wrote to Stamfordham putting Desborough (or Mildmay) forward as Captain of the Guard. Stamfordham replied that either would be acceptable but doubted whether either would accept. On 29 November 1924 Stanley Baldwin wrote to the King recommending Desborough.

24. Lord Stamfordham, Royal Archives, K2223/99.

25. Lord Desborough to Stamfordham, Royal Archives, K2223/129.

26. King George to Desborough, 13 June 1929, Royal Archives, K2223/121.

27. There were occasional flurries of activity: he gave sixty 'speeches' (these could be brief interjections) on amendments to the Petroleum Bill in 1928 and fifty-seven on the Land Drainage Bill in 1930.

28. Grenfell took on the role of mayor in a fallow period in politics between resigning as an MP and winning a new seat. High Steward is an honorific title for life granted by a limited number of towns and cities. High Sheriff is a royal appointment for one year; it is honorific.

29. Grenfell to Ettie Grenfell, Lochmore, 26 September 1897, Hertfordshire Archives and Local Studies, Hertford, D/ERvC1159/163.

30. Maidenhead Golf Club has, somewhat controversially, been selling up this land. At the back of an appointments diary for 1900–06 is a list of Desborough's subscriptions paid to local organisations between 5 December 1905 and 3 September 1906, which totals 132, including support to fourteen cricket clubs, various football and many other sporting clubs, together with numerous local charities, ranging from cottage hospitals to flower shows. Maidenhead United Football Club established itself in 1870 at York Road on land acquired from Grenfell, it is now 'officially acknowledged as the oldest continually used football ground in the world by the same club', according to the Club's website.

31. Obituary in *Maidenhead Advertiser*, 10 January 1945.

32. *Maidenhead Advertiser*, 23 October 1889.

33. As reported in the *Maidenhead Advertiser*, 23 October 1889.

34. The initial landscaping was by Robert Stuchbery, uncle of a future five times Mayor, Thomas Stuchbery.

35. The Freshwater Fish Committee under Desborough's leadership produced at least two reports, one of which in 1917 was on the cultivation of eels as a food source in wartime.

36. Note found among papers in the Hertfordshire Archives and Local Studies, Hertford.

37. There were some who would argue this was the putative start of a British Revolution, building on events in Russia.

38. Desborough to Ettie Desborough in Paris, 8 May 1919, Hertfordshire Archives and Local Studies, Hertford, D/ErvC1159/819.

39. Initial terms for the Police Report, p.3.

40. Committee on the Police Service. *Report of the Committee on the Police Service of England, Wales and Scotland. Part I.* 1919, Cmnd 253; *Part II.* 1920, Cmnd 574; *Part III.* 1924, Cmnd 2086. The second Committee report was based around a further nine sittings and two re-called witnesses and was focused on 'Recruiting and Training, Discipline, Promotion, Leave, Medical Arrangements, the other questions relating to Pensions, Grouping of Police Authorities for purposes of control, and the merging of the smaller Borough Forces in the County Forces' as set out on p.19 of the First Report.

41. Police Bill, House of Lords debate, 5 August 1919, vol.36, cc456-60. He went on, 'The Committee have not yet finished their work . . . but this Bill contains all that is necessary to enable the carrying into effect of the recommendations of Lord Desborough's Committee . . . [enabling] the Secretary of State to standardise the pay, allowances, pensions, clothing, expenses and conditions of service of the police forces throughout the country.'

42. The Police Federation, created to act as the representative body of different strata of police, has on occasions used the motto 'What we have we hold – the Desborough Report upon which we take our stand'. Delightfully, a retired police officer named his house after Desborough. A note by Pam Turner in the *Burntwood Family History Group Journal*, 2005, reports, 'In 1927 eight years after my great-grandfather has his pay increase, he retired from the police force and consequently had to vacate Bloxwich Police Station, his home for the previous 11 years. As a consequence, he purchased and moved into a reasonably sized newly built property in Bloxwich. This house was the one he named "Desborough". In 1919 his Inspector's annual salary had risen from £195.00 p.a. to £355.00 p.a., an increase of over 80 per cent.'

43. See, for example, his letter to Lancaster Town Council as reported in the *Yorkshire Post*, Tuesday 11 November 1919.

44. Lady Desborough, response to the Thames Conservators, January 1945, as reproduced in their centenary publication, *The Thames Conservancy, 1857-1957*, p.xv.

Chapter 13: The Lords and Socialism

1. The Chancellor was effectively the Chairman of its Council, above whom was the Grand Master, the titular leader of the League. Lord Desborough was Chancellor for 1909–10 and again in 1910–11; it was an annually elected post.

2. Just before a large Primrose League meeting in 1910, Willy wrote to Ettie: 'I believe you are going to be asked to present the Banner. The Primrose League is booming, they are coming in at the rate of 3400 a week.' Desborough to Ettie Desborough, Taplow, 23 April 1910, Hertfordshire Archives and Local Studies, Hertford, D/ErvC1159/464.

3. The *Pall Mall Gazette* was an evening London newspaper published between 1865 and 1923, when it became part of the *Evening Standard*.

4. 'Concerning the question of the House of Lords and Socialism', *Pall Mall Magazine*, vol.5, January–April 1895, pp.671–83.

5. *Ross Gazette*, Thursday 10 August 1893.

6. *Yorkshire Gazette*, Saturday 5 August 1893. The *Daily Chronicle* added that Grenfell had Whig proclivities and was very much out of touch with the general attitudes of the Liberal Party before concluding, somewhat harshly, that 'A great athlete, he has never been more than a tepid and wavering politician'; cited in the *Maidenhead Advertiser*, 9 August 1893.

7. William Grenfell joined the Conservative Party in either 1896 or 1898, both dates being given in different sources.

8. *South Bucks Standard*, Friday 28 September 1900.

9. *Pall Mall Magazine*, 1895, p.674.

10. Ibid., p.677.

11. Ibid., p.680.

12. The agricultural depression that had started with the flooding of cheaper grain into Britain from America and Canada in the 1870s continued into the 1890s.

13. There is an impressively wide range of references here, from British figures such as John Burns and Ben Tillett to European theorists such as Marx and Bakunin.

14. *The Spectator*, 29 July 1893.

15. *Pall Mall Magazine*, 1895, p.683.

16. At times he appeared to be close to the Radical Unionist faction led by Joseph Chamberlain within the Liberal Unionist Party.

Chapter 14: Passionate Campaigner

1. This is well documented by J. T. Vurpillat in 'The Other Cross of Gold: The United States and the Search for Global Monetary Stability, 1867–1900', Ph.D. Dissertation, Graduate School of The University of Texas at Austin, 2014.

2. Grenfell to Ettie Grenfell, 1890, undated, Hertfordshire Archives and Local Studies, Hertford, D/ErvC1159/1.

3. Letter from Shane Leslie, Buckinghamshire Archives, Aylesbury, D/GR/14/89/7.

4. This was set out in Grenfell's article 'Mr Gladstone and the Currency', *The Fortnightly Review*, 1893.

5. Grenfell to Ettie Grenfell, 1893, undated, Hertfordshire Archives and Local Studies, Hertford, D/ErvC1159/102.

6. Grenfell to Ettie Grenfell, Brussels, 25 April 1896, Hertfordshire Archives and Local Studies, Hertford, D/ErvC1159/132.

7. Lord Desborough, *On Money*, privately printed at William Lea and Co, London, 1904, edns 1928, 1930, 1933. It was reprinted in the *Empire Review and Magazine*, no.385, February 1933, pp.70–75.

8. Lord Desborough, 'The Real Yellow Peril', *The Financial Review of Reviews*, September 1909.

9. Lady Rolleston, illustrations in pamphlet 'Silver Money – the Case for its Restoration', with a Foreword by Lord Desborough, Lord Greeenway, Lord Hunsdon, Sir Henri Deterding, and Sir Montagu de P. Webb, August 1934.

10. See, for example, Milton Friedman's 1990 article 'Bimetallism Revisited', *The Journal of Economic Perspectives*, vol.4, no.4 (Autumn 1990), pp.85–104, and a more recent paper for the National Bureau for Economic Research by Christopher Meissner, 'The Limits of Bimetallism', Working Paper 20852 National Bureau of Economic Research Review, January 2015.

11. House of Lords debate, 2 July 1920, vol.41, cc381-93.

12. Desborough to Ettie Desborough, Taplow, 11 August 1920, Hertfordshire Archives and Local Studies, Hertford, D/ErvC1159/859.

13. Rt. Revd Randall Davidson, House of Lords debate, 27 April 1921, vol.45, cc45-67.

14. Desborough to Ettie Desborough, Dunrobin Castle, 9 October 1921; he sounds hopeful when he writes: 'The Pope has set up a Committee under Cardinal Mercier on Fixing Easter and Calendar Reform, which I suppose is the result of my Bill in the Lords.' Hertfordshire Archives and Local Studies, Hertford, D/ErvC1159/899.

15. Lord Desborough to Ettie, Grand Hotel de Russie, Rome, 23 March 1923, Hertfordshire Archives and Local Studies, Hertford, D/ErvC1159/941.

16. Desborough to Ettie Desborough, Hotel Excelsior, Rome, 24 March 1923, Hertfordshire Archives and Local Studies, Hertford, D/ErvC1159/942.

17. In early 1925 Desborough wrote to Ettie that 'I preached yesterday from a platform in the Church, very different from my usual surroundings and was expected to go on for ¾ of an hour, which I did. I don't expect that they will want ever to hear of Easter again.' Desborough to Ettie Desborough, Taplow, 10 January 1925, Hertfordshire Archives and Local Studies, Hertford, D/ErvC1159/977.

18. Lord Birkenhead, House of Lords debate, 2 July 1928, vol.71, cc794-805.

19. For a 2017 summary by Andrew Defty of subsequent attempts to bring the Act into force, see 'What happened to the Easter Act? Who Runs Britain?', 17 April 2017, whorunsbritain. blogs.lincoln.ac.uk/2017/04/17/what-happened-to-the-easter-act/

20. Rev. David R. Fotheringham, *The Date of Easter and other Christian Essays*, Society for Promoting Christian Knowledge, Macmillan, London, 1928.

21. House of Lords debate, 10 July 1930, vol.78, cc401-14.

22. The Easter Act, House of Lords debate, 15 March 1932, vol.83, cc868-80.

Chapter 15: Bringing the Games to Fruition

1. Lord Desborough, *Official Report for the London Olympic Games*, British Olympic Council, Summer 1908.

2. Lincoln Allison points out in *The Politics of Sport* that 'the members [of the IOC] he recruited shared a similar aristocratic lifestyle and worldview. He chose people of independent means who were free from governmental influences, who themselves were influential and so could promote Olympism effectively, and who could make decisions reflecting the enlightened consensus of civilised men.' Initially the members were required to be able to pay their own expenses for international meetings. Lincoln Allison, *The Politics of Sport*, Manchester University Press, Manchester, 1986, p.222.

3. Keith Baker, *The 1908 Olympics: The First London Games*, Sportsbooks, Cheltenham, 2008, p.90.

4. Frank Deford, 'The Little-Known History of How the Modern Olympics Got Their Start', in *Smithsonian Magazine*, July 2012.

5. Desborough to Ettie Desborough, 24 April 1906, Hotel Imperial, Athens, Hertfordshire Archives and Local Studies, Hertford, D/ErvC1159/370.

6. Desborough to Ettie Desborough, 26 April 1906, Hotel Imperial, Athens, Hertfordshire Archives and Local Studies, Hertford, D/ErvC1159/374.

7. Desborough to Ettie Desborough, 18 April 1906, on board SS *Branwen*, Hertfordshire Archives and Local Studies, Hertford, D/ErvC1159/380.

8. Desborough to Ettie Desborough, 10 May 1906, SS *Branwen* moored in Venice, Hertfordshire Archives and Local Studies, Hertford, D/ErvC1159/377; Count Eugenio Brunetta d'Usseaux was an Italian representative to the IOC; de Coubertin had deliberately *not* travelled to Athens for the Intercalated Games.

9. See Theodore Andrea Cook, *The Cruise of the Branwen*, privately published, London, 1908 and Grenfell to Ettie Grenfell, 26 April 1906, Hotel Imperial, Athens, Hertfordshire Archives and Local Studies, Hertford, D/ErvC1159/373.

10. Matthew P. Llewellyn, *Rule Britannia: Nationalism, Identity and the Modern Olympic Games*, Routledge, Abingdon, 2012, p.36. The Athens 1906 Intercalated Games were later downgraded and are no longer regarded as part of the official sequence of Olympiads.

11. Theodore Cook writing in *Baily's Magazine of Sports and Pastimes*; quoted in Llewellyn, *Rule Britannia*, p.37.

12. Lord Desborough, Chairman's Report, British Olympic Council, Summer 1908.

13. Theodore Andrea Cook, *The Olympic Games of 1908 – A Reply to Certain Criticisms*, London, 31 October 1908, p.14.

14. Llewellyn, *Rule Britannia*, p.26. The fact that other major international sporting events were staged without government support allowed the British government to believe that subsidy was not appropriate for the Olympics.

15. Philip Barker, 'The story of the first Lord of the London Olympic Rings', www.insidethegames.biz/articles/17153/lord-desborough-the-niagara-falls-swimmer-who-helped-save-the-london-1908-games-

16. See H. C. G. Matthew, 'Asquith, Herbert Henry, first Earl of Oxford and Asquith (1852–1928)', *Oxford Dictionary of National Biography*, Oxford University Press, Oxford, 2004.

17. The title of 'White City' for the west-London site emerged from the white-painted pavilions that Kiralfy commissioned for the 1908 exhibition; the name came to be attached to the stadium as well.

18. Llewellyn, *Rule Britannia*, p.47.

19. Paul Greenhalgh, 'Art, Politics and Society at the Franco-British Exhibition of 1908', *Art History*, vol.8, no.4, December 1985, pp.433–52. The name 'White City' will have resonance for some in relation to this term, having already been used to describe the pavilions of the Chicago World's Columbian Exposition of 1893.

20. Desborough to Ettie Desborough, 1 May 1908, Bath Club, Hertfordshire Archives and Local Studies, Hertford, D/ErvC1159/410.

21. Desborough to Ettie Desborough, 17 May 1908, 16 Queen Street, London, Hertfordshire Archives and Local Studies, Hertford, D/Erv C1159/412.

22. Rebecca Jenkins, *The First London Olympics 1908: The definitive story of London's most sensational Olympics to date*, Piatkus, London, 2008, 'Introduction'.

23. See Bob Wilcock, *The 1908 Olympic Games, the Great Stadium and the Marathon: A Pictorial Record*, The Society of Olympic Collectors, London, 2008.

24. George Orwell, 'The Sporting Spirit', in *The Tribune*, London, December 1945, quoted in Llewellyn, *Rule Britannia*, p.78.

25. As reported in *Throne* magazine, 15 August 1908.

26. Llewellyn, *Rule Britannia*, p.59.

27. 'Dinner for Competitors', *The Times*, 13 July 1908.

28. Jenkins, *The First London Olympics*, p.75.

29. Baker, *The 1908 Olympics*, p.14; Baker makes the point that by the end of the Games the BOC ended with a remarkable profit of £6,000. Eugen Sandow was a celebrity bodybuilder and strongman. Members of the Bath Club, which Desborough had helped found, donated a total of £500.

30. Ibid., p.20.

31. Quoted in Deford, 'The Little-Known History of How the Modern Olympics Got Their Start'.

32. *The Daily Graphic*, Tuesday 14 July 1908, p.2.

33. De Coubertin said this on various occasions and it has become known as the 'Olympic creed'; see the 'De Coubertin Speaks' website: coubertinspeaks.com/quotes/jan/03

34. 'Ethelbert Talbot: His Life and Place in Olympic History' by Ture Widlund, *Journal of Olympic History*, special issue, Olympic Congress Copenhagen, 2009, p.113.

35. 'King Edward and the Olympic Games', the *Daily Telegraph*, 13 July 1908; reprinted in Martin Smith, *The Telegraph Book of the Olympics*, Aurum Press, London, 2012.

36. See Baker, *The 1908 Olympics*, pp.27–8; much discussion swirled around the Ralph Rose 'incident', at the time and subsequently.

37. Quoted by Llewellyn, *Rule Britannia*, p.65.

38. A photographic illustration featured a young model, Miss Pattie Wells, wearing a 'traditional Greek costume' of a light pleated dress which finished well above the knee; *The Sketch*, 22 July 1908, supplement p.10.

39. Quoted in Keith Baker, *The 1908 Olympics: The First London Games*, Sportsbooks, Cheltenham, 2008, p.75.

40. At the Holborn Restaurant, as reported in the *Daily Mail*, 24 July 1908; quoted by Jenkins, *The First London Olympics*, p.196.

41. Jenkins, *The First London Olympics*, p.196.

42. Wilcock, *The 1908 Olympic Games*, p.31; Jack Andrew was the Honorary Secretary of the Polytechnic Harriers and laid out the marathon course into London, with runners separated from spectators who lined the route from below the castle into west London.

43. As reported in *The Globe*, 25 July 1908.

44. Wilcock, *The 1908 Olympic Games*, p.102.

Chapter 16: Olympic Dreams and Reality

1. G. K. Chesterton, 'Americans in Sport and Jingoism', *The Illustrated London News*, 15 August 1908, p.161.

2. Matthew P. Llewellyn, *Rule Britannia: Nationalism, Identity and the Modern Olympic Games*, Routledge, Abingdon, 2012, p.72.

3. Theodore Andrea Cook, *The Olympic Games of 1908 – A Reply to Certain Criticisms*, London, 31 October 1908, p.18.

4. Quoted by Llewellyn, *Rule Britannia*, pp.72–3.

5. Desborough knew Roosevelt through his North American connections relating to hunting and conservation. President Roosevelt to Desborough, 28 August 1908, Theodore Roosevelt Center at Dickinson State University; www.theodorerooseveltcenter.org/; see also Llewellyn, *Rule Britannia*, pp.74–6.

6. Jenkins, Rebecca, *The First London Olympics 1908: The definitive story of London's most sensational Olympics to date*, Piatkus, London, 2008, p.81.

7. *Daily Mail*, 13 June 1899; from a website on the history of bartitsu; see www.artof manliness.com/articles/bartitsu-gentlemen/

8. See Lincoln Allison, *Amateurism in Sport: An Analysis and a Defence*, Frank Cass, London, 2001, p.29; he adds on p.30 that 'De Coubertin was not a particularly clear or original thinker; his genius lay in image-making and publicity.'

9. Ibid., p.30.

10. Lincoln Allison, 'Sport and Politics', in *The Politics of Sport*, ed. Lincoln Allison, Manchesster University Press, 1986, p.9.

11. Allison makes reference to the Grantland Rice poem of 1941 called 'Alumnus Football'.

12. Llewellyn, *Rule Britannia*, p.50.

13. Allison explains that 'The period between 1860 and 1890 was an adaptive phase in which many modern sporting institutions were established. It was marked by a transition from local rules and one-off agreements on rules to standardisation and bureaucratisation of sporting arrangements. In this period a few national sports themselves were at the core of popular culture and the modern reporting of sport began.' *Amateurism in Sport*, p.9.

14. Lord Desborough, Chairman's Report, British Olympic Council, Summer 1908.

15. Cited by Barker, 'The story of the first Lord of the London Olympic Rings', 3 June 2012, www.insidethegames.biz/articles/17153/lord-desborough-the-niagara-falls-swimmer-who-helped-save-the-london-1908-games-

16. *Vanity Fair*, 'A Weekly Show', London, 29 July 1908.

17. An Olympic webpage on the parliament.uk site makes the comparison: 'In 2011, despite major protests over public sector pensions, there were fewer working days lost to strikes

and other labour disputes than in 1948. There were eight times as many days lost in 1908, when there were disputes in the engineering and shipbuilding industries in the North East, and strikes in the cotton industry over proposals to reduce wages.' See www. parliament.uk/business/publications/research/olympic-britain/employment/picket-up/

18. Keith Baker, *The 1908 Olympics: The first London Games*, Sportsbooks, Cheltenham, 2008, pp.90–91.

19. Ibid., p.93; later in his book Baker refers again to the 'inspirational role played by Lord Desborough, although he has yet to receive the full biography he deserves', p.177.

20. Desborough noted in a letter to Ettie from Stockholm, 'I find the English are the most popular winners next to the Swedes, & the Germans the least, while the Americans are suspected though they are behaving much better, as men like Wendell, Col. Thompson, Professor Sloane . . . have taken the direction out of the hands of the Irish American gang which has been running them hitherto.' Kingl. Slottet, Stockholm, 10 July 1912, Hertfordshire Archives and Local Studies, Hertford, D/ErvC1159/573.

21. Llewellyn, *Rule Britannia*, p.92.

22. Ibid., p.99.

23. Ibid., p.108.

24. The White City stadium was used for a match as part of the 1966 World Cup.

Chapter 17: The Thames Remade

1. *Derby Daily Telegraph*, 10 January 1945.

2. The list includes the Desborough Cut (originally called Channel) and Desborough Island near Sunbury. In 1953 the TC instituted the Desborough Medal – an award to certain approved rowing, punting, sailing and swimming clubs to encourage the increased use of the Thames for sport and recreation. For whatever reason it was a short-lived experiment.

3. In a moving speech Sir Jocelyn Bray, long-term successor to Lord Desborough, at the first Board meeting in 1945 after his death, commented that 'in the Churchyard at Taplow, on the banks of the Thames he loved so well and within sound of the murmur of its waters in the summer and the rushing riots of the floods in winter, Lord Desborough has gone to his rest, but surely, his spirit will ever keep watch and ward and a never-ending vigil over the waters of his River', quoted in *The Thames Conservancy 1857–1957*, p.xiv. The Conservators of the Thames (or the Thames Conservancy as it was commonly known) published a centenary report in 1957. This report, along with the archives of the Conservancy held at the Berkshire Record Office in Reading, together with newspaper commentaries and other archival materials, provide much of the source material for this chapter. We have benefited from advice from Mr Tom Christie, himself a former Conservancy employee and expert on the River Thames, and from John Eade, whose website, Where Thames Smooth Waters Glide, is an extensive resource on all matters to do with the river: thames.me.uk

4. *The Thames Conservancy 1857–1957*, p.xv.

5. We are grateful to Anthony Quinn and his Magforum archive for helping with identifying this illustration and to Deborah Gage for establishing that the original is in the collections at Firle Place.

6. Writers such as G. D. Leslie (1888), Hilaire Belloc (1930), Robert Gibbings (1945), A. P. Herbert (1966), Peter Ackroyd (2007) and Christina Hardyment (2016) are among the many writers who have published books on different aspects of the Thames. Each writer has woven various strands of the river's history and culture together, capturing its many dimensions.

7. Jerrold's illustrated book portrays a largely bucolic Upper Thames, but once the narrative reaches Staines, the story and the pictures are increasingly about things urban rather than rural and the frequency with which, for example, punts are portrayed diminishes quite rapidly. Walter Jerrold, *The Silvery Thames*, Alf Cooke, London, 1906.

8. First Report (Thames) I Report, pp.11–12. Anthony Wohl succinctly comments that 'the benefit of hindsight might encourage us to condemn the Victorians for polluting their rivers, but water, after all, runs silent and deep and, although it also was beginning to run turgidly and polluted as early as 1860, the danger to health was not imminent'. Anthony S. Wohl, *Endangered Lives: Public Health in Victorian Britain*, Dent, London, 1983, p.239.

9. In 1892 the London County Council, the successor body to the Metropolitan Board of Works, finally adopted a system by which solid matter in the form of sludge was conveyed by vessels to a point below the Conservators' jurisdiction.

10. In his absence one of the Conservators could be appointed, though it seems the Lord Mayor often exercised his right to take the Chair.

11. As reported in the *South Bucks Standard*, Friday 25 July 1902.

12. As reported in the *South Bucks Standard*, Friday 13 January 1905, p.2.

13. Although these positions were remunerated, we understand that he chose to remain unpaid throughout.

14. He may have been ex-officio for many of these, giving him the right of attendance.

15. *The Thames Conservancy 1857–1957*, p.42.

16. An obituary in *The Scotsman* in January 1945 noted that 'it is claimed Lord Desborough knew every creek and current of the Thames'.

17. J. E. Vincent, *The Story of the Thames*, Smith, Elder and Co., London, 1909.

18. Thames Conservancy records, Berkshire Record Office, Reading.

19. See Lisa Tickner, 'Messing about in Boats: E. J. Gregory's "Boulter's Lock: Sunday Afternoon" (R.A. 1897)', *Oxford Art Journal*, vol.25, no.2, 2002, pp.1–28.

20. *The Thames Conservancy 1857–1957*, p.33; Desborough had it on his mind, writing to Ettie, on 28 September: 'I hope I have settled about buying Fullers Mill [on Ray Mill island] for the Conservancy: unfortunately, I shall not be at their meeting – but I have seen as many of them as are about and am sending a printed manifesto to all of them.

I shall have great fun, if the property is bought, in superintending the building of the lock, & suggesting boat slides etc., and two days later, 'I do hope the Board will buy Fullers Mill – £7000 – they meet on Monday 4th & will have to settle then. I have worked hard at it, & convinced those I have seen – it will be a great mistake if they let the opportunity go' and again on 3 October, 'they meet tomorrow: I hope they will buy the Ray Mill Property: it is just as well for them to decide in my absence, as they may consider me personally interested.' Hertfordshire Archives and Local Studies, Hertford, D/ErvC1159/454 and 455 and 456.

21. *The Times* reported on 23 June 1913, in 'The Scene at Boulter's Lock', how, in its first year in full use, 'the "conveyor" . . . simply hitches itself to your craft, with its full company on board, and transports you to the higher waters . . . It was the scene of a continuous procession from morning until night, and the congestion in the lock and outside its gates was in consequence less than it has been for years.' The conveyor was illustrated in a special Thames supplement of *Mayfair (and Country Society)*, 4 July 1914.

22. No more mechanical conveyor belts were built. In the official Thames Conservancy account, it says rather dryly that 'it is significant that the experiment was not repeated elsewhere on the Thames'; *The Thames Conservancy 1857–1957*, p.33.

23. *Lakes Herald*, 24 January 1913.

24. *Belfast Telegraph*, 2 January 1936.

25. *Oxford Journal Illustrated*, iss.9998, 16 June 1926.

26. Elsewhere this is referred to as having cost £500,000 – c. £40 million today. Understandably the scheme is given great prominence in the Conservancy's official history, *The Thames Conservancy 1857–1957*, p.53.

27. See *Thames Improvement Scheme; Opening of the Desborough Channel, Walton on Thames by the Rt. Hon. Lord Desborough*, Thames Conservancy, 1935.

28. Ibid., p.4.

29. Chairman's statement 1935; Conservancy Board meeting, 13 January 1936; minute books held at the River and Rowing Museum, Henley-on-Thames.

30. The works are grouped by period: 1894–1908, 1908–19, 1919–30 and 1930–45, with dramatic instances such as the centre of Kingston-upon-Thames being under 11' 6" of water in 1894.

31. *Richmond Herald*, 28 January, 1928, p14

32. *The Sphere*, 21 January 1928. Desborough's own copy of the 'Expert Studies and Reports' published in 1907 under the title *The Port of London and the Thames Barrage*, on behalf of the Thames Barrage Committee, has, inside the covers, various pieces of correspondence relating to curbing the tidal Thames.

33. J. O. Bunge, 'Tideless Thames' in *Future London*, Thames Barrage Association, London, 1944.

34. See, for example, T. W. Barber, 'The Great Thames Barrage', *Public Works*, 16 November 1903, pp.1–15. This was published around the time of the Royal Commission on the Thames.

35. Sir Jocelyn Bray, Chairman Thames Conservancy; *The Thames Conservancy 1857–1957*, p.xiv.

36. The text of the address is given in *The Thames Conservancy 1857–1957*, Appendix 1.

37. For a description of the Taplow Sword, which was dredged up opposite Messum's Boathouse at Bray on 19 November 1936 by Thames Conservancy employees, see C. F. C. Hawkes, 'A Hallstatt bronze sword from the Thames at Taplow', *The Antiquaries Journal*, vol.XVIII, Notes, pp.185–7; see also 'A Friend Of The Thames', *The Times*, 13 July 1937, p.19.

Chapter 18: Commerce, Empire, War and Peace

1. President, London Chamber of Commerce, 1910–13 and 1916–19.

2. As reported in the Proceedings of the Eighth Congress, 1912, British Imperial Council of Commerce, London Metropolitan Archives.

3. The Congress of the Chambers of Commerce in the Empire was reconvened in London in 1892, 1896 and 1900, before meeting in Montreal in 1903, followed by London in 1906, Sydney in 1909 and London again in 1912. The planned 1915 meeting in Toronto was held over until 1920 (the last congress took place in 1972 and the organisation was wound down in 1975).

4. Nicholas Mosley married Rosemary Salmond, one of William Grenfell's grand-daughters.

5. This led Willy to set up the Desborough Settlement Trust in 1910, buying farmland and estates in different parts of England in order to minimise death duties, as cited in Richard Davenport-Hines, *Ettie: The Intimate Life and Dauntless Spirit of Lady Desborough*, Weidenfeld & Nicolson, London, 2008, p.366. According to Mosley, Desborough and Lloyd George were, for periods, not on speaking terms and the latter was never invited to Panshanger, (or presumably, Taplow).

6. Along with a supertax and steep increases in death duties (introduced in 1894), the proposed land tax would have the greatest impact on the landed classes. It resulted in the 1909 Finance Bill being rejected by the House of Lords and causing a serious constitutional crisis. The 1909 Finance Bill, though delayed, nevertheless received Royal Assent in April 1910.

7. *Pall Mall Magazine*, January–April 1895, vol.V.

8. As reported in the Proceedings of the Eighth Congress, 1912, British Imperial Council of Commerce, London Metropolitan Archives.

9. Typically, Desborough presented the BICC with a presidential badge inscribed with the words 'Unity in Commerce, Unity in Defence' above and below a picture of Britannia surrounded by the flags of the dominions.

10. Report of Proceedings of the 1st Annual Meeting of the British Imperial Chamber of Commerce, held on 2 June 1915, page 4. After his statement Lord Desborough

withdrew and Mr Stanley Machin took over as chairman. Before he began the business of the meeting Mr Machin proposed that a vote of sincere sympathy be passed on the great bereavement Lord Desborough and his family had suffered. The quotation is from page 5 of the same Report of Proceedings. The BICC records are held in the London Metropolitan Archives.

11. At the 7th Annual Meeting in 1921 Desborough retired as President (and became a Vice President, albeit remaining active in BICC after he stood down). In the 8th Annual Report published the following year Desborough apologised for the great length of time that they had put up with his services.

12. Grenfell to Ettie Grenfell, 16 September 1888, Hertfordshire Archives and Local Studies, Hertford, D/ErvC1159/39.

13. Davenport-Hines, *Ettie*, p.115.

14. Ibid., p.240. Given his appetite for outdoor activity, Canada would have suited Desborough greatly, but that was less true of the urbane Ettie. In 1921, when his name emerged as the first candidate in relation to the governorship, he no longer thought it of interest, and Ettie was still against it.

15. From on board RMS *Olympic* he wrote to Ettie on 10 August: 'My dearest . . . Charlie Beresford & Argy Stanley are with us and Pierpont Morgan is on board . . . This is like a Ritz Hotel as long as St James's Street with water on each side. My cabin is much more gorgeous than any room at Taplow, and has a double & single bed in it . . . I have my journal of 1888 with me, which I kept very fully, & it will be very interesting to compare the Canada of today with the Canada of the 1880s.' Hertfordshire Archives and Local Studies, Hertford, D/ERvC1159/522.

16. In an account by R. McCuaig, a local resident, and published as *Our Pointe au Baril*, 1984, we learn that Lord Grey bought the island for his family, then purchased fifteen more properties for friends in England, including Desborough (who came to see the property in 1911 and subsequently mentions it in 1920).

17. Grenfell to Ettie Grenfell, 11 September 1888, Hertfordshire Archives and Local Studies, Hertford, DERvC1159/35 and 38.

18. Desborough to Ettie Desborough, 10 August 1911, Hertfordshire Archives and Local Studies, Hertford, D/ErvC1159/522; 3 September 1911, D/ErvC1159//536; 5 September 1911, D/ErvC1159//537.

19. Desborough to Ettie Desborough, 7 September 1911, D/ErvC1159/538.

20. Desborough to Ettie Desborough, 8 September 1911, D/ErvC1159/539. He also wrote that 'Tomorrow we go to Calgary – I have a small interest in a coal syndicate there. They all think it will be worth double in three years: they ask $36 an acre for it this year, and $50 next year & expect that in 3 years it will fetch $150 when the water is laid on. Anyhow it is very unlikely that one should lose anything.' 9 September 1911, Hertfordshire Archives and Local Studies, Hertford, D/ErvC1159/540.

21. See J. F. Gilpin, 'The Canadian Agency and British Investment in Western Canadian

Land, 1905–1915', thesis submitted for the degree of Doctor of Philosophy at the University of Leicester, June 1992.

22. A List of Securities deposited with Lloyds Bank Ltd, Law Courts Branch, The Strand, in the name of the Rt Hon. Lord Desborough, Buckinghamshire Archives, Aylesbury, D86/3 and D 11/10/4c.

23. Basil Hansard, *Leaders of the Empire*, vol.iv, Virtue and Co., London, 1912, photograph by Reginald Haines, p.64.

24. There was quite a long list of possible candidates with differing qualities. See Mary Kathleen McManus, 'The End of Imperial Diplomatic Unity, 1919–1928: Anglo-Canadian Relations from the British Perspective', thesis submitted for the degree of Doctor of Philosophy, University of London, March 1992, f/n.13, ch.7.

25. Underhill, Colonial Office, writing to the King's Private Secretary, 11 May 1921, Royal Archives, L1615.72.

26. Churchill also wrote to Desborough (from 10 Downing Street): 'My dear Willie, I have received a telegram from Canada which tells me your appointment as Governor-General will give the greatest satisfaction; and with the approval of the Prime Minister, I have the pleasure of inviting you to undertake this most important and responsible task, and allow me to submit your name to the King accordingly. The utmost secrecy must be observed until the King's pleasure is known. With all good wishes, your most sincere friend, Winston S. Churchill.' Buckinghamshire Archives, Aylesbury, D 86/19.

27. Davenport-Hines offers a revealing view of this through the eyes of Ettie, who clearly did not like Canada or Canadians, pp.240–41.

28. According to the *Belfast Evening Telegraph*, 28 December 1909.

29. Ettie Desborough, *Pages from a Family Journal*, p.397; and letters from Julian Grenfell quoted, p.458.

30. Davenport-Hines, *Ettie*, p.178. In March 1914 Willy had written to Ettie, referring to 'going to a demonstration in Hyde Park against Lloyd George & co.' and mentions that 'if one is governed by liars, and swindlers, it is only what should be expected' . . . 'Asquith will go down in history as a drunken timeserver with no moral character and prostituted abilities. However, you will know what is happening 4 days before you get my letters.' 22 March 1914, Taplow, Hertfordshire Archives and Local Studies, Hertford, DERvC1159/671.

31. Davenport-Hines, *Ettie*, p.179.

32. He had also been a Captain in the Harrow Volunteers. The *London Gazette*, 10 November 1876, refers to W. H. Grenfell resigning his commission as a Sub-lieutenant in the Royal Bucks Militia.

33. Somewhat confusingly, *Debrett's* 1901 has him listed as a Major in the 3rd Volunteer Battalion, Oxfordshire Light Infantry. In reality, following repeated reorganisations, it was the conjoined Oxfordshire and Buckinghamshire Light Infantry (which existed 1881–1958).

34. Lord Desborough to the King, March 1915, Royal Archives, PS/PSD/GV/PSQQ14,1720.

35. The Marquess of Lincolnshire added that 'My noble friend worked early and late, and was fortunate enough to secure General Sir O' Moore Creagh, V.C., late Commander-in-Chief in India, as his military adviser; Mr. Percy Harris, of the London County Council, who was one of the initiators of the movement, as his hon. secretary; and Mr. Charles J. Stewart, the Public Trustee, as hon. treasurer. These men set to work and got the disjointed units into one great whole.' House of Lords debate, 26 October 1915, vol.20, cc4-18, para.5.

36. House of Lords debate, 16 November 1915, vol.20, cc343-345. Without this protection it was suggested a volunteer who, for sake of example, shot an escapee from a prison which the VTC was guarding could be hanged for murder.

37. In his entry on Lord Desborough in the *Oxford Dictionary of National Biography*, Ian Beckett refers to the VTC work as 'his most prominent public-service'. Beckett is himself an author on many aspects of the First World War and will feel justified in this statement. However, while recognising that Desborough played a key role in the creation and running of the VTC, we might argue that his other public service roles, most notably his long service overseeing the Thames Conservancy, had a more lasting legacy. It seems that at the start of the Second World War Desborough, well into his eighties, possibly enrolled in the Home Guard as a private.

38. David Cannadine describes how Lord Montagu of Beaulieu, having opened a training school in the grounds of his country house, 'began to take an interest in the military implications of powered flight. In 1909, he established the Aerial Defence Committee . . . Until 1914 he was a severe critic of the government's lack of interest.' *Aspects of Aristocracy-Grandeur and Decline in Modern Britain*, Yale University Press, New Haven, 1994, p.68.

39. In a letter to *The Times* published on 12 June 1913, Desborough set out the aims and objects of the Imperial Air Fleet Committee.

40. British Pathé news footage (wrongly dated) shows Desborough's letter of thanks to the German authorities of 14 April 1913: www.britishpathe.com/video/imperial-air-fleet-committee-letter/query/correspondence

41. Hamel's father, Gustav Hugo Hamel, became British after being appointed physician to the King; he lived in Kingston-upon-Thames.

42. Ettie Desborough, *Pages from a Family Journal*, p.304.

43. In a letter published in *The Globe*, Monday 15 December 1913.

44. *The People*, Sunday 27 September 1914.

45. Gustav Hamel and Monica Grenfell were reported as both being guests of the Duchess of Westminster at Combermere Abbey in December 1913.

46. Julian Grenfell to Ettie Desborough, Potchefstroom, 4 December 1913, reprinted in *Julian Grenfell, Soldier and Poet*; Hertfordshire Archives and Local Studies, Hertford, DE/RvC1135/640.

47. *Oxfordshire Weekly News*, Wednesday 3 June 1914.

48. An excellent website for the Hull and Humber Chamber of Commerce gives details of this occasion: www.hull-humber-chamber.co.uk/pages/camel. He wrote to Ettie that 'Saturday following I have to go to Hull to give an aeroplane. I have just had a telephone call from the Air Force Ministry to say that they think a very great deal of our aeroplane functions, and they want me to go up and see them on Thursday next with an idea of combining our aeroplane activities with them, with a view to recruiting for the aeroplane services, and of bringing home to the workers in aeroplane factories the very great importance of speeding up their work. When I was up at Liverpool there was a squad drawn up of young volunteers who are doing a bit of drill and learning aeroplane mechanics in their spare time, and I inspected them, besides Volunteers, Motor Volunteers, and Cadets, all of which are flourishing at Liverpool, and when I go to Hull I shall stir them up to do something of the same kind.' And by the end of May, 'Hull was a great function: 20,000 people: I spoke well.' 14 May and 26 May 1918, Hertfordshire Archives and Local Studies, Hertford, DERvC1159/782 and 787.

49. On 25 May 1918; the plane was flown by 2nd Lt W. J. Walford, having been manufactured by Clayton & Shuttleworth in Lincoln.

50. Writing to Monica, he noted that 'Our Southend Hospital is doing splendidly now, and I think has achieved a great reputation. It is practically under professional management now, and the Committee look after the finances and raise the money and make suggestions, the last of which is to get large recreation grounds for the convalescents, which would be a great boon for them.' Desborough to Monica Grenfell, 26 April 1915, Hertfordshire Archives and Local Studies, Hertford, DERvC1163/14. Taplow as a rest home was described in a *Daily Mirror* article of 1918.

51. A 'huge gathering' according to *The Times*, Wednesday 8 January 1919.

52. There were (and are) two societies: the Pilgrims of Great Britain and the Pilgrims of the United States of America. A short history can be found on the website of the Pilgrims of Great Britain: pilgrimsociety.org/history.php

53. Desborough to Ettie Desborough in Cairo, 24 January 1924, Hertfordshire Archives and Local Studies, Hertford, DERvC1159/953.

54. 'Birdsong and Findhorn' in *Time International*, Monday 1 June 1929. At the dinner in question there was the newly arrived US Ambassador, the past and present Foreign Secretary and the Ambassadors of France, Germany, Japan, Belgium, Brazil and Italy.

55. Whiteslea Journal, vol.2, 20 April 1933, Buckinghamshire Archives, Aylesbury, D86/11.

56. Frank Kellogg, US Secretary of State, had signed the Kellogg-Briand Pact on 27 August 1928, an international agreement to outlaw war, which added to the work of the League of Nations and pointed towards the founding of the United Nations. The brochure for Lord Desborough's retirement dinner on 12 February 1930 is in the Pilgrims Society section of the London Metropolitan Archive.

Chapter 19: Great Losses

1. *Julian Grenfell, Soldier and Poet*; Hertfordshire Archives and Local Studies, Hertford, DE/RvC1135/640, p.223.

2. Julian Grenfell to Ettie Desborough, 15 October 1914, *Julian Grenfell, soldier and poet*, p.225.

3. Nicholas Mosley, *Julian Grenfell: His life and the times of his death*, 1888–1915, Weidenfeld & Nicolson, 1976, p.233.

4. Julian Grenfell to Ettie Desborough, 24 October 1914, *Julian Grenfell, soldier and poet*, p.231.

5. Julian Grenfell to Ettie Desborough, 24 October 1914, *Julian Grenfell, soldier and poet*, p.229.

6. Julian Grenfell to Ettie Desborough, 3 November 1914, *Julian Grenfell, soldier and poet*, p.237.

7. Julian Grenfell to Ettie Desborough, 13 November 1914, *Julian Grenfell, soldier and poet*, p.242.

8. Mosley, *Julian Grenfell*, p.243.

9. Julian Grenfell to Ettie Desborough, 4 December 1914, *Julian Grenfell, soldier and poet*, p.247.

10. Julian Grenfell to Lord Desborough, 22 November 1914, *Julian Grenfell, soldier and poet*, p.246.

11. Julian Grenfell to Lord Desborough, 3 March 1915, *Julian Grenfell, soldier and poet*, p.265.

12. Letter from Julian Grenfell, quoted in Salmond, *Tracery*, Book IV, pp.200–1.

13. Ettie Desborough to Monica Grenfell, 12 May 1915, *Julian Grenfell, soldier and poet*, p.309.

14. Mosley, *Julian Grenfell*, p.260.

15. Julian Grenfell to Ettie Desborough, 14 May 1915, *Julian Grenfell, soldier and poet*, p.287.

16. Ettie Desborough, *Pages from a Family Journal*, p.397; and letters from Julian Grenfell quoted, p.546.

17. Salmond, *Tracery*, Book IV, p.205.

18. Billy Grenfell to Lord Desborough, 25 May 1915, *Julian Grenfell, soldier and poet*, p.312.

19. Salmond, *Tracery*, Book IV, p.217.

20. Lord Desborough to Lord Kitchener, 25 May 1915, *Julian Grenfell, soldier and poet*, p.311.

21. Phoebus Apollo was the god of light. Ettie Desborough, *Pages from a Family Journal*, p.397; and letters from Julian Grenfell quoted, p.556.

22. Quoted in Mosley, *Julian Grenfell*, p.266.

23. Lord Desborough to Lord Kitchener, 28 May 1915, *Julian Grenfell, soldier and poet*, p.311; in a further note from Hardelot to Lord Kitchener, Desborough ended by saying, 'All that can be done now is to see that Julian and his like shall not have laid down their lives in

vain: each in the way that is open to him', Hertfordshire Archives and Local Studies, Hertford, D/ERvC1170/3; for a note on Julian's death and gravestone, see www.unofficialroyalty.com/may-1915-royalty-and-world-war-i/#A1; in some instances Julian's death and the publication of 'Into Battle' in *The Times* are referred to as being on Thursday 27 May rather than Friday 28 May.

24. Billy Grenfell to Ettie Desborough, 1 June 1915, *Julian Grenfell, soldier and poet*, p.313.

25. Lord Desborough to the King, 1915, Royal Archives, GV A A48/66.

26. Mary, Countess of Wemyss, *A Family Record*, p.289, quoted in Angela Lambert, *Unquiet Souls: The Indian Summer of the British Aristocracy 1880–1918*, Macmillan, London, 1984, p.186.

27. Edmund Gosse, 'Some Soldier Poets', *Edinburgh Review*, vol.226, no.4, October 1917, pp.296–316.

28. Salmond, *Tracery*, Book IV, p.251.

29. Ibid., pp.252, 258 and 262.

30. Her letter was returned unopened, and marked 'Killed in Action 30/7/15'.

31. Quoted in Richard Davenport-Hines, *Ettie: The Intimate Life and Dauntless Spirit of Lady Desborough*, Weidenfeld & Nicolson, London, 2008, p.198.

32. Quoted in ibid., p.199; Nancy Astor had become a close friend of Billy.

33. Angela Lambert discusses the issue of how disproportionately more of the sons of the British upper classes were killed in the First World War, *Unquiet Souls*, p.186.

34. Quoted in Davenport-Hines, *Ettie*, p.201.

35. Margot Asquith, *The Autobiography of Margot Asquith, 1962*; originally published in two volumes in 1920 and 1922, edited by Mark Bonham Carter, Weidenfeld & Nicolson, London, 1995, p.313.

Chapter 20: Dynastic Tragedy

1. Quoted in Jane Abdy and Charlotte Gere, *The Souls*, Sidgwick & Jackson, London, 1984, p.67.

2. Quoted by Richard Davenport-Hines, *Ettie: The Intimate Life and Dauntless Spirit of Lady Desborough*, Weidenfeld & Nicolson, London, 2008, p.205.

3. Quoted by ibid., p.209.

4. The text of the book is available online at: archive.org/stream/in.ernet.dli.2015.210735/2015.210735.Pages-From_djvu.txt

5. Letters to Ettie quoted by Davenport-Hines, *Ettie*, p.210.

6. Davenport-Hines, *Ettie*, p.210. Violet Meynell's essay about Julian, published in *The Dublin Review* in 1917, and then as a short book, *Julian Grenfell*, Burns & Oates Ltd., London, 1917, will have amplified the public recognition of the loss of Julian.

7. See section on war memorials in Sandy Nairne and Nicholas Serota, eds, *British Sculpture in the Twentieth Century*, Whitechapel Art Gallery, London, 1981.

8. In 1959 the artist's son John Rothenstein presented the three unfinished cartoons to the

University of Southampton collection; they were exhibited at Taplow Court in 2005 and a subsequent display, titled *The Sons of the Souls*, included reproductions. Information courtesy of Taplow Court; see also Samuel Shaw, 'Under Fire: William Rothenstein's war memorial designs', posted on ArtUK.org, 14 May 2019, artuk.org/discover/stories/under-fire-william-rothensteins-war-memorial-designs

9. 'The Rothenstein Mural', University of Southampton pamphlet, available online: www.southampton.ac.uk/assets/imported/transforms/content-block/UsefulDownloads_Download/66DDAC4504D547CF9DAE450E368F46C2/52911_RothensteinMural_COMBINED%20compressed.pdf

10. Desborough to Ettie Desborough, 17 September 1915, Hertfordshire Archives and Local Studies, Hertford, D/ERvC1159/682.

11. Willy's journal from visiting the Front in 1915 includes a letter of 1 February 1916 from Lloyd George praising how his 'constant presence and solicitude gave to the Deputation a degree of success which it could not otherwise have attained'. Buckinghamshire Archives, Aylesbury, D/86/8.

12. Desborough to Ettie Desborough, 14 December 1915, Hertfordshire Archives and Local Studies, Hertford, D/ERvC1159/701.

13. Desborough to Ettie Desborough, 16 December 1915, Hertfordshire Archives and Local Studies, Hertford, D/ERvC1159/703.

14. Desborough to Ettie Desborough, 20 December 1915, Hertfordshire Archives and Local Studies, Hertford, D/ERvC1159/707.

15. Desborough to Ettie Desborough, 18 May 1916, Hertfordshire Archives and Local Studies, Hertford, D/ERvC1159/710.

16. Desborough to Ettie Desborough at Beacon Hotel, Hindhead, 22 May 1917, Hertfordshire Archives and Local Studies, Hertford, D/ERvC1159/737.

17. Davenport-Hines, *Ettie*, p.218.

18. Hilaire Belloc to Ettie Desborough, August 1915, *Pages from a Family Journal*, pp.644–5.

19. Ettie Desborough, entry for 5 December 1918, The Children's Journal vol. IV, Grenfell family collections.

20. For an excellent survey of life in country houses and the fate of the British aristocracy in the inter-war period see Adrian Tinniswood, *The Long Weekend: Life in the English Country House Between the Wars*, Vintage, London, 2018. Typical of visits to Taplow in the 1920s and '30s are those recorded by Siegfried Sassoon in his journals and correspondence with Ettie; see Cambridge University Archive, archivesearch.lib.cam.ac.uk/agents/people/10718

21. British Pathé News: www.britishpathe.com/asset/48535/

22. *Birmingham Gazette*, 1 December 1920.

23. As told in Jonathan Rice, *Presidents of the MCC*, Methuen Publishing, London, 2006.

24. Desborough to Ettie Desborough, 30 August 1916, Bath Club, Hertfordshire Archives and Local Studies, Hertford, D/ERvC1159/716.

25. Davenport-Hines, *Ettie*, p.243.

26. Desborough to Ettie Desborough, 10 January 1925, Hertfordshire Archives and Local Studies, Hertford, D/ERvC1159/978.

27. Reprinted in Maurice Baring, *Poems 1892–1929*, privately printed at the Fanfare Press, 1929.

28. Abdy and Gere, *The Souls*, p.68.

29. Letters from Desborough to Monica Salmond, Grenfell family papers, Hertfordshire Archives and Local Studies, Hertford.

30. Letter from Ettie Desborough to Monica Salmond quoted by Davenport-Hines, *Ettie*, p.276.

Chapter 21: Last Years

1. See Jon Edgar, 'A Balliol Broadland Story', jonedgar.wordpress.com/2014/08/22/a-pulborough-sculpture-a-balliol-broadland-story/

2. Desborough to Monica Salmond, Whiteslea, 28 September 1928, Grenfell family papers, Hertfordshire Archives and Local Studies, Hertford.

3. *The Illustrated Sporting and Dramatic News*, 31 August 1934, no page numbers.

4. Whiteslea Diary No.2, 20 April 1933 to 15 October 1938, Buckinghamshire Archives, Aylesbury, D/86/11.

5. Diary entry, April 1936, Whiteslea Diary No.2, Buckinghamshire Archives, Aylesbury, D/86/11.

6. Desborough to Monica Salmond, Whiteslea, 18 September 1936, Grenfell family papers, Hertfordshire Archives and Local Studies, Hertford.

7. Desborough to Ettie Desborough, 12 October 1937, Hertfordshire Archives and Local Studies, Hertford, D/ERvC1159/1273.

8. David Cannadine, *Aspects of Aristocracy: Grandeur and Decline in Modern Britain*, Yale University Press, New Haven, 1994, p.245.

9. Richard Davenport-Hines, *Ettie: The Intimate Life and Dauntless Spirit of Lady Desborough*, Weidenfeld & Nicolson, London, 2008, p.247.

10. Ibid., pp.284–5.

11. 'Who, When and Where', *The Bystander*, 23 May 1928.

12. We are grateful to Deborah Gage for sharing her research on the Cowper collections, about which she and Dr Charles Ellis have lectured. Hugh Belsey and Charles Sebag-Montefiore have both written about the Cowper collections.

13. Desborough to Ettie Desborough, 27 January 1936, Grenfell family papers, Hertfordshire Archives and Local Studies, Hertford.

14. For a full account see Jenny Balston, *The Story of St Stephen's College*, published by the Old St Stephenites Society, 1994.

15. There were advantages to Taplow Court as at this date apparently it still had seven outdoor tennis courts, one of which was a hard court.

16. See 'The Second Evacuation' by E. A. Williams, in *Hertfordshire Countryside*, February

1969, pp.30–31, in which the author describes how 'Lord Desborough walked up and down shaking hands and telling people what wonderful birds they would see in the Hertfordshire countryside.' We are grateful to Matthew Beckett of Lost Heritage for this reference.

17. Desborough to Ettie Desborough, Panshanger, 17 January 1941, Hertfordshire Archives and Local Studies, Hertford, D/ERvC1159/1286.

18. See article on Norfolk Wildlife Trust website: www.norfolkwildlifetrust.org.uk/news-and-articles/articles/all-articles/the-story-of-hickling-broad

19. In these years Ettie Desborough assembled a collection of short pieces, some of which had been published as letters to *The Times* under the title of *Flotsam and Jetsam*, and dedicated to her granddaughter Camilla, which was privately printed in 1949. A copy is located at Hertfordshire Archives and Local Studies, Hertford, DE/X1050/1/2/1/2.

20. Davenport-Hines, *Ettie*, p.369.

21. Thursday 29 May 1952, *Henry 'Chips' Channon: The Diaries (Volume 3): 1943–57*, edited by Simon Heffer, Hutchinson, London, 2022, p.787.

22. See John Martin Robinson, section on Pansangher in *Felling the Ancient Oaks: How England Lost its Great Estates*, Aurum History, London, 2011, pp.156–69; and Charlotte Mclaughlin, 'Meet the Lord and Lady who sold their estate to the founders of Welwyn Garden City', *Welwyn Hatfield Times*, 24 December 2020.

23. Letter from Eric Turrell, Hutchins and Co., 3 December 1939, Hertfordshire Archives and Local Studies, Hertford, D86/19/20; Desborough replied on 7 December. Although Willy kept diaries and journals at different points in his life, he never found time to attempt a memoir.

24. Strachey wrote that Ettie was 'less insincere than usual', and went on to refer, very unfairly, to Willy as 'almost completely gaga'. Davenport-Hines, *Ettie*, pp.270–71; Davenport-Hines claims that 'when bored by excessively brittle conversation at dinner: he used to shut himself off from the repartee, and practise punting strokes to himself at the end of the table'.

25. Harry Mount, 'A Sporting Life', *The Spectator*, 16 June 2012; www.spectator.co.uk/article/a-sporting-life-

26. *Lancashire Evening Post*, Thursday 30 October 1930, p.4.

27. Edward Emmett set down that the surviving recording 'is taken from a single-sided Shellac 78rpm disc passed down through my family. It was recorded for use during the 1938 BBC boat race commentary, and it carries the BBC library number 2707, dated May 1938 (running time 03:52).'

28. As reported in *Newcastle Sun*, Tuesday 16 August 1938, p.13; we are grateful to Bernadette and Roger Hurcombe for help with the translation.

29. Whiteslea Diary No.2, 20 April 1933 to 15 October 1938, Buckinghamshire Archives, Aylesbury, D/86/11; on 10 October he wrote to Monica: 'I was very pleased to get your letter and to see that you approved of what I sent to the "Times" – we only just

escaped a silly war, in which we could have done no good.' Hertfordshire Archives and Local Studies, Hertford, D/ERvC1163/39.

30. Ettie Desborough to H. A. L. Fisher, 30 September 1939, quoted in Davenport-Hines, *Ettie*, p.331.

31. Davenport-Hines, *Ettie*, p.353.

32. Dittons Skiff and Punting Club was founded in 1923 and Lord Desborough was Patron from 1924 until his death in 1945. Letter written from Panshanger, 25 April 1944, DSPC Archive.

33. Myocardial degeneration is a disease of the heart and oedema involves excessive swelling of parts of the body.

34. Ettie Desborough to HM The Queen, 15 June 1945, Royal Archives, CC47/2211.

35. Richard Davenport-Hines, *Ettie*, p.356.

36. Ibid., p.356.

37. Wednesday 10 January 1945, *Henry 'Chips' Channon: The Diaries (Volume 3): 1943–57*, pp.215–16. Channon was close with Ivo Grenfell at Oxford, and later was a friend of George, Lord Gage, and his wife Imogen (Grenfell).

38. Walter de la Mare, letter to Ettie Desborough, 26 January 1945, Hertfordshire Archives and Local Studies, Hertford, D/ERvC675/31; to this letter was appended Walter de la Mare's poem 'The Rapids'.

39. Lord Gage to Ettie Desborough, 10 January 1945, Hertfordshire Archives and Local Studies, Hertford, D/EVrC892/100.

40. Walter de la Mare, 'The Rapids', manuscript, Hertfordshire Archives and Local Studies, Hertford, D/ERvC675/31.

Index

Unbound is the world's first crowdfunding publisher, established in 2011.

We believe that wonderful things can happen when you clear a path for people who share a passion. That's why we've built a platform that brings together readers and authors to crowdfund books they believe in – and give fresh ideas that don't fit the traditional mould the chance they deserve.

This book is in your hands because readers made it possible. Everyone who pledged their support is listed below. Join them by visiting unbound.com and supporting a book today.

Sponsors

Charles Chubb
Joan and Simon Liefer
Lisa Tickner
Esther Williams

Supporters

Nigel à Brassard
Drew Adams
Kerry Ahearn
Geoffrey Allen
Richard Ansell
Melanie Aram
Ian & Chris Arter
Anjali Arya
Pam Atkinson
Richard Baines
Ashleigh Barnes-Brooks
Kevin Batchelor
Ian Bathgate
Pim & Andrew Baxter
Alex Beard
Philip Beckett
Andy Beer
Shahin Bekhradnia
David Bell
Christopher Bellew
Jurij Benn
Jackie Bennett OBE
Duncan Berry

Mike Berry
Thomas and Victoria Berry
Roger Bettridge
Chris Bilton
Rosalind P. Blakesley
Mark Blandford-Baker
Richard Boddie
Geoffrey Bond OBE DL FSA
Adam Boon
Alexander Borg
Jeremy Bradshaw
Jonny Briggs
Karen Brine
Brian Browne
Caroline & Tim Bunting
John Burnett
Corin Campbell Hill
David Cannadine
Sebastian Cannings
David Carney-Haworth OBE
John Carpenter
Nigel Carrington
Camilla Cazalet
David Cazalet
Hal Cazalet
Penny Chuter OBE
Peter Clark
Sarah Clarke
Adrian Coles
Steve Collins

Jacquiline Creswell

Stephen Cross

Tom Dacey

Huw Alban Davies

Kate Davies

Simon Davis

Philip Defriez

Katrina Desborough

Christopher Dodd

Keith Dugmore

John Eade

Fionnuala Earley

Patrick Eccles

James Elder

Andrew Ellis

Angela Evans

Mark Evans

Richard Faithfull

Brian Felske

Patrick & Deirdre Fennessy

For Paul Byrne

Paul Forster

Susan Foster and Catherine Mallyon

Claire Foster-Gilbert

Paul John France

Deborah Gage

Nicolas Gage

Tom Gentleman

Tim Gerrard

Julie Giles

Matthew Gordon

Antony Gormley

Orlando Gough and Joanna Osborne

Jaedon Green

Fiona Greenwood

Melissa Greenwood

Tim Gutch

Tony Hall

Jack Hanbury-Tenison

Christina Hardyment

Dom Harlow

Leigh Hatts

John Hawkes

Michael Hebbert

Richard Heffer

Richard Hermon

Andrew Heywood

John Holden

Alan Hollinghurst

Derek Holmes

Graham Hubbard

Richard Humphreys and Joanna Banham

Michael Humphries

Perdita Hunt

Roger Hurcombe

Andrew Jacob

Mike James

Roger Jarman

Ivan Jones

Colin Joseph

Donal Kerrigan

Dan Kieran

Christopher King

Ellie King

Oliver Kinsey

Malcolm Knight

Ariane Koek

Elias Kupfermann

Nigel Lax

Laura Lee

Martin Levy

James Lingwood

Fred Lockwood

Natalie MacLean

Bruce Maidment

Paul E Mainds BEM

Eliza Manningham-Buller

Pete, Julia, Ben & Holly Marfleet

Stephen & Debbie Marfleet

Steph Marsh

His Honour John Martin QC

Richard Mason

Alex May

Linda Maynard

Richard Mayon-White

David McCulloch

Richard McLauchlan

Debbie McMullen

John Mitchinson

Neil Morgan

Araminta Morris

Andrew Motion

Jock Mullard

Andrew Nairne

Charles Hoare Nairne
Christopher Nairne
Kathy Nairne
Carlo Navato
Rebecca Neusteter
Jesse Norman
Gemma Oakley
Michael Pakenham
Bob Pannell
Beven J Parrish
Alexandra Patchett
Zarin Patel
David Percy
John Perry
Michael Perry
Justin Pollard
Nick Pollard
Anna Price
Caroline Pulver
Alice Purkiss
Paul Ramsbottom
Nick Rawlins
Jonathan Reekie
Kate Ribay
Paul Richards
Gray & Liz Rigge
Richard Robinson
Christopher Rodrigues
Penny Rose
Victoria Sambunaris
Marian Schmidt
Tom Serpell
Matthew Shaw
Paul Smee
Dr Brian L. Smith
Robert Smith
Stephen Smith
Colin Snowdon

Sally Stanley
Shaun Stevens
Jim Stevenson
Tamsin Stirling
Oliver Stocken
Barbara Story
Graham Summer
Katie Tait
Sarah Teuten
Tom Tew
The Desborough Lawn Tennis Golf Cup
The Library, University College Oxford
Nick Thomas
Dora Thornton and Jeremy Warren
John Tindale
Sarah Tinsley
David Tweedy
Dame Julia Unwin
Fabio van den Ende
Mark Vent
Oliver Vicars-Harris
Ian Volans
Sheena Wagstaff
William Waldegrave
Sarah Waller CBE
Dominic Wallis
Peter Walters
Anthony Ward
Lalla Ward
Robin Warwick
Penny Watts-Russell
Paul Webb
Katy Wellesley Wesley
Amy Whitaker
Steve Wilcox
Paul Willcox
Michael Williams
David Worthington